Comparative Legal Metrics

Comparative Law in Global Perspective

VOLUME 5

The titles published in this series are listed at *brill.com/clgp*

Comparative Legal Metrics

Quantification of Performances as Regulatory Technique

Edited by

Mauro Bussani, Sabino Cassese, and Marta Infantino

BRILL | NIJHOFF

LEIDEN | BOSTON

Cover illustration: hands covering a face. Courtesy of the artist Darya Tsymbalyuk.

Library of Congress Cataloging-in-Publication Data

Names: International Academy of Comparative Law. General Congress (21st : 2022 : Asunción, Paraguay) | Bussani, Mauro, editor. | Cassese, Sabino, editor. | Infantino, Marta, editor.
Title: Comparative legal metrics : quantification of performances as regulatory technique / edited by Mauro Bussani, Sabino Cassese, and Marta Infantino.
Description: Leiden ; Boston : Brill/Nijhoff, 2023. | Series: Comparative law in global perspective, 2772-5332 ; 5 | Includes bibliographical references and index.
Identifiers: LCCN 2023026326 (print) | LCCN 2023026327 (ebook) | ISBN 9789004680937 (hardback) | ISBN 9789004680944 (ebook)
Subjects: LCSH: Justice, Administration of–Evaluation–Congresses. | Legal research–Evaluation–Congresses. | Performance–Evaluation–Congresses. | Social responsibility of business–Evaluation–Congresses.
Classification: LCC K2100.A6 I55 2023 (print) | LCC K2100.A6 (ebook) | DDC 347–dc23/eng/20230608
LC record available at https://lccn.loc.gov/2023026326
LC ebook record available at https://lccn.loc.gov/2023026327

Typeface for the Latin, Greek, and Cyrillic scripts: "Brill". See and download: brill.com/brill-typeface.

ISSN 2772-5332
ISBN 978-90-04-68093-7 (hardback)
ISBN 978-90-04-68094-4 (e-book)

This book is printed on acid-free paper and produced in a sustainable manner.

Contents

PART 2
National Policy Making

PART 3
Transnational and International Market-Related Activities

Figures and Tables

Figures

Tables

Notes on Contributors

Basak Chiradeep
Assistant Professor of Law, Government Centre of Legal Education, West Bengal Education Services, Kolkata, India.

Béjar Luis José
Contract Faculty, Faculty of Politics and International Studies, Bishop's University, Sherbrooke, Québec, Canada; member of the Researchers' National System of Mexico (CONAHCYT).

Borges Fortes Pedro Rubim
Professor of Constitutional Law at the State University of Rio de Janeiro (UERJ), Rio de Janeiro, Brazil.

Bussani Mauro
Full Professor of Comparative Law, Law Department, Trieste University, Trieste, Italy; Adjunct Professor, Law School, University of Macau, Macau, SAR of the People's Republic of China.

Casanovas Juan Antonio
Full-Time Professor, Law Faculty, Universidad Panamericana, Ciudad de México, México; member of the Researchers' National System (CONACTY).

Cardillo Ivan
Adjunct Professor holder of the chair of Chinese Law at Trento University, Italy; Adjunct Professor at China University of Political Science and Law, People's Republic of China; Senior Advisor Faren Think Tank of the Chinese Government Ministry of Justice.

Cassese Sabino
Emeritus Judge of the Italian Constitutional Court, Rome, Italy; Emeritus Professor, Scuola Normale Superiore of Pisa, Pisa, Italy.

Corselli Livio
Contract Researcher, Faculty of Political Science and Diplomatic Relations, Palermo University, Palermo, Italy.

Davis Kevin E.
Beller Family Professor of Business Law, School of Law, New York University, New York, United States.

Farysheuskaya Viyaleta
Postgraduate Associate, Yale Economic Growth Center, Yale University, Yale, United States.

Gottardo Raenette
Independent consultant and international relations specialist, Cape Town, South Africa.

Heckendorn Urscheler Lukas
Deputy Director of the Swiss Institute of Comparative Law, Lausanne, Switzerland; Lecturer, Law Faculty, University of Fribourg, Switzerland.

Inatani Tatsuhiko
Professor of Law, Graduate School of Law, Kyoto University, Kyoto, Japan.

Infantino Marta
Associate Professor of Comparative Law, Department of Political Science, Trieste University, Trieste, Italy.

Jakubowski Andrzej
Professor (in affiliation with the UNESCO Chair in Cultural Property Law), Faculty of Law and Administration, Opole University, Opole, Poland; former Chair of the ILA Committee on Participation in Global Cultural Heritage Governance (2017–2022).

Kinoshita Masahiko
Professor of Constitutional Law, Graduate School of Law, Kobe University, Kobe, Japan.

Lienhard Andreas
Full Professor of constitutional and administrative law, Centre for Public Management, University of Bern, Bern, Switzerland.

Mancuso Salvatore
Professor of Comparative Law, Faculty of Political Science and Diplomatic Relations, Palermo University, Palermo, Italy.

McGrogan David
Senior Lecturer, Faculty of Law and Business, Northumbria University, Newcastle upon Tyne, United Kingdom.

Piraino Patrizio
Associate Professor of Education, Labor, and Development, Keough School of Global Affairs, University of Notre Dame, Notre Dame, United States.

Rodríguez de las Heras Ballell Teresa
Associate Professor of Commercial Law, University Carlos III of Madrid, Madrid, Spain; Sir Roy Goode Scholar, UNIDROIT, Rome, Italy.

Sunder Raj Manjeri Subin
Assistant Professor of Law, School of Law, Christ (Deemed to be University), Bangalore, India; Knowledge Network Expert, United Nations Harmony with Nature.

Villanueva Carlos A.
Ph. D. Candidate Law Faculty, Universidad Panamericana, Ciudad de México, México; Lecturer at Post-Secondary Courses, Master in Administrative Law Programme, Law Faculty, Universidad Panamericana, Ciudad de México, México.

CHAPTER 1

Quantification of Performance as a Regulatory Technique: An Introduction

Mauro Bussani, Sabino Cassese and Marta Infantino

1 The Aim of the Book

This volume collects fourteen essays prepared for a Workshop on 'Comparative Legal Metrics: Quantification of Performance as a Regulatory Technique', held in Asunción, Paraguay, on October 2022, within the framework of the 21st General Congress of the International Academy of Comparative Law (IACL)[1]. The overall aim of the volume is to comparatively investigate how performance-based measurements may work as a regulatory tool. These processes of social quantification are herein called 'legal metrics'.

Our research originated from an empirical observation. Over the last decades, a shift towards the use of performance-based measures in order to improve management and to steer behavior towards desired goals has become noticeable in many areas and sectors – and increasingly more so since the so-called digital revolution[2].

The proliferation of performance measurements has produced fundamental changes in the ways in which the social world is seen and acted upon. The spread of social quantification is related to, and accompanies, substantial turns in the techniques of governance, whereby preference is given to carrot-and-stick approaches and form over substance. When performance quantification matters, what becomes important is less the quality of performance per

1 See <https://aidc-iacl.org> (accessed 10 January 2023). According to Art. 2 of the IACL Statute (<https://aidc-iacl.org/statutes-by-laws/>) (accessed 10 January 2023), "[t]he purpose of the Academy is the comparative study of legal systems". The editors acknowledge funding from the Italian Ministry of University and Research, under the project 'Digital Vulnerability in European Private Law' (DiVE), 2022-2025.

2 Cf. Alain Supiot, *La gouvernance par les nombres* (Faynard 2015), also published in English as *Governance by Numbers. The Making of a Legal Model of Allegiance* (translated by Saskia Brown, Bloomsbury 2017); Michael Power, *The Audit Culture* (Demos 1994).

 | DOI:10.1163/9789004680944_002

se, but rather the results that the actor measured can produce (and that its supervising authority can check)[3].

This shift to performance-based measures also entails the emergence of new sets of methodologies for intervening in the social world, new competencies and new loci of authorities. In a world where performances are counted, there is the need for people, offices and tools whose main function is collecting data and monitoring activities. Quantitative expertise thus becomes a factor of specialization and, at the same time, a source of technocratic legitimacy[4].

Perhaps more importantly, performance quantification triggers intended and unintended behavioral changes in the processes and activities being measured. This happens because of the well-known behavioral propensity of human beings to react to measurements in co-reflexive ways[5]. Human reactivity to measures is actually the main reason why performance-based quantification can qualify as a form of regulatory intervention – that is, as one of the many elements (including politics, policies, formal and informal institutions, controls and compliance) that intentionally attempt to shape society[6].

---

3 See for all Siddharth Peter de Souza, *Designing Indicators for a Plural Legal World* (CUP 2022) 27–50, 112–173; AnnJanette Rosga and Margaret L. Satterthwaite, 'The Trust in Indicators: Measuring Human Rights' (2009) 27 *Berkeley Journal of International Law* 253–315.

4 For all, see de Souza, *supra* fn 3, 112–162; Kevin E. Davis, Benedict Kingsbury, Sally Engle Merry, 'Introduction: Global Governance by Indicators', in Kevin E. Davis, Angelina Fisher, Benedict Kingsbury, Sally Engle Merry (eds), *Governance by Indicators. Global Power through Quantification and Rankings* (OUP 2012) 3–28, at 19–21.

5 Human reactivity to measurements is undisputed in a number of disciplines – from sociology to psychology, from economics to anthropology. Cp. Henry A. Landsberger, *Hawthorne Revisited* (Cornell University Press 1958) (discovering what would be later called 'the Hawthorne effect': individuals modify their behavior in response to their awareness of being observed); Donald T. Campbell, *Assessing the Impact of Planned Social Change* (The Public Affairs Center 1976) (who, as a psychologist, noted "[t]he more any quantitative social indicator (or even some qualitative indicator) is used for social decision-making, the more subject it will be to corruption pressures and the more apt it will be to distort and corrupt the social processes it is intended to monitor": Id. at 49); Charles Goodhart, 'Problems of Monetary Management: The U.K. Experience', in Anthony S. Courakis (ed), *Inflation, Depression, and Economic Policy in the West* (Rowman & Littlefield 1981) 111–132 (remarking, from an economic point of view, that "any observed statistical regularity will tend to collapse once pressure is placed upon it for control purposes": Id. at 116); Marilyn Strathern, 'From Improvement to Enhancement: An Anthropological Comment on the Audit Culture' (1996/7) 19 *Cambridge Anthropology* 1–21 (noting, from an anthropological perspective, that "when a measure becomes a target, it ceases to be a good measure": Ead. at 5).

6 Governance is generally used as a broader term than 'regulation'. In the words of Braithwaite, Coglianese, and Levi-Faur, while governance is "about providing, distributing, and regulating", regulation can be conceived as "that large subset of governance that is about steering the flow of events and behavior": John Braithwaite, Cary Coglianese, David Levi-Faur, 'Can regulation and governance make a difference?' (2007) 1 *Regulation*

Needless to say, quantification of performances may take a variety of shapes and sizes. We will define what is meant by 'legal metrics' in this book in Section 2, while Section 3 will illustrate some of the instances of legal metrics that will be more closely investigated in the following chapters. A survey of the fragmented state of art of the legal literature on social quantification in Section 4, will make it clear that this is the first study focusing on the legal implications of the phenomenon as a whole. As we will explain in more detail in Section 5, the present volume fills a gap in legal research by exploring whether and how performance-based quantification has permeated selected legal systems, and has therein affected the way in which the law is perceived and enforced. Section 6 will provide an overview of the specific contexts investigated in the contributions that follow.

2 What We Mean by Legal Metrics

There is no agreed definition of 'legal metrics'.

The expression may be thought to cover all the sectors in which the adoption of quantitative processes or yardsticks is required by law or entails legal consequences. In this sense, legal metric lies at the heart of a number of well-established legal fields: companies' accounting and public budgeting, finance, banking and insurance, antitrust law, tax and monetary policies, employees' incentives, technical standards for products and services, quantification of damages, calculation of fines, regulatory impact assessments, international aid law, and so on and so forth.

Such a meaning is not the one embraced here. With the term 'metrics', we refer to the use of quantitative tools (e.g., points-based systems, black/white-lists, scores, outcome evaluations, indicators, rankings, algorithms) that continuously or repeatedly measure the performance of processes, people or organizations. Iteration through time is a fundamental feature of these tools: the threat of measuring again in the future is what triggers the behavioral response by the measured (and in turn leads to changes in the conduct of the measured and of the measurers themselves)[7]. As to the adjective 'legal', this refers to the

& Governance 1–7, at 3; see also David Levi-Faur, 'Regulation and Regulatory Governance', in David Levi-Faur (ed), *Handbook on the Politics of Regulation* (EE 2011) 3–21, at 3 (David Levi-Faur ed., 2011); Sabino Cassese, 'Administrative Law Without the State? The Challenge of Global Regulation' (2005) 37 *NYU Journal of International Law and Politics* 663–694.

7 See the authors quoted *supra* fn 5, as well as Judith G. Kelley, *Scorecard Diplomacy. Grading State to Influence Their Reputation and Behavior* (CUP 2017) 12–13, 18, 50, 246–247; Marta Infantino, 'Global Indicators', in Sabino Cassese (ed), *Research Handbook*

direct or indirect regulatory effects that the act of measuring produces on the behavior of the subjects involved in the measurement process, including not only the measured, but also the measurers and those who rely on the measurements. We intentionally decided to keep the notions of performance, processes/people/organizations, and regulatory effects as broadly as possible in order to avoid imposing any artificial limit on our contributors' search for social activities that are quantified, and hence regulated, through legal metrics.

This kind of metrics noticeably entails the application of quantitative techniques to areas that are traditionally not considered to be quantifiable, such as the quality of public administration, the strength of legal research, the efficacy of the law and the regularity of people's behavior. It is important to stress that the 'legal' character of such metrics does not necessarily stem from the object being quantified, which may, or may not, be related to the law. Neither does it stem from the legal status and the source mandating the adoption of the performance measure. The use of quantitative tools is sometimes required by international commitments, statutory law or contractual arrangements; in other cases it is imposed by code, and still in other cases it is simply applied by relevant actors on a voluntary basis. Similarly, the legal effects of performance measurements are sometimes established by law, but most of the times they derive from the perception of such measurements as authoritative, and the spontaneous reliance on them by the communities concerned.

When we talk of legal metrics, therefore, we do not refer only to performance metrics dealing with legal issues or regulated by law, but also to performance metrics of any kind producing legal effects. This implies that, while some of the quantitative tools analyzed in the books satisfy all the requirements of legality under a formalistic vision of the law, the legal nature of others can be established only by adopting a wider lens on the life of law, including its unofficial, soft and pluralistic manifestations[8].

---

on Global Administrative Law (EE 2016) 347–367, at 348–349; Alexander Cooley, 'The emerging politics of international rankings and ratings. A framework for analysis', in Alexander Cooley and Jack Snyder (eds), *Ranking the World. Grading States as a Tool of Global Governance* (CUP 2015) 1–38, at 14; Kevin E. Davis, Benedict Kingsbury, Sally Engle Merry, 'Introduction. The Local-Global Life of Indicators: Law, Power, and Resistance', in Sally Engle Merry, Kevin E. Davis, Benedict Kingsbury (eds), *The Quiet Power of Indicators. Measuring Governance, Corruption, and Rule of Law* (CUP 2015) 1–24, at 12, 19.

8 On the necessary use of these lenses to investigate the contemporary dynamics of the law at any level – be it global, transnational, domestic or micro-local level –, see Mauro Bussani, 'Strangers in the Law: Lawyers' Law and the Other Legal Dimensions' (2019) 40 *Cardozo Law Review* 3126, 3127–3142; Marta Infantino, 'Legal Pluralism in the Western Law of Obligations', in Francesca Fiorentini and Marta Infantino (eds), *Mentoring Comparative Lawyers: Methods, Times, and Places. Liber Discipulorum Mauro Bussani* (Springer 2019) 43–56; Sabino Cassese (with Elisa d'Alterio), 'Introduction: The Development

3 Instances of Legal Metrics

Examples of legal metrics as defined above take a variety of shapes and sizes, and run across boundaries and sectors.

In many countries justice and education services are subject to domestic assessments intended to check their quality, to decide on the allocation of resources and to foster improvement[9]. At the same time, the performance of countries as to justice and education are also evaluated and compared by a plethora of transnational actors. Suffice it to think of the judicial statistics developed, within the Council of Europe, by the European Commission for the Efficiency of Justice[10], and of the many available global rankings of academic institutions by specialized journals and companies[11]. Similar trajectories are visible in the health sector. At the domestic level, the assessment of doctors' performances and the (self-)tracking of people's health are increasingly

---

of Global Administrative Law', in Sabino Cassese (ed), *Research Handbook on Global Administrative Law* (EE 2016) 1–21.

9 See the Chapters in Part 1 of this book. See also, with regard to measurement of law schools, Kimberlee G. Weatherall and Rebecca Giblin, 'Inoculating Law Schools Against Bad Metrics', in Kathy Bowrey (ed), *Feminist Perspectives on Law, Law Schools and Law Reform: Essays in Honour of Professor Jill McKeough* (The Federation Press 2021) 191–223 (Australia); Wendy Nelson Espeland and Michael Sauder, 'Rankings and Reactivity: How Public Measures Recreate Social Worlds' (2007) 113 *American Journal of Sociology* 1–40 (United States); as to the measurement of legal scholarship (in both Europe and North America), Rob van Gestel, 'Ranking, Peer Review, Bibliometrics and Alternative Ways to Improve the Quality of Doctrinal Legal Scholarship', in Rob van Gestel, Hans-W. Micklitz, Edward L. Rubin (eds), *Rethinking Legal Scholarship. A Translatlantic Dialogue* (CUP 2017) 351–398; with regard to justice, Kwai Hang Ng and Peter C. H. Chan, '"What Gets Measured Gets Done": Metric Fixation and China's Experiment in Quantified Judging' (2021) 8 *Asian Journal of Law and Society* 255–281 (China); Juan Carlos Botero, Angela Maria Pinzon-Rondon, Christine S. Pratt, 'How, When and Why Do Governance, Justice and Rule of Law Indicators Fail Public Policy Decision Making in Practice?' (2016) 8 *Hague Journal on the Rule of Law* 51, 54–58 (Colombia); James J. Spigelman, 'Measuring Court Performance' (2006) 16 *Journal of Judicial Administration* 69–80 (2006) (Australia).

10 See <https://www.coe.int/en/web/cepej/eval-tools> (accessed 10 January 2023).

11 The most famous ones include the 'Shanghai's Academic Ranking of World Universities' (<https://www.shanghairanking.com> (accessed 10 January 2023)), launched in 2003 by the Center for World-Class Universities (CWCU) and the Graduate School of Education of the Shanghai Jiao Tong University, and now published by the Chinese independent agency ShanghaiRanking Consultancy; the 'Times Higher Education in the World University Rankings' (<https://www.timeshighereducation.com/content/world-university-rankings> (accessed 10 January 2023)), published since 2004 by the British weekly magazine Times Higher Education; and the 'QS World University Rankings' (<https://www.topuniversities.com> (accessed 10 January 2023)), published since 2009 by the US company Quacquarelli Symonds.

common, especially in common law countries[12]; but healthcare performance is also measured transnationally, as the deluge of trackers of Covid-19 related data that have proliferated since the outbreak of the Covid-19 pandemic in 2020 have dramatically shown[13].

Performance quantification is by no means limited to justice, education, and healthcare. The creditworthiness of sovereign states (and of companies and people) has long been measured by credit rating agencies, with the biggest share of the market being taken by the three American sisters Standard and Poor's, Fitch and Moody[14]. Between 2003 and 2020, investment climates of all countries around the globe were (in)famously ranked by the World Bank's Doing Business Reports[15], which is now about to be replaced by their successor, the Business Enabling Environment (BEE) project[16].

---

12 Jerry Z. Muller, *The Tiranny of Metrics* (Princeton University Press 2018) 103–125 (on hospitals); Shoshana Zuboff, *The Age of Surveillance Capitalism* (Public Affairs 2019) 200–206, 213; Steffen Mau, *The Metric Society: On the Quantification of the Social* (Polity 2019) 69–74, 151–153; Deborah Lupton, *The Quantified Self: A Sociology of Self-Tracking* (Polity 2016); Catherine O'Neil, *Weapons of Math Destruction. How Big Data Increases Inequality and Threatens Democracy* (Crown 2016) 161–178 (all on self-measurements and their use, especially by insurance companies).

13 See for instance the statistics and worldmap published in the 'COVID-19 Dashboard' by the Johns Hopkins University in Baltimora, Maryland (<https://coronavirus.jhu.edu/map.html> (accessed 10 January 2023)), the online Covid dataset of the 'Our-World-in-Data' project by Oxford University (<https://ourworldindata.org/coronavirus> (accessed 10 January 2023)), the 'COVID-19 Projections' published by the Institute for Health Metrics and Evaluation in Seattle, Washington (<https://covid19.healthdata.org/global> (accessed 10 January 2023)). On these and similar initiatives, see Marta Infantino, 'Hazards and fallacies of social measurements: global indicators in the pandemic' (2021) 17 *International Journal of Law in Context* 168–185.

14 Rawi Abdelal and Mark Blyth, 'Just who put you in charge? We did: CRAs and the politics of ratings', in Cooley and Snyder (eds), *supra* fn 7, 39–59; Mauro Bussani, 'Credit Rating Agencies' Accountability: Short Notes on a Global Issue' (2010) 10 *Global Jurist* 1–13.

15 See <https://archive.doingbusiness.org/en/doingbusiness> (accessed 10 January 2023). Literature examining (and critizing) the Doing Business Reports, their methodology and their effects is abundant. See Chapter 15 in this book, as well as Gerard McCormack, 'Why 'Doing Business' with the World Bank May Be Bad for You' (2018) 19 *European Business Organization Law Review* 649–676; Mathias M. Siems, 'Taxonomies and Leximetrics', in Jeffrey N. Gordon and Wolf-Georg Ringe (eds), *The Oxford Handbook of Corporate Law and Governance* (OUP 2018) 228–248; Nuno Garoupa, Carlos Gómez Ligüerre, Lela Mélon, *Legal Origins and the Efficiency Dilemma* (Routledge 2016); Guangdong Xu, *Does Law Matter for Economic Growth? A Re-examination of the 'Legal Origin' Hypothesis* (Intersentia 2014); Simon Deakin and Katharina Pistor (eds), *Legal Origin Theory* (EE 2012).

16 See <https://www.worldbank.org/en/programs/business-enabling-environment/bee> (accessed 10 January 2023).

Outside the economic field, the Sustainable Development Goals developed by the United Nations, like their predecessors, the Millennium Development Goals, are nothing but a set of measurement tools to assess the comparative performance of countries and to help governments identify and steer appropriate interventions to achieve the targets set out in the General Assembly 2030 Agenda[17]. Compliance by states and companies with environmental, human rights and sustainable development standards is also measured by a number of domestic, trans-national and supra-national private and public actors, often on the basis of self-evaluation by the concerned actors[18].

Performance quantification as a regulatory tool applies well beyond the level of the state administration and corporate conduct. Besides the case of private credit ratings mentioned above, within (and among) a number of jurisdictions private and public actors employ low-or high-tech techniques in different contexts – from service delivery to the management of punishments – in order to score the actual and prospective behavior of people, whether as consumers, criminals, or citizens in general[19]. Finally, performance metrics is a

17 Siobhán McInerney-Lankford and Hans-Otto Sano, 'Human rights indicators in development: definitions, relevance and current trends', in Stephen P. Marks and Balakrishnan Rajagopal (eds), *Critical Issues in Human Rights and Development* (EE 2021) 368–394; Sakiko Fukuda-Parr, 'Sustainable Development Goals', in Thomas G. Weiss and Sam Daws (eds), *The Oxford Handbook of the United Nations* (2nd edn, OUP 2018) 764–779; Sharmila Murthy, 'Translating Legal Norms into Quantitative Indicators: Lessons from the Global Water, Sanitation, and Hygiene Sector' (2018) 42 *William & Mary Environmental Law and Policy Review* 385–446.

18 This is for instance the way in which the United Nations Office of the High Commissioner for Human Rights (UNOHCHR) and the United Nations' Global Compact work: see <https://www.ohchr.org/en/issues/indicators/pages/hrindicatorsindex.aspx> and <https://www.unglobalcompact.org> (accessed 10 January 2023). On performance quantification in these fields, see Chapters 11 and 14 of this book, as well as Larry Catá Backer, 'Governance Polycentrism or Regulated Self-Regulation – Rule Systems for Human Rights Impacts of Economic Activity Where National, Private and International Regimes Collide', in Kerstin Blome, Hannah Franzki, Andreas Fischer-Lescano, Nora Markard, Stefan Oeter (eds), *Contested Collisions: Interdisciplinary Inquiries into Norm Fragmentation in World Society* (CUP 2016) 198–225; Rosga and Satterthwaite, *supra* fn 3.

19 See Chapters 8–10 (on South Africa, China, Japan respectively) and 12–13 (on Africa and Europe). See also Noah Vardi, *Creditworthiness and 'Responsible Credit'. A Comparative Study of EU and US Law* (Brill 2022) and Asress Adimi Gikay, 'The American Way – Until Machine Learning Algorithm Beats the Law?' (2021) 12 *Case Western Reserve Journal of Law, Technology, and the Internet*, issue 1, <https://scholarlycommons.law.case.edu/jolti/vol12/iss1/3> (accessed 10 January 2023) (both on consumer credit scoring in the United States and Europe); Christopher Slobogin, *Just Algorithms. Using Science to Reduce Incarceration and Inform a Jurisprudence of Risk* (CUP 2021) (on the use of algorithms to identify and punish individuals in the United States); Marta Infantino and Weiwei Wang, 'Challenging Western Legal Orientalism. A Comparative Analysis of Chinese Municipal

new vogue on digital markets. Tech companies, digital platforms, social media and sharing economy actors widely employ algorithmic scorings for products, services, news, opinions, search results, and customers themselves for a variety of purposes[20].

The list of illustrations of performance quantification could certainly be longer, but the examples set out above are enough to show how pervasive the phenomenon investigated in this volume is. As highlighted above, in Section 1, the scope of quantification of the social world now covers issues – justice, compliance with international law obligations, the appropriateness of private conduct – that were until recently approached in non-quantitative terms only. In these fields, the exercise of measuring performances, whether embedded in official law or not, has provoked intended and unintended changes in the management styles in the sectors concerned, in the institutional frameworks applying to them, in the behavior and role of the people involved, as well as in the latter's expectations and entitlements. In other words, reliance on performance-based measurements has changed the way in which these sectors are regulated, officially or not.

The great variety of situations covered by the notion of legal metrics suggested us to limit the scope of our inquiry in a way that could better serve the aim of our research. We therefore invited our contributors to focus on the use and the consequences of legal metrics in a specific legal system or area of the legal world in one of these three sectors: state-administered justice and education (Part 1), policy-making (Part 2), and market-related activities (Part 3). These sectors were chosen for a number of reasons, besides their being closer to the editors' competences. They are sectors where the regulatory effects of quantification of performance are of the utmost evidence; they constitute

Social Credit Systems' (2021) 8 *European Journal of Comparative Law and Governance* 46–85; Daithí Mac Síthigh and Mathias M. Siems, 'The Chinese Social Credit System: A Model for Other Countries?' (2019) 82 *Modern Law Review* 1034–1071 (both on Chinese social credit); Virginia Eubanks, *Automating Inequality: How High-tech Tools Profile, Police, and Punish the Poor* (St. Martin Press 2018) (on the use of rating programs for the management of social services in the United States).

20 See Chapters 12–13 of this book (on Africa and Europe, respectively), as well as Zuboff, *supra* fn 12; Mau, *supra* fn 12; Safiya Umoja Noble, *Algorithms of Oppression. How Search Engines Reinforce Racism* (NYU 2018); Sofia Ranchordás, 'Online Reputation and the Regulation of Information Asymmetries in the Platform Economy' (2018) 5 *Critical Analysis of Law* 127–147; Btihaj Ajana (ed), *Metric Culture: Ontologies of Self-Tracking Practices* (Emerald Publishing 2018); Lupton, *supra* fn 12; Frank Pasquale, *The Black Box Society* (Harvard University Press 2015) 58–100; Hassan Masum and Mark Tovey (eds), *The Reputation Society: How Online Opinions Are Reshaping the Offline World* (MIT Press 2011).

subjects matters that are easy-to-identify and amenable to comparison; they concern issues in which the lack of comparative research is particularly acute.

4 The State of the Literature

As already noticed, the notion of 'legal metrics' employed in this volume is not limited to a single, well-defined field. Many distinct strands of legal scholarship have dealt with one or more instances of legal metrics as defined above, or with its methodological and foundational aspects. The most important lines within this literature deserve to be mentioned here, in order to better contextualize the present research and to clarify its added value.

In this regard, two preliminary caveats are in order.

First, the emergence of legal metrics in the last decade has occurred in parallel with an intellectual and academic turn to quantitative methods that has affected, although in different forms and with different timeframes, all social sciences, including legal ones (and somewhat paradoxically, as social research has increasingly relied on quantitative methods, its outputs have also increasingly been quantified and subject to performance assessments by peers, universities, funders and journals)[21]. We do not intend to explore here how the quantitative drive has progressively taken hold of social sciences. Our aim is different: we wish to identify and to summarize the main lines of research that have either paved the way for or otherwise investigated experiments of *legal* metrics as defined above.

Secondly, there is a burgeoning literature on the disruption brought by reliance on quantitative tools in domestic and transnational governance, authored by researchers taking perspectives other than the legal one. The quantification of the social world through the measurement of performances has attracted the attention of historians[22],

21 See for all Imad A. Moosa, *Publish or Perish. Perceived Benefits versus Unintended Consequences* (EE 2018), as well as Chapter 7 in this book. The turn described in the text is for instance of the utmost evidence in the field of comparative constitutional law, in which large cross-national studies have proliferated in recent years: see, among many others, Niels Petersen and Konstantin Chatziathanasiou, 'Empirical research in comparative constitutional law: The cool kid on the block or all smoke and mirrors?' (2021) 19 *International Journal of Constitutional Law* 1810–1834; Ran Hirschl, *Comparative Matters: The Renaissance of Comparative Constitutional Law* (OUP 2014) 151–191.

22 Cf. Alain Desrosières, *La politique des grands nombres. Histoire de la raison statistique* (2nd edn, La Découverte 2000; the first edition was also published in English as *The Politics of Large Numbers. A History of Statistical Reasoning* (translated by Camille Naish, Harvard University Press 1998)); Theodore M. Porter, *Trust in Numbers. The Pursue of Objectivity*

anthropologists[23], sociologists[24], international relations theorists[25], political scientists[26], economists[27]. Although the present book stands on the shoulders of this previous research (among many other studies), we will not be concerned here with such developments, insofar as we are mainly interested with what occurs in the legal domain.

At the beginning of the 1970s, legal scholars involved in the Stanford-based Studies in Law and Development (SLADE) project collected a massive amount of empirical data on a small sample of countries in order to investigate the relationship between law and development[28]. As is well known, the project was swiftly discontinued: the information gathered was too much and too hard to manage. The lack of immediate results rapidly cooled down the enthusiasm of the scholars involved and, most importantly, of the development agencies that were funding the program[29]. In what follows, we will focus on three bundles of legal scholarship that emerged from the 1980s onwards: the first is more or less closely linked to the spread of managerial and economic approaches to the law (Section 4.1); the second looks at law-making through rankings and indicators in the global sphere (Section 4.2); and the third explores the evolution of the law in our increasingly digitalized and algorithmic contemporary societies (Section 4.3). We will then briefly assess what these strands of literature have

---

in Science and Public Life (Princeton University Press 1995); Mary Poovey, *A History of the Modern Fact. Problems of Knowledge in the Sciences of Wealth and Society* (University of Chicago Press 1998).

23 See for all Sally Engle Merry, *The Seductions of Quantification. Measuring Human Rights, Gender Violence, and Sex Trafficking* (University of Chicago Press 2015); Chris Shore and Susan Wright, 'Audit Culture Revisited: Rankings, Ratings and the Reassembling of Society' (2015) 56 *Current Anthropology* 421–444.

24 Cf. Sarah Brayne, *Predict and Surveil. Data, Discretion, and the Future of Policing* (OUP 2021); Mau, *supra* fn 12; Lupton, *supra* fn 12.

25 See especially Judith G. Kelley and Beth A. Simmons (eds), *The Power of Global Performance Indicators* (CUP 2020); Kelley, *supra* fn 7.

26 See, among the many, Eubanks, *supra* fn 13; André Broome, Alexandra Homolar, Matthias Kranke, 'Bad science. International organizations and the indirect power of global benchmarking' (2018) 24 *European Journal of International Relations* 514–539; André Broome and Joel Quirk, 'The Politics of Numbers: The Normative Agenda of Global Benchmarking' (2015) 41 *Review of International Studies* 813–818.

27 Cf. Morten Jerven, *Poor Numbers. How We Are Misled by African Development Statistics and What to Do About It* (Cornell University Press 2013); Power, *supra* fn 2.

28 John H Merryman, 'Law and Development Memoirs II: SLADE' (2000) 48 *American Journal of Comparative Law* 713–727. One of the authors of this chapter, Sabino Cassese, was directly involved in the project as the rapporteur from Italy.

29 David M. Trubek, 'Law and Development: 40 Years after Scholars in Self-Estrangement – A Preliminary Review' (2016) 66 *University of Toronto Law Journal* 301–329.

in common and how they have contributed to shedding light on the regulatory effects of performance quantification (Section 4.4).

4.1 *Economic-Oriented Legal Studies*

Since the 1980s, the emergence of the so-called New Public Management (NPM) paradigms, inspired by neo-classical economic theories, fueled the widespread adoption by governments of approaches characterized by deregulation, pro-market culture, and result-based performance[30]. NPM paradigms called for the introduction of forms of performance benchmarking protocols that could be applied to public sector employees, and for the imposition of limits on the regulatory power of the administration through the adoption of governance arrangements that outsourced rule-making to the regulatees. This is known as 'performance-based' regulation': regulatory authorities do not specify what is required but rather set a performance target for the regulatees and monitor the achievement of that target over time[31].

In the meantime, the concurrent global rise of law-and-economics (L&E) has contributed to legitimizing the idea that legal rules should be understood not to much in terms of value-driven ought-to-be, but rather as a matter of costs and incentives, and that they should be assessed in the light of their ability to achieve expected outcomes and to induce changes in behavior[32]. Two well-known off-shoots from this view have been, on the one hand, the launch in the late Nineties of the so-called 'legal origins' project, which sought to measure quantitatively the extent to which how countries' legal origins affect their economic performance[33], and, on the other hand, the development of

---

30 Muhammad Shamsul Haque, 'New Public Management: Origins, Dimensions, and Critical Implications', in Krishna K. Tummala (ed), *Public Administration and Public Policy* (Eolss 2004) 209–229, at 210–211.

31 See Cary Coglianese, 'Performance-based regulation: concepts and challenges', in Francesca Bignami and David Zaring (eds), *Comparative Law and Regulation. Understanding the Global Regulatory Process* (EE 2016, reprinted 2018) 403–429; Cary Coglianese, Jennifer Nash, Todd Olmstead, 'Performance-Based Regulation: Prospects and Limitations in Health, Safety, and Environmental Protection' (2003) 55 *Administrative Law Review* 705–729. However, performance-based regulation has also been advocated for other purposes, e.g., as a tool for protecting consumers in post-industrial economies: cf. Lauren E. Willis, 'Performance-Based Consumer Law' (2015) 82 *University of Chicago Law Review* 1309–1409; Stephen D. Sugarman, 'Salt, High Blood Pressure, and Performance-Based Regulation' (2009) 3 *Regulation & Governance* 84.

32 For a summary of these shifts, see Lewis A. Kornhauser, 'The Normativity of Law' (1999) 1 *American Law and Economics Review* 3–25.

33 See, e.g., Rafael La Porta, Florencio C. Lopez de Silanes, Andrei Shleifer, Robert W. Vishny, 'Legal Determinants of External Finance' (1997) 52 *Journal of Finance* 1131–1150; Rafael La Porta, Florencio C. Lopez de Silanes, Andrei Shleifer, Robert W. Vishny, 'Law and Finance'

behavioral L&E research on how non-regulatory measures, such as nudges, smart disclosures and choice architecture, influence people's behavior and could be used by regulators to channel social conduct in desired directions[34].

Economic-inspired modelling approaches have thus made a powerful contribution to the creation of an intellectual milieu in which performance-based assessments are normalized and are seen as a core strategy for social and legal intervention.

4.2 *Indicators in the Global Sphere*

In contrast from economic-centered approaches, two other strands within the literature have considered the quantification of the social from an external perspective, investigating the regulatory implications of performance-based practices in, respectively, global arenas and the every day's digital world. Let us start with the former line of inquiry.

We already noted that in 2003 the World Bank launched the Doing Business Reports, which translated the legal origins theory into a global indicator of countries' business friendliness[35]. Following their launch, the evident limitations of the Reports led many legal scholars to criticize them and their regulatory effects[36]. Some even worked on alternative projects. For instance, the frustration with the Doing Business Reports inspired three (at that time) Cambridge-based scholars to develop the 'CBR Leximetric Datasets', coding countries for labor regulation and shareholder protection[37]. A similar sentiment led the French 'Fondation pour le droit continental' to inaugurate the

(1998) 106 *Journal of Political Economy* 1113–1155 (1998); Edward L. Glaeser and Andrei Schleifer, 'Legal Origins' (2002) 107 *Quarterly Journal of Economics* 1193–1229.

34 This is the very well-known and influential thesis of Richard H. Thaler and Cass R. Sunstein, *Nudge. Improving Decisions About Health, Wealth and Happiness* (1st edn 2008, Penguin 2021).

35 See *supra* fn 15.

36 See the authors referred *supra* fn 15. See also the articles collected in the special issues on 'Symposium on Legal Origins' (2009) 57(4) *American Journal of Comparative Law* 765–876, 'Economics and Comparative Law' (2009) 59(2) *University of Toronto Law Journal* 179–235, 'Law and Finance' (2009) *Brigham Young University Law Review* 1413–1906, 'Jurimetrics' (2010) 166(1) *Journal of Institutional & Theoretical Economics*, 'Misurare il diritto' (2012) *Annuario di diritto comparato* 7–353, as well as Mathias M. Siems, 'Legal Origins: Reconciling Law & Finance and Comparative Law' (2007) 52 *McGill Law Journal* 55–81; Association Henri Capitant des amis de la culture juridique francaise, *Les droits de tradition civiliste en question. A propos des rapports Doing Business* (2 vols, Société de législation comparée 2006); Bertrand du Marais (ed), *Des indicateurs pour mesurer le droit? Les limites méthodologiques des rapports Doing Business* (La Documentation Française 2006).

37 See <https://www.repository.cam.ac.uk/handle/1810/256566> (accessed 10 January 2023).

'Index de la sécurité juridique' (published twice, in 2015 and 2018), aiming to compare countries' degrees of 'legal certainty'[38]. The experience with the Doing Business team induced Juan Carlos Botero to conceive the 'Rule of Law Index®', which has been published since 2008 within the 'World Justice Project' and is sponsored, inter alia, by the American Bar Association[39].

The multiplication of global indicators of this kind has attracted the attention of a growing number of legal scientists, especially since the end of the 2000s. On the one hand, scholars interested in global governance, global administrative law and global legal pluralism have studied in particular the increased use of global quantitative tools for data collection in inter-and transnational relations as instruments for establishing and enforcing normative standards[40]. On the other hand, scholars from other fields, such as law-and-development, comparative constitutional law, and human rights law, have emphasized the many unintended consequences that the growing reliance on quantitative, performance-based tools for controlling performance often precipitate in their respective domains[41].

---

38 Bruno Deffains and Micheal Séjan, *Index de la sécurité juridique. Rapport pour la Fondation pour le droit continental* (Dalloz 2018).

39 See <https://worldjusticeproject.org> (accessed 10 January 2023); but see also Botero, Pinzon-Rondon, Pratt, *supra* fn 9.

40 From the perspective of global governance, see Debora Valentina Malito, Gaby Umbach, Nehal Bhuta (eds), *The Palgrave Handbook of Indicators in Global Governance* (Palgrave 2018). From the perspective of global administrative law, see Engle Merry, Davis, Kingsbury (eds), *supra* fn 7; Davis, Fisher, Kingsbury, Engle Merry (eds), *supra* fn 4 (and in particular the chapter of Sabino Cassese and Lorenzo Casini, 'Public Regulation of Global Indicators', 465–474). From the perspective of global legal pluralism, see David Nelken, 'The Legitimacy of Global Social Indicators: Reconfiguring Authority, Accountability and Accuracy' (2018) 59 *Cahiers de Droit* 35–84; David Restrepo Amariles, 'Legal indicators, global law and legal pluralism: an introduction' (2015) 47 *Journal of Legal Pluralism & Unofficial Law* 9–21; Benoît Frydman and Arnaud Van Waeyenberge (eds), *Gouverner par les standards et les indicateurs. De Hume aux rankings* (Bruylant 2014).

41 From the law-and-development perspective, see de Souza, *supra* fn 3; Michael Trebilcock Michael and Mariana Mota Prado, *What Makes Poor Countries Poor? Institutional Determinants of Development* (EE 2011); from the perspective of comparative constitutional law, see Mila Versteeg and Tom Ginsburg, 'Measuring the Rule of Law: A Comparison of Indicators' (2017) 42 *Law & Social Inquiry* 100–137; from the human rights perspective, Simon Walker, 'Challenges of human rights measurement', in Bård A. Andreassen, Hans-Otto Sano, Siobhán McInerney-Lankford (eds), *Research Methods in Human Rights. A Handbook* (EE 2017) 306–332; Sakiko Fukuda-Parr, *The MDG s, Capabilities, and Human Rights: The Power of Numbers to Shape Agendas* (Routledge 2015).

4.3 *Algorithmic Law*

A more recent strand of legal scholarship has mainly focused on the changes to and challenges for legal systems brought about by mass digitalization and datification.

The starting point for such research has been the consideration that, especially in wealthy contemporary societies, social activity and human behavior are increasingly tracked, quantified and managed by powerful (private and public) actors through technology.

This is why some scholars in this group, especially from the United States and Europe, have investigated the potential of algorithmic metrics for profiling individuals and automating the personalization of legal rules. Discussion have considered how smart algorithms are increasingly devised in order to provide people with ex ante, context-dependent behavioral prescriptions, or with individually-appropriate levels of information and disclosure, or with personally-tailored suggestions as to which standard of care and conduct should be adopted[42].

Nevertheless, the majority of studies on digitalization, algorithms and the law have adopted a rather more critical stance concerning the wider consequences of automating performance quantification. Some have examined in selected jurisdictions the drawbacks associated with the use of algorithmic quantification and automation by police, courts, governments and private companies[43]. Other scholars have investigated and denounced how, through choice architecture, big data analytics and practices of (self-)measurement, algorithmic coding can constrain and regulate social behavior, reducing

---

42 Cf. Christoph Busch, 'Implementing Personalized Law: Personalized Disclosures in Consumer Law and Data Privacy Law' (2019) 86 *University of Chicago Law Review* 309–331; Philipp Hacker, 'Personalizing EU Private Law: From Disclosures to Nudges and Mandates' (2017) 25 *European Review of Private Law* 651–677; Omri Ben-Shahar and Ariel Porat, 'Personalizing Negligence Law' (2016) 91 *NYU Law Review* 627–688. But see also, in a more critical perspective, Timothy Endicott and Karen Yeung, 'The death of law? Computationally personalized norms and the rule of law' (2021) *University of Toronto Law Journal*, <https://doi.org/10.3138/utlj-2021-0011> (accessed 10 January 2023); Dan L. Burk, 'Algorithmic Legal Metrics' (2021) 96 *Notre Dame Law Review* 1147–1203; Jordan M. Barry, John W. Hatfield, Scott D. Kominers, 'To Thine Own Self Be True? Incentive Problems in Personalized Law' (2021) 62 *William & Mary Law Review* 723–790.

43 Cf. Tania Sourdin, *Judges, Technology and Artificial Intelligence. The Artificial Judge* (EE 2021); Andrew Guthrie Ferguson, *The Rise of Big Data Policing Surveillance, Race, and the Future of Law Enforcement* (NYU Press 2019); Michael Veale and Irina Brass, 'Administration by Algorithm? Public Management Meets Public Sector Machine Learning', in Karen Yeung and Martin Lodge (eds), *Algorithmic Regulation* (OUP 2019) 119–149; Brendan McGurk, *Data Profiling and Insurance Law* (Hart 2018).

decision-making autonomy and leaving people vulnerable to digital nudging[44]. Both kinds of studies have emphasized the many weak spots that affect big data analytics and algorithmic automation, such as proneness to bias, inherent opaqueness and limited (if any) accountability.

4.4 *Common Threads*

The above lines of research are variously related to one another.

Overall, they should all be credited for shedding light on how traditionally non-regulatory tools, such as nudges, indicators and algorithms, may be used to shape and channel individual and collective behavior.

Studies on the normative power of indicators and algorithms have further helped single out how performance-based, quantitative tools have an impact on (and are impacted by) the legal contexts in which they are adopted and deployed. Reliance on performance-based quantitative tools may for instance highlight correlations that would not otherwise be visible, and also simplify procedures, reshape processes and competencies for dealing with social issues, inform policy-making processes, inspire legal reforms, promote best practices, and stimulate worthy legal behavior[45].

However, as the above literature has also emphasized, performance-based, quantitative tools often suffer from methodological weaknesses (such as the entrenchment of their producers' biases), empower unaccountable technocratic elites with substantial and unleashed normative power, divert social attention from what counts towards what is counted and produce more and less dangerous unintended effects (including the inducement of rank-seeking and gaming strategies by the measured) that may frustrate or run counter the very purpose of the measurement[46].

---

44 See, in addition to the critical voices mentioned *supra* fn 42, Pedro Rubim Borges Fortes, Pablo Marcello Baquero, David Restrepo Amariles, 'Artificial Intelligence Risks and Algorithmic Regulation' (2022) *European Journal of Risk Regulation* 357–372; Helga Nowotny, *In AI We Trust* (Polity Press 2021); Karen Yeung, 'Hypernudge? Big Data as a Mode of Regulation by Design' (2016) 20 *Information, Communication & Society* 118–136; Mireille Hildebrandt, *Smart Technologies and the End(s) of Law: Novel Entanglements of Law and Technology* (EE 2015); Danielle K. Citron, 'Technological Due Process' (2008) 85 *Washington University Law Review* 1249–1313; Lawrence Lessig, *Code and Other Laws of Cyberspace, Version 2.0* (Basic Books 2006).

45 See especially the authors cited *supra* fns 36 and 40-42.

46 See authors cited *supra* fns 36 and 40-44.

5 Uncharted Perspectives

The present volume builds on the academic background just outlined, but also enriches it from multiple perspectives.

Existing legal researches on the transformative impact of quantification of social phenomena have so far focused on reliance on specific quantitative techniques (e.g., indicators, ratings, algorithmic scoring) in specific sectors (e.g., human rights measurements, finance and corporate law, business-to-consumer digital transactions), examining the implications of such reliance either in selected jurisdictions or in the abstract. From this point of view, the current legal literature on performance quantification and the law is either anecdotal, providing fragmentary information whose general value remains unclear, or highly decontextualized, apparently resting upon the assumption that the quantitative turn gives rise to the same effects irrespective of where it occurs.

By contrast, this book is concerned with the use of performance-based measurements as a regulatory technique in general. The volume looks at the legal consequences produced by a range of quantitative performance-based tools (no matter whether low-or high-tech, domestic or supranational, official or unofficial) in a variety of fields and legal systems. The chapters collected in this volume thus offer empirical, quantitative and qualitative data about the overall impact of different performance-based tools across different sectors and places. In this light, the book represents the first comparative study on the legal effects triggered by the reliance on performance measurements, providing cross-sectoral and cross-country comparative data that, simply put, were not available before.

Reasons of space constraints and of matching of contributors' availability and competencies explain why only some selected sectors and countries are covered. Sectors include national state-administered justice, education, and policy-making, as well as transnational and international measurements of market-related activities, while regions and jurisdictions covered include Brazil, China, the European Union, Mexico, India, Japan, Poland, South Africa, Switzerland, and the United Kingdom. Each chapter in Parts 1–3 analyzes the regulatory impact of performance-based quantitative tools in a specific legal system or region of the world. Contributors freely chose the most interesting sector(s) to deal with in the region/jurisdiction of their concern. Notwithstanding the methodological limitations of such an inquiry, which is also dependent upon the take of individual contributors on the issue, the national chapters provide a first empirical basis for the comparative assessment of the dynamics triggered by legal metrics in many of its various forms.

6 Plan of the Book

The first two Parts of the book are dealing with the spread of legal metrics in the management of core functions and services (such as justice, education, and policy-making) at the domestic level, while the last Part analyzes how legal metric is used within and across state boundaries.

More in particular, the seven contributions in the first Part investigate whether, to what extent and with what consequences performance-based quantitative assessments permeate the justice system in Brazil (Chapter 2), Mexico (Chapter 3), India (Chapter 4) and Switzerland (Chapter 5)[47]. These contributions analyze whether the performance of judges and courts is subject to measurement and whether there are overall quantitative assessments of the performance of the justice system. The other two chapters in Part 1 deal with the actual or prospective uses of legal metrics in the education systems in South Africa (Chapter 6) and Poland (Chapter 7)[48].

The four chapters in Part 2 address the use of performance-based tools in policy making from a variety of perspectives. Chapter 8 on South Africa (and on Africa in general) examines how the digitalization of the public administration is providing for new quantitative tools of governance that may help ensure the transparency and accountability of public sector management. Chapters 9 and 10, on China and Japan respectively, navigate through the many local uses of performance-based instruments for the management and supervision of public and private conduct. Chapter 12 on the United Kingdom reports how performance-based assessments lie at the core of the human rights review carried out by the UK's Equality and Human Rights Commission.

The four chapters in Part 3 look at reliance upon performance-based tools in the transnational and international arenas. Taking the sub-Saharan region as a case-study, Chapter 12 explores the potential benefits and perils of mass consumer algorithmic profiling. From a similar angle, but with the focus on Europe, Chapter 13 investigates how reputational feedback systems are the backbone of digital economy and provide regulatory and enforcement tools that apply regardless of national boundaries. Chapter 14 examines the development of hard and soft-law quantitative tools of self-measurement for controlling and channeling corporate activity within and outside state's boundaries. Finally, Chapter 15 focuses on the ways in which the measurement of countries' legal

---

47 Additional insights on the effect of performance-based assessments on justice systems are provided by Chapter 9 on China.

48 In this regard too, additional information on the effect of performance-based assessments on education are provided by Chapter 9 on China.

institutions by international organizations have influenced policy-making and regulation in national legal systems.

Chapter 16 summarizes the comparative findings emerging from national contributions. As chapters in Parts 1–3 show, the turn to quantification and performance-based tools is global, but the different ways and extent to which quantitative techniques permeate the law, call for a comparative study of the varied effects they give rise to.

PART 1

Justice and Education

CHAPTER 2

Revisiting 'Justice in Numbers' in Brazil: Quantified Justice, Managerial Judges, and Numeroids as a Regulatory Technique

Pedro Rubim Borges Fortes

1 Introduction

This chapter builds on an article that I published on the Brazilian National Council of Justice and the program 'Justice in Numbers' almost ten years ago[1]. It is an updated version of my previous research on the quantification of justice in Brazil with original reflections about new developments. More in particular, my research question examines how the statistical information related to quantification of the justice system may influence the judicial profession. To be sure, I should reexamine how the rise of legal indicators influence the administration of justice and judicial behavior. Importantly, the core of the response comes from the explanation that judges become managers and quantified justice provides legal indicators – or 'numeroids' – which function as a mechanism of control and a regulatory technique to assess judicial performance. In this context, my contribution to the research agenda on comparative legal metrics and quantification of performance as a regulatory technique will be divided in three parts. First, I will revisit the program 'Justice in Numbers', describing its evolution since 2015. Second, I will analyze the relationship between a quantified justice, managerial judges, and 'numeroids' as a regulatory technique. Third, I will provide a few reflections on the current setting and institutional challenges for Brazilian justice based on information that emerges from these reports.

1 Pedro Rubim Borges Fortes, 'How legal indicators influence a justice system and judicial behavior: the Brazilian National Council of Justice and 'justice in numbers'' (2015) 47 *Journal of Legal Pluralism and Unofficial Law* 39–55.

 | DOI:10.1163/9789004680944_003

2 Revisiting 'Justice in Numbers' in Brazil

The original article focused on the establishment of the Brazilian National Council of Justice (NCJ) as new body for overview and control of the judiciary branch based on 15 interviews conducted in 2009 and 2010 as part of a project from FGV on the oral history of the NCJ[2]. The NCJ produces statistical reports on judicial procedures and sentences for every state, type of tribunal, and hierarchical level, which originated the project 'Justice in Numbers'. Politically, the NCJ uses statistical information as *disciplinary power* and *bio-power* with political control exercised over the population of judges through regimes of incentives and sanctions that affect their behavior, including planning, guiding, protecting, or eventually disciplining individual judges[3]. Importantly, the quantitative administration of justice in Brazil also involves dynamics of institutional coordination and competition. In terms of sanctioning judges, for instance, the NCJ would normally refer the disciplinary case to the local ombudsman and supervise the proceeding without direct intervention, except if necessary. In terms of incentives, the NCJ stimulates competitions between state tribunals by comparing the efficiency of all different tribunals in the 'Justice in Numbers' annual reports.

Theoretically, the original article demonstrated that the so-called 'mathematical turn' in law may influence the transformation of the internal structure of a legal order through internalization of legal indicators and pressure for judicial efficiency[4]. Even if we may not consider these mathematical elements as part of the official law, we must acknowledge their impact as 'irritants' through a built-in structure that influences the judicial branch and changes its program, structure, and operations[5]. Politically, the origins of the NCJ involved sensitive discussions on its composition with definition of members, especially because of concerns on the political control of this new body and the potential risks of a subordination of the judiciary power to other powers or to the civil society. The establishment of the NCJ brought the old question of *'Quis custodiet ipsos custodes?'* into a new and more complex perspective, because the question on 'who controls the controllers?' invites us to reflect on the necessity of checks

2 Borges Fortes, *supra* fn 1.

3 Michel Foucault, *Security, territory, population: lectures at the Collège de France, 1977–78* (Palgrave Macmillan 2009).

4 Restrepo Amariles, *supra* fn 1, 9–21.

5 Niklas Luhmann, *Law as a social system* (Oxford University Press 2004); Gunther Teubner, 'Legal irritants: good faith in British law or how unifying law ends up in new divergencies' (1998) 61 *Modern Law Review* 11–32.

and balances for the NCJ, but also on the risks of political capture by the judiciary or of political domination from powerful actors.

Lessons of legal realism are also relevant for our reflection as the *law-jobs* and the *institutional machinery of justice* influence the administration of justice and judicial behavior, especially because numerical indicators of judicial performance are considered for promotion of efficient judges and punishment of inefficient ones[6]. State systems developed electronic overview mechanisms capable of identifying cases awaiting a judicial decision for long periods of time, discouraging judges to retain processes in their offices. Because judges are concerned with the quantity of decisions they produce and need to deliver judicial sentences routinely, they are encouraged to prepare templates that may be easily adjusted to the particularity of the cases by their clerks. The managerial rationality imported from the new public management rationale into adjudication affects the quality of decision-making, depth of legal analyses, and the credence of judge-made law[7].

Looking back to the original article now, the research was based on the oral history of the NCJ, which focused primarily on its foundation and the origins of the project 'Justice in Numbers'. As the interviews were conducted in 2009 and 2010 with interviewees from the original composition of the board of counsellors, the original article did not explain in detail the institutionalization of the judicial statistical system defined by the Resolution n. 76, published by the NCJ in 2009. This resolution established the principles of the judicial statistical system, the responsibility of Presidents of Tribunals to provide comprehensive data annually and defined the categories of mandatory general statistical indicators that must be produced. According to these rules, the NCJ must produce general statistical indicators related to (I) incomes, budgets, and degrees of use, especially (a) revenues and expenses; (b) structure; (II) litigiosity, especially (a) workload, (b) index of procedural traffic jam, (c) index of appealability and reform of decisions; (III) access to justice; (IV) profile of cases. Even if the original 'Justice in Numbers' report was produced in 2004

6 Karl N. Llewellyn, 'The normative, the legal, and the law-jobs: the problem of juristic method' (1940) 49 *Yale Law Journal* 1355–1400; William Twining, *Karl Llewellyn and the realist movement* (Cambridge University Press 2012); Pedro Rubim Borges Fortes, 'An explorer of legal borderlands: a review of William Twining's jurist in context, a memoir' (2019) 5 *REI-Revista Estudos Institucionais* 777–790.

7 Benoît Frydman, 'Le management judiciaire comme alternative à la procédure', in Benoît Frydman and Emmanuel Jeuland (eds), *Le nouveau management de la justice et l'indépendance des juges* (Dalloz 2011) 101–110; Benoît Frydman, 'Concilier le management avec les valeurs du judiciaire', in Thierry Marchandise (ed), *Quel management pour quelle justice?* (Larcier 2013) 81–88.

and the twentieth report is expected to be produced in 2023, the NCJ refers to the series of reports since 2009 as a new historical series based on these institutional rules and principles set by the Resolution n. 76/2009.

As the original research reflected on the foundation and the initial decade of the NCJ and the 'Justice in Numbers' projects, the present text should consider their second decade and the reports produced between 2015 and 2022. In the introduction of the eleventh report, there are mentions to the celebration of ten years of the NCJ and important transformations made in the statistical analysis[8]. Innovations included detailed information on the organization of the judicial branch and the judicial bodies in every unit of the Brazilian federation. Likewise, the report announced that there was an organizational effort to produce uniformity regarding the types of cases, the procedural categories, and the themes of disputes to facilitate judicial management. This report also informed that there were new analytical frames for subjects like digital justice, the differences between the first and the second degrees of jurisdiction, and the distinction between judgments of merit ('*ações de conhecimento*') and of law enforcement ('*ações de execução*'). Additionally, the report contained a specific section on management of judicial performance, which included the Comparative Index of Judicial Productivity ('*Índice de Produtividade Comparada da Justiça – IPCJus*'). Furthermore, this report anticipated two changes of methodology for the following report, which would include information on cases decided through ADR mechanisms and cases suspended awaiting mandatory decisions from the superior courts under the regime of judicial precedents for repetitive appeals.

Interestingly, the subsequent reports were produced according to the benchmark of the eleventh report. The twelfth report provided an interesting clarification about the identity between the statistical research of the 'Justice in Numbers' project and the institutional agenda of NCJ[9]. Many of the issues that appeared in the reports were object of investigations, requests and opinions produced by counsellors or the Presidency of the NCJ. Therefore, the statistical analysis of 'Justice in Numbers' reports often echoed concerns related to judicial management, like tax law enforcement, imbalances between personnel from the first and second degrees of jurisdiction, expansion of digital justice through judicial electronic procedures, and indexes for procedural traffic jam and judicial productivity. This report also highlighted the importance

8 Conselho Nacional de Justiça, *Justiça em Números 2015 – Ano-Base 2014* (CNJ 2015). All the reports are available at <https://www.cnj.jus.br/pesquisas-judiciarias/justica-em-numeros/> (accessed 15 January 2023).

9 Conselho Nacional de Justiça, *Justiça em Números 2016 – Ano-Base 2015* (CNJ 2016).

to analyze the length of procedures according to the different categories. Furthermore, there was new information on the percentage of cases closed by conciliation and mediation. Even if ADR was already part of the institutional agenda of the NCJ, the inclusion of this issue was motivated by a legal reform of the civil procedure that included a mandatory ADR stage at the beginning of every judicial procedure. Importantly, according to the twelfth report, the creation of a Comparative Index of Judicial Productivity (*'Índice de Produtividade Comparada da Justiça – IPCJus'*) in 2013 transformed the conception of productivity and analyses of productive capacities, use of resources, and judicial management.

Beyond the conception explained above, the description of the data presented in the subsequent reports may illustrate this judicial statistical information. The thirteenth report informed us that by the end of 2016 there were 79,7 million active procedures in the judicial dockets[10]. Coincidently, the number of new cases brought in 2016 was equivalent to the number of judicial cases closed by judiciary during the year: 29,4 million judicial cases. In terms of productivity, on average, each Brazilian judge decided 1,749 judicial procedures in 2016. Additionally, this thirteenth report showed that 70,1% of all judicial procedures were electronic. Interestingly, the length of procedures with judgments of merit (*'ações de conhecimento'*) was, in average, 1 year and 4 months, and the length of procedures with judgments of law enforcement (*'ações de execução'*) was, in average, 4 years and 6 months. In terms of budget, the total expenses with the judiciary branch comprised R$ 84,6 billion (equivalent to roughly 24,7 billion euros), which meant a cost per capita of R$ 411,73 (equivalent to roughly 120,22 euros per individual)[11]. This report also revealed a policy effort to mobilize more resources to the first degree of jurisdiction, because of relatively bigger workload – 94% of the volume of work – and relatively smaller mobilization of personnel – 66% of free appointment positions and 84% of tenured civil servants. Regarding ADR mechanisms, according to the report, 12% of the disputes were solved through settlement in 2016.

While reexamining how the rise of legal indicators influence the administration of justice and judicial behavior, we should consider the annual number of judgments per individual judge. In 2017, in average, each judge produced 1,819 judicial sentences or 7,2 judicial sentences for every working day[12]. In 2018, in average, each judge produced 1,877 judicial sentences or almost 8 judicial

10 Conselho Nacional de Justiça, *Justiça em Números 2017 – Ano-Base 2016* (CNJ 2017).

11 According to the website <exchangerates.org.uk> (accessed 15 January 2023), 1 BRL was equivalent to 0,292 euros on 31 December 2016.

12 Conselho Nacional de Justiça, *Justiça em Números 2018 – Ano-Base 2017* (CNJ 2018).

sentences for every working day[13]. In 2019, in average, each judge concluded 1,877 cases or almost 8,4 for every working day[14]. According to the sixteenth report, there was a consistent growth in productivity for five years and, in comparison with 2014, the judicial productivity was 24,2% higher in 2019. The seventeenth report explained that 2020 was an unusual year because of the global pandemic of COVID-19 and the productivity of judges was 22% lower in comparison with the previous year[15]. In numerical terms, in 2020, in average, each judge concluded 1,643 judicial cases or some 6,5 judicial sentences for every working day. These numbers remained stable in 2021 as it was the second year of the global pandemic and, in average, each judge concluded 1,588 cases or some 6,3 judicial sentences for every working day[16].

The 'Justice in Numbers' reports reveal that the judiciary receives and finishes a very large number of judicial procedures every year but continues to retain a huge volume of cases in the judicial dockets. For instance, there were 80,1 million active procedures in the judicial dockets by the end of 2017[17], 78,7 million by the end of 2018[18], 77,1 million by the end of 2019[19], 75,4 million by the end of 2020[20], and 77,3 million by the end of 2021[21]. By the end of 2022, there are certainly tens of millions active procedures in the judicial dockets, but we will have to wait for the next report to know precisely the total numbers. In terms of closure of judicial cases, this number reached more than 30 million cases for the first time in 2017, when the judiciary closed 30,4 million judicial cases. Because the NCJ monitored old cases awaiting a judicial decision and established targets for terminating these old cases, the numerous judicial sentences of old cases had an impact on the length of judicial procedures, which was registered in the 'Justice in Number' reports. The average length of a judicial case was 5 years and 6 months in 2015, being reduced to 4 years and 10 months in 2018. Interestingly, in 2019, the 'index of procedural traffic jam' ('*taxa de congestionamento*') reached a historical low number: 68,5% – meaning that 31,5% of all active judicial cases were solved within that year. On the other hand, the number of new judicial cases annually remains very large. For instance, even

13 Conselho Nacional de Justiça, *Justiça em Números 2019 – Ano-Base 2018* (CNJ 2019).
14 Conselho Nacional de Justiça, *Justiça em Números 2020 – Ano-Base 2019* (CNJ 2020).
15 Conselho Nacional de Justiça, *Justiça em Números 2021 – Ano-Base 2020* (CNJ 2021).
16 Conselho Nacional de Justiça, *Justiça em Números 2022 – Ano-Base 2021* (CNJ 2022).
17 Conselho Nacional de Justiça, *supra* fn 12.
18 Conselho Nacional de Justiça, *supra* fn 13.
19 Conselho Nacional de Justiça, *supra* fn 14.
20 Conselho Nacional de Justiça, *supra* fn 15.
21 Conselho Nacional de Justiça, *supra* fn 16.

in 2020, the first year of the global pandemic of COVID-19 witnessed a volume of 25,8 million new cases in the Brazilian judicial dockets.

The 'Justice in Numbers' reports also monitored the percentage of conciliation and of electronic procedures in Brazilian tribunals. The evolution of the 'Index of Conciliation' is the following one: 11,1% in 2015; 11,9% in 2016; 12,1% in 2017; 12% in 2018; 12,5% in 2019; 9,9% in 2020. According to the reports, the global pandemic of COVID-19 caused a reduction in the success rate of ADR mechanisms and the 'Index of Conciliation' remained lower than before. On the other hand, this period of global pandemic of COVID-19 witnessed the consolidation of the digitalization of the justice system and a point of maturity of the electronic procedures in Brazilian tribunals. For instance, in 2019, 90% of the new judicial cases were initiated through electronic procedures. In contrast, ten years before, in 2009, only 11,2% of the new judicial cases were initiated electronically. By 2019, the percentage of electronic cases in the Brazilian judicial dockets was around 73%. Furthermore, the judiciary developed some technological strategies to provide judicial services during the global pandemic through 100% digital courts, virtual counter, and a package of initiatives implemented through the program Justice 4.0.

One important component of these reports is the Comparative Index of Judicial Productivity (*'Índice de Produtividade Comparada da Justiça – IPCJus'*). According to the NCJ, this index measures the relative efficiency and productivity of tribunals through a unified score to compare the optimal efficiency with the actual efficiency measured in each judicial unit. This methodology permits comparisons between units of the same kind of tribunal (federal, state, labor, electoral or military tribunals), independent of its size, because it considers what was produced by the unit based on the available resources. The IPC-Jus also measures how many additional judicial procedures should be closed for a judicial unit to reach maximal efficiency. In several annual reports, for instance, the Tribunal of Justice of Rio de Janeiro (TJRJ) was the most efficient and reached 100% in terms of optimal efficiency, becoming the benchmarking for calculating what other state tribunals could have done, if they used their resources optimally like the TJRJ did.

This numerical indicator also fosters competition between different tribunals, influencing the administration of justice and judicial behavior. Examining the numbers from 2017, for instance, the Tribunal of Justice of Rio Grande do Sul (TJRS) managed to reach 100% of efficiency in both first and second degree of jurisdiction, and the TJRJ reached 100% of efficiency for first degree and 99% of efficiency for second degree of jurisdiction. However, the Tribunal of Justice of Paraná (TJPR) reached 100% of efficiency in the lower courts, but only 66% of efficiency in its higher courts. In contrast, the Tribunal of Justice for the Federal District (TJDFT) reached 100% of efficiency in its higher courts, but only 78% of efficiency in the lower courts. These numbers were a prodigious example of how the 'Justice in Numbers' reports may produce 'irritants' for the internal operations of a justice system, as the publicization of this numbers stimulated discussion and reflection on the relative efficiency and productivity of judges and tribunals. These numbers matter for the recognition of merit of individual judges, especially when they apply for promotion.

Likewise, the NCJ established some forms of institutional awards and prizes, like the 'Seal Justice in Numbers' (*'Selo Justiça em Números'*) implemented in 2013 and replaced in 2019 by the 'NCJ Quality Award' (*'Prêmio de Qualidade CNJ'*). All the ninety different Brazilian tribunals are considered for the 'NCJ Quality Award' and they may be deemed 'diamond', 'gold', or 'silver', after being evaluated in terms of their (a) governance; (b) productivity; (c) transparency; (d) data and technology. The top tribunal among all the 90 tribunals, with the highest total score, receives the 'excellency award' (*'Prêmio Excelência'*). As this award considered various factors beyond the IPC-Jus, courts like the TJRJ – deemed 100% efficient – did not receive this award in its initial years of 2019 and 2020, but eventually scored better in 2021 and 2022 to receive the 'silver award'.

In 2022, the NCJ added new criteria for evaluation of tribunals, like (1) support for victims of crimes; (2) accessibility and inclusion of handicapped persons; (3) capacitation of judges for rights of children and adolescents; (4) development of policy for innovation management; (5) implementation of centers for judicial cooperation; (6) existence of judicial units with 'Index of Response to Demand' (*'Índice de Atendimento à Demanda'*) superior to 100%; (7) procedural speed and impulse for judgment of environmental actions; (8) provide information for the 'DataJud' through judicial units; (9) implementation of digital platform of the judiciary power; (10) implementation of the Codex platform. In recent years, the 'Justice in Numbers' reports added sections on environmental protection and human rights protection and these criteria are aligned with their initiative of recognizing the importance of diffuse and collective rights.

The sixteenth report referred to the Brazilian commitment with the UN Agenda 2030 for sustainable report. The seventeenth report provided specific information on environmental actions, indicating a total number of 57,168 judicial cases in 2020 with a growth of 17,9% in comparison with 2019. This report also included information on 'human rights' but acknowledged that this is an essentially contested concept by excluding the themes of 'right to healthcare' and 'right to education' and prioritizing themes like 'constitutional guarantees' and 'social assistance'. With the global pandemic of COVID-19 and the explosion of number of cases of social assistance, there was a total number of 64,978 judicial cases of human rights in 2020 with a growth of 342% in comparison with 2019. The eighteenth report described a total number of 89,588 new judicial cases of environmental actions in 2021 with a growth of 10,4% in comparison with 2020.

The eighteenth report was also marked by an important technological innovation. Because of the point of maturity of the electronic procedures, the NCJ extracted the statistical information directly from the 'DataJud' system. The NCJ eliminated the previous format of manual procedures and the provision of information through electronic forms filled by the Presidency of all 90 tribunals. Without intermediaries, the statistical measurement becomes more precise and trustworthy. Additionally, the CODEX platform is an innovative mechanism for data extraction that functions as a *data lake* with the consolidation of procedural information from electronic cases that may translate textual content and structured data into panels, graphs, and reports of business intelligence, unified research, automated provision of statistical data, and provision of data for models of artificial intelligence.

Therefore, the 'Justice in Number' reports indicate a managerial effort of the judiciary branch to deal with a huge volume of active judicial cases, that requires a quantified justice system, efficient performance of managerial functions by magistrates, and use of legal indicators as technological tools for governance of the judiciary and regulation of judicial behavior. The next section analyzes these subjects.

3 Quantified Justice, Managerial Judges, and 'Numeroids' as a Regulatory Technique

The 'Justice in Numbers' project was developed in the context of the global demand for legal indicators that could demonstrate the operations of a justice system. In a certain sense, there was a protectionist spirit of preparing the national indicators as a tool for resistance to economic imperialism disseminated through the Washington Consensus[22]. In another sense, there was

22 Amanda Perry-Kessaris, 'Prepare your indicators: economics imperialism on the shores of law and development' (2011) 7 *International Journal of Law in Context* 401–421; Kevin E. Davis, Benedict Kingsbury, Sally Engle Merry, 'Indicators as a technology of global governance' (2012) 46 *Law & Society Review* 71–104; Tor Krever, 'Quantifying Law: legal indicator projects and the reproduction of neoliberal common sense' (2013) 34 *Third World Quarterly* 131–150.

a public policy concern of preparing the national indicators as means for aggregation of a new picture of a coherent and uniform quantified justice system. Like the image of Thomas Hobbes' Leviathan with the sovereign being composed by the aggregation of multiple fragmented units, the 'Justice in Numbers' reports provide the image of a coherent and uniform quantified justice system emerging from the aggregation of tens of thousands judicial units that manage tens of millions judicial procedures with a continuous dynamic flow of new cases being received and old cases being concluded[23]. Not surprising this statistical information of the quantified justice system may be referred metaphorically as a radiography of the judiciary.

The annual report published in 2020, for instance, referred to this metaphor of the x-ray and suggested that 'Justice in Numbers' reveals the internal operations of the justice system "with detailed information of the performance of the bodies that compose the judicial branch, their expenses, and their structures"[24]. According to the opening remarks made by the Chief-Justice, transparency is a powerful managerial tool, and the knowledge of this data permits the adoption of a policy of case management based on technical information, strong responsibility, and accountability. Importantly, legal indicators have been used for analysis of professional performance and justification of the existence of judicial, prosecutorial and defense organs and bodies.

Assessing the performances of processes, people and organizations became one of the important functions of the NCJ, whose annual report titled 'Justice in Numbers' provides a series of legal indicators related to legal fields, judges, and courts. Measuring the volume of cases processed by judges, prosecutors, and defenders is essential for the decision to create, eliminate, or transform new professional positions, organs, and bodies within these organizations. Interestingly, the pressure created by the large quantity of cases could lead to new strategies to simplify formalities, inform decision-making, and promote best-practices and legal reforms.

Additionally, judicial precedents also evolved as a managerial technique. Originating from an initiative of Justice Victor Nunes Leal in the 1960s[25], the Supreme Court established an institutional protocol to define judicial precedents that should have a binding effect within the judiciary. The Constitutional reform of the justice system in 2004 included additional methods for expanding the binding effects of these judicial precedents towards lower courts. These

23 Thomas Hobbes, *Leviathan* (Cambridge University Press 1991).

24 Conselho Nacional de Justiça, *supra* fn 14, 5.

25 Victor Nunes Leal, 'Passado e futuro da súmula do STF' (1981) 145 *Revista de Direito Administrativo* 1–20.

new regulatory techniques have been applied by the Brazilian Supreme Court to provide more efficient judicial decisions, reduce sentencing delays and economic costs, and transform the legal experience. As quantification of performance permeates the Brazilian legal system, the application of judicial precedents was internalized within the judiciary branch as a control mechanism, but eventually judges may resist against uniformization of adjudication.

Moreover, algorithms may also be used as regulatory techniques for the internal operations of the justice system, even if current technology is not sufficiently developed for artificial intelligence to substitute human intelligence in terms of judicial sentencing[26]. The State-Administered Justice employs algorithms as tools for identifying repetitive claims, sorting, and grouping thematic clusters, and applying document assembly and automation. There are pilot projects of robots to facilitate case management within the Brazilian Supreme Court, the Superior Tribunal of Justice, regional tribunals, the Attorney General's Office, and the Office for Public Defenders.

Maurice Duverger makes a balanced analysis of the potential use of mathematical methods in political science, praising how translation of phenomena into numbers and symbols may introduce the comparative precision of quantification and improve the tools for analysis with such a difference like the one between walking and flying with a jet[27]. On the other hand, the French jurist criticizes investigations restricted to quantification and mathematical analysis[28]. In this sense, statistical investigation could be complemented by other means of empirical investigation, to cast new light into the administration of justice and the performance of managerial functions by magistrates.

One important consequence of the emergence of these indicators is the rise of managerial rationality in law[29]. As David Restrepo Amariles correctly puts it, indicators become entrenched in institutional practices and interconnect with other normative devices and eventually drive the institutional behavior of organizations towards a managerial rationality that pervades legal

26 Pedro Rubim Borges Fortes, 'Paths to digital justice: Judicial robots, algorithmic decision-making, and due process' (2020) 7 *Asian Journal of Law and Society* 453–469; Pedro Rubim Borges Fortes, Pablo Marcello Baquero, David Restrepo Amariles, 'Artificial intelligence risks and algorithmic regulation' (2022) 13 *European Journal of Risk Regulation* 357–372; Pedro Rubim Borges Fortes and David Restrepo Amariles, 'Law-jobs in the algorithmic society' (2022) 18 *International Journal of Law in Context* 1–12.

27 Maurice Duverger, *Ciência política* (Zahar 1981, 3rd edn).

28 Duverger, *supra* fn 27.

29 David Restrepo Amariles, 'Supping with the Devil? Indicators and the rise of managerial rationality in law' (2017) 13 *International Journal of Law in Context* 465–484.

processes[30]. Revisiting the 'Justice in Numbers' in Brazil and establishing a link between the quantification of justice and judicial behavior, the empirical reality is that Brazilian judges exercise typical managerial functions nowadays. The managerial rationality behind statistical information and behavioral control over judges by the NCJ requires that magistrates produce an average of six to eight judicial sentences every working day, so that they may be efficient and productively control dockets of their judicial unities.

The view of a magistrate alone in his cabinet, examining the evidence of the case and consulting his legal library to prepare his opinion on a judicial procedure, based on his careful analysis of the facts and reflections on the merit of his judgment seems to be a romantic image nowadays. Like clothes no longer are tailormade in the garment industry, but rather previously produced and ready for use (or *prêt-à-porter*), judges now prepare templates of opinions for different sorts of cases and significant parts of these templates are copied and pasted into the sentences produced for different judicial processes. Additionally, judges must manage a team of freely appointed clerks, judicial civil servants, temporary interns, and other officials to run their judicial units and guarantee a continuous line of production of judicial sentences. Under the pressure to produce a high number of judicial sentences every day and in parallel with all responsibilities related to judicial hearings, production of evidence, interim decisions, and other acts of ordinary impulse of judicial procedures, the exercise of judicial functions depends on a teamwork managed by the judge.

Inevitably, the function of the judicial clerk becomes decisive for efficient case management, since a judge alone would be unable to produce eight sentences, in average, per working day, without the support of highly qualified professionals to collaborate with the magistrate. Judicial clerks must provide support for judges in the mass production of judicial sentences, but the necessity for a line of production negatively affects the quality of judicial decisions. Criticisms about exercise of judicial power by clerks in substitution of judges as if the judicial branch became a '*clerkocracy*' instead of a '*juristocracy*' are exaggerated, because judges normally keep control over content of the judicial decisions they sign and for which they are responsible[31].

30 Restrepo Amariles, *supra* fn 29.

31 Ran Hirschl, *Towards juristocracy: the origins and consequences of the new constitutionalism* (Harvard University Press 2009); Helen J. Knowles, 'Clerkish Control of Recent Supreme Court Opinions?: A Case Study of Justice Kennedy's Opinion in Gonzales v. Carhart' (2009) 10 *Georgetown Journal of Gender and the Law* 63–86; M.R. Kumara Swamy, 'Clerkocracy in India' (1968) 3 *Intereconomics* 86–87.

On the other hand, pressure for quantitative production means that Brazilian judges have very limited time to dedicate to each individual judicial procedure. Considering that each judge produces between six and eight sentences per working day and must manage thousands of active judicial procedures in their dockets, there is little time for reading files, conducting legal research, reflecting about legal issues, and approaching judicial controversies from original perspectives. Therefore, quantification of justice requires rigid performance management and control. Solutions are replicated to many judicial processes to facilitate case management of around 80 million judicial procedures by some 18,000 magistrates.

Institutional design of measurements of judicial performance produces incentives for simplification and against complexity. As explained in the original article, complex litigation, collective actions, and high-profile cases may be considered radioactive and problematic for the performance, productivity, and efficiency of judges. Even if more recent reports refer to the UN Agenda 2030 and to statistical information on environmental protection and human rights, the NCJ did not develop mechanisms of control and monitoring of complex litigation and collective actions that adequately consider their potential for promoting justice and making a difference in society[32]. Likewise, the NCJ considers that 'closing a case' is the efficient resolution of a civil procedure without considering the merits, the substance, or the values embedded in the judicial sentence. However, a magistrate may 'close a case' unfairly, as often happens with execution of judicial sentences in extremely complex collective actions which are challenging in terms of effective law enforcement. As NCJ and 'Justice in Numbers' have not developed criteria for normatively evaluating the merits of judicial decisions, wrong 'closures' may be classified as efficient, even if they promote injustice.

Consider, for instance, that judges from TJRJ have been considered highly efficient and productive and this tribunal often reached 100% in terms

---

32 See Pedro Rubim Borges Fortes, 'O impacto regulatório da tutela coletiva de direitos: a definição das regras e o desenvolvimento socioeconômico' (2019) *Repensando a regulação no Brasil: novas visões e propostas. Rio de Janeiro: Synergia* 213–242; Pedro Rubim Borges Fortes and Pedro Farias Oliveira, 'A insustentável leveza do ser? A quantificação do dano moral coletivo sob a perspectiva do fenômeno da ilicitude lucrativa e o 'caso Dieselgate'' (2019) 2 *Revista IBERC* 1–28, available at <https://revistaiberc.responsabilidadecivil.org/iberc/article/view/85/65> (accessed 15 January 2023); Pedro Rubim Borges Fortes, 'O Fenômeno da Ilicitude Lucrativa' (2019) 5 *REI-Revista Estudos Institucionais* 104–132; Pedro Rubim Borges Fortes, 'O consumidor contemporâneo no Show de Truman: a geodiscriminação digital como prática ilícita no direito brasileiro' (2020) 124 *Revista de Direito do Consumidor* 253–260.

of Comparative Index of Judicial Productivity (*'Índice de Produtividade Comparada da Justiça – IPCJus'*). However, during the last decade, the state of Rio de Janeiro suffered from severe political corruption, territorial control by organized crime, militia, and drug lords, and economic decadence due to geographical relocation of businesses to other jurisdictions[33]. Additionally, reports refer to an increasing number of environmental procedures, but destruction of the Amazon Forest also significantly grew in this period. Likewise, increasing numbers of human rights cases coincided with a significant number of human rights violations in Brazil. Therefore, reflecting on the original purpose of developing these legal indicators as proxies for the good quality of institutions that could define valuable rules of the game to foster development, the NCJ and 'Justice in Numbers' project should reconsider their perspective that considers 'closing the case' to be an efficient and productive action, regardless of the merits or the substance of the cases. In other words, the quantitative analysis of the internal operations of the justice system also needs to be complemented by a qualitative analysis that considers the impact of the judicial system in terms of promoting justice, citizenship, the rule of law, and socioeconomic development.

At their current stage, the legal indicators adopted by the NCJ and the 'Justice in Numbers' project do not seem to be normative, but measurements of facts related to the opening, closure, size, and length of procedures in the dockets of judicial units. Even if these indicators are relevant for control of numbers, volume, and duration of procedural acts, the NCJ does not evaluate the quality of a judicial decision, its fairness, and the legitimacy of its merits. At the original article, I borrowed Karl Llewellyn's concept of a '*legaloid*' – an external element from the general culture that becomes partially legal through a process of fusion – to imagine a legal indicator as a '*numeroid*', that is, a number with normative weight that indicates the quality of rule of law, efficiency of law enforcement, and substant justice through mathematical formulas and indexes[34]. In this second decade of functioning of the 'Justice in Numbers' project, the NCJ maintained the similar catalog of indicators that provides incentives for speedy, simple, and less risky decisions. Strategic behavior may affect judge's perspectives and this managerial rationality may negatively

33 See Pedro Rubim Borges Fortes, 'Vigilante Justice and the Rule of Death: The Existential Threat to the State and Its People in Brazil', in Peter Robson and Ferdinando Spina (eds), *Vigilante Justice in Society and Popular Culture* (Farleigh Dickinson University Press 2022) 295–321; Pedro Rubim Borges Fortes, 'Imagining Bossa Nova: Possibilities and Limits of Charter Cities' (2020) 6 *REI-Revista Estudos Institucionais* 769–779.

34 Borges Fortes, *supra* fn 1, 39–55.

affect quality of decision-making, depth of legal analyses, and credence of judge-made law.

Reflecting on 'numeroids' as a regulatory technique, the normative character of indicators adopted by the NCJ should be considered as part of our analysis. According to the Resolution n. 76/2009, there are general statistical indicators related to (I) incomes, budgets, and degrees of use, especially (a) revenues and expenses; (b) structure; (II) litigiosity, especially (a) workload, (b) index of procedural traffic jam, (c) index of appealability and reform of decisions; (III) access to justice; (IV) profile of cases. The 'Justice in Numbers' reports contain a catalog of these 'numeroids' – numerical formulas with normative weight that indicate measurements of the functioning of the justice system. For instance, the section on the 'landscape of the judiciary power' provides statistical data on the structure of the first degree of jurisdiction, with geographical distribution of judicial units, classification of size of tribunals, budget comparisons, measurement of workforce, and indicators on average time for procedural duration. The section on financial resources and human resources provides historical records on income and expenses. The section of judicial management contains legal indicators for measurement of litigiosity, indicators related to access to justice and legal aid, index of procedural traffic jam, index of response to the demand, index of external and internal appealability, and a specific analysis of the law enforcement stage. The index of electronic procedures provides information on the percentage of new cases brought to court through digital form. The index of conciliation provides information on the percentage of cases closed by a mutual agreement between the parties. There are also indicators on time length of duration of each case. Regarding efficiency, there is an index for judicial productivity and the Comparative Index of Judicial Productivity (*'Índice de Produtividade Comparada da Justiça – IPCJus'*). These indicators reflect external elements – for instance, economic costs, degree, and volume of social conflict – that are incorporated into the legal discourse and become decisive for judicial behavior through the influence of the NCJ and the impact of a regime of incentives that is shaped by numbers of efficiency and productivity.

4 Reflections on Institutional Possibilities and Challenges for the Judiciary

Interestingly, the statistical information on quantification of the justice system, development of a managerial rationality as part of judicial performance and emergence of these 'numeroids' as a regulatory technique and part of the contemporary discourse provide food for thought on institutional possibilities and challenges for the judiciary. There is a correlation between the development of judicial organizations and application of the institutional rules of the game. In this sense, mapping judicial structure provides detailed information on judicial units based on subject matter and their distribution within tribunals, geographical areas, and degree of jurisdiction. In comparison with other jurisdictions, for instance, the criminal justice system remains very inefficient, formalistic, slow, and subject to numerous appeals and claims of nullification. Likewise, measures for law enforcement (*'ações de execução'*) may last three times longer than judgment of merits of a cause (*'ações de conhecimento'*), which means that judgments may symbolic, as the party may win the case, but not benefit from the positive verdict. Instead of securing previously potential resources for effective law enforcement after a judgment of merits of a case, judges may provide an opportunity for the party to divert assets and create obstacles for payment after trial.

Another challenge comes from the budget and the regime of access to justice in operation at the Brazilian judiciary. In 2021, for instance, the total annual budget of the Brazilian judiciary power consisted of a total of R$ 103.921.103.891,00 (roughly equivalent to 16.409.142.304,39 euros)[35]. 91,5% of these resources were allocated to pay salaries of a total of 424,911 individuals in the judicial workforce, including the 18,035 active judges. These expenses correspond to 9,64% of the total public expenses spent annually on governmental budget and would be equivalent to approximately 1,2% of the total Brazilian Internal Production. The cost of judicial services per capita in 2021 would be approximately R$ 489,91 for individual (roughly equivalent to 77,35 euros). Importantly, 19,5% of these expenses are allocated for the payment of retired workforce. According to the 'Justice in Numbers' report, the judiciary brought back many incomes for the Brazilian state in 2021, which would be roughly equivalent to 71% of the total expenses with the judiciary power. However, this calculation includes not only money from court's fees and judicial taxes, but also money resulting from law enforcement of favorable decisions to the government. In fact, the incomes directly from court fees and judicial taxes were equivalent to R$ 24,8 billion, which would correspond to approximately 23,8% of total costs with the judicial branch. Therefore, judicial services are largely covered with public resources from taxpayers. One important challenge is related to the large number of cases exempted from

35 According to the website <exchangerates.org.uk> (accessed 15 January 2023), 1 BRL was equivalent to 0,1579 euros on 31 December 2021.

court fees not paid directly by the parties. On one hand, this exemption from court fees gives a false impression that the judiciary is freely accessible to the population at large. On the other hand, a generous philosophy of wide access to justice opens the judicial system for a large volume of judicial procedures which are expensive and do not generate sufficient revenue to cover all expenses.

This institutional setting leads us to problems revealed by the indexes of litigiosity, procedural traffic jam, and judicial productivity. All 'Justice in Number' Reports reveal a large volume of active cases in judicial dockets, with tens of millions of new cases being received and old cases being closed every year. With judges producing around 6 to 8 new sentences per working day, there is a continuous sense of working under pressure to perform and to deliver many fast, speedy, and short sentences. The level of attention that judges may give to these cases is very limited. Lack of time for examining evidence, reading thousands of pages, and conducting research on legal doctrine negatively affects quality of sentences produced by Brazilian judges. None of these critical points are found in 'Justice in Numbers' reports, but these are effects of an evaluation of judicial performance based on quantity instead of quality. Development of indicators and measurement of quality instead of quantity would be desirable. Likewise, our political community could also assess the sustainability of the means for financing litigation primarily through general taxation instead of court fees directly paid by the parties. Furthermore, law enforcement could become even more effective in the future than it is now in the present. These are some of the challenges for the judiciary that emerge from the careful analysis of 'Justice in Numbers' reports from 2015 until today.

5 Final Remarks

By examining the evolution of reports and development of new legal indicators by the NCJ in Brazil, 'Justice in Numbers' is revisited. The rise of legal indicators influences the administration of justice and judicial behavior. The judiciary receives and finishes a very large number of judicial procedures every year but continues to retain a huge volume of cases in judicial dockets. Percentage of conciliation and of electronic procedures in Brazilian tribunals is increasing with consolidation of ADR mechanisms and digitalization of the justice system. The managerial effort of the judiciary branch to deal with a huge volume of active judicial cases requires a quantified justice system, efficient performance of managerial functions by magistrates, and legal indicators as technological tools for governance of the judiciary and regulation of judicial behavior. Continuous challenges involve the effectiveness of law enforcement, high costs of adjudication, and qualitative measurement of judicial performance.

CHAPTER 3

Performance-Based Evaluation in Mexico's Federal Administrative Justice Tribunal and the Federal Judiciary Power: A Comparison

Luis José Béjar, Juan Antonio Casanovas and Carlos A. Villanueva

1 Introduction

In Mexico, being a Federation, different levels of jurisdictions, courts and tribunals coexist. Even when they look similar, there remain many differences between courts of different states and between state and federal courts.

For the purposes of this paper, we will focus on a comparative analysis of the performance models that regulate two of our federal judicial bodies. On the one hand, we will look at the judicial power of the Federation (*Poder Judicial de la Federación*, PJF), which is responsible for ordinary federal justice, but also plays the role of a constitutional judge through the *Amparo* trial. On the other hand, our analysis will centre on the Federal Tribunal of Administrative Justice (*Tribunal Federal de Justicia Administrativa*, TFJA), which is endowed with constitutional autonomy and responsible for the administrative litigation trial and the imposition of sanctions for serious misconduct by public employees.

The structure of the judicial power of the Federation has been inspired by the North American model, while the Federal Tribunal of Administrative Justice is modeled after the French Council of State and, therefore, does not technically belong to the judicial power, although its rulings are reviewable by the federal courts, through the so-called direct *Amparo* trial (in the admnistration of which federal courts function as a cassation court).

The appointment of the personnel of these two sets of courts follows completely different mechanisms. In the case of the judicial branch, all employees, from the position of Court Clerk (notifier) to the position of Magistrate of the Circuit Plenary, are part of the judiciary. They are subject to assessment through their entire career – from the procedure for their appointments, which is based on resolutions of the Federal Judicature Council, to the procedures for their permanence, promotions and incentives. At the appointment stage, the assessment entails the examination of prospective judges' theoretical and practical knowledge, but for purposes of permanence, promotions and incentives, performance-based evaluations are carried out as well, so as to

 | DOI:10.1163/9789004680944_004

test theoretical and practical knowledge of the subject matter. Performance-based evaluation is carried out through an interview phase with a commission appointed for such purpose, which has to take objective quantitative and qualitative elements into account, in accordance with the provisions of the Judicial Career of the Federal Judiciary Act (2021). Only new personnel who is hired directly by the head of a jurisdictional body, and the justices of the Supreme Court of Justice of the Nation, who are appointed by means of a shortlist of three candidates submitted by the President of the Republic to the Senate, are exempt from this system. As a result, the performance of a civil servant during his or her legal career is fundamental for his or her promotion, if not for maintaining the position he or she occupies. The standards for such performance-based evaluation are established by means of general dispositions issued by the Judiciary Council.

By contrast, the Magistrates of the Federal Tribunal of Administrative Justice, both of the Superior and Regional Chambers, are appointed directly by the President of the Republic with the approval of the Senate. The Federal Tribunal of Administrative Justice also has a performance-based evaluation system, although this is not expressly established by the rules that regulate the federal administrative judiciary. The Federal Tribunal of Administrative Justice Organisational Act (2016) only provides for a professional jurisdictional career system, and contemplates a system that seeks excellence through competitions and periodic evaluations for promotion and permanence purposes, in terms of the regulations issued by its Board of Government and Administration. However, this performance evaluation system is restricted to only a part of the personnel of the Tribunal, such as clerks and actuaries of the jurisdictional bodies. Under these conditions, the performance evaluation is excessively limited to the intermediate personnel of the administrative justice administration bodies.

This chapter revolves around a comparative analysis of the above performance-based evaluation models, at the level of the personnel of the courts and tribunals. The debate that arises is whether these mechanisms for measuring results based on performances contribute to improving the quality of judicial decisions or whether they are a form of exercise of power that the legal community has met with resistance. Although we are inclined to side with the latter view, it is undeniable that performance-based evaluation strongly influences decisions about the need for creating new courts and chambers, and their redistribution in the territory, as well as the division of labor between courts and tribunals by specific subjects. Performance-based evaluation can also influence (although this is very difficult to appreciate empirically) the assignment of judges and the stability of their assignment, as a system of reward and punishment.

In order to highlight the convergences and divergences of these career systems inside the Mexican federal system, this paper will engage in a functional comparison, all internal to the Mexican judiciary, between the two above-mentioned levels of courts. In order to reduce the complexity of the variables considered, we will not refer to the local career systems, which could be the object of a future comparative exercise.

In short, our work proves that, even though it has been relatively few years since these performance evaluation measurement systems have been in place, they contribute objectively and positively to the improvement of the professional career service and, at least, result in measurable and objective information that is available to all legal operators to analyze and understand the quality of justice in relation to the workload of the courts and tribunals.

2 The Context

Mexico falls in the category of presidential systems. By presidentialism, following Mainwaring & Shugart[1], we mean a regime in which the president is always the chief executive and is elected by popular vote, and the terms of office for the president, the assembly and the Supreme Court are fixed. The separation of powers is distinctive: the independence of the president is based on a constitutionally stipulated term of office, and the congress has an equally autonomous term[2]. Also, the term for the Supreme Court's Judges is fixed at 15 years.

More in particular, under article 83 of the Political Constitution of the Mexican United States (*Constitución Política de los Estados Unidos Mexicanos*, CPEUM) the president is appointed by direct vote and for a period of six years without re-election. According to the article 80 of the CPEUM, the president is the head of the executive power and of the public administration. This denotes a series of implicit and explicit powers such as decision-making power, appointment of Secretaries of State, power of command, disciplinary power[3], as well as the power to promote new pieces of legislation and reforms to existing

1 Scott Mainwaring and Matthew S. Shugart, 'Juan J. Linz: presidencialismo y democracia (una revisión crítica)' (1993) 33 *Foro Internacional* 653–683. All translations in what follows are responsibility of the authors.

2 Fred W. Riggs, 'The survival of presidentialism in America: Para-Constitutional practices' (1988) 9 *International Political Science Review* 248.

3 Miguel Acosta Romero, *Teoría general del derecho administrativo* (Porrúa 1999) 284–292.

statutes[4] and to propose to the Senate the names of Supreme Court's judges[5] and magistrates for the TFJA[6].

Looking at the Mexican history since the 19th century, one can observe a tendency to authoritarian regimes, in spite of a well-established set of strong rules for accountability and political-administrative liability of high-ranking officers, of reasonably independent courts and tribunals, and even of a pluralistic press. All this notwithstanding, political élites have often been able to turn back on accountability, provoking a series of practices, if not entirely illegal, at least morally questionable, and to justify antiliberal actions with the invocation of national security or public interest[7].

In the present day, the political institutions, and especially the presidency, has demonstrated a political ambivalence and chameleonic qualities to take the color of the environment in which unfolds, building its own narrative, myth, and symbols[8], creating a sort of bureaucratic authoritarianism[9] centered in the president. Current president López Obrador is pictured by many as a populist leader, who bases his government power on support from a large number of followers: besides the election (which he won by a landslide), plebiscites, mass demonstrations and opinion polls are crucial instruments through which he mobilises and demonstrates his power capability[10].

Be it as it may, there is no doubt that Mexico does in fact have a democracy, at least a basic one (in terms of quality), with a highly developed administrative structure, a fair number of autonomous agencies, and substantial judicial autonomy. Yet, it should also be kept in mind that: (a) Mexico does have a mixed system, with elements of two contradictory concepts: authoritarianism and democracy, and (b) the legal framework grants the president a wide power in policy design and implementation, with little to no contraints from the legislation[11].

---

4 Article 71 of the CPEUM.

5 Article 96 of the CPEUM.

6 Article 73, section XXIX-H, sixth paragraph, of the CPEUM.

7 Marlies Glasius, 'What authoritarianism is … and is not: a practice perspective?' (2018) (93) *International Affairs* 513–533.

8 Paul Taggart, *Populism* (Open University Press 2000) 3–4.

9 Guillermo O'Donnell, *Modernization and Bureaucratic-Authoritarianism. Studies in South American Politics* (IIS-University of California 1979).

10 Kurt Weyland, 'Clarifying a Contested Concept: Populism in the Study of Latin American Politics' (2001) 34 *Comparative Politics* 1–22.

11 Lorenzo Meyer. *Nuestra tragedia persistente: la democracia autoritaria en México* (Debate 2013) i.

As to the relationship between the president and the judiciary, suffice it to mention that President López Obrador has appointed four members of the Supreme Court in its current composition; five other members were appointed by the presidents elected with the support of the Partido Acción Nacional (PAN) (2000–2006 and 2006–2012), while the other two members of the Court were appointed by the president Peña Nieto, elected with the Partido Revolucionario Institucional (PRI) (2012–2018). All of them were appointed for a term of 15 years without renewal.

On the other hand, the Upper Chamber of the TFJA is composed of 16 Magistrates; however, only 13 Magistrates are currently sitting in the Upper Chamber, since the missing three belong to a section specialised on anticorruption issues, which is in the process of being implemented since 2015. Of the currently 13 appointed Magistrates of the TFJA, only two have been appointed by the current president, while the rest have been appointed before, up to 2007. The term of appointment of these Magistrates is fixed on 15 years without renewal[12].

Except for the Supreme Court of the Nation and the Upper Chamber of the TFJA, it is fair to say the political context has not affected the Mexican current performance-based system in both federal courts and administrative tribunals. Nevertheless, it is important to acknowledge at least an indirect influence of the current political situation over the appointment of judges and magistrates.

3 The Method

A good part of comparative law research is proposed without mentioning the approach or the epistemological background upon which the research is based[13] and, in fact, it is only in exceptional cases that methodological choices are explained[14]. For this reason, in this paper we decided to analyse, albeit briefly, the methodological bases chosen for the comparative analysis between TFJA and PJF rulings in the Mexican case.

12 Article 43 of the Federal Administrative Justice Tribunal Organisation Act (*Ley Orgánica del Tribunal Federal de Justicia Administrativa*, LOTFJA).

13 Jorge Silvero Salgueiro, El método funcional en la comparación constitucional', in José María Serna de la Garza (ed), *Metodología del derecho comparado. Memorias del Congreso Internacional de Culturas y Sistemas Jurídicos Comparados* (Universidad Nacional Autónoma de México 2005) 405–419.

14 John Henry Merryman and Pérez-Perdomo, Rogelio, *La tradición Jurídica Romano Canónica* (3rd edn, translation by de Eduardo L. Suárez Galindo and José María Imaz, Fondo de Cultura Económica 2014) 122–132.

Evidently, the functional method is only one of several tools used by comparativists. Even those who have advocated the functionalist method have used other alternative methods[15]. For the purposes of this paper, the proposed microcomparative exercise will be carried out using the functional method, and this section will explain very briefly some of its most important features.

We have opted for the aforementioned methodology, as it implies a very interesting proposal that has gained followers in recent decades, specifically for exercises such as the one carried out here at the micro-comparative level, that is, the comparison of specific legal institutions.

The approach proposed by the functionalist method implies a change in the traditional conception of legal science, as it is not interested in discovering the essence of rules or institutions. What instead is relevant is to identify how legal institutions function and how they respond to concrete social needs. Thus, it is not unusual that comparativists, to explain their own methodology, also adopt a functionalist approach, that is, they often prioritise the study of function(s) rather than that of essences. In the words of Michaels, "[i]f the substance of a functional method in comparative law is unclear, our analysis should move from a substantive to a functional one and focus on what it does, instead of what it is"[16].

However, the complications in defining the notion and contents of functionalism have been one of the main criticisms of the functionalist method. Indeed, according to Michele Graziadei, functionalism has two connotations in the field of comparative law. First, it has been used as a comparative methodology. Secondly, it evokes the idea that law responds to social needs and that it is precisely the product of social demands[17].

In this respect, we should not lose sight of the fact that in comparative law and, in particular, in functionalism, the authors have been little concerned with developing or justifying an epistemological basis for its method. However, law as a science has not been concerned with developing a methodology in recent times either, and scholars have had no problems in this regard[18].

Indeed, according to Gustav Radbruch, if sciences have to take care of their methodology, it is because they are sick sciences. To this statement, Konrad

15 Michele Graziadei, 'The funcionalist heritage', in Pierre Legrand and Roderick Munday (eds), *Comparative Legal Studies: Traditions and Transitions* (CUP 2003) 101.

16 Ralf Michaels, 'The Functional Method of Comparative Law', in Mathias Reimann and Reinhard Zimmermann (eds), *The Oxford Handbook of Comparative Law* (1st edn, OUP 2006) 340, 363.

17 Graziadei, *supra* fn 152, 100.

18 Konrad Zweigert and Hein Kötz, *Introduction to comparative law* (3rd edn, OUP 1998) 33.

Zweigert and Hein Kötz famously responded that the sickness to which Radbruch refers cannot be assigned to comparative law but to law in general, to which comparative law is precisely a remedy[19].

In this sense, few scholars have developed the epistemological assumptions on which the functional method is based. According to Michaels, one of the reasons why the functional method has been little explored doctrinally is because its creators were more interested in solving concrete problems than in proposing a methodological basis. For this reason, functionalism in comparative law has developed mostly through examples and particular cases, rather than doctrinal development[20].

Although the doctrine developed around the methodological assumptions and epistemological bases of the functional method is scarce, comparativists such as Konrad Zweigert, Hein Kötz and Ralf Michaels have provided important bases and foundations in this respect, which is why in this paper we will use the concept of functional equivalence, which has been developed by Niklas Luhmann in the field of sociology and by the jurists just mentioned in the field of comparative law.

According to the method of equivalent functionalism, legal systems face similar problems by providing for different institutions. If the problems are similar, the institutions that solve these problems, even if they are different in structure, fulfil the same function. This is functional equivalence. Therefore, the methodological principle of comparative law that we have proposed is that of functionality. It is also the case that the functional method has little interest in discovering the essence of institutions and in the present work we have not set ourselves such an objective[21].

The legal systems are very different in conceptual and doctrinal terms. They are so different in that respect that comparison is sometimes frustrated. For example, when civil law jurists set out to compare one of their own legal institutions with one from the common law system, they will often be forced to conclude that the latter has nothing to offer, since they will not find something that fits conceptually and doctrinally with the institution being compared. This is not an impediment to the functional method, for if one shifts the focus to comparing functions, i.e., institutions in relation to a particular problem, one will certainly find an institution that fulfils the same function in the other

19 Zweigert and Kötz, *supra* fn 18, 35.
20 Michaels, *supra* fn 16, 362.
21 Michaels, *supra* fn 16, 364–365.

system, i.e. one will find something that is functionally equivalent to the original term, despite any structural difference in the solutions[22].

Therefore, functional equivalence fulfils a first epistemological function, since it forces us to understand our law from a different perspective than the one we are used to. It invites us to move to a scheme in which it is assumed that institutions fulfil functions, that is, that they seek to solve social problems, instead of analysing their doctrinal assumptions[23]. This is certainly a highly pragmatic approach, which we assume in this paper.

In this way, we come to the second function of functional equivalence. Since legal institutions solve social problems and all legal systems face similar problems, our measure of comparison appears: the measure of comparison or *tertium comparationis*. It is therefore the problems at the core of the research that allow us to make the comparison. But it is not just a matter of comparing problems in isolation; it is necessary to locate them in their functional relationship with institutions in context[24]. This is key to the functional methodology: it is not only the problems that will be compared, but the problems in relation to the institutions.

Thus, a third function of functional equivalence appears. If legal systems face the same problems, they are presumed to respond to them with functionally equivalent institutions[25]. Indeed, in view of the above, this paper will focus on analysing the way in which, within the Mexican legal system, the TFJA and the PJF are functional equivalents, even inside the same legal system, due to the nature of both jurisdictions. Therefore, we can assert that the internal comparison must be done functionally to fully appreciate the convergences and divergences between their way of working.

Fourth, we find that functional equivalence allows us to construct a conceptual system and terminology that are particularly fitting to describe and juxtapose the similarities and differences between the results found[26].

There are two other functions that have generally been attributed to functional equivalence and that we will not adopt in the present comparative work. The first one offers to use the functional method to propose which solution is best among the compared legal systems[27]. The reader will find here a comparative work, but we have left for another occasion to evaluate which of the

22 Michaels, *supra* fn 16, 356–358.
23 Michaels, *supra* fn 16, 363.
24 Michaels, *supra* fn 16, 367–369.
25 Michaels, *supra* fn 16, 369–372.
26 Michaels, *supra* fn 16, 372–373.
27 Michaels, *supra* fn 16, 373–376.

institutions is optimal, as this goes beyond the functional method itself. In close relation with the previous point, we do not find it optimal in the present work to develop proposal for legal unification[28]. In relation to the objectives we have set ourselves, this is irrelevant, and perhaps not even advisable.

4 The Players

It is important to point out that we recur to the functional method to make this comparative exercise due to the particularities of the Mexican justice system, which is dualist, insofar as it attributes the administrative process to jurisdictional organs – with technical autonomy – as part of the Public Administration[29]. Mexico has a further variant of this dualist model, because administrative justice is inspired by the French model, while the system of ordinary courts is highly influenced by the US model.

On the one hand, the TFJA is constitutionally established as an autonomous body outside of the executive power, but it does not belong to the judicial power either. On the other hand, the federal judiciary is inspired, as stated before, by the US model of justice, though with the additional power of performing constitutional judicial review through the *Amparo* trial.

Although both structures oversee the delivery of justice services in Mexico, administrative justice is therefore entrusted to an autonomous body, whose rulings could however be reviewed by the federal Circuit Courts. On the other side of the formula, the rulings of the federal judges of first instance can be overturned by the Circuits' Courts.

Both structures could rule on administrative issues. Yet, the TFJA does it through the administrative process, verifying the legality of the administrative acts and decisions. The judiciary could rule on the same subjects, but does so through the *Amparo* trials, which is the qualification of the constitutionality of administrative acts and decisions (including policies and bylaws).

Regarding performance-based evaluations, both models have a career system for their civil servants, but we find several divergences and little to no convergences, which strengthen our selection of the functional method for the comparison.

---

28 Michaels, *supra* fn 16, 376–378.

29 Augusto Durán Martínez, *Contencioso Administrativo* (Fundación Cultura Universitaria de Montevideo 2007) 14–15.

4.1 *The Federal Administrative Justice Tribunal*

The history of the TFJA is quite interesting. There were some attempts to establish an administrative court during the 19th century to consolidate our legal system, but amidst profound political differences (bear in mind that Mexico became an independent country in 1821). Most of the century was torn between a centrist/conservative/French-like system and a federalist/liberal/US-like system. The result was the creation of an administrative tribunal during the governments ruled by the conservative party, but that tribunal was rapidly declared unconstitutional by the judiciary in the 1850s[30].

It is not until 1936, when the Taxation Justice Act (*Ley de Justicia Fiscal*) appeared and created the Federal Taxation Tribunal (*Tribunal Fiscal de la Federación*) as part of the executive branch, not without controversy[31], that an autonomous system of administrative justice reappared. The Federal Taxation Tribunal slowly began to evolve into an administrative tribunal, changed its name in the year 2000 to Federal Justice of Fiscal and Administrative Tribunal (*Tribunal Federal de Justicia Fiscal y Administrativa*), later on shortened to TFJA as part of the Anticorruption Constitutional reform in 2012.

According to article 1 of the Federal Administrative Justice Tribunal Organisation Act (*Ley Orgánica del Tribunal Federal de Justicia Administrativa*, LOTFJA), the TFJA is a jurisdictional organ with autonomy to rule with full jurisdiction, according to the principles of legality, maximum publicity, respect for human rights, material truth, reasonableness, proportionality, presumption of innocence, typicity and due process. Its budget is to be exercised with full independence and the TFJA is liable and accountable for its proper exercise.

The TFJA is formed by an Upper Chamber, the Board of Government and Administration and Regional Chambers (*Junta de Gobierno y Administración*)[32].

The Upper Chamber is formed, as stated earlier, by 16 Magistrates, functioning in Plenary or in Three Sections. 14 of the Magistrates are required to perform jurisdictional duties, with one of them acting as the President of the TFJA, while the other two are part of the Board. The Magistrates of the Upper Chamber have a fixed term of 15 years.

---

30 Luis José Béjar Rivera, 'La dualidad jurisdiccional en materia administrativa en México', in Jaime Rodríguez-Arana Muñoz, William Vázquez Irizarry, María del Carmen Rodríguez Martín-Retortillo (eds), *Contenciosos administrativos en Iberoamérica* (Universidad de Puerto Rico 2015) 273, 278.

31 José Luis Vázquez Alfaro, *El control de la Administración Pública* (Universidad Nacional Autónoma de México 1996) 180–181.

32 Article 6 LOTFJA.

The plenary and the three sections of the Upper Chamber are authorised by law to create case-law, modify it, suspend it or solve controversies regarding their case-law[33]; they further have special jurisdiction over specific cases (and the Third section has exclusive juridsdiction regarding the fight against corruption). The Upper Chamber can also choose whether to attract a case to its jurisdiction, in matters that are considered particularly important.

The Board of Government and Administration, formed by the President of the Tribunal, two Upper Chamber Magistrates and two Regional Chamber Magistrates, is responsible for the proposition of the Internal Regulations or bylaws, the expedition of the General Agreements for the Tribunal, the preparation of the budget, and – most importantly for us – the evaluation of all personnel, including civil servants, based on objective and statistical data about the latter's performances[34]. Also, the Board of Government and Administration is responsible for the creation of new Chambers and the appointment of the civil servants[35].

The Regional Chambers are formed by three Magistrates and the civil servants who are required to ensure their proper functioning. These servants can be ordinaries, auxiliaries (entitled to make the final rulings), or specialised, for the exercise of special jurisdictions such as those on intellectual property, environmental law, antitrust law and administrative liability.

The body of civil servants is formed by Upper Chamber Magistrates, Regional Chamber Magistrates, Administrative Liability Specialised Chamber Magistrates, Supernumerary Magistrates, General Secretary, Adjunct Secretaries, Upper Chamber Secretaries, Regional Chamber Secretaries, Actuaries and Tribunal Officers, Head of the Internal Control Body, Operative and Technical secretaries, Head of the Centre of Administrative Justice Studies, and the rest of the support personnel[36].

All the Magistrates, in both the Upper and Regional Chambers, are appointed by the President of the Republic, ratified by a majority of the Senate or the Legislative's Permanent Commission. The Upper Chamber Magistrates cannot be renewed[37]. The Regional Chamber Magistrates are appointed for a term of 10 years and could be renewed for a similar period once[38]. The Administrative Liability Specialised Regional Chambers' Magistrates can only be appointed

33 Article 17 LOTFJA, sections I and II.

34 Article 27 LOTFJA, section IV.

35 Article 27 LOTFJA.

36 Article 42 LOTFJA.

37 Article 43, first paragraph, LOTFJA.

38 Article 43, second paragraph, LOTFJA.

for a term of 10 years without renewal[39]. In accordance with the Internal Regulation of the Tribunal (*Reglamento Interior del Tribunal Federal de Justicia Fiscal y Administrativa*), the Supernumerary Magistrates fill the temporal vacancies of the Regional Magistrates but also assist the Board by performing inspections, such as visits to Regional Chambers to verify their performance[40].

Focusing on the evaluation of performances, the Board of Government and Administration is responsible for devising and managing the career status of the personnel[41], as well as for providing the general provisions and policies in this regard[42]. The Board of Government and Administration is also responsible for the management of the jurisdicitonal career. It is however fundamental to point out that this provision about the jurisdictional career only applies to the Adjunct Secretaries, the Upper and Regional Chamber Secretaries, and Actuaries within the ranks of civil servants[43]. Therefore, the scope of the above provision is limited by the nature of the posts it refers to. According to article 50 of the Internal Regulation, the management of the jurisdictional career, which is carried out by an Executive Office within the Board, should be based on principles of efficiency, capacity, and experience. More in particular, under article 53, last paragraph, of the Internal Regulation, the evaluation of the personnel should be based on "objective elements and statistical data on performance, as well as on the quantitative and qualitative criteria determined by the Board".

As to the evaluation of Magistrates, the Internal Regulation provides that the Board of Government and Administration will yearly identify some visiting Magistrates, who will be entrusted with the task of visiting the Regional Chambers. During the visits, the correct functioning of the chambers will be verified at least on the basis of: a) qualitative and quantitative productivity, b) regularity of the chamber, c) the compliance of Magistrates' rulings with the law, d) the respect of deadlines and procedural phases, e) the compliance with the court's rules of order, vigilance and discipline, f) the regularity of the administrative performance by the court's civil servants, g) the conditions of the working environment[44]. For the renewal of the Magistrates, the Board files a report on each Magistrate's performance.

39 Article 43, second paragraph, LOTFJA.
40 Article 31, sub-section c), Internal Regulation.
41 Article 23 LOTFJA, sections IV, IX, and XXXII.
42 Article 52 of the Internal Regulation.
43 Article 51 LOTFJA.
44 Article 54 of the Internal Regulation.

4.2 *The Federal Judiciary Power*

The Federal judicial power in Mexico is of a complex design, as disposed by the Constitution. Regulated by the Chapter 4 of the CPEUM, the Judiciary reposes on a Supreme Court of Justice (SCJN), an Electoral Tribunal, Collegiate Circuit Tribunals, Collegiate Appeal's Courts and District Courts[45]. For the purposes of administration, vigilance (that is, accountability) and discipline, except for the Supreme Court, the federal judicial power is overseen by the Federal Council of Magistracy (*Consejo de la Judicatura Federal*, CFJ)[46], which is also in charge of determining the number and division of circuits, their territorial jurisdiction, and the subject specialisation of the Circuit Tribunal and District courts[47].

The Supreme Court, as said earlier, is composed by eleven Ministers[48] or judges, functioning either in Plenary or in two chambers of five members each, made up of all members but for the President of the Court (who is elected every four years, without the possibility of immediately be re-elected). The Ministers of the Supreme Court are appointed for a period of 15 years non-extendable by any means[49]. For the appointment of Ministers, the President presents before the Senate a shortlist of three candidates, preferably chosen from the judicial civil service[50], who will then appear before the Senate. The Senate will then vote to choose one by a qualified majority of two thirds; if the shortlist is rejected or neither of the candidates obtain the required votes, the President will send another shortlist (which might contain the same names). If the new list gets again rejected, then the President directly appoints the new Justice[51].

It is important to notice that neither Chambers nor the Plenary of the Court are at liberty to choose which cases to rule on, since they have hear all the disputes indicated in Article 105, Sections 1 and 2, of the Mexican United States Constitution and in the Amparo Act (*Ley Reglamentaria de las fracciones I y II del Artículo 105 de la Constitución Política de los Estados Unidos Mexicanos*, so-called *Ley de Amparo*). The Supreme Court, therefore, does not control its working agenda, although, exceptionally, it can assert jurisdiction over cases

45 Article 94, first paragraph, CPEUM.

46 Article 94, second paragraph, CPEUM.

47 Article 94, sixth paragraph, CPEUM.

48 Under the Mexican system, the title of Minister (*Ministro*) is reserved exclusively to the eleven judges of the Supreme Court. The heads of the Public Administration are called Secretaries, as Mexico does not have ministries, but only secretariats, although the latter are clearly a functional equivalent of the former.

49 Article 94, twelfth paragraph, CPEUM.

50 Article 95, last paragraph, CPEUM.

51 Article 96, CPEUM.

that involve a first-time interpretation of fundamental rights regarding an act, a statute or a regulation (that is, a statutory disposition), but only if a lower judge requests its intervention, over cases dealing with matters that are considered politically and socially significant or highly salient, and over cases requiring the interpretation of an international treaty.

Essentially, the Supreme Court have statutory jurisdiction and is duty-bounded by the Constitution: to rule on case-law contradictions between tribunals or the chambers; to review certain cases ruled by the Circuit Tribunals through a procedure akin to an appeal (more properly, to a recourse for judicial review); to adjudicate constitutional controversies (*controversias constitucionales*), which are conflicts between different branches and levels of government; to rule on unconstitutionality actions (*acciónes de inconstitucionalidad*), which are similar to constitutional controversies, but are promoted by congress minorities, the General Attorney, the political parties, national and local, and the human rights ombudspersons. The two latter functions enshrine two types of constitutional review that, by granting the Supreme Court the power to hear conflicts among the executive and the legislative branches, the federal government and the states, the municipalities and the governors, allow the Court to ensure the enforcement of order among different political agents[52]. In addition, the Plenary of the Supreme Court must validate any questionnaire presented by the president in popular consultations[53].

Although inspired by the model of American courts, the truth is that Mexico's legal system is highly kelsenian; therefore, every legal rule is lawful by virtue of another, higher-order, legal rule. Thus, a ministerial decree or a police action taken in pursuance of a statute must respect the terms of that statute or otherwise can be declared invalid by judicial authorities; and the statute itself must conform to constitutional dictates, being otherwise at risk of being invalided by judicial authorities. The constitutional legality of a norm (or of a policy) and the legitimacy of the legal system are virtually one and the same[54]. In this model, courts performing judicial review ensure the normative superiority of

52 Beatriz Magaloni, 'Enforcing the Autocratic Political Order and the Role of the Courts: The Case of Mexico', in Tom Ginsburg and Mousfata Tamir (eds), *Rule by Law: The Politics of Courts in Authoritarian Regimes* (Cambridge University Press 2008) 180, 199.

53 For the first time this attribution was used in 2020 for a popular consultation where the President was asking if the people wanted the government to pursue criminal conducts by the former presidents, including the last five ones.

54 Alec Stone Sweet, 'Path Dependence, Precedent, and Judicial Power', in Martin Shapiro and Alec Stone Sweet (eds), *On Law, Politics, and Judicialization* (OUP 2002) 112, 131.

the Constitution[55], and effectively become a negative legislator by annulling statutes when the parliament's law conflicts with the Constitution[56].

As to the other members of the federal judiciary, judges in lower federal courts, the Magistrates of the Circuit Tribunals and the District Judges are all appointed by the Magistracy Council, according to the procedures established by the Federal Judiciary Power Organization Act (*Ley Orgánica del Poder Judicial de la Federación*, LOPJF). They are first appointed for six years, but, if this appointment is ratified or they are promoted, they will be appointed for life[57].

With the only exception is for Ministers sitting in the SCJN, the executive does not have any power in appointing the Federal Judges and Magistrates. The structure of federal courts is therefore mainly based on a Weberian civil service system of merit[58], which includes the clerks, the notifiers and the assistants. Federal courts thus form a very unique bureaucratic organization, that fulfills all the following conditions: a) it is a very large organization, b) its members are full-time workers, who are in most cases forbidden to have any other income besides their salary, c) their hiring and promotion procedure is theoretically based on some type of assessment of their capabilities and performances, and, d) a major portion of the output of the organization is not directly or indirectly evaluated by any markets external to it[59].

Only federal judicial clerks or judges from local jurisdictions (something which however is not very common) can be appointed as Judges; only District Judges can be appointed as magistrates. These appointments are made in accordance with the Title 7th of the LOPJF, on the basis of the principles of excellence, professionalism, objectivity, impartiality, independence, and seniority. This, at least in principle, ensures the full independence of the judges and magistrates, although of course there is no guarantee that the judicial power will be independent once politics begins to unfold[60].

But as Vanberg explains, following Landes & Posner's seminal work[61], an independent judiciary provides 'credibility' for the political actors;

55 Stone Sweet, *supra* fn 54, 135.

56 Martin Shapiro, 'The Success of Judicial Review and Democracy', in Shapiro and Stone Sweet (eds), *supra* fn 54, 149.

57 Article 97 of the Constitution.

58 Merilee S. Grindle, *Jobs for the Boys. Patronage and the State in Comparative Perspective* (Harvard University Press 2012) ix.

59 Anthony Downs, *Inside Bureaucracy* (Rand Corporation 1964) 2–3.

60 Georg Vanberg, 'Establishing and Maintaining Judicial Independence', in Keith E. Whittington, R. Daniel Kelemen, and Gregory A. Caldeira (eds), *Oxford Handbook of Law and Politics* (OUP 2008) 101, 102.

61 William M. Landes and Richard A. Posner, The Independent Judiciary in an Interest-Group Perspective (1975) 18 *Journal of Law & Economics* 875–901.

we may also add, following Whittington[62], that, if certain decisions carry a political risk, the official charged with these decisions will often choose to pass such issues off to someone else, including the judiciary. Finally, even parties and politicians who occupy offices at different times have an embedded interest in supporting judicial independence whenever there is sufficient electoral uncertainty and parties and politicians expect to rotate in and out of office. All this is part of what Vanberg[63] calls endogenous explanations for judicial independence, while exogenous factors include public support and the belief of citizens in judicial independence as an important constitutional value.

Defining with precision what judicial independence exactly means is not necessarily an easy task, due to the many possible interpretations of the expression, at least from the legal perspective. For the limited purposes of this paper, we might take judicial independence as implying: 1) the (collective and individual) autonomy of judges vis-à-vis other individuals and institutions (usually the executive and legislative branch) and 2) the judges' capacity to have an independent thinking and ruling, which is not necessarily the result of the first condition[64]. Conceived as such, the principle of judicial independence is enshrined in many constitutions, that demand judicial freedom for all dependency and obstacle, external or internal, that could subordinate them to elements other than the law[65]. In line with previous scholars, Ferejohn noted that there are several ways to avoid interferences from public officials, such as the adoption of legal rules – statutory or constitutional – restraining public officials from infringing on judicial authority and the enforcement of such rules with sanctions for violations; also, a set of conventions or norms of self-restraint might work as a kind of political morality[66]. It should however be added that, if a wider conception of judicial independence is to be adopted, its protection could not confine itself to restraining the actions of public officials,

---

62 Keith E. Whittington, 'Legislative Sanctions and the strategic environment of judicial review' (2003) 1 *International Journal of Constitutional Law* 446–474.

63 Vanberg, *supra* fn 60, 106–108.

64 Karlos Castilla Juárez, 'Judicial independence in the called inter-American convencionality control' (2016) 14 *Estudios Constitucionales* 53, 65.

65 Norbert Lösing, 'Independencia y función del Poder judicial en el Estado democrático de derecho' (2011) 17 *Anuario de Derecho Constitucional Latinoamericano* 413, 414; see also Castilla Juárez, *supra* fn 64, 66.

66 John Ferejohn, 'Independent Judges, Dependent Judiciary: Explainign Judicial Independence' (1999) 72 *Southern California Law Review* 353–384.

but would rather aim at preventing any interference with the legal process, wherever it may originate[67].

It is true that for many years, during the PRI's autocratic period, the Supreme Court has functioned as the *legalizing* arm of the executive, who was (and still is) propense to make several constitutional changes[68] to accommodate and imprint each president's policy agenda[69]; in fact, most of the judges of the Supreme Court were loyal agents of the party and the president from time to time in power. Magaloni argues that the Supreme Court began to be gradually strengthened after 1988 and became a fully independent political player until the PRI lost power in 2000[70]. Now, it is apparent that, with the change in the government and the current presidency of the Supreme Court and the presidency of both chambers, the independency of the SCJN, if not the rest of the Federal Judiciary, is at peril.

The District Courts and the Circuit Tribunals have jurisdiction over federal cases dealing with: criminal law, provided that the Federal Criminal Code applies; civil law, provided that the Federal Civil Code is applied (a not very common occurrence)[71] and civil contracts involving public administrative bodies; commercial law, in which there exists a dual jurisdiction with the local courts, due the existence of a sole commercial code; administrative law by exception, because on this issue there exists the jurisdiction of the Federal Administrative Justice Tribunal, which, as already said, does not belong to the judiciary.

Above and beyond this, the main reason for the existence of the federal judiciary is the constitutional review through the *Amparo* proceedings. As is well known, the *Amparo* trial is a type of judicial constitutional review of acts and actions of public authorities, including the executive, legislative and other judicial bodies. Its origins go all the way back to the Mexican Constitution of 1836, where it was first introduced for protecting fundamental rights[72]. It has

67 Ferejohn, *supra* fn 66, 365–366.

68 It has been 105 years since the current constitution was enforced and there are more than 500 changes in its text, although the constitutional reform process is not flexible.

69 Magaloni, *supra* fn 52, 184.

70 Magaloni, *supra* fn 52, 187.

71 Under the Mexican federalism, each State regulates civil law, with the result that each one of them has a Civil Code, more or less with the same contents.

72 Marcos Francisco Del Rosario, 'El juicio de amparo: origen y evolución hasta la Consstitución de 1917. Tres casos paradigmáticos que determinaron su configuración', in Eduardo Ferrer Mac-Gregor and Alfonso Herrera García (eds), *El juicio de amparo en el centenario de la Constitución Mexicana de 1917* (Instituto de Investigaciones Jurídicas-Universidad Nacional Autónoma de México 2017) 123–126.

since then continuously evolved throughout the years, transforming the federal judiciary in a network of constitutional courts. Following Shapiro[73], we should emphasize that constitutional courts present special problems of judicial independence because of the inevitable political impact of their decisions, because of the great lawmaking discretion that the broadly worded language of constitutions gives to their judicial interpreters, and because of the final character of their decisions, which is somewhat more 'final' than that of decisions by judges interpreting statutes[74]. For the purposes of this research, we claim that, on general terms, the independence of federal Judges and Magistrates is a reality in Mexico. Even if the president has some control over the Supreme Court, most of the times this presidential control does not affect or interfere in the activities of lower courts and tribunals, thanks to the institutional design of these courts and their budgetary independence from the executive.

Now, regarding the regulation of the civil service career, this has been recently reformed and is now regulated by the Judicial Career of the Federal Judiciary Power Act (*Ley de Carrera Judicial del Poder Judicial de la Federación*, LCJPJF) (2021). This is specifically regulated by Title 2nd of the Act, whose article 4 defines the judicial career as an institutional system designed to regulate the entry procedures, preparation, promotion, performance-based evaluation, stability and exit of judicial civil servants, on the basis of merit and respecting equal opportunities. Article 7 of the LCJPJF provides that the development of the career of judicial civil servants should be based on the principles of excellence, professionalism, objectivity, impartiality, independence, seniority and gender equality.

According to article 10 of the LCJPJF, the judicial career includes Circuit Magistrates, followed by Judges, General Secretary of the Supreme Court or the Upper Chamber of the Electoral Tribunal, Undersecretary, Supreme Court's and Upper Chamber of the Electoral Tribunal's clerks, Chamber's clerks, Chamber's Deputy clerks, Circuit's and Regional Chamber's clerks, Circuit's projects clerks, Court's clerks, Assistants, Court's projects clerks, Actuaries and Court officers.

As a general rule, for being promoted on the judicial career, the civil servant must be already part of the system and usually pass a closed internal competition. However, in some cases, the Magistracy Council could call for an open competition. The system includes both school-based mode and a non-school-based mode as a means to be eligible for promotion (articles 25 and 26).

---

73 Martin Shapiro, 'Judicial Independence: New Challenges in Established Nations' (2013) 20 *Indiana Journal of Global Legal Studies* 253–277 (2013).

74 Shapiro, *supra* fn 73, 270.

Moreover, the Third Section of Title 2nd of the LCJPJF expressly regulates the performance-based evaluation for all members of the judicial career, based on quantitative and qualitative compliance with the functions and the goals entrusted to civil servants, and in line with the purpose of reinforcing the efficiency, the efficacy and the quality of the administration of justice (article 34).

This performance-based evaluation aims to detect the strengths of the system and the opportunities for improvement of the performances of civil servants according to their post (article 35). The Magistracy Council is required to publish general framework agreements detailing the criteria and specific evaluation mechanisms to measure efficacy and efficiency in the performance of the civil servant's duties (article 36). The results of this evaluation will form the basis for granting incentives and awards, and also for evaluating the promotion process inside the judicial career. Still, for the purposes of this work, we decided not to approach one of the main problems affecting judicial career, that is, nepotism, which has been widely denounced and documented[75], and should be explored in future works, regarding the subject, specially, its effects on the performance-based evaluation.

The General Framework Agreement (*Acuerdo General del Pleno del Consejo de la Judicatura Federal que reglamenta la Carrera Judicial*) was published by the Magistracy Council on October 28th, 2021. More specific criteria for performance-based evaluation of the civil servants will be established by the Judicial Inspection Unit (*Visitaduría Judicial*) through a General Framework[76], which, to this date, has not been published yet. It is important to note that article 128 of the General Framework Agreement, lists a positive performance-based evaluation as one of the requirements for all Judges and Magistrates to be confirmed in their post or advance in the judicial career.

5 The Findings

Once we have explored the regimes related to the civil servants' career both before federal courts and the Federal Tribunal of Administrative Justice, we can conclude that performance-based evaluation is part of both systems.

On the one hand, in the case of the federal judicial power, performance-based assessments are used by the Magistracy Council from the lower levels

75 Valeria Durán, Dulce González, Raúl Olmos, 'El poder familiar de la Federación', Mexicanos Contra la Corrupción, at <https://contralacorrupcion.mx/web/magistrados/> (accessed May 2022).

76 Article 136 of the General Framework Agreement.

of the judicial career, the actuaries, up to Circuits' Magistrates, and therefore includes most of the judiciary personnel. On the other hand, the Board of the Federal Tribunal of Administrative Justice, as a functional equivalent of the Magistracy Council, also has its own evaluation system, starting bottom-up from the actuaries up to Adjunct Secretaries. The evaluations concern by far less personnel before the TFJA than the PJF.

Another significant difference between the two systems is that the federal judicial power has a more structured process of evaluation, insofar as it does include not only performance-based evaluation but also scholarity programmes to certify the personnel and give them better access to promotions and competitions.

Moreover, the performance-based evaluation of the Judges and Magistrates in the PJF is more complete and more directly related to the quality of justice services than performance-based evaluations of the Magistrates within the TFJA. Before the Federal Tribunal of Administrative Justice, performance-based evaluations are softer, insofar as the evaluation could or not have an impact on the renewal on posts; it is still is up to the President to propose the appointment or the renewal.

Before federal courts, Magistracy Council has a specialised unit in charge of the visitations and audits, the Judicial Inspection Unit, the tasks of which are amply outlined by the Rules and regulations of the judicial career and might be further corrected and improved by the Magistracy Council itself. At the Federal Tribunal of Administrative Justice, many of the visits and audits are performed by Supernumerary Magistrates, who are yearly appointed as Inspectors. From this point of view, the legal framework of performance-based evaluations for career in the federal judicial power is by far more developed than the thin regulation governing assessment for the career before the TFJA.

Finally, on practical terms, it should be noted that the federal judicial career is aspirational within its own bureaucratic model. The federal personnel can always aspire to further advancements within the federal judicial power, including the appointment as Ministers of the Supreme Court. By contrast, before the TFJA, the members of the jurisdictional career who follow the path can be promoted up to Adjunct Secretary, since the appointment as Magistrate does not depend on the previous career. Therefore, the performance-based evaluation performed within the TFJA has little to no impact on the behavior of its personnel.

Further, the executive power intervenes on the appointment of federal judges only by proposing the shortlist of candidates for the position of Ministers of the SCJN before the Senate, which is then required to vote on their appointment. The Magistrates of the TFJA are instead directly appointed by the President, although their appointment has to be ratified by the Senate. Obviously, this could affect not only the quality of administrative justice, but even the independence of the TFJA as a court. There are not enough empirical data, however, to make a judgement on this issue.

6 Conclusions

The above features of convergence and divergence between the federal judicial power and the TFJA, due to their inherently different design and functions, fully justify the adoption of the functional methodology for analysing Mexican justice. The coexistence of these two models within Mexican dualism proves to be the perfect scenario for a micro-comparison under the functional method.

The career systems of civil servants and judges within the two models has gradually improved over the years, but it is clear the federal judiciary (most likely due to its size and budget, although we did not explore the issue) has developed a more complete and complex system than the TFJA.

Although both career systems have an element of performance-based evaluation, this has a significantly lower impact in the TFJA and a much higher impact on the federal judiciary. This difference could be easily explained by the fact that, in the appointment of the Magistrates of the TFJA, the results of performance-based evaluation results do not influence the President's decision to make the designation. By contrast, the career advancement in the federal judiciary, the modification of posts and the promotions up to Circuit Magistrate, are very much influenced by the performance-based evaluation of the concerned personnel.

Empirical data do not provide information regarding the independence of both structures as judges, but one could venture to assume that the federal judicial power is more independent than the TFJA. It is a fact that for neither the Executive nor the Legislative intervenes on the designations of federal judges and magistrates, while the designation of the TFJA's Magistrates is a direct and discretionary decision of the President, and the intervention of the Senate ratifying the appointments is a mere formality.

Despite the not so flattery scenario about performance-based evaluation at the TFJA, it is also true that it is relatively too soon to make a judgment about the system, because the administrative tribunal is constantly changing and improving its practice. In fewer words, evaluation before the TFJA is to a good extent a work in progress. That passage of time is crucial in this regard is demonstrated by the situation within the federal judiciary. The road taken a few years ago by the federal judiciary is now starting to pay off. The performance-based evaluation has been and is a fundamental part of the advancement in the judicial career. This evaluation translates into better prepared judges, and therefore has a direct impact on the quality of justice.

Nevertheless, there is still much to explore about the correlation between the performance-based measures and the quality of justice; we simply presented here an introductory work on the subject.

In this sense, our intention was to test new methods to analyse old phenomena and to open the debate about the quality of justice offering a different point of view that certainly deserves to be considered.

CHAPTER 4

Judicial Performance Index in India: Charting a New Course

Manjeri Subin Sunder Raj and Chiradeep Basak

1 Preface

Evaluation is one common term that we all are well aware of; it is used in numerous fields and oft treated as the benchmark. Extending evaluation related aspects to various walks of life has helped us gauge performances and outcomes, and also put forth standards and ideals. While one thinks about the different machineries that exist together and function in tandem, and give rise to a state, the concern is all about as to how well they will be able to gel together and function for the benefit of the state. Whether it is the Executive, the Legislature or the Judiciary, each branch should – on their own as well as together – function smoothly for the state to perform well. While the first two branches can be said to have a lot more of a direct connection with the populace, as far as India is concerned, the same cannot be said about the judiciary – which is, to a large extent, and should be as well, an independent authority, that is, free from an untoward influences from the other two powers.

As far as the first two powers are concerned, evaluation is a key aspect for the Legislature, because of its connection with the populace; it is a bit on the easier side. That the same cannot be extended to the Judiciary has created its own set of challenges and problems[1]. But this does not, in any way, take away the

1 The main problem about evaluating the judiciary is made clear by an observation made by Bernard Schwartz. It succinctly and effectively delves into the simple, yet profound problem that every evaluator mechanism would posses: "How should we go about evaluating the Justices' performance? If we were to give the Justices an annual report card, what subjects would we want to grade? Some old favorites would appear. Math – can they add to five, the magic number that Justice Brennan used to say could do anything at the Court" [Bernard Schwartz, *Decision: How The Supreme Court Decides Cases* (Oxford University Press 1996) 6]. A similar problem can be identified based on the method used for grading judges, as has been opined by Laura Krugman Ray: "English-do they write clearly and concisely, so that we don't have to struggle to understand what they say? And what about what used to be called deportment? Do they work well with others, are they courteous and respectful, do they participate effectively in group activities? And finally, should the Justices be graded, as many law students are, on a curve? That is, should we measure the Rehnquist Court against an

 | DOI:10.1163/9789004680944_005

possibility and the necessity to bring the performance of the judiciary under the scanner – for that is what a healthy democracy should possess and aim for. That is exactly why the judiciary too has been sought to be brought under the realm of evaluation – assessing the qualities and the capabilities of the judges, which in turn would help the system to function smoothly and effectively. One has to delve into the history of such an exercise in India, its objectives and the methods used to achieve those objectives, and to examine as to whether such a system could possibly work out in a country like India, which is so vast, and has a judicial setup like no other.

The challenges pertaining to judicial reforms in India have always been revolving around the institutional and financial frame. Lack of judges, state of art courtrooms and requisite funds have been regarded as the hindrances to judicial reformation. Judges obviously play a critical role in our system of justice and therefore, the quality of their performance heavily influences the system's operation and the public's perception of it.

Like other institutions, the quality of the judicial system turns upon the quality of the work performed by those involved in that system. Any serious attempt to make a significant improvement in the quality of justice must necessarily focus upon improving the performance of members of lawyers and judges. Judicial performance evaluations are generally centered around responses to standardized, scaled surveys provided by individuals who have had direct dealings with a judge during an evaluation period. Performance measures are also a useful way of ensuring judicial accountability without impinging judicial independence.

The concept of judicial performance evaluation is not a new one, as is evident from the history attached to. In 1975, Alaska became the first state in the United States of America to start the evaluation of judges for judicial retention elections. Alaska Judicial Council was bestowed with the responsibility of evaluating the judges appearing on a retention election ballot because the said evaluation would help the concerned voters to decide over the retention of a justice in office. Subsequently, several other American States took the initiative to evaluate judges standing for retention election. The trend of judicial performance evaluation is not uncommon in Western countries. The International Framework for Court Excellence was developed by an international consortium consisting of the Australasian Institute of Judicial Administration (Australia & New Zealand), the National Center for State Courts (United

absolute standard of judicial excellence, or should we take into account the quality of earlier Courts or the particular challenges of the present day?". See Laura Krugman Ray, 'Judging the Justices: A Supreme Court Performance Review' (2003) 76 *Temple Law Review* 209.

States), the Federal Judicial Center (United States), and the Subordinate Courts of Singapore (Singapore).

Keeping in mind that the objective of a Judicial Performance Index is to evaluate different aspects of justice delivery, the paper tries to encapsulate different aspects which play an integral part in deciphering this index – pointers which would help and possibly aid an impartial evaluation of judges, and highlight the changes that needs to be brought about in the system, the steps that have been taken to that effect and the outcome so far of such steps.

2 What Is Judicial Performance Evaluation?

As was pointed out earlier, the United States of America was the first nation which had in place a judicial performance evaluation system, which provided for all necessary information about judges, and on the basis of which voters could decide judges' fate. Way back in 1978, Alaska introduced the first state sponsored programme, where judicial performance was evaluated[2]. The idea and the rationale behind such a programme were obviously to increase levels of accountability amongst judges[3] – which in turn increased transparency in the whole judicial process, and contributed to increasing the efficiency and effectiveness of the judiciary as a whole[4]. Soon, this model of evaluation spread, obviously furthered by the large amount of support that it was able to garner, and a number of other states in the United States of America followed suit. While this can be said to be an institutionalized version of assessment of judicial performances, there were also informal ways of assessment that prevailed in many bar-polls that were conducted to test the opinions shared between the bar members[5]. Currently too, there are instances of formalized bar opinion polls in many states in the United States of America.

While one can definitely point out that such polls have serious limitations, out of which one is definitely the sample that is chosen to provide the

2 Michael L. Rubenstein, 'Alaska's Judicial Evaluation Programme: A Poll the Voters Rejected' (1977) 60(10) *Judicature* 478.

3 For more see, Francis Bremson, Alan Handler, Janet Franz, 'Judicial Performance Evaluation' (1986) 4 *Law & Inequality* 77. Also see Joe McIntyre, 'Evaluating Judicial Performance Evaluation: A Conceptual Analysis' (2014) 4 *Oñati Socio-legal Series* 898.

4 Richard C. Kearney, 'Judicial Performance Evaluation in the States' (1999) 22 *Public Affairs Quarterly* 468.

5 Richard J. Young, 'The New Jersey Judicial Performance Evaluation Program: An Assessment of the Program's Impact on Judicial Performance' (1997), available at <https://cdm16501.contentdm.oclc.org/digital/collection/judicial/id/43> (accessed on 6 May 2022).

evaluation, bar-pools have nevertheless played an important role in eliciting the opinion of stakeholders, asking them to assess judicial performances. Though various concerns can be raised, particularly the low response rate to such polls, the reliability of such information, and the personal connections which might influence respondents' appraisal or criticism, this method has nevertheless opened new doors, aiming at securing the best interests of justice. These problems that were galore, soon led to discussions about a better system to be put in place to evaluate judicial performances; with the passage of time the debate was able to mould itself into a better scheme.

In the United States of America, a number of states have adopted a Judicial Performance Evaluation system which helps combine public opinion and sentiment and translate it into better judicial performance. With the advent of consumer mass society, one cannot but help to bring within the system some sort of accountability, as justice can be termed to be considered as a 'service' rendered to the public at large[6]. The extension of the concept of *consumer* was definitely mooted and the end result was that consumers too had some sort of a say as regards the justice that they were served with. With the passage of time, a number of concerns about the need of hearing the voice of justice consumers were raised, and soon states in the United States of America started using different methods and processes to conduct their judicial performance evaluation. This can definitely be said to be a welcome change and brought different contours and considerations to the whole discussion surrounding evaluation of the performance of judges and the justice delivery mechanism.

It was not just in the United States of America, but also in various other countries, that this evaluation system gained prominence. This fact does bring to one's attention and notice that the concept of evaluating the performance of judges has been a global phenomenon and that many countries around the globe have worked to devise mechanisms for assessing justice that could be acceptable as well as appreciated, and that, more importantly, could change the perception that evaluating the judges' performance was beyond scrutiny. Europe has been no exception, for, even before it had a formalised system to evaluate judicial performance, it used to have a traditional quality control mechanism[7]. Countries did also resort to setting up formalised mechanisms, which were more often than not, allowed by a formal legislation. Apart from these country specific mechanisms, the European Commission for the

---

6 N. R. Madhava Menon, 'Evaluating Judicial Performance: A Consumer Perspective' (2008) 50 *Journal of the Indian Law Institute* 468.

7 Richard Mohr and Francesco Contini, 'Judicial Evaluation in Context: Principles, Practices and Promise in Nine European Countries' (2007) 1 *European Journal of Legal Studies* 254.

Efficiency of Justice nowadays collects and analyses all relevant information about state courts' functioning, thereby evaluating judicial function across the member states in the Council of Europe. Setup in 2002, this body ensures that judicial reforms are brought about in Europe, which would help cater to better justice delivery mechanisms[8]. As already mentioned, the quest for evaluation systems also exists at the national level. One could for instance notice, in the United Kingdom, the presence of a Report of the Advisory Panel on Judicial Diversity, which lays down reasons to conduct an appraisal[9], the Auld Review of the Criminal Courts of the England and Wales[10], and the Lord Chief Justice's Report[11] – all of which called for performance tools being used. There have actually been a number of indicators being used in England to assess performance and these indicators have been instrumental in bringing about a change in the functioning of the judicial system.

However, care and caution need to be exercised in reading the outcomes of all these evaluation mechanisms, as it needs not always be in the interests of justice or put forth a picture that justice is served, if a large number of cases are being decided – quantity should definitely not be a benchmark for assessing quality! A performance index should definitely be a yard-stick, but not an absolute one. Keeping in mind the constraints and problems that exist in setting up an evaluation mechanism for justice, is by far the most important thing that needs to be taken into account when devising such mechanism. Coming up with a balanced approach is quite a challenge.

3 Need and Necessity

Even though the establishment of a system for assessing justice and of a Judicial Performance Index is a novel idea and a revolutionary concept, the very need and necessity to have these mechanisms in place, is something which, it is felt, takes a lot of time to be digested. This is probably because of the fact that the judiciary is seen as a separate body, assuming a lot of significance

8 For more information, see European Union Justice Scoreboard, available at <https://ec.europa.eu/info/policies/justice-and-fundamental-rights/upholding-rule-law/eu-justice-scoreboard_en> (accessed on 9 May 2022).

9 Available at <https://www.judiciary.uk/wp-content/uploads/JCO/Documents/Reports/advisory-panel-judicial-diversity-2010.pdf> (accessed on 9 May 2022).

10 Available at <https://www.criminal-courts-review.org.uk/auldconts.htm> (accessed on 4 June 2023).

11 See <https://www.judiciary.uk/wp-content/uploads/2016/01/lcj_report_2015-final.pdf> (accessed on 9 May 2022).

and maintaining a level of independence as well – something which has been not really attached with the other two organs of the state. Bordering on areas related to accountability and transparency, in a field as nuanced as the judicial field, an evaluation system, it can be argued, can actually instil in the general public some sort of an increased level of faith[12]. It is sure that a system which is perceived as accountable and transparent would definitely be held more in public trust – and this is what we would want as well for a state to function better. Such as system may form part of a well-oiled machinery, helping attain legitimacy to the institutions and also to the people who helm it. By following such a method, both at an institutional level as well as an individual level, the importance of the judiciary may be upheld. This, in turn, promotes public confidence[13], which caters well as far as the judiciary's functioning too is concerned. Assessments place an onus on judges, as their abilities and outputs are recorded and analyzed, and this in turn would help them function better, and in turn would help the system function better as well, creating a sort of a managerial accountability which can be attached to the judicial institutions of the country. Is it not human tendency that if someone is keeping watch on us, then we probably would be more careful and concerned about our actions? Certain countries, like France and the Netherlands, for example, have studies carried out to collect information about the number of cases which are pending and the number of judges required so as to dispose of these cases in an effective manner[14]. This definitely helped the judiciary and the judicial setup in these respective countries perform better.

It should also be kept in kind that, while such measures are taken to increase transparency and accountability, a balance is to be maintained so as not to interfere with judicial independence. The reason underlying the need for such a balance is that a judge's independence is one of the most valued assets, and any evaluation should not, in any way, create a sense of it affecting a judge's independent decision-making power. That would definitely hamper the process and would be counter-productive. Undue interference from external quarters is one of the last things that we would want! We would definitely

12 Peter Cappelli and Anna Tavis, 'The Performance Management Revolution', available at <https://hbr.org/2016/10/the-performance-management-revolution> (accessed on 9 May 2022).

13 Jean Dubofsky, 'Judicial Performance Review: A Balance between Judicial Accountability and Judicial Independence' (2007) 34 *Fordham Urban Law Journal* 315.

14 See EU Justice Scoreboard, available at <https://ec.europa.eu/info/policies/justice-and-fundamental-rights/upholding-rule-law/eu-justice-scoreboard_en> (accessed on 9 May 2022).

not want judges who would, for example, give decisions that fall in line with the mandate of the executive or any other power wielding government functionary, rather than on what their opinion is. That could be the worst possible scenario as judges would want to toe the line of external mandates eyeing post retirement job opportunities. As independent as a judge would like himself to be, the manner and the way in which he enjoys this should definitely reflect in his decision-making powers too. After all, this is also how any populace would want the judiciary to function as well. Justice should not only be done, but also seem to be done – says the adage.

4 The Indian Scenario

India, which has a large number of courts and judges, can be taken as an interesting case study, in order to further the idea of a Judicial Performance Index and check the ways in which it could possibly be implemented in a better fashion. Though multiple attempts have been made, in India, to create some sort of a mechanisms to deal with judicial performance – more from an accountability perspective, there is not yet a concrete law in force to deal with it – rather India has a largely informal system in place which deals with it[15].

India has a centralised judicial setup with the Supreme Court of India being the highest court in the country and its decisions binding on lower courts. There are High Courts for each state, with some states sharing the same High Court. These constitutional courts are the highest courts within the respective state jurisdictions. Appeals from the High Courts are to the Supreme Court. The judgments rendered by the High Courts are binding on the lower courts in the state, but have only persuasive value as far as other High Courts are concerned. Below the High Courts, each state would have a lower judiciary with the Munsiff-Magistrate Courts at the lowest level, with appeals to the Sub-Courts and from there to the District and Session Court. With quite an intricate system of courts, India has been at the fore of many a change that has been brought about in judicial arena – and the concept of judicial accountability and standards too had been broached about.

It was in 2010 that the first Judicial Standards and Accountability Bill was introduced in India[16]. It laid down certain judicial standards under S. 3, which

15 For more see, Bhairav Acharya, 'The Evolution of Judicial Accountability in India' (2017) 1 *Journal of Public Affairs and Change*.

16 The Preamble of the Bill stated that its objective thus are "to lay down judicial standards and provide for accountability of Judges, and, establish credible and expedient

clearly mentioned the dos and donts'[17]. The assets and liabilities of the judge is

---

mechanism for investigating into individual complaints for misbehaviour or incapacity of a Judge of the Supreme Court or of a High Court and to regulate the procedure for such investigation; and for the presentation of an address by Parliament to the President in relation to proceedings for removal of a Judge and for matters connected therewith or incidental thereto".

17 S. 3 – Judicial Standards: "3. (1) Every Judge shall continue to practice universally accepted values of judicial life as specified in the Schedule to this Act. \ (2) In particular, and without prejudice to the generality of the foregoing provision, no Judge shall – (a) contest the election to any office of a club, society or other association or hold such elective office except in a society or association connected with the law or any court; (b) have close association or close social interaction with individual members of the Bar, particularly with those who practice in the same court in which he is a Judge; (c) permit any member of his immediate family (including spouse, son, daughter, son-in-law or daughter-in-law or any other close relative), who is a member of the Bar, to appear before him or associated in any manner with a cause to be dealt with by him; (d) permit any member of his family, who is a member of the Bar, to use the residence in which the Judge actually resides or use other facilities provided to the Judge, for professional work of such member; (e) hear and decide a matter in which a member of his family, or his close relative or a friend is concerned; (f) enter into public debate or express his views in public on political matters or on matters which are pending or are likely to arise for judicial determination by him: Provided that nothing contained in this clause shall apply to,— (i) the views expressed by a Judge in his individual capacity on issues of public interest (other than as a Judge) during discussion in private forum or academic forum so as not to affect his functioning as a Judge; (ii) the views expressed by a Judge relating to administration of court or its efficient functioning; (g) make unwarranted comments against conduct of any Constitutional or statutory authority or statutory bodies or statutory institutions or any chairperson or member or officer thereof, in general, or at the time of hearing matters pending or likely to arise for judicial determinations. (h) give interview, to the media in relation to any of his judgment delivered, or order made, or direction issued, by him, in any case adjudicated by him; (i) accept gifts or hospitality except from his relatives; (j) hear and decide a matter in which a company or society or trust in which he holds or any member of his family holds shares or interest, unless he has disclosed his such holding or interest, and no objection to his hearing and deciding the matter is raised; (k) speculate in securities or indulge in insider trading in securities; (l) engage, directly or indirectly, in trade or business, either by himself or in association with any other person: Provided that the publication of a legal treatise or any activity in the nature of a hobby shall not be construed as trade or business for the purpose of this clause; (m) seek any financial benefit in the form of a perquisite or privilege attached to his office unless it is clearly available or admissible; (n) hold membership in any organisation that practices invidious discrimination on the basis of religion or race or caste or sex or place of birth; (o) have bias in his judicial work or judgments on the basis of religion or race or caste or sex or place of birth. Explanation. – For the purposes of this sub-section, "relative" means – (i) spouse of the Judge; (ii) brother or sister of the Judge; (iii) brother or sister of the spouse of the Judge; (iv) brother or sister of either of the parents of the Judge; (v) any lineal ascendant or descendant of the Judge; (vi) any lineal ascendant or descendant of the spouse of the Judge; (vii) spouse of the person referred to in clauses (ii) to (vi)".

to be furnished within a specific period[18], and the same shall be exhibited on the website for the public to access[19]. It envisaged an Oversight Committee[20] to deal with complaints that were raised against judges[21]. From the Committee, any complaint would be referred to the Scrutiny Panel[22], which has all the powers of a civil court[23] under the Code of Civil Procedure, 1908. The complaint would also be investigated into by an Investigation Committee[24].

The Bill was criticised on a large number of fronts by alleging that the judicial independence which was said to be one of the cardinal principles of the Indian polity, as has been perceived by the Constitution as well, was being threatened. There were certain revised versions of the Bill that was later circulated, but nothing much has materialised.

If one were to look into certain concerns which the Bill did try to portray, one cannot but help realize that a judicial performance index, which was one of the final intended outcomes of the Bill, would only materialise if certain standards of accountability and standards are prescribed for judges. *No one is above the law* being one of the cardinal principles of jurisprudence, one can definitely argue that judges who decide cases and lay down the law too should be brought within its ambit and scope.

4.1 *Further Trysts and Proposed Steps*

The Niti Aayog, in April 2017, came out with a Three-year Action Agenda, which was revised in August 2017, following comments from various stakeholders, and chalked a path towards achieving a number of goals and reforms; judicial reforms too formed an integral part of it. One of the most notable ideas that were proposed was to introduce a Judicial Performance Index, which could help the High Courts[25], and their Chief Justices, to keep a track on judges and their performances in court. The idea was to check the performance of the lower-level district courts, and to increase the speed in which cases were decided, and to a large extent do away with the delay that was plaguing the

18 S. 4 – Declaration of assets and liabilities.

19 S. 5 – Making available document or information in relation to a declaration of assets and liabilities of Judges on website.

20 S. 17 – Establishment of Oversight Committee. S. 18 speaks about the composition of the same.

21 S. 7 – Complaints.

22 S. 9 – Reference to Scrutiny Panel.

23 S. 14 – Power relating to scrutiny of complaints.

24 S. 22 – Investigation by investigation committee.

25 The highest court in a state.

legal systems. These were, for sure, the most urgent problems that plagued the Indian judiciary.

Getting rid of delay was something easier said than done, as shown by the history of attempts to deal with the problem. Having a set time limit for a case to be tried and trying to figure out as to whether there has been any delay, and finding out those causes which have led to the delay, is a tedious and onerous task. As is the case with other jurisdictions, India too did face similar problems, and there was a general opinion prevalent amongst the various stakeholders in the judicial system which led to a conclusion that a case could probably be classified as one in which a decision has been delayed. The report also tried to delve into certain best practises that were being followed, in different parts of the globe, and criteria that were being followed internationally. The Global Measures of Court Performance[26] is one tool that has been developed which tries to delve into a number of concerns that are to be addressed to increase court efficiency. The European Commission for the Efficiency of Justice[27] also strives to increase judicial efficiency in Europe.

An important point that has been raised in the report is the workload on judges which in turn affects their efficiency. This assumes a lot of significance in India, especially where the judges are under huge pressure to perform their duties, and hear a lot of present-day cases and more importantly have to deal with a huge set of cases which have been piling over the years. Freeing judges from day-to-day activities and ensuring that these activities are taken care of by administrative officials are one way that has been put across by the report, which, it is felt, is a sure shot method of easing the judges' burden. As every other appraisal method, this evaluation process should also be able to put across, in clear terms, to judges as to whether exactly they have not been able to meet the standards, and where exactly they have failed – so that a fix can be identified.

Especially in countries like India where the judiciary functions at various levels, care and caution should be exercised wherein the members of the subordinate judiciary, which falls under the administrative control of the High

---

26 This is a joint creation by the Australasian Institute of Judicial Administration (Australia and New Zealand), the Federal Judicial Center (United States), the National Center for State Courts (United States), and the State Courts of Singapore. For more see International Consortium for Court Excellence, *Global Measures of Court Performance* (3rd edn, Secretariat for the International Consortium for Court Excellence 2020), available at <https://www.courtexcellence.com/__data/assets/pdf_file/0030/54795/GLOBAL-MEASURES-3rd-Edition-Oct-2020.pdf> (accessed on 13 May 2022).

27 For more information see <https://www.coe.int/en/web/cepej> (accessed on 13 May 2022).

Courts of the respective states, are clearly evaluated. A bottoms-up approach is highly advisable and would definitely bring about a clearer picture as to what the situation is on the ground. This in turn would help focus more on relevant points and concerns and thereby lead to pointed and precise solutions. What the report does say is that a 'competitive reform' is the need of the hour.

Another suggestion laid down in the report[28] is that an administrative cadre, on the lines of the existing Indian Police Services, the Indian Administrative Services and the Indian Foreign Services, should be formed. The report tries to put forth the idea that such a cadre, in the judiciary, will help reduce the burden of the judges, who have had to juggle judicial functions along with administrative functions. As a result of this cadre being formed, its personnel would directly report to the Chief Justice of the respective High Courts, which in turn would ensure that the judges would have enough and more time to handle and perform their judicial functions. Division of labour and creation more job opportunities would be a win-win situation as far as India is concerned, given the high rates of unemployment.

The report also suggested that a better, efficient, and increased used of Information and Communication Technology (ICT)[29] could help in court processes. By prioritising automation and electronic ways of courts management, efficiency and efficacy could be increased. It also suggested the usage of a national court application system so as to ensure that uniformity is present as regards court procedures. Prioritizing ways in which such systems can be implemented in jails and in law enforcement agencies was yet another novel method that was proposed.

A major issue that India as a country did face is timely judicial appointments. The report did touch upon this aspect and suggested that an online mechanism which keeps track of real-time statistics and details as to how a judge performs in his court, would definitely be able to put across the need and the necessity to prioritize judicial appointments. Introducing a correct identification of the number of cases at hand and a calculation which aims to find out the number of judges that would have to be dealing with the pending cases, in order to ensure that there is no delay or unnecessary piling up of cases, was yet another idea that was mooted. The Niti Aayog Report had proposed a judicial appointment process which should be able to iron out all the problems that currently exist and rationalize the whole same[30].

28 Point 19.11 of the Niti Aayog Report.
29 Point 19.12 of the Niti Aayog Report.
30 Point 19.13 of the Niti Aayog Report.

The Report also tried to identify certain specific instances of workload division, wherein it was mooted that large workloads be handed over to separate sections – for example like the one proposed in the Commercial Courts, Commercial Division and Commercial Appellate Division of High Courts Act, 2015. This was opined to be a sure shot way to reduce the burden on existing courts. The Report also made a note that a special court be established to tackle traffic and police *challan* cases (*challan* is a report sent by the police to the Magistrate, after completion of investigation), as they did constitute more that 37% of the total number of cases that were examined during the period in which the report was prepared. It was suggested that offenders did not have to come to court to pay the fines, which in turn would reduce the workload of the judges.

5 An Appraisal

While it is a no-brainer that the Niti Aayog Report has been one which has kick started a long-drawn-out process of identifying and evaluating judicial performances, the ideas that it mooted and proposed to be put into practice need to be delved into a bit more – especially to gauge their effectiveness, practicality and probability of being implemented.

The Judicial Performance Index part, which would allow the higher judiciary to keep a tab on the lower judiciary and its functioning, by evaluating the judges, seems to put across a clear path, but one which, it is thought, is still a bit incomplete. The idea of entrusting the Index to higher courts and of evaluating only up to a certain level of the judiciary, it is felt, defeats the very aim underlying the initiative. Statistics do note that, in India, cases are piled up not just in the lower judiciary, but in the higher judiciary as well – which should lead one to make a safe assumption that judicial performance should be evaluated at every level. The very fact that pendency of cases if present at all levels in the judiciary should help one understand and realise that a judicial performace index should be not limited to the lower judiciary, but should definitely encompass the higher judiciary as well.

While references have been made to global standards that have been followed and put into practice in various places, a way in which it can be imbibed or at least, proposed to be imbibed in India, could have been a welcome addition. Tools which would certainly increase judicial efficiency and the best ways to properly incorporate them into the Indian legal system, could have been further discussed.

Determining the workload of judges was yet another point that was under scrutiny. Quite often than not, we notice that judges are bogged down with a lot of administrative work, that they seldom do find time and the energy to perform their primary function – decide cases, which, as it can easily be understood, is a clear reason for the pendency of cases. Identifying administrative help which can be afforded to judges would definitely help them a lot. This has also been reiterated by the report wherein it proposed the establishment of a separate administrative cadre like the ones that we do have in the police department as well as for administrative services, which, it is felt, is a wonderful move. By ensuring that a talented set of people do join the administrative side of the judiciary and help the judges in performing their duties better, the *elephant in the room* can be addressed.

Technological advancements have been nothing short of a boon, and the impact that they have had on the justice delivery mechanisms in India is commendable. The use of ICT, automation and various electronic methods, which help speedy, effective and efficient delivery of justice, could be another way of ensuring that the judges perform impeccably.

Appointment of an adequate number of judges is one major factor that does play a great role in ensuring better judicial performance. The ratio of the number of judges and the cases which they have to decide is a matter of concern and unless of course we have a clear, transparent process whereby judges are appointed, based on merit, this problem cannot be tackled. Appointing as many judges as needed would definitely ensure that courts are not overloaded with work and would be able to ensure that the wheels of justice tread surely.

Judicial Performance Index to be a reality in India, as it should be, in its original form, seems to be a distant dream – but for sure is achievable given the positive steps that have been initiated. It is high time that such a mechanism is put in place, not just for the lower judiciary, but also for the higher judiciary, for justice, rather its lack, should not be discriminative.

CHAPTER 5

Performance Assessment in Courts – the Swiss Case

Andreas Lienhard

1 Introduction

Courts find themselves under an increased pressure to perform, and there are several reasons for this: the workload is rising, whereas the available resources are limited[1]. The quality of the justice system is increasingly being discussed and questioned[2] by the authorities responsible for the supervision and (re-) appointment of judges[3]. Judges are also becoming the subject of assessment[4]. Judicial performance is compared through rankings[5] and judicial[6] activity is critically debated by

---

1 Andreas Lienhard, Daniel Kettiger, Daniela Winkler, *Stand des Justizmanagements in der Schweiz* (Stämpfli 2013) 3 f., with further references; Rainer Klopfer, 'Management der Justiz – Richterbild im Wandel' (2007) (2) *Richterzeitung* para. 17, available at <http://richterzeitung.weblaw.ch/rzissues/2007/2/r318.html> (accessed 10 October 2022). This chapter is a slightly revised version focussed on Switzerland, of Andreas Lienhard, 'Performance Assessment in Courts – The Swiss Case, Constitutional appraisal and thoughts as to its organisation' (2014) 6(2) *International Journal for Court Administration* 26–42.

2 Stephan Gass, 'Professionalisierung des Richteramts' (2010) 19(9) *Aktuelle juristische Praxis* (*AJP*) 1149; Hans Wiprächtiger, 'Recht und Richter', in Pierre Tercier (ed), *Gauchs Welt. Recht, Vertragsrecht und Baurecht. Festschrift für Peter Gauch zum 65. Geburtstag* (Schulthess 2004) 327; Christoph Bandli, 'Die Rolle des Bundesverwaltungsgerichts', in Pierre Tschannen et al. (eds), *Neue Bundesrechtspflege, Auswirkungen der Totalrevision auf den kantonalen und eidgenössischen Rechtsschutz* (Stämpfli 2007) 195 ff. and 205 f., with further references.

3 Andreas Lienhard, 'Oberaufsicht und Justizmanagement' (2009) (1) *Richterzeitung* para. 71 ff., available at <http://richterzeitung.weblaw.ch/rzissues/2009/1/r587.html> (accessed 10 October 2022).

4 Daniel Grosse, 'Assessmentcenter für Richter' (2013) *Legal Tribune online*, available at <www.lto.de/recht/job-karriere/j/assessmentcenter-richter-gerichte> (accessed 10 October 2022).

5 See for example the comparative studies by the European Commission for the Efficiency of Justice (CEPEJ), *European Judicial Systems* (2022), available at <https://www.coe.int/en/web/human-rights-rule-of-law/-/efficiency-and-quality-of-justice-in-europe-council-of-europe-publishes-its-2022-report> (accessed 10 October 2022); European Commission, *The 2022 EU Justice Scoreboard* (2022), available at <https://ec.europa.eu/info/sites/default/files/eu_justice_scoreboard_2022.pdf> (accessed 10 October 2022).

6 Hans Peter Walter, 'Interne richterliche Unabhängigkeit' (2005) (1) *Richterzeitung* para. 29, available at <http://richterzeitung.weblaw.ch/rzissues/2005/1/r3.html> (accessed

 | DOI:10.1163/9789004680944_006

politicians and the media. The demands for court management have risen accordingly[7].

In many areas of public administration, performance assessment has become a fixed date on the management calendar and a crucial element of quality assurance and development[8]. The performance of each authority is recorded and evaluated in reports (such as public office annual reports). In addition, performance records (for example, course evaluations) are also kept and performance assessments (in particular staff appraisal interviews) are undertaken at employee level.

This inevitably raises the question of whether and how judicial performance can and should be assessed. In particular the performance of judges is singled out as an issue. This has been a topic of discussion in Switzerland for some time[9] and was the subject of an international conference of the Swiss Judges' Association (*Schweizerische Vereinigung der Richterinnen und Richter*, SVR) in 2013[10]. The importance and current relevance of the topic was underlined by a 2013 decision not to re-appoint a supreme court judge due to perceived shortcomings in his working methods and organisation[11]. In the canton of Lucerne, a change to cantonal law has given rise to a debate on the principles for deciding who should be appointed as a judge[12]. The canton of Geneva's new

10 October 2022); Ulrich Zimmerli, 'Wenn die Politik Druck macht – Richtertätigkeit unter Beeinflussungsversuchen' (2009) (4) *Richterzeitung*, available at <http://richterzeitung.weblaw.ch/rzissues/2009/4/r700.html> (accessed 10 October 2022); Stephan Gass & Peter Stolz, 'Institutionen der Richterkontrolle im internationalen Vergleich' (1998) *Schweizerische Juristen*-Zeitung (SJZ) 128; see also the 'Court Test' in the Beobachter magazine from 22 June 2001 (13 *Beobachter*).

7 Michael Meisenberg, 'Die Justiz als modernes Dienstleistungsunternehmen', in Reinhard Böttcher, Götz Hueck, Burkhard Jähnke (eds), *Festschrift für Walter Odersky zum 65. Geburtstag* (De Gruyter 1996) 61 ff.

8 See for example, Adrian Ritz & Norbert Thom, *Public Management: Innovative Konzepte zur Führung im öffentlichen Sektor* (Gabler Verlag 2019, 6th edn) 501 ff.; Kuno Schedler & Isabella Proeller, *New Public Management* (utb 2011) 257 f.

9 See already Daniel Kettiger, 'Auf dem Weg zu einer leistungs-und wirkungsorientierten Justiz: Erkenntnisse – offene Fragen – Ausblick', in Daniel Kettiger (ed), *Wirkungsorientierte Verwaltungsführung in der Justiz – ein Balanceakt zwischen Effizienz und Rechtsstaatlichkeit* (SGVW 2003) 189 f., with further references.

10 *Richterliche Unabhängigkeit und Leistungsbeurteilung – Die Beurteilung richterlicher Tätigkeit im Spannungsverhältnis zur richterlichen Unabhängigkeit, Internationale Tagung der Schweizerischen Vereinigung der Richterinnen und Richter* (SVR), 23 May 2013.

11 *Aargauer Zeitung*, 23 August 2013.

12 Bill for consultation dated 21 January 2013, 13 f.; Motion No. 740 of 14 September 2010 on improving the basis for decision-making in appointing judges; Motion No. 406 of 9 September 2013 on the qualification and performance assessment of judges and public prosecutors as the basis for re-appointment and increasing workloads. See also Schweizerische Vereinigung der Richterinnen und Richter (SVR), 'Consultation Procedure.

constitution even contains the following regulation: "Before each appointment to the judiciary, the Magistrates Supervisory Council shall evaluate the qualifications of the candidates. It shall prepare a preliminary opinion"[13].

The following paper addresses the question of the performance assessment of judges from the point of view of constitutional law and shows examples from the judiciary of Switzerland.

2 Constitutional Framework in Switzerland

2.1 *Requirements*

Courts and their judges are expected to perform appropriately and efficiently, and judicial performance is partly guaranteed by the prohibition of judicial delays and the requirement of prompt procedures contained in Article 29 Paragraph 1 of the Swiss Federal Constitution[14], according to which judgments must be issued within a reasonable time[15]. At the same time, basic procedural

---

Gesamtrevision der Geschäftsordnung des Kantonsrats etc.', 25 April 2014, and Thomas Stadelmann, 'Überlegungen zur Wahl und Wiederwahl von Richterinnen und Richtern, Kritische Anmerkungen anlässlich eines Gesetzgebungsprojekts im Kanton Luzern' (2014) (3) *Richterzeitung*, available at <http://richterzeitung.weblaw.ch/rzissues/2014/3/uberlegungen-zur-wah_14215af798.html__ONCE> (accessed 10 October 2022).

13 Art. 127 Constitution of the Republic and Canton of Geneva of 14 October 2012 (KV-GE, SR 131.234).

14 The Swiss Federal Constitution is available at <https://www.fedlex.admin.ch/eli/cc/1999/404/en> (accessed 10 October 2022). The cantonal constitutions have increasingly analogous provisions, where the federal constitutional law does not apply in any case to the cantons as well. In some cases, the framework is also marked out in international law, e.g. in the European Convention on Human Rights (ECHR) and in the UN Covenant on Civil and Political Rights. On the international discussion, see for example Pim Albers, 'Performance indicators and evaluation for judges and courts', available at <https://rm.coe.int/performance-indicators-and-evaluation-for-judges-and-courts-dr-pim-alb/16807907b0> (accessed 10 October 2022); Richard Mohr & Francesco Contini, 'Judicial Evaluation in Context: Principles, Practices and Promise in Nine European Countries' (2007) 1(2) *European Journal of Legal Studies*, available at <https://ro.uow.edu.au/lawpapers/49/> (accessed 10 October 2022).

15 Excessively long proceedings reduce both the legal protection afforded to the parties to the proceedings and to third parties. Avoiding excessively long proceedings is therefore a feature of a good judge (see for example Klaus Rennert, 'Was ist ein guter Richter? – Fünfzehn Thesen für eine Annäherung' (2013) 68(6) *JuristenZeitung* (JZ) 297–299. More recently on the issue, see Beat Brändli, *Prozessökonomie im schweizerischen Recht: Grundlagen, bundesgerichtliche Rechtsprechung und Auswirkungen im schweizerischen Zivilprozess* (Stämpfli 2013), in particular 21 ff. as well as Christoph Bürki, *Verwaltungsjustizbezogene Legalität und Prozessökonomie* (Stämpfli 2013), in particular 128 ff.; Kettiger, *supra* fn 9, 200).

rights must be respected, particularly the right to an impartial court (Article 30 Paragraph 1 Federal Constitution) and the right to a fair hearing, which includes the requirement to provide adequate justification for any decision (Article 29 Paragraph 2 Federal Constitution)[16]. In addition to these procedural (formal) aspects of the judicial process, court decisions are expected to be of a high content-related (material) quality: judgments should guarantee legal protection and contribute to legal harmony[17]; the practices of the supreme courts should also function as a guide and as an example for legal development[18].

This touches on the effectiveness and efficiency of the justice system[19], qualities that must be considered in relation to all state tasks (cf. at federal level Article 43a Paragraph 5, and Article 170 Federal Constitution)[20]. Even courts have only limited resources – despite the fact that the need for sufficient financial support is constantly being reiterated[21]. Therefore the need to use the available funds economically becomes more and more important, just as

16 For an overview of the constitutional procedural guarantees see for example Gerold Steinmann, 'Art. 29 BV', in B. Ehrenzeller et al. (eds), *Die schweizerische Bundesverfassung. St. Galler Kommentar* (Dike/Schulthess 2014, 3rd edn) para. 4 ff.

17 Giovanni Biaggini, '§ 73 Rechtsprechung, para. 1', in Daniel Thürer, Jean-François Aubert, Jörg Paul Müller (eds), *Verfassungsrecht der Schweiz* (2001); Kettiger, *supra* fn 9, 201; Regina Kiener, 'Das Bundesgericht und weitere richterliche Behörden', in Giovanni Biaggini, Thomas Gächter, Regina Kiener (eds), *Staatsrecht* (Dike 2021, 3rd edn) 285 ff.; Heinrich Koller, 'Art. 1', in Marcel Alexander Niggli et al. (eds), *Basler Kommentar. Bundesgerichtsgesetz* (Schulthess 2018, 3nd edn) para. 14.

18 See for example Biaggini, *supra* fn 17, para. 1 and para. 34.

19 See Andreas Lienhard, 'Controllingverfahren des Bundesgerichts' (2007) (2) *Richterzeitung* para. 4, available at <http://richterzeitung.weblaw.ch/rzissues/2007/2/r300.html> (accessed 10 October 2022); Lienhard, *supra* fn 3, para. 29 f. See also for example Kettiger, *supra* fn 9, 199 ff.; Etienne Poltier, 'L'organisation et le fonctionnement interne de l'ordre judiciaire et des tribunaux' (2011) 20(8) *AJP* 1020; Niccolò Raselli, 'Richterliche Unabhängigkeit' (2011) (3) *Richterzeitung* para. 19, available at <http://richterzeitung.weblaw.ch/rzissues/2011/3/r972.html> (accessed 10 October 2022); Thomas Stadelmann, 'Richterliche Unabhängigkeit und Leistungsbeurteilung' (2013) (1) *Richterzeitung* para. 1, available at <http://richterzeitung.weblaw.ch/rzissues/2013/1/2246.html> (accessed 10 October 2022). The requirement of efficiency of the courts and of judges is also stressed with reference to Art. 6 ECHR by the Committee of Ministers of the Council of Europe in of its recommendation 'On judges: independence, efficiency and responsibilities' (Recommendation CM/Rec[2010]12).

20 See also Jan-Marie Doogue, Colin Doherty, Jeff Simpson, 'Accountability for the Administration and Organisation of the Judiciary' (2013), paper presented to the Asia Pacific Courts Conference 10, available at <https://aija.org.au/wp-content/uploads/2017/08/DoogueDoherty.pdf> (accessed 10 October 2022).

21 Raselli, *supra* fn 19, para. 31; Patrick Guidon, 'Von der gleichmässigen Verteilung von Enttäuschungen' (2013) (1) *Richterzeitung*, available at <http://richterzeitung.weblaw.ch/rzissues/2013/1/2092.html> (accessed 10 October 2022); BGE 107 Ib 160 E. 3c, 165.

it is with the entire national budget (see at federal level Article 126 Paragraph 1 Federal Constitution).

Judicial performance and economy are, when taken with legality, the main criteria applied in supervision[22]. This applies first of all to parliamentary oversight (at federal level Article 169 Paragraph 1 Federal Constitution)[23]; the control over the content of individual judgments is out of the question and oversight is limited in principle to court management[24]. However, judicial performance is a significant element in general procedural matters. The oversight authority must investigate whether the courts generally comply with their constitutional duties and whether they efficiently use the available resources in the judicial process. The oversight authority or its advisory committees must be allowed to look into judge-related matters (such as the number of cases dealt with by individual judges) where there are multiple, objectively inexplicable anomalies[25].

The ongoing transition to self-government by courts (for the Swiss Federal Supreme Court [*Schweizerisches Bundesgericht*] regulated by Article 188 Paragraph 3 Federal Constitution)[26] brings with it the requirement of in-court supervision (supervision of management and administrative bodies) for both

---

22 Lienhard, *supra* fn 3, para. 15 f.

23 In relation to judicial councils (equipped with various powers), see Lienhard, *supra* fn 3, para. 22, with further references.

24 Lienhard, *supra* fn 3, para. 8 ff., with numerous further references; Regina Kiener, 'Aspekte der parlamentarischen Justizaufsicht im Kanton Bern' (1997) *Bernische Verwaltungsrechtsprechung* (*BVR*) 394 ff.; Peter Stolz & Stephan Gass, 'Kontrolle und Bewertung von Richterarbeit aus rechts-und wirtschaftswissenschaftlicher Sicht' (1996) 14(5) *recht* 170 f.; Thomas Sägesser, 'Art. 26 ParlG', in Martin Graf, Cornelia Theler, Moritz von Wyss (eds), *Parlamentsrecht und Parlamentspraxis der Schweizerischen Bundesversammlung. Kommentar zum Parlamentsgesetz (ParlG)* (Helbing Lichtenhahn Verlag 2014) para 56 f.

25 See already Andreas Lienhard, *Staats-und verwaltungsrechtliche Grundlagen für das New Public Management in der Schweiz – Analyse, Anforderungen, Impulse* (Stämpfli 2005) 467.

26 Andreas Lienhard, 'Die bernische Gerichtsbarkeit auf dem Weg zur Selbstverwaltung', in Ruth Herzog & Reto Feller (eds), *Bernische Verwaltungsgerichtsbarkeit in Geschichte und Gegenwart* (Geiger AG 2010) 401 ff., in particular 411 ff.; see also for example Hans Wipfli, 'Justizielle Selbstverwaltung', in Benjamin Schindler & P. Sutter (eds), *Akteure der Gerichtsbarkeit* (Dike 2007) 115 ff.; Klopfer, *supra* fn 1, para. 4 ff.; Andreas Lienhard & Daniel Kettiger, 'Die Selbstverwaltung der Gerichte, Erkenntnisse der Auslegung von § 112 Abs. 2 der Verfassung des Kantons Basel-Stadt' (2013) (3) *Richterzeitung*, available at <http://richterzeitung.weblaw.ch/rzissues/2013/3/2258.html> (accessed 10 October 2022); Marta Niquille-Eberle, 'Das Bundesgericht verwaltet sich selbst (Art. 188 Abs. 3 BV)' (2013) 22(9) *AJP* 1358 ff.; Beat Frey, 'Die selbständige Gerichtsverwaltung im Kanton Solothurn oder: Wie der Justizdirektor sich fast selber abschaffte', in Andreas Eng et al. (eds) *Festgabe Walter Straumann* (Staatskanzlei 2013) 154 ff.

higher and lower judicial authorities, depending on their structure. This supervisory activity concerns itself mainly with court management. The supervisory authority must query excessively long lists of pending cases and inefficiencies (also in relation to individual judges)[27]. Self-government makes high demands with regard to (management) quality. Caseload management is an important element of self-government[28]; case allocation takes the workload and the performance of individual judges into account[29]. Self-government also includes personnel management and career development; performance assessments are an essential basis for employee appraisal interviews and status reviews, not to mention employers' references. Unlike most EU states[30], Switzerland has no particular law on the judiciary in the sense of comprehensive public service legislation[31]. Judges of first instance especially are usually subject to general public service law, sometimes with modifications specific to the judiciary[32].

---

27 Georg Müller, 'Politik und Medien', in Peter Hänni (ed), *Mensch und Staat – L'homme et l'Etat. Festschrift für Thomas Fleiner* (Schulthess 2003) 545 ff.

28 Andreas Lienhard & Daniel Kettiger, 'Geschäftslastbewirtschaftung bei Gerichten: Methodik, Erfahrungen und Ergebnisse einer Studie bei den kantonalen Verwaltungs- und Sozialversicherungsgerichten' (2009) 110(8) *Schweizerisches Zentralblatt für Staats- und Verwaltungsrecht* (*ZBl*) 413 ff.; Andreas Lienhard, 'Caseload Management in the Law Courts: Methodology, Experiences and Results of the first Swiss Study of Administrative and Social Insurance Courts' (2010) 3 *International Journal for Court Administration* (*IJCA*) 30 ff., available at <https://www.iacajournal.org/articles/abstract/10.18352/ijca.52 /> (accessed 10 October 2022).

29 Arthur Aeschlimann, 'Justizreform 2000 – Das Bundesgericht und sein Gesetz' (2008) 109(8) *ZBl* 397 ff., 404 und 413; Christoph Bandli, 'Das Bundesverwaltungsgericht als Eckpfeiler der Justizreform: Bewährtes und Anpassungsbedarf' (2012) *Zeitschrift des Bernischen Juristenvereins* (*ZBJV*) 101 ff., 111 f.

30 See Stephan Gass, 'Die Stellung des Richters im neuen Personalgesetz', in Kanton Basel-Landschaft (ed), *Aspekte der richterlichen Unabhängigkeit und Richter(aus)wahl* (Verlag des Kantons Basel-Landschaft 2000) 84 ff.

31 See however for example the German Judges Act of 8 September 1961 (DriG, available at <http://www.gesetze-im-internet.de/bundesrecht/drig/gesamt.pdf> (accessed 10 October 2022)) and the judges acts of the individual Bundesländer.

32 For the federal courts, there are largely self-contained regulations (the Federal Supreme Court Act of 17 June 2005 [FSCA; SR 173.110], the Federal Assembly Act and the Ordinance of 6 October 1989 on the Remuneration and Occupational Pensions of Senior Government Officials and Supreme Court Judges [SR 172.121 and SR 172.121.1 respectively] for Federal Supreme Court judges, and the Patent Court Act of 20 March 2009 [PatGG; SR 173.141], the Administrative Court Act of 17 June 2005 [FACA; SR 173.32], the Criminal Justice Authorities Act of 19 March 2010 [StBOG; SR 173.71] and the Federal Assembly Ordinance of 13 December 2002 on the Employment and Remuneration of Judges of the Federal Administrative Court, the ordinary judges of the Federal Criminal Court and the Full-time Judges of the Federal Patent Court [Judges Ordinance; SR 173.711.2] for the other federal judges).

This means that, where applicable, even a judge can demand an employer's reference, which not only confirms the judge's employment as such, but includes details concerning performance and conduct. This is important, in part because Switzerland has no regulated or customary career paths for judges, and changes of occupation from the judiciary to public administration and the private sector are common[33]. Guaranteeing that an employer's reference will be provided requires a continual assessment of performance and conduct. This is particularly essential in the case of judges, who often have no designated superiors or whose governing committee members change annually or at regular intervals.

In Switzerland, judges are appointed for a fixed term of office (at federal level in accordance with Article 188 Paragraph 4 Federal Constitution) either by parliament or by plebiscite (at federal level in accordance with Article 168 Paragraph 1 Federal Constitution, they are elected by the United Federal Assembly). The criteria for eligibility vary from canton to canton. The process of judicial selection is generally prepared by a parliamentary judicial committee. However, affiliation to a political party usually plays a crucial role. Switzerland does not have a career judiciary and has no procedure for promotion to higher courts[34]. The system of reappointment is mainly justified by "[…] the necessity, for the very sake of his independence, to occasionally place the judge under the spotlight of measurable control, measurable by whether the superior authority continues to recognise and respect his judicial qualities"[35]. This inevitably

33 If available, candidates for new judicial positions, for example in the canton of Aargau, must also submit employers' references or the minutes of any performance review interviews. See Adrian Schmid, 'Vorbereitung der Wahlen von Richterinnen und Richtern durch das Parlament des Kantons Aargau' (2013) (2) *Parlament – Mitteilungsblatt der Schweizerischen Gesellschaft für Parlamentsfragen* 37 ff., in particular 39.

34 For selection, appointment and reappointment of judges, see Regina Kiener, 'Judicial Independence in Switzerland', in Anja Seibert-Fohr (ed), *Judicial Independence in Transition* (Springer 2012) 403 ff., 411 ff. For an overview on the various systems of (re-) appointment in Switzerland, see Pascal Mahon & Roxane Schaller, 'L'élection des juges entre tradition démocratique et exigences de l'Etat de droit' (2013) (2) *Parlament – Mitteilungsblatt der Schweizerischen Gesellschaft für Parlamentsfragen* 3 ff. For criticism of the principle of having a term of office, see in particular Walter, *supra* fn 6, para. 29; Kiener, *supra* fn 17, 263 f.; Stadelmann, *supra* fn 12, para. 7, with further references. An exception to the principle of having a term of office is only found in the canton of Freiburg (see Kiener, 'Judicial Independence in Switzerland', *supra* in this fn, 419).

35 Kurt Eichenberger, 'Sonderheiten und Schwierigkeiten der richterlichen Unabhängigkeit in der Schweiz', in Richard Frank (ed), *Unabhängigkeit und Bindungen des Richters in der Bundesrepublik Deutschland, in Österreich und in der Schweiz* (Helbing &Lichtenhahn 1997) 69 ff., 81; for further justification (in particular the specific weighting of the principle

raises the question of (re-)appointment criteria, aside from affiliation to any political party[36]. It is self-evident that individual performance should be among these criteria[37]. Accordingly, it must be possible to assess a number of professional and personal characteristics (in particular professional expertise, personal and social skills and management abilities)[38]. Insofar as appointments are considered decisions and thus fundamental procedural guarantees must be observed in (re-)appointments (Article 29 Federal Constitution), such

---

of democracy, restraint of powers and regulatory law aspects) Regina Kiener, 'Sind Richter trotz Wiederwahl unabhängig?' (2001) 5 *Plädoyer* 37 f.

36 See for example Hansjörg Seiler, 'Richter als Parteivertreter, Parteienproporz und Richterwahl' (2006) (3) *Richterzeitung* para. 1 ff., available at <http://richterzeitung.weblaw.ch/rzissues/2006/3/r193.html> (accessed 10 October 2022); Peter Albrecht, 'Richter als (politische) Parteivertreter?' (2006) (3) *Richterzeitung* para. 1 ff., available at <http://richterzeitung.weblaw.ch/rzissues/2006/3/r191.html> (accessed 10 October 2022); Raselli, *supra* fn 19, para. 6 ff., with further references. On the criticism of the dominant position of political parties in the appointment procedure, see Stadelmann, supra fn 12, para. 2, with further references.

37 See also Thomas Hugi Yar & Andreas Kley, 'Art. 9 BGG', in Niggli et al. (eds), *supra* fn 17, para. 3f; see also Daniel Rietiker, 'Qualitätskontrollen für Strassburger Richter' (2012) (2) *Richterzeitung*, available at <http://richterzeitung.weblaw.ch/rzissues/2012/2/r1102.html> (accessed 10 October 2022); electing judges on the basis of the performance of the candidates (a 'merit-selection system') is also derived from Art. 14 Sec. 1 UN Covenant II (reference from Regina Kiener, 'Verfahren der Erneuerungswahlen von Richterinnen und Richtern des Bundes' (2008) (3) *Verwaltungspraxis der Bundesbehörden* 363). For appointments to the federal courts, although reference is made to professional and personal suitability in the invitation for applications, these criteria are not laid down in the legislation; in the case of re-appointments, the judicial committee preparing for the appointments does not obtain an overview of performance to date (see Katrin Marti, 'Die Gerichtskommission der Vereinigten Bundesversammlung' (2010) (1) *Richterzeitung*, in particular para. 7, available at <http://richterzeitung.weblaw.ch/rzissues/2010/1/r719.html> (accessed 10 October 2022)). The principles of conduct of the judicial committee on the Committee procedure for removal from office or non-re-appointment of 3 March 2011 (*Bundesblatt* (*BBl*) 2012 1271 ff.) indeed cover the procedure, but say nothing further on professional or personal eligibility criteria.

38 See for example Peter Albrecht, 'Was zeichnet gute Richterinnen und Richter aus?', in Schindler & Sutter (eds), *supra* fn 26, 3; Frank Bieler & Jürgen Lorse, *Die dienstliche Beurteilung* (Erich Schmidt 2012) 373; Johannes Riedel, 'Training and Recruitment of Judges in Germany' (2013) 5(2) *IJCA* 48 f., available at <https://iacajournal.org/articles/10.18352/ijca.12 > (accessed 10 October 2022); Johannes Riedel, 'Individual Evaluation of Judges in Germany' (2014) 4(5) *Oñati Socio-Legal Series* 974; Jordan M. Singer, 'Knowing Is Half the Battle: A Proposal for Prospective Performance Evaluations in Judicial Evaluations' (29) 2006–2007 *University of Arkansas Little Rock Law Review* 725 ff.; for a critical appraisal see Doogue, Doherty, Simpson, *supra* fn 20, 14.

acts of applying the law must also be adequately justified[39]. In this case, the pre-defined[40] suitability or appointment criteria must be referred to[41].

As non-re-appointment for personal rather than organisational reasons is equivalent to dismissal from office to the individual concerned, it is essential that proper justification is given[42]. In any case, non-re-appointment must not be abused in order to avoid proceedings to dismiss a judge from office[43]. The necessity of adequate justification, and, where applicable, justification that considers individual performance, is further accentuated in the context of disciplinary proceedings.

Where objectively inadequate justification is given for non-re-appointment, dismissal or disciplinary decisions, this is also problematic from the point of view of judicial independence (Article 30 Paragraph 1, 191c Federal Constitution)[44].

2.2 *Barriers*

Judicial independence is the key constitutional barrier that prevents external influencing of judicial decisions (Article 30 Paragraph 1 and Article 191c Federal Constitution)[45]. In this context, binding performance targets for judges seem constitutionally problematic, especially if they are not set by the Constitution

39 At any rate in relation to re-appointment of federal judges, see Kiener, *supra* fn 37, 357 ff., 360, 379.

40 In this sense, see also Mahon & Schaller, *supra* fn 34, 13 f.

41 For example in the canton of Aargau: Schmid, *supra* fn 33, 39 f.

42 Kiener, *supra* fn 37, 369; similarly Stadelmann, *supra* fn 12, para. 8.

43 Kiener, *supra* fn 37, 369.

44 See for example Martin Kayser, 'Richterwahlen: Unabhängigkeit im Spannungsfeld von Rechtsstaatlichkeit und Demokratie', in Schindler & Sutter, *supra* fn 26, 60 f. The grounds for not re-electing judges must be substantial, such as permanent disruption of the judicial process, damage to the trust in/credibility of the justice system, incompetence/inappropriate conduct, serious/repeated breaches of official duties (Kiener, *supra* fn 35, 42).

45 See for detail Regina Kiener, *Richterliche Unabhängigkeit. Verfassungsrechtliche Anforderungen an Richter und Gerichte* (Stämpfli 2001), in particular 235 f.; in this connection see Hans-Jacob Mosimann, 'Richterliche Unabhängigkeit und Leistungsbeurteilung: Schweiz', in Thomas Stadelmann, Stephan Gass, Richard McCombe (eds), *Performance Appraisal of the Judiciary and Judicial Independence* (Dike 2015) 87 ff., 92 ff., with further references [hereinafter 'Richterliche Unabhängigkeit'] and Hans-Jacob Mosimann, 'Leistungsbeurteilung von Richterinnen und Richtern – Qualitätsmerkmal oder Angriff auf die richterliche Unabhängigkeit?' (2011) (1) *Richterzeitung*, available at <http://richterzeitung.weblaw.ch/rzissues/2011/1/r871.html> (accessed 10 October 2022) [hereinafter 'Leistungsbeurteilung']. See, on the international agreements, declarations and standards on judicial independence, Stephan Gass, Regina Kiener, Thomas Stadelmann (eds), *Standards on judicial independence* (Editions Weblaw 2012).

itself (for example by the prohibition of judicial delays) or by law (for example case processing deadlines prescribed by law)[46]. However, performance targets such as planning measures within the judicial sector in relation to the number of cases are increasingly viewed as acceptable and necessary[47]. "Court administration necessitates management. Management does not necessarily violate personal judicial independence as long as it contributes to the self-government of the court. [...] Binding goals of an organisational nature or that concern the management of the justice system are not merely acceptable, but absolutely necessary"[48].

The ongoing problem of how to assess judicial performances in qualitative terms is often mentioned in connection with judicial independence[49]. The problem with judicial activity is that its influence on society cannot easily be measured[50]. Performance indicators are often quantitative measurements that give little indication of the quality of a judgment[51]. Efficiency analyses therefore must always consider qualitative aspects as well, otherwise judicial independence could be affected[52].

However, judicial independence does not preclude effective quality control in principle. Indeed, it could even ensure it: "Adequacy or inadequacy in office is not a question of independence, and suitable preventive or repressive measures in order to guarantee quality foster, and do not counteract, the right form of independence. In particular, the nimbus of independence does not trivialise the seriousness of professional or social shortcomings, and a judge's autonomy must not allow him to treat his office as a comfortable sinecure. Despite the

---

46 Lienhard, *supra* fn 25, 465 ff.; Paul Tschümperlin, 'Gerichtsmanagement am Bundesgericht: Stand und Entwicklungstendenzen', in Daniel Kettiger (ed), *Wirkungsorientierte Verwaltungsführung und Justiz – ein Balanceakt zwischen Effizienz und Rechtsstaatlichkeit* (Verlag SGVW 2003) 93; Kettiger, *supra* fn 9, 189.

47 Ulrich Cavelti, 'Der Gerichtspräsident – primus inter pares oder Justizmanager', in Peter Mäusli-Allenspach & Michael Beusch (eds), *Steuern und Recht – Steuerrecht! Liber amicorum für Martin Zweifel* (Helbing Lichtenhahn Verlag 2013) 330; in the same context, see also Paul Tschümperlin, 'Die Aufsicht des Bundesgerichts' (2009) SJZ, 237.

48 Cavelti, *supra* fn 47, 332.

49 Walter, *supra* fn 6, para. 28.

50 Lienhard, *supra* fn 26, 424.

51 Raselli, *supra* fn 19, para. 20; Mosimann, 'Leistungsbeurteilung', *supra* fn 45, para. 50, who comments critically in particular on numbers of appeals and reversed decisions.

52 Cf. Uwe Berlit, 'Richterliche Unabhängigkeit und Organisation effektiven Rechtsschutzes im 'ökonomisierten' Staat', in Helmut Schulze-Fielitz & Carsten Schütz (eds), *Justiz und Justizverwaltung zwischen Ökonomisierungsdruck und Unabhängigkeit* (Duncker & Humblot 2002) 135 ff., in particular 156.

shield of independence, effective quality control is a matter of means, not of principle"[53].

Yet, the imperative of efficiency as part of the guarantee of justice[54] must not undermine that guarantee. It has been established, for example, that judicial performance increases with an increasing workload – though only to a certain degree[55]. Excessive pressure on courts and judges to be efficient must therefore be avoided[56].

As long as performance assessments concern individual judges, the constitutional protection of privacy could be affected[57]: in particular, under Article 13 Paragraph 2 Federal Constitution, every person has the right to be protected against the misuse of their personal data. Therefore, judgment-related performance data for individual judges is not made available to the general public[58].

2.3 *Conclusion*

Constitutional law offers certain principles that underline the appropriateness of performance assessments of judicial activity: judicial performance is an element of effectiveness and efficiency, the subject matter of self-government, supervision and oversight, and a criterion in appointments, re-appointments and dismissals or disciplinary proceedings. The assessment of the performance of judges is therefore essential to guaranteeing justice.

However, constitutional law also lists a number of substantial barriers to performance assessment in order to protect the judiciary. Judicial independence

---

53 Walter, *supra* fn 6, para. 34; see also Sec. 2.1 above.

54 On the requirement of efficiency, see Sec. 2.1 above.

55 Kamil Jonski & Daniel Mankowski, 'Is the sky the limit? – Revisiting 'exogenous productivity of judges' argument' (2014) 6(2) *IJCA*, available at https://www.iacajournal.org/articles/abstract/10.18352/ijca.135/ (accessed 11 October 2022).

56 See for example Franzen von Ruben, 'Der Druck der Überforderung. Wenn Richter überfordert sind mit dem Anspruch, nur der Wahrheit und Gerechtigkeit zu dienen ...', (2013) 113 *Betrifft Justiz* 24 ff.

57 The protection of privacy may have compensatory significance for judges, because they cannot themselves call on judicial independence in its form as a fundamental right (Kiener, *supra* fn 45, 381); in the present context Peter Bieri, *Bearbeitung von Daten über Richterinnen und Richter, Bedarf und Schranken, Schriftenreihe zur Justizforschung* (Stämpfli 2017) 82 ff.

58 See BGE 137 I 1 ff. relating to the disclosure of daily allowances for commercial court judges for a specific case (see Andreas Lienhard & Daniel Kettiger, 'Keine Absage an ein zeitgemässes Justizmanagement' (2011) (2) *Richterzeitung*, available at <http://richterzeitung.weblaw.ch/rzissues/2011/2/r923.html> (accessed 10 October 2022)); see also Doogue, Doherty, Simpson, *supra* fn 20, 13.

above all other factors is meant to allow courts and judges to perform their duties without performance targets that directly influence judicial activity. Certain special requirements regarding the conduct of performance assessment of judges also arise from the law on the protection of privacy.

Performance assessments cannot be equated with performance targets; however, they can indirectly exert a certain pressure on the level of performance. Even this effect is problematic when considering the importance of judicial independence[59]. It can only be justified when set against the background of other principles relating to the organisation of the judiciary – but only as long as the procedurally prescribed care in case processing is not adversely affected[60].

Therefore, from a general constitutional standpoint, it is not a question of whether performance assessments in the judiciary are permitted. Rather, it is a question of how these assessments should be organised in a fair and balanced manner in accordance with the various principles of constitutional law[61]. The conflict between guaranteeing justice and protecting the judiciary raises the following key questions[62]:

- What purpose do performance assessments serve (case allocation, quality assurance, career development, re-appointment, agreeing salaries) and what are the consequences?
- What is the subject of a performance assessment (judicial activity, management) and what are the assessment criteria?
- How is performance recorded in order to form the basis for a performance assessment (statistics, surveys, meetings)?

---

59 Roland Rechtsreport, *Sonderbericht: das deutsche Rechts-und Justizsystem aus Sicht von Richtern und Staatsanwälten* (Institut für Demoskopie Allensbach 2014) 54 (34 or 45% of judges interviewed, with or without management duties, admit that the assessment system influences their personal or professional independence).

60 Lienhard & Kettiger, *supra* fn 26, para. 18; Lienhard & Kettiger, *supra* fn 58, para. 18 ff.

61 Sie also Stephan Gass & Thomas Stadelmann, 'Leistungsbeurteilung in der Justiz und richterliche Unabhängigkeit im Spannungsfeld von Recht und Politik, Wirtschaft und Gesellschaft', in Stadelmann, Gass, McCombe (eds), *supra* fn 45, 3 ff.; basically, to balance different constitutional principles in the judiciary see Andreas Lienhard & Daniel Kettiger, 'The Judiciary between Management and the Rule of Law – Introduction', in Andreas Lienhard & Daniel Kettiger (eds), *The Judiciary between Management and the Rule of Law* (Stämpfli 2016) 7.

62 See also Gass & Stolz, *supra* fn 6; Gass & Stadelmann, *supra* fn 61, 7 ff.; Stadelmann, supra fn 12, para. 1; Mosimann, 'Richterliche Unabhängigkeit', *supra* fn 45, 102; Madeleine Keel, *Die Leitungsstrukturen der Justiz im Bund und in ausgewählten Kantonen – Eine Studie im Spannungsfeld von Führung und verfassungsrechtlichen Prinzipien* (Diss. St. Gallen 2014) 312 ff.

- Who is the subject of a performance assessment (courts, divisions, judges, clerks of court) and should there be a differentiation between members of higher and lower courts?
- Who conducts a performance assessment (judges themselves, presidents of divisions, court management boards, higher courts, supervisory authorities) and what are the rights of recourse?
- To whom are the results of the performance assessment addressed (judges, presidents of divisions, court management boards, supreme courts, the oversight authorities, the general public)?

The following observations focus on the performance assessment of judges. The challenges raised by judicial independence do not affect the performance assessment of courts[63] or clerks of court[64] as significantly[65].

3 Examples of Performance Assessment in Swiss Courts

3.1 *Preliminary Remarks*

The following section gives an overview of approaches to the performance assessment of judges in Switzerland with the help of selected, succinct examples. The simple supervision of court business, as is standard in courts[66], is not the subject of this overview. Likewise, this section will not review the performance targets for or within courts or divisions[67].

3.2 *Number of Cases Dealt with by Specific Judges*

In order to implement the Federal Assembly's Ordinance on Judicial Positions at the Federal Supreme Court (*Verordnung der Bundesversammlung über die Richterstellen am Bundesgericht*) of 30 September 2011[68], the Federal Supreme Court runs a controlling procedure devised in consultation with the

63 As a whole or of specific collegial panels of judges (divisions, chambers).

64 See, in this context, Mosimann, 'Richterliche Unabhängigkeit', *supra* fn 45, 91, 102; in general Peter Uebersax, 'Die Stellung der Gerichtsschreiberinnen und Gerichtsschreiber in der Gerichtsverfassung', in Schindler & Sutter (eds), *supra* fn 26, 77 ff.

65 See on this issue, for example Uebersax, *supra* fn 64, 77 ff.; Michael Beusch, 'Die Zusammenarbeit zwischen Richterinnen und Gerichtsschreibern' (2007) (2) *Richterzeitung*, available <http://richterzeitung.weblaw.ch/rzissues/2007/2/r311.html> (accessed 10 October 2022).

66 Lienhard, Kettiger, Winkler, *supra* fn 1, 14 f.

67 See for an overview of this, Lienhard, Kettiger, Winkler, *supra* fn 1, 18 f., with further references.

68 SR 173.110.1.

parliamentary supervisory committees[69]. As a result of the observations made, this procedure has recently been revised and presented to the supervisory committees. With regard to the accessibility of the statistical data obtained, the controlling concept differentiates between public data in its annual report, special controlling data for the parliamentary committees and internal controlling[70]. The controlling records inter alia the performances of the individual divisions (for example the number of judgments issued). The number of cases completed by individual judges is recorded as part of the internal controls[71]. The supervisory committees receive details of the average number of cases per judge for each division. Deficiencies in individual judges are brought to the attention of the parliamentary Judiciary Committee (*Gerichtskommission*) if these are significant and could potentially jeopardise re-appointment[72].

The Federal Administrative Court (*Bundesverwaltungsgericht*) allocates cases to individual judges in an electronically automated procedure (known as the Bandlimat). It therefore possesses performance data pertaining to individual judges that are drawn from the electronic administrative process and can be combined with each other[73].

The Cantonal Supreme Court in Graubünden (*Kantonsgericht* Graubünden) and the Cantonal Supreme Court in Neuchatel (*Tribunal cantonal* Neuchâtel) both use a similar automated case allocation system[74]. The Social Insurance Court of the Canton of Zurich (*Sozialversicherungsgericht des Kantons* Zürich) takes the current workload of the judges in each division into consideration

69 Federal Supreme Court Controlling Concept for the attention of the Control Committee, 5 March 2007; for detail, see Lienhard, *supra* fn 19, para. 10 ff.

70 On this cascade-type structure, see Lienhard, *supra* fn 19, para. 8 ff.; Lienhard, *supra* fn 3, para. 65 ff.

71 Lienhard, *supra* fn 19, para. 13.

72 Lienhard, *supra* fn 19, para. 12; according to a draft of the ordinance it was intended to provide the Commission with statistics on the number of cases dealt with by the individual judges.

73 Bandli, *supra* fn 29, 111 f.; for more detail on how panels of judges are formed in courts, see Christoph Bandli, 'Zur Spruchkörperbildung an Gerichten: Vorausbestimmung als Fairnessgarantin', in Ruth Reusser & Benjamin Schindler (eds), *Aus der Werkstatt des Rechts: Festschrift für Heinrich Koller* (Schulthess 2006) 209 ff. On the current criticism, Konstantin Büchel et al., 'Automatisierte Spruchkörperbildung an Gerichten, Grundlagen und empirische Erkenntnisse am Beispiel des Bundesverwaltungsgerichts', Die Schweizer Richterzeitung' (2021) (4) Justice – Justiz – Giustizia, available at <https://richterzeitung.weblaw.ch/rzissues/2021/4/automatisierte-spruc_30c90b8de3.html__ONCE> (accessed 10 October 2022).

74 Lienhard, Kettiger, Winkler, *supra* fn 1, 16, with further references.

when allocating cases to judges[75]. Caseload management systems that record the judges' workload can likewise be found in other higher cantonal courts[76]. Many cantonal courts regard the work output of the individual judges as an element in quality management[77].

3.3 *Employee Appraisal and Status Interviews*

At the civil and criminal courts of first instance in the canton of Bern, annual status interviews with the judges are carried out[78]. These meetings are considered to be a factor in the quality of institutional independence and serve to maintain and encourage the judges' professional and social skills. The subject of the discussions is the judges' activities in office, including the duration and number of concluded cases, but not the content of judicial decisions. Senior judges of the courts of first instance conduct the interviews (although a representative of the supervisory authority can be called on in exceptional cases). The President of the Cantonal Supreme Court receives the results in anonymised form and is responsible for providing the annual management feedback to the senior judges. The individual reports may not be used in connection with judicial appointments and are only available as reference information with consent. The status interviews have no effect on salary[79].

---

75 Hans-Jacob Mosimann, 'Geschäftslastbewirtschaftung am Sozialversicherungsgericht des Kantons Zürich' (2009) (3) *Richterzeitung*, para. 6, available at <http://richterzeitung.weblaw.ch/rzissues/2009/3/r658.html> (accessed 10 October 2022).

76 Supreme Court of the Canton of Basel-Landschaft, Administrative Court of the Canton of Bern, Supreme Court and Administrative Court of the Canton of Graubünden, Supreme Court of the Canton of Lucerne, Administrative Court of the Canton of St. Gallen, Administrative Court of the Canton of the Ticino, Supreme Court and Administrative Court of the Canton of Thurgau, Supreme Court of the Canton of Vaud, Supreme Court of the Canton of Valais, Supreme Court and Administrative Court of the Canton of Zug, Administrative Court of the Canton of Zurich (Lienhard, Kettiger, Winkler, *supra* fn 1, 15 f.).

77 The performance of the judges and the court staff is used at the following courts as one of several indicators for measuring quality: Supreme Court of the Canton of Aargau, Supreme Court of the Canton of Bern, Supreme Court of the Canton of Lucerne, Administrative Court of the Canton of St. Gallen, Supreme Court of the Canton of Schaffhausen, Administrative Court of the Canton of the Ticino, Administrative Court of the Canton of Zug (Lienhard, Kettiger, Winkler, *supra* fn 1, 17 f., with further references).

78 Lienhard, Kettiger, Winkler, *supra* fn 1, 26.

79 Supreme Court of the Canton of Bern, Status discussions with judges, 25 November 2013; Myriam Grütter, 'Leitungskompetenz in der Justiz' (2012) (3) *Richterzeitung*, in particular para. 10 f., available at <http://richterzeitung.weblaw.ch/rzissues/2012/3/2015.html> (accessed 10 October 2022); Regula Müller Brunner, 'Richter darf niemand beurteilen' (2014) (1) *Plädoyer* 73.

Staff appraisal interviews at courts of first instance are also held in the canton of Zurich[80]. Under the rules on personnel management, each year superiors assess judges on their performance and conduct (such as expeditiousness in dealing with cases, and personal development corresponding to the judges' portfolio)[81]. Judicial decisions as such are not the subject of this assessment, but the assessment is relevant to increases in salary[82].

Staff appraisal interviews with judges at courts of first instance are also conducted in the canton of Lucerne; the court presidents hold the meetings with the judges annually[83].

The higher courts in the canton of St. Gallen[84] and the Social Insurance Court in the canton of Zurich also carry out regular staff appraisal interviews with judges[85].

3.4 *Quality Circles and Peer Reviews*

Judges discuss questions of judicial activity and management at regular sessions (plenary, divisional or chamber) at numerous cantonal supreme courts and federal courts.

In addition, colleagues discuss individual cases at most cantonal supreme courts, the Federal Supreme Court and at the Federal Criminal Court (*Bundesstrafgericht*)[86].

In recent years, voluntary 'collegial feedback' has been an option at the Federal Criminal Court. This assessment focuses on efficiency and professional, management and social skills. Around half of the judges make use of it[87].

---

80 Lienhard, Kettiger, Winkler, *supra* fn 1, 26.

81 See Rainer Klopfer & Daniel Preckel, 'Das 'Richterportfolio' – ein neuer Weg in der schweizerischen Richterausbildung?', in Schindler & Sutter (eds), *supra* fn 26, 23 ff.

82 On implementation, see Mosimann, 'Leistungsbeurteilung', *supra* fn 45, para. 22 f.; Müller Brunner, *supra* fn 79, 72. The relevance of the performance assessment for an increase in salary must be distinguished from the initial allocation to a salary class, which is not considered in this paper (on the latter, see Daniel Kettiger, 'Zur Gehaltseinreihung von Richterinnen und Richtern: Anmerkungen zu BGE 138 I 321' (2013) (1) *Richterzeitung*, available at <http://richterzeitung.weblaw.ch/rzissues/2013/1/2137.html> (accessed 10 October 2022)).

83 Lienhard, Kettiger, Winkler, *supra* fn 1, 26.

84 Lienhard, Kettiger, Winkler, *supra* fn 1, 26 (the interviews are conducted by the president of the Administrative Court).

85 Hans-Jacob Mosimann, 'Erfahrungen mit NPM am Sozialversicherungsgericht des Kantons Zürich', in Kettiger (ed), *supra* fn 9, 70.

86 Lienhard, Kettiger, Winkler, *supra* fn 1, 27, with further references.

87 Müller Brunner, *supra* fn 79, 72.

3.5 *Surveys*

A survey of the performance of judicial authorities has been carried out in the Canton of Bern at least once[88]. Court management was the subject of the survey, which identified points such as the accessibility of the authorities or interaction with parties to the proceedings and the legal profession. Participation in the survey was anonymous and the evaluation made no comments on particular individuals.

Surveys on satisfaction with the quality of service in courts were also carried out in five other cantons[89].

3.6 *Preliminary Findings*

The overview reveals that there are various approaches to assessing the performance of judges at federal and cantonal courts. These approaches range from the simple quantitative recording of processed judgments to staff appraisal interviews, and they can concern management and/or judicial activity. The performance assessment is the responsibility of the judges themselves (peer review and quality circles), the court or divisional management (case allocation, status discussions and staff appraisal interviews) or, in the case of re-appointment, of the advisory parliamentary committee. Surveys, when carried out, do not pertain to specific individuals. Performance assessments – with one apparent exception – have no effect on salary.

However, not enough experience has been gained in order to provide meaningful information on the structure and effects of the performance assessment of judges.

---

88 BEJUBE, 'Beurteilung der Justiztätigkeit im Kanton Bern oder Was halten die Kunden von unserer Arbeit?, Zusammenfassung der Ergebnisse' (April 2001), an extract of which is available in (2001) (2) *In dubio* 99 ff.; François Paychère, 'Les enquêtes de satisfaction conduites auprès des tribunaux des cantons de Berne et de Genève' (2013) (1) *Les cahiers de la justice* 37 ff.

89 Lienhard, Kettiger, Winkler, *supra* fn 1, 29, with further references. The surveys were conducted in the following courts: Supreme Court of the Canton of Appenzell-Innerrhoden (on which see Irene Kobler-Bryner, 'Kundenzufriedenheit mit den Gerichtsverfahren im Kanton Appenzell-Innerrhoden' (2013) (4) *Richterzeitung*, available at <http://richterzeitung.weblaw.ch/rzissues/2013/4/2413.html> (accessed 10 October 2022)), Supreme Court of the Canton of Geneva, Supreme Court of the Canton of Solothurn (on which see Pascal Haussener, 'Zweite Umfrage der Gerichtsverwaltungskommission des Kantons Solothurn unter der Anwaltschaft zur Zufriedenheit mit den Gerichten' (2013) (4) *Richterzeitung*, available at <http://richterzeitung.weblaw.ch/rzissues/2013/4/2354.html> (accessed 10 October 2022)), Supreme Court of the Canton of Valais and Supreme Court of the Canton of Zurich.

4 Conclusions for Performance Assessment in Switzerland

4.1 *Basic Estimation*

From a general constitutional point of view, the recording and assessment of the performances of individual judges seems to be permissible subject to certain requirements and, indeed, expedient, subject to those requirements. The assessment results aid internal court management (in particular caseload management and balancing the workload) as well as career development[90] (e.g. with a view to taking on management duties) and are therefore an integral element of quality management. Ultimately, this is meant to consolidate or raise the performance of the court[91]. Additionally, assessment results for individual judges can, when processed appropriately, aid authorities (committees or judicial councils)[92] in (re-)appointment, dismissal or disciplinary procedures[93].

Adequately publicising the performance of individual judges aids transparency and makes general discussions around the performance of individual judges that inevitably take place at all levels ('corridor conversations') more objective[94], thereby contributing to legal harmony in the court system.

Accordingly, it seems important that the courts do not obstruct the ongoing discussion on performance assessments, but rather indicate methods themselves and express their views on the assessment process before others decide on it for them[95].

4.2 *Organisation*

The specific process for performance assessments of individual judges that conform to the Constitution depends, as has been shown, on various elements, in particular the purpose of the assessment, the subject matter, who is responsible for it, the target group, the opportunity to participate in the assessment process, to have a say in it and to question its findings.

---

90 See in particular Bieler & Lorse, *supra* fn 38, 365 ff.

91 For a sceptical view in relation to this, see Mosimann, 'Richterliche Unabhängigkeit', *supra* fn 45, 103.

92 On the latter in this connection, see Stolz & Gass, *supra* fn 24, 177 f.

93 See already Lienhard, *supra* fn 19, para. 8, and the findings in Kettiger, *supra* fn 9, 190; for a more critical view, see Daniel Kettiger & Andreas Lienhard, 'Möglichkeiten und Grenzen von WOV in der Aargauer Justiz', legal opinion dated 29 August 2002 (unpublished, on file with the author), 28, with further references.

94 See Raselli, *supra* fn 19, para. 30.

95 See also Bandli, *supra* fn 2, 206; see also Walter, *supra* fn 6, para. 28, who regards quality controlling as a personal task for judges themselves.

In relation to the purpose of performance assessments of individual judges, caseload management systems that aim to optimise caseload allocation internally in the courts, based on a quantitative recording of the number of cases[96] handled by the individual judges, seem essential to courts in general and, in view of the requirement of judicial independence, not simply reasonable, but necessary. Employee appraisal interviews and status discussions serve to ensure quality throughout the court as well as personal development[97]. Performance assessments can additionally aid bodies responsible for (re-)appointment, dismissal or disciplinary procedures: in order to fulfil their tasks, they require relevant information on the performances of the individual judges[98]. However, it appears problematic to use information gathered in performance assessments when deciding on salaries[99], as this could obviously lead to false incentives. It is clear that the pecuniary aspect is an unsound basis for legitimising the performance assessment of judges. What is not permitted, according to the opinion represented here, is the reinterpretation of performance assessments as specific, binding performance requirements[100].

With regard to the subject matter of performance assessments of individual judges, initially only the number and nature of the proceedings involved (personal case statistics including duration of proceedings)[101] seem appropriate in relation to judicial process.

In contrast, further quantitative statistics (such as rates of appeal) seem less suitable, especially where there is a lack of causality (apart from special or obvious cases)[102]. A content-based (qualitative) analysis of individual judgments (material quality) or the procedural process (formal quality) is, in contrast, not compatible with judicial independence[103], unless it has been initiated and

96 Taking account of the differences in weighting the cases.

97 For an opinion against formalised performance assessments, see Mosimann, 'Richterliche Unabhängigkeit', *supra* fn 45, 105, 108.

98 On this, see immediately below.

99 See also Kettiger, *supra* fn 9, 196 f.; Mosimann, 'Richterliche Unabhängigkeit', *supra* fn 45, 103 f.; Kiener, *supra* fn 45, 290; Cavelti, *supra* fn 47, 330; Consultative Council of European Judges (CCJE), Opinion No. 17, on the evaluation of judges' work, the quality of justice and respect for judicial independence (2014), available at <https://www.coe.int/en/web/ccje/opinion-n-17-on-the-evaluation-of-judges-work-the-quality-of-justice-and-respect-for-judicial-independence> (accessed 10 October 2022), para. 28, 45, 49.13.

100 See Sec. 2.3 above.

101 See also Mosimann, 'Richterliche Unabhängigkeit', *supra* fn 45, 99 ff.; for a critical view of case statistics, see Walter, *supra* fn 6, para. 26.

102 See also Mosimann, 'Richterliche Unabhängigkeit', *supra* fn 45, 98 f., 104 f.; CCJE, *supra* fn 99, para. 35.

103 See for example Poltier, *supra* fn 19, 1028. This is more often the subject of appeal proceedings; see also Mosimann, 'Richterliche Unabhängigkeit', *supra* fn 45, 98 f.

carried out by the relevant judges for the purpose of quality assurance or personal development[104] (for example in the form of an exchange of experiences in quality circles, peer-reviews or 360-degree feedback)[105]. The required parallel assessment of the quality of the judicial process thus reaches its limits[106]. The subject matter of performance assessment is therefore, primarily, aspects of court management (management quality), such as the management of proceedings, personnel management, communication or team skills[107]. These aspects should also be a priority in employee appraisal interviews or status discussions, or in employers' references, and only these aspects can be assessed in surveys, although these surveys must not be related to specific persons.

What always appears to be essential is that various criteria are evaluated in the performance assessment, so as to obtain what is at least an approximate picture of the (measurable) performances of judges[108]. It must not be the case that only the number of concluded cases or the average duration of proceedings is assessed, for example, as this would undoubtedly lead to false incentives. In addition, the different requirements and particularities of judicial activity in the lower and upper courts must be taken into account (such as the type of proceedings, how the facts are established, speed of proceedings and the creation of case law)[109].

As far as responsibility for conducting performance assessments is concerned, it should be noted that performance assessments are an element of management and an essential counterpart to setting objectives. Superiors usually carry out employee appraisal interviews. In a court, this task is usually given (even if these are not superiors in the proper sense) to the president of the plenary court, or in the case of larger courts, of the division concerned[110].

104 For a sceptical view in relation to the purpose as regards changes of function, See Mosimann, 'Richterliche Unabhängigkeit', *supra* fn 45, 104.

105 See for example Kettiger & Lienhard, *supra* fn 93, 43. Stolz & Gass, *supra* fn 24, 177, and Walter, *supra* fn 6, para. 28, emphasize the importance of internal mechanisms; on the topic of 360-degree feedback see Marylin Warren, 'Enhancing our self-perception: 360-degree feedback for judicial officers' (2011) *Journal of Judicial Administration* (*JJA*) 3 ff.

106 See also Walter, *supra* fn 6, para. 27; Tschümperlin, *supra* fn 46, 93.

107 See, on the various areas of competence, Sec. 2.1 above.

108 On the unmeasurable qualities of judges, see Mosimann, 'Richterliche Unabhängigkeit', *supra* fn 45, 104 f.; Raselli, *supra* fn 19, para. 20; Walter, *supra* fn 6, para. 27; Gass & Stolz, *supra* fn 6, 128 f.; see also CCJE, *supra* fn 99, para. 35, 49.6.

109 On the necessary differentiation between assessment criteria for judges of lower and higher court, see for example Natalie Knowlton & Malia Reddick, 'An informed opinion: Direct Opinion Review and Appellate JPE', in National Centre State Courts (ed), *Trends in State Courts* (NCSC 2013) 91 ff.

110 For a sceptical view on the role of superiors, see Mosimann, 'Richterliche Unabhängigkeit', *supra* fn 45, 104 (pleading instead for a consideration of individual strengths and

The presidents must be given the corresponding management authority in terms of the judicial organisational law. This will confer on them the required democratic legitimacy and the duty to manage (court management) which is compatible with their role as a primus inter pares in the judicial process[111]. As an alternative, collegial models or judicial councils could be considered.

Additionally, a distinction must be made between the addressees of the performance assessment data on individual judges. The data primarily aids the court management board in fulfilling its managerial role[112]. Conventional supervisory authorities generally do not need this data – other than in certain exceptional cases, as their supervisory purview concerns the efficiency of the lower court as a whole rather than the performances of individual judges[113]. This must be evaluated differently only in the case of the performance of judges entrusted with the management of the lower courts. The same applies to a greater extent to oversight authorities (normally parliaments or parliamentary supervisory committees), whose supervisory activity is generally characterised by additional distance[114]. Authorities concerned with the preparation of (re-)appointments (parliamentary committees or judicial councils)[115] have the right to additional information[116]. In principle, generalised, condensed information from the court management board on the performances of individual judges should suffice. The bodies responsible for the preparation of (re-) appointments must only receive additional information if an accumulation of

weaknesses in a collegial exchange: Id. at 107). In this context, see also Walter, *supra* fn 6, para. 28, who calls for personal responsibility in an open discussion within the court; see also above in the text.

111 Cavelti, *supra* fn 47, 327 ff.

112 See already the findings in Kettiger, *supra* fn 9, 189; Raselli, *supra* fn 19, para. 29.

113 Calling for the supervisory authorities to have a duty to report failures to achieve annual objectives, see Bandli, *supra* fn 29, 114.

114 See Sec. 2.1. above; for detail on the differences between oversight and administrative supervision, see Tschümperlin, *supra* fn 47, 233 ff., 235 ff.

115 On the requirements for independent election bodies, see Markus Felber, 'Richterwahlen sind nichts für Politiker', *Neuen Zürcher Zeitung* (NZZ) *am Sonntag*, 13 April 2014, 19 – a requirement also accentuated by the existence in some cases of appointments of judges by the people. For the current discussion in Switzerland, see for example Alexander Tichy, 'Die Wahl ins Bundesgericht, Im Spannungsfeld zwischen Unabhängigkeit und demokratischer Kontrolle' (2022) (3) *Richterzeitung*, available at <https://richterzeitung.weblaw.ch/rzissues/2022/3/die-wahl-ins-bundesg_b14d5a0af5.html__ONCE&login=false> (access 10 October 2022).

116 See already Lienhard, *supra* fn 19, para. 7, and the findings in Kettiger, *supra* fn 9, 190.

deficiencies occurs that is not objectively explicable[117]. Special rights to information are also necessary in disciplinary or dismissal procedures.

Judges must have appropriate opportunities to have their say and, if necessary, rights of recourse when undergoing a performance assessment. In the case of employee appraisal interviews, this can initially entail a meeting with the supervisory authority, and in the second phase an appeal to an impartial authority. In the case of dismissal or disciplinary procedures, as well as non-re-appointments (where appropriate), existing or yet to be established appeal mechanisms must be used. Here, models involving judicial councils are an obvious option.

4.3 *Outlook*

The performance assessment of judges remains a subject that has not been researched much. Even if the constitutional framework has been roughly defined and various empirical principles have been established abroad in the meantime, further research into performance assessment systems that conform to the constitution is required.

Additionally, Switzerland still has little experience of assessing the performance of judges. Carefully conducted practical projects in cantonal and federal courts could provide valuable findings.

Only then can carefully developed performance assessment systems which successfully strike the balance between guaranteeing justice and protecting the judiciary begin to be incorporated into judicial organisational law.

117 See already Lienhard, *supra* fn 19, para. 7; see also Lienhard, *supra* fn 25, 467; for Mosimann, 'Richterliche Unabhängigkeit', *supra* fn 45, 103, however, it is inconceivable to penalise poor performance assessments by not re-electing the judges concerned.

CHAPTER 6

Admission Algorithms for Affirmative Action in Higher Education: The South African Experience

Viyaleta Farysheuskaya and Patrizio Piraino

1 Introduction

Despite multiple legislative changes targeted at addressing inequality, South Africa remains one of the most unequal countries in the world[1]. Inequalities are pervasive and persistent in several domains of socioeconomic life, including higher education[2].

During the Apartheid regime, the legal framework institutionalized the separation of higher educational institutions along racial lines. This created a system where resource-rich educational institutions were mostly inaccessible for the vast majority of the population, especially for African Black and Coloured students. With the transition to democracy in the 1990s, these restrictions were removed and some historically white universities introduced special admission considerations for previously discriminated students. These often included admission algorithms that used diversity targets, point systems, or a combination of both. Despite these actions, the share of non-white students in many institutions has remained below their demographic representation in the general population.

In this paper, we explore admission procedures at five historically white universities in South Africa, focusing on policies that were aimed at redressing historical disadvantage. Our analysis and findings are exclusively based on publicly available information, which might not capture the entirety of affirmative action policies at each university. Where applicable, we describe the regulations implemented to facilitate admission of historically disadvantaged applicants, with particular attention to the different proxies used to define disadvantage. We conclude by discussing the advantages and challenges of different admission 'algorithms' and by outlining the potential for further research

1 OECD, 'Income Inequality (Indicator)', available at <https://data.oecd.org/inequality/income-inequality.htm> (accessed 19 May 2022).

2 Amnesty International, *Broken and Unequal* (Amnesty International Ltd. 2020).

 | DOI:10.1163/9789004680944_007

on the desirability of introducing machine learning tools in the admission processes of higher education institutions in South Africa.

2 Historical and Legal Overview of the Education System in South Africa

The election of the National Party in 1948 signs the onset of a series of policies known as Apartheid, a regime that lasted until 1994[3]. Under Apartheid, South Africa as a whole, including the education system, was characterized by strong racial segregation. The legal basis for racial segregation came from the Population Registration Act of 1950, which defined three racial groups: whites, Black Africans (also called natives), and Coloured, with the latter defined as "not a white person or a native." Another racial group – Indians – was later added to the Act[4].

Universal schooling for white South Africans was introduced at the beginning of the 20th century, while African and Coloured children continued to receive education mainly at mission schools. The Bantu Education Act of 1953 enforced racial segregation at schools, and the 1959 Extension of University Education Act limited the capacity of historically white universities to accept Black students[5]. It also established separate universities for Black, Coloured, and Indian students[6]. As a result, four English-medium universities and four Afrikaans-medium universities mainly served white South African students through the end of the 20th century (see Table 6.1). It is also worth noting that, under Apartheid, there were only two official languages, Afrikaans and English, despite South Africa being a multilingual nation[7].

3 Linda Chisholm, 'Apartheid Education Legacies and New Directions in Post-Apartheid South Africa' (2012) 8 *Storia delle donne* 81.

4 Deborah Posel, 'What's in a Name? Racial Categorisations under Apartheid and Their Afterlife' (2001) 47 *Transformation: Critical Perspectives on Southern Africa* 50.

5 Black students needed special permission issued by the Ministry of Education to attend a white university. See Reitumetse Obakeng Mabokela and Yeukai Angela Mlambo, 'Access and Equity and South African Higher Education: A Review of Policies after 20 Years of Democracy' (2017) 61 *Comparative Education Review* 780.

6 Bridget Terry Long and Laura Kavazanjian, 'Affirmative Action in Tertiary Education: A Meta-Analysis of Global Policies and Practices' (2012) *World Bank Report*; Amnesty International, *supra* fn 2.

7 James Colins, 'Dilemmas of Race, Register, and Inequality in South Africa' (2017) 46 *Language in Society* 39.

The end of Apartheid and the transition to democracy brought several changes to the education system. In 1993, the Interim Constitution proclaimed education as one of the fundamental rights, promoting universal basic education and equal access to educational institutions. In 1996, higher education became a part of the new Constitution of the Republic of South Africa, focusing on the state making higher education "progressively available and accessible" through "reasonable measures". The Higher Education Act of 1997 highlighted the need to "redress discrimination and ensure retrospectivity and equal access" and mandated public higher education institutions to establish non-discriminatory admission policies to redress past inequalities. At the same time, redressing past inequalities became a focus of public higher education funding.

While these pieces of legislation mainly provided a vision for developing the higher education system in the country, a more comprehensive analysis of the system was presented in the Education White Paper 3 issued by the Ministry of Education in 1997. White Paper 3 reported the existing challenges in higher education, the vision of its transformation, and the vision of functions, operations, and governance of higher education[8]. A significant share of the report was dedicated to conveying existing inequalities, including racial inequalities, and suggesting how to make the higher education system more equitable[9]. In 2001, many of the points from White Paper 3 were included in the National Plan for Higher Education, which was meant to ensure "the fitness of the higher education system to contribute to the challenges that face South Africa in the 21st century"[10]. Among the goals of the National Plan for Higher Education were increasing student enrolment in higher education and their graduation rates. Importantly, the plan required student bodies to be representative of the demographic reality in South Africa. The plan also suggested reforming the higher education system through institutional mergers (see Table 6.1).

As a result of these legislative changes, there was a significant increase in the share of Black students among enrolled students. However, representation relative to the overall racial makeup of South Africa remained rather low (12.1% in 2009)[11]. This low representation questions whether there was substantial

8 Department of Education, 'Notice 1196 of 1997. Education White Paper 3: A Programme for the Transformation of Higher Education', available at <https://www.gov.za/sites/default/files/gcis_document/201409/18207gen11960.pdf> (accessed 31 August 2022).

9 Ibid.

10 Ministry of Education, 'National Plan for Higher Education' (2001), available at <https://www.justice.gov.za/commissions/feeshet/docs/2001-NationalPlanForHigherEducation.pdf> (accessed 31 August 2022), § 1.1.

11 Mabokela and Mlambo, *supra* fn 5.

TABLE 6.1 Historically white universities

Language of instruction	University	Status (as of 2021)
English	University of Cape Town	Active
	University of Natal	Merged with University of Durban-Westville, now University of KwaZulu Natal
	Rhodes University	Active
	University of Witwatersrand	Active
Afrikaans	Potchefstroom University	Merged with University of Bophuthatswana, now North-West University
	Rand Afrikaans University	Merged with Technikon Witwatersrand and Vista University, now University of Johannesburg
	University of Pretoria	Active
	Stellenbosch University	Active

SOURCE: THE SOURCE FOR THIS TABLE IS CLAYTON G MACKENZIE, 'BLACK STUDENTS IN "WHITE" UNIVERSITIES: THE CHARACTER AND PROVISION OF LIBERAL HIGHER EDUCATION INSTITUTIONS IN POST-APARTHEID SOUTH AFRICA' (2006) 24 *COMPARE: A JOURNAL OF COMPARATIVE AND INTERNATIONAL EDUCATION* 67; SEE ALSO THE WEBSITE OF THE DEPARTMENT OF HIGHER EDUCATION AND TRAINING AT <HTTPS://WWW.DHET.GOV.ZA/> (ACCESSED 19 MAY 2022).

progress in making student bodies representative of the demographic reality in the country. Additionally, Black students reported lower graduation rates (69%) than other racial groups (76% for Indian, 77% for Coloured, and 82% for White students), which might be attributed to lower quality instruction at the basic education levels[12]. As for institutional mergers, the plan was often seen

12 Ibid.

as an excessive focus on historically white institutions and the lack of effort to strengthen historically Black institutions[13].

In 2014, the Department of Higher Education and Training released the White Paper for Post-School Education and Training. This new white paper suggested building a coordinated post-school system that could provide different educational opportunities for people with different levels of prior educational experience[14]. This coordinated post-school system was seen as a means to reduce inequalities, including racial inequalities[15]. The Draft National Plan for Post-School Education and Training provided a framework for building this coordinated post-school system until 2030, mainly through strengthening different post-secondary institutions, with a focus on Technical and Vocational Education and Training Colleges and Community Colleges.

3 Admission Policies at Historically White Universities

Figure 6.1 displays changes in the racial composition of the student body at five prominent historically white universities. These are universities that did not undergo significant structural changes (e.g. merging of campuses). As seen from Figure 6.1, the vast majority of undergraduate students at these universities before the democratic transition were white. For benchmarking, the average share of the white population in the three provinces where the universities are located (Eastern Cape, Gauteng, Western Cape) was around 17% in 1996[16]. The transition to democracy in the 1990s led to a significant increase in the share of non-white students at all universities. Figure 6.1 also shows that the enrollment trends have not been uniform, partly due to differences in regional racial demographics, but also because of different admission procedures.

With the enactment of the Constitution of 1996 and the Higher Education Act of 1997, universities began to change their admission procedures to broaden access to previously excluded applicants. While some universities tried to

13 Ibid.

14 Department of Higher Education and Training, 'Government Notice No. 37229 of 2014. White Paper for Post-School Education and Training: Building an Expanded, Effective and Integrated Post-School Education System' (2014), available at <https://www.gov.za/sites/default/files/gcis_document/201409/37229gon11.pdf> (accessed 31 August 2022).

15 Ibid.

16 Statistics South Africa, 'The People of South Africa. Population Census, 1996', available at <https://apps.statssa.gov.za/census01/Census96/HTML/default.htm> (accessed 20 June 2022); Statistics South Africa, 'Community Survey 2016' (2016) <http://cs2016.statssa.gov.za/> (accessed 23 May 2022).

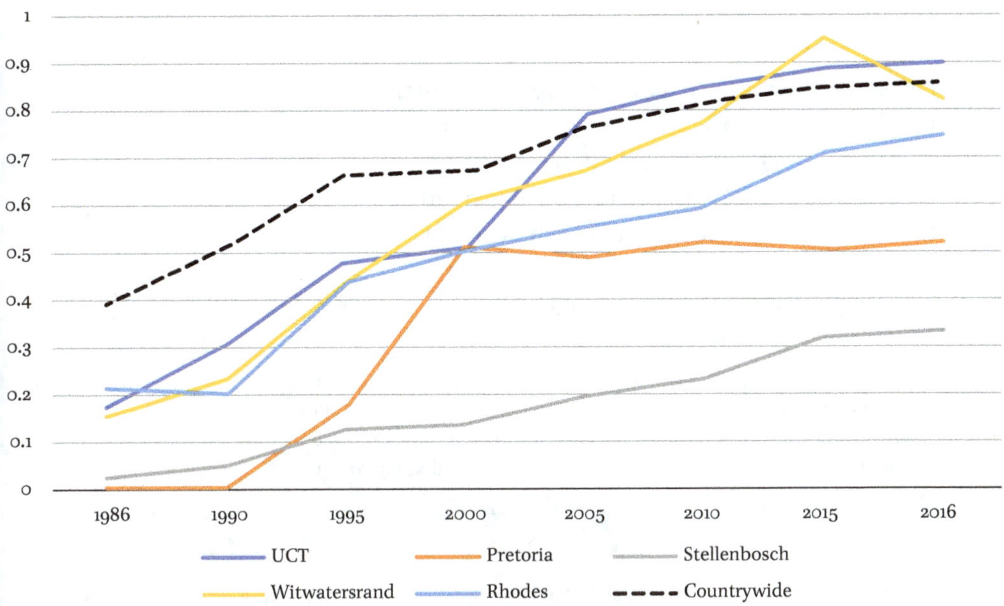

FIGURE 6.1 Share of non-white students among enrolled undergraduates
DATA ARE FROM DEPARTMENT OF HIGHER EDUCATION AND TRAINING, 'HIGHER EDUCATION MANAGEMENT INFORMATION-SYSTEM', AVAILABLE AT <HTTPS://WWW.DHET.GOV.ZA/SITEPAGES/HIGHER-EDUCATION-MANAGEMENT-INFORMATION-SYSTEM.ASPX> (ACCESSED 22 JUNE 2022).

establish color-blind policies, giving equal access to all applicants regardless of race, other universities designed policies that had different admission requirements for students from different backgrounds. In addition, most universities enacted extended study programs to provide additional support for previously excluded students. Such programs were developed on the foundations laid by the earlier Academic Development Programmes (ADPs) that were introduced in the 1980s by some universities (e.g. University of Cape Town, Witwatersrand University, and Rhodes University)[17].

For most universities, the general admission policy is established at the central level, while individual faculties are responsible for indicating minimum requirements for their programs. In most cases, this takes the form of an Admission Point Score (APS) computed on the basis of the applicants' performance on the National Senior Certificate (NSC), which is the high school

17 Eli Blitzer and Annette Wilkinson, *Higher Education as a Field of Study and Research* (Sun Press 2009).

TABLE 6.2 Seven-point grading scale based on the NSC results

Level 7	80–100% (outstanding achievement)
Level 6	70–79% (meritorious achievement)
Level 5	60–69% (substantial achievement)
Level 4	50–59% (moderate achievement)
Level 3	40–49% (adequate achievement)
Level 2	30–39% (elementary achievement)
Level 1	0–29% (not achieved – fail)

SOURCE: THE SOURCE FOR THIS TABLE IS DEPARTMENT OF EDUCATION, 'THE NATIONAL SENIOR CERTIFICATE: A QUALIFICATION AT LEVEL 4 ON THE NATIONAL QUALIFICATIONS FRAMEWORK (NQF)' (2005), AVAILABLE AT <http://education.pwv.gov.za> (ACCESSED 19 MAY 2022).

matriculation certificate at the national level[18]. The APS normally comprises an aggregate value of the six best subjects, excluding Life Orientation[19]. It is a common practice to convert the NSC percentage system to a seven-point grading scale so that the maximum score is 42 (see Table 6.2).

In addition to the minimum aggregate APS, some programs establish minimum APS for certain subjects. In the past, many universities required applicants to also submit the National Benchmark Test (NBT) results[20], though this changed during the COVID-19 pandemic[21].

18 Eligible groups for the NSC include current Grade 12 learners and those who want to improve their prior NSC results. The requirements for passing are (i) scoring at least 40% in three subjects, (ii) scoring at least 30% in the other three subjects, and (iii) providing evidence of the knowledge in these subjects in School Based Assessment. See Department of Basic Education, 'NSC Examinations', available at <education.gov.za/Curriculum/NationalSeniorCertificate(NSC)Examinations.aspx> (accessed 16 August 2022).

19 Applicants are often conditionally admitted based on their Grade 11 performance.

20 NBT is a measurement of "academic readiness for university" through the assessment of an applicant's proficiency in (i) Academic Literacy and Quantitative Literacy or (ii) Mathematics. See Centre for Educational Testing for Access and Placement, 'FAQ – National Benchmark Test Project', available at <https://nbt.uct.ac.za/content/faq-0> (accessed 16 August 2022).

21 To our knowledge, all faculties of the University of Cape Town require all applicants residing in South Africa to take the test in the 2022 application cycle, with the only exception of the Faculty of Engineering and the Built Environment.

4 Affirmative Action Policies at Five Historically White Universities

Affirmative action regulations, referred to as 'Transformation' in South Africa, vary among universities, but they can be broadly grouped into three categories:

1. diversity targets;
2. differential points by race and proxy for disadvantage in the computation of Application point score (APS);
3. extended programs, typically including an additional year of study.

Some universities use a hybrid approach, combining more than one of the elements above. We describe below the policies adopted by five historically white universities included in our analysis.

4.1 *University of Cape Town* (UCT)

UCT computes applicants' score by adding the percentages – rather than points – of the NSC results from six subjects. This aggregated APS score is used to compute the Faculty Point Score (FPS), which is used to evaluate applicants[22]. In recent years, UCT admission policy shifted the focus of affirmative action from using race as the only proxy for historical disadvantage to multiple socio-economic and demographic factors. As a result, in the admission policy for 2023, UCT evaluates applicants in three 'bands':

- Band A: applicants are ranked based on their academic performance;
- Band B: applicants are ranked accounting for their socioeconomic disadvantage;
- Band C, applicants are ranked accounting for their race[23].

Students are first selected in *Band A* based on their FPS, i.e. best-ranked applicants are admitted as part of Band A, even if they are eligible for Band B or C. Depending on the program, the share of applicants in Band A ranges from 10% to 40%[24].

---

22 For example, if an applicant's APS score for English is 67%, her FPS for English would be 67 points.

23 University of Cape Town, 'Undergraduate Prospectus 2023 Admission' (2022), available at <http://www.students.uct.ac.za/sites/default/files/image_tool/images/434/prospective/ug_prospectus/ug_prospectus.pdf> (accessed 19 May 2022).

24 Ibid.

Approximately 60% of all incoming students in all programs are selected from *Band B,* which is designed to target disadvantaged students. In Band B, UCT assigns a weighted FPS (referred to as WPS) to each applicant by adjusting the raw FPS to account for disadvantage. This disadvantage factor normally accounts for up to 10% of the total score (except for the Faculty of Health Sciences, where it could be up to 20%) and is determined by the applicant's school background, parental level of education, financial support from the state, and home language (see Table 6.3). Thus, if the disadvantage factor is x%, an applicant's WPS would be:

$$WPS = FPS + (x*FPS)$$

Our examination of the admission process showed that UCT allocates the weights to disadvantage factors as described in Table 6.3.

In addition to the three disadvantage factors from Table 6.3, the applicant's school background is also included in the point system and has a large impact on the disadvantage score. All schools in South Africa are ranked into one of five quintiles, with Quintile 1 representing the poorest schools, and Quintile 5 the most affluent. The unemployment and literacy rates of the community where a school is located are amongst the factors that determine the ranking[25]. If an applicant's school is from Quintile 1 to 4, the application receives a 10% disadvantage factor regardless of the other disadvantage factors described above.

Finally, approximately 25% of incoming students are selected in the race-based *Band C.* UCT defines four redress categories, using the racial classification of the applicants' parents under apartheid as shown in Table 6.4.

Depending on the faculty and/or program, the admission in Band C can be limited to certain redress categories (e.g. category 1 and 2 in the Faculty of Health Sciences) or to applicants with a certain disadvantage factor (e.g. disadvantage factor greater than one in the Faculty of Commerce)[26].

In addition to the admission policy described above, UCT also offers Academic Development Programmes to help integrate previously disadvantaged students. These programs typically include extended degree options at several faculties[27].

---

25 H van Dyk and CJ White, 'Theory and Practice of the Quintile Ranking of Schools in South Africa: A Financial Management Perspective' (2019) 39 South African Journal of Education S1.

26 Ibid.

27 University of Cape Town, 'Undergraduate Teaching – Academic Development' (2022), available at <http://www.adp.uct.ac.za/undergraduate-teaching> (accessed 19 May 2022).

TABLE 6.3 UCT's disadvantage factor breakdown

Factor	Disadvantage weight (in %)
Family received a social pension from the state OR a child-support grant on behalf of the applicant	1
Mother's first language other than English or Afrikaans	6
Highest degree attained by each family member (including mother, father, and the highest degree by any grandparent) is below University or Technikon degree	1 each (up to 3 total)

SOURCE: THE SOURCE FOR THIS TABLE ARE OUR OWN CALCULATIONS BASED ON UNIVERSITY OF CAPE TOWN, 'DISADVANTAGE FACTOR CALCULATOR' (2022), AVAILABLE AT <HTTPS://PUBLICACCESS.UCT.AC.ZA/PSP/PUBLIC/EMPLOYEE/SA/C/UCT_PUBLIC_MENU.UCT_SS_DISADVANTAG.GBL?> (ACCESSED 19 MAY 2022).

TABLE 6.4 Redress categories at UCT

Redress category 1	At least one parent classified as Black
Redress category 2	At least one parent classified as Coloured (and the other not as Black)
Redress category 3	At least one parent classified as Indian (and the other not as Black or Coloured)
Redress category 4	At least one parent classified as Chinese (and the other not as Black, Coloured or Indian)

SOURCE: THE SOURCE FOR THIS TABLE IS UNIVERSITY OF CAPE TOWN, *SUPRA* FN 26.

4.2 *University of Pretoria* (UP)

The University of Pretoria uses a standard seven-point grading scale (see Table 6.2), considering the 6 best subjects (excluding life orientation) to calculate the APS. The highest APS score that can be achieved is 42 (= 7 × 6).

In their admission process, UP faculties can divide applicants into 'open' or 'designated' categories, where the designated category is fully based on race (comprising South African Black and Coloured candidates). Target numbers for these categories are set for each program separately.

The affirmative action policies are more pronounced in the programs offered by the Faculty of Health Sciences and Medicine than in other faculties. It is outside our scope to go into the details of each faculty's admission policies, so we focus on this faculty as it houses some of the most selective programs. According to the faculty's admission policy for 2023, for both designated and open categories, students with the highest merit point score (MPS) are admitted. The MPS is calculated as follows:

> *MPS = 0.5*(average NSC score) + 0.3*(Significant Subject Score) + 0.2*(Suitability and Equity Score)*

where the Significant Subject Score equals (*NSC score in English in % + NSC score in Mathematics in % + NSC score in Physical Sciences in % + NSC score in Life Sciences in %)/4* and the Suitability and Equity Score is calculated based on factors that include student origin, schooling, family background, and language[28]. Similar to UCT, each program first selects students for the open category (i.e. regardless of race). When the target number for the open category is reached, programs start to review applications from the designated category, which is reserved for Black and Coloured students and can account for a significant share of all seats (the share varies depending on the program)[29].

The seat allocation at the Clinical Medical Practice program is different from the rest of the university. In addition to allocating applicants to open or designated categories, a substantial share of seats (62%) is also reserved to ensure 'provincial representation', with 20% of places in this category being allocated to each of the following provinces – Gauteng, Mpumalanga, Limpopo, and KwaZulu Natal – and the remaining 20% allocated to all other provinces combined.

---

28 University of Pretoria, Faculty of Health Sciences, 'Selection Criteria BChD and BOH Degree Programmes' (2021), available at <https://www.up.ac.za/media/shared/8/bchd-and-boh-selection-criteria-2022.zp201993.pdf> (accessed 19 May 2022); University of Pretoria, Faculty of Health Sciences, 'Selection Criteria Dietetics, Nursing Science, Occupational Therapy, Radiology, Physiotherapy' (2021), available at <https://www.up.ac.za/media/shared/8/2022/2022-for-2023-selection-of-sohcs-programmes_25-march-2022.zp218143.pdf> (accessed 19 May 2022); University of Pretoria, Faculty of Health Sciences, 'Selection Criteria of BCMP AND BSportSci. Degree Programmes 2022 for 2023' (2022), available at <https://www.up.ac.za/media/shared/8/2022/2022-for-2023-selection-of-bcmp-and-bsportsci-students_25-march-2022.zp218141.pdf> (accessed 19 May 2022); University of Pretoria, Faculty of Health Sciences, 'Selection Criteria of MBChB Students. Degree Programmes 2022 for 2023' (2022), available at <https://www.up.ac.za/media/shared/8/2022/2022-for-2023-selection-of-bcmp-and-bsportsci-students_25-march-2022.zp218141.pdf> (accessed 19 May 2022).

29 Ibid.

Finally, the Faculty of Natural & Agricultural Sciences offers extended programs for applicants that are likely to succeed but may lack prior academic preparation. The extended programs have lower minimum requirements and include an additional year of study[30].

4.3 *Rhodes University*

The main objective of the admission policy at Rhodes University is to "enable academic access and success based on social equity"[31]. To ensure equity, in addition to student academic achievement, the university reserves a right to consider other factors in the admission process, including the applicant's school location, origin, race, gender, family income, home language, civil involvement, certain talents and abilities, nationality, and past hardships[32].

At Rhodes University, the APS is computed by dividing the percentage of each of the six best subjects' results (excluding life orientation) in the NSC by 10[33] and then aggregating the results. Taking the National Benchmark Test (NBT) is recommended for all applicants and used in cases when applicants do not meet automatic entry requirements.

Rhodes also offers extended studies programs in three faculties (Humanities, Commerce and Science) to a limited number of students. The extended studies program is designed for students coming from disadvantaged backgrounds who show potential to succeed. Similarly, students who do not qualify for automatic acceptance but score higher than the minimum threshold can be considered for admission at the Dean's discretion, with the preference given to students from disadvantaged backgrounds[34].

4.4 *Stellenbosch University*

Stellenbosch University introduced student diversity targets in 2017. According to the new university-wide policy, each faculty should set "aspirational"

30 University of Pretoria, Faculty of Natural & Agricultural Sciences, 'BSc – Extended Programmes' (2022), available at <https://www.up.ac.za/faculty-of-natural-agricultural-sciences/article/16226/bsc-extended-programmes> (accessed 19 May 2022).

31 Rhodes University, 'Student Admissions' Policy' (2019), available at <https://www.ru.ac.za/media/rhodesuniversity/content/institutionalplanning/documents/Rhodes_University_Student_Admissionsâ%C2%80%C2%99_Policy.pdf> (accessed 31 August 2022).

32 Ibid.

33 For example, if an applicant scores 78% in English, her APS for this subject would be 7.8.

34 Rhodes University, 'Entry Requirements' (2021), available at <https://www.ru.ac.za/admissiongateway/application/entryrequirements/> (accessed 19 May 2022); Rhodes University, 'Extended Studies Unit' (2021), available at <https://www.ru.ac.za/teachingandlearning/esu/> (accessed 19 May 2022).

TABLE 6.5 Determinants of an applicant's socio-economic status (SES)

Disadvantage	Proxies	Maximum points
Economic	– Family is a recipient of a social grant – Applicant is a recipient of a need-based bursary/scholarship	4
Educational	– School quintiles or school fees	4
First-generation student status	– Highest qualification of parents/ guardian(s)	2

SOURCE: THE SOURCE FOR THIS TABLE IS STELLENBOSCH UNIVERSITY, 'ADMISSIONS POLICY' (2017), AVAILABLE AT <HTTPS://SUNRECORDS.SUN.AC.ZA/CONTROLLED/C4%20POLICIES%20AND%20REGULATIONS/ADMISSISIONS%20POLICY_2017.PDF> (ACCESSED 20 MAY 2022).

enrollment targets for students from different (i) racial (Black, Coloured, and Indian or Asian) and (ii) socio-economic backgrounds. The latter is determined by three disadvantage factors: economic, educational, and first-generation student status (see Table 6.5).

For applicants satisfying the minimum criteria, faculties should first allocate seats based on student APS (regardless of race and SES). Stellenbosch calculates APS by computing an average percentage of 6 NSC subjects so that the final value ranges from 0% to 100%. After faculties reach the target in this category, they start allocating seats to best-performing students in racial and SES categories. If at the end of this three-stage cycle, there are still not enough applicants to meet race and SES targets, the remaining best-performing applicants are admitted regardless of their race and/or SES categories[35].

The policy also requires deans to develop admission policies for individual faculties that would be in line with the university-wide admission policy. Having revised admission procedures at different faculties at Stellenbosch, we could determine that two faculties explicitly outline their plan for achieving diversity in their admission policies. The Faculty of Education does so by allocating 26% of all seats to Black, Coloured, and Indian students[36]. The Faculty

35 Ibid.

36 Stellenbosch University, Faculty of Education, 'Guidelines and Procedures for Selection: BEd (Foundation Phase Teaching)' (2021), available at <https://www.sun.ac.za/english/maties/Documents/Education%20BEd%20Foundation%20Phase.pdf> (accessed 20 May 2022).

of Medicine and Health Sciences uses both race and SES in the admission process. Applicants with a SES score of 6 and higher should comprise a fraction of the whole student body, where the share is determined individually for each program within that faculty. Some programs also consider additional characteristics, such as regional representation[37].

Similar to the other universities, Stellenbosch also offers extended degree programs to students who are not admitted to the mainstream program, with the preference given to applicants with the highest SES score[38].

4.5 *University of Witwatersrand* (*Wits*)

Unlike the universities above, Wits computes APS based on the best seven subjects, including Life Orientation. Additionally, Wits uses its own percentage conversion system to determine applicants' APS.

Wits's admission policy recognizes the need for fair discrimination in the admissions process in order to promote redress for historical inequity. To this end, they committed themselves to the development of access principles that do not rely solely on academic achievement criteria, so as to identify candidates from scholastically and socio-economically disadvantaged backgrounds[39].

We could not find a university-wide policy specifying the admission process for disadvantaged applicants, but some faculties and programs do have equitable policies. For example, the Bachelor of Architectural Studies program offered by the Faculty of Engineering and Built Environment considers 'demographic balance' when deciding between applicants that score in the same range[40]. Additionally, programs offered by the Faculty of Health Sciences develop admission targets for applicants based on their race (African and Coloured only), location (rural), and school background (low quintiles), with each of the three categories accounting for 60% of the total number of

---

37 As of May 2022, this admission policy is pending consideration and approval from the Faculty. See Stellenbosch University, Faculty of Medicine and Health Sciences, 'Guidelines for the Selection of MBChB Students' (2022), available at <https://www.sun.ac.za/english/maties/Documents/MB,ChB.pdf> (accessed 20 October 2022).

38 Stellenbosch University, *supra* fn 40.

39 University of the Witwatersrand, 'University Policies' (2022), available at <https://www.wits.ac.za/about-wits/governance/university-policies/> (accessed 20 October 2022).

40 University of the Witwatersrand, 'Guide for Undergraduate Applicants 2023' (2022), available at <https://www.wits.ac.za/undergraduate/guide-for-undergraduates/> (accessed 19 May 2022).

students and allocating the remaining 40% of the seats based on student academic achievement[41].

The broad admission guidelines for the 2022 cycle mention academic achievement criteria based on the applicant's index score, composed of (i) results for five subjects (English, Mathematics, Physical Science/Life Sciences and the best two other subjects) and (ii) NBT scores, i.e. Index score = 0.5*(APS in % for five subjects) + 0.5*(NBT scores)[42].

5 Proxies for Disadvantage in Affirmative Action Practices

Our review of admission policies at five prominent historically white universities shows that these institutions follow a somewhat similar approach to diversify their student bodies, with some specific modifications to a common 'algorithm'. The general algorithm follows three main steps:

- *Step #1.* Create an open admission category based on academic credentials only. For most universities, there is a specified quota of applicants that can be admitted under this category. Three of the five universities reviewed (UCT, UP, and Stellenbosch) clearly state that disadvantaged applicants are first considered in this category alongside other applicants.
- *Step #2.* Applicants who do not satisfy the minimum requirement for admission in step #1 are considered for admission based on a disadvantage criteria and/or other criteria. This second step usually involves creating different groups of applicants. Within each group, students are ranked according to their academic credentials, or to an 'adjusted' academic score. This within-group ranking may require two sub-steps:
    a. Applicants' scores are adjusted on a predefined criteria. For example, in Band B, UCT adjusts applicants' FPS accounting for their disadvantage (based on the pre-defined criteria). If an applicant does not meet any of the disadvantage criteria, they may still compete

41 This policy is ambiguous in terms of its target, i.e. it is unclear whether it targets all programs offered by the Faculty of Health Sciences or only the Medicine and Surgery (MBBch) program. See University of the Witwatersrand, 'Wits University Revises Its MBBch Degree Admissions Policy' (2017), available at <https://www.wits.ac.za/media/wits-university/faculties-and-schools/health-sciences/student-documents/undergraduate/Revised%20Health%20Sciences%20Admissions%20Policy.pdf> (accessed 20 October 2022).

42 University of the Witwatersrand, *supra* fn 40.

within this category with WPS = FPS. Similar approaches are used in the UP's Clinical Medical Practice program.

b. Only certain groups are allowed to compete within a predefined category. For example, in Band C, UCT only allows applicants with a certain racial background to compete. Similarly, UP's designated category is only open for Black and Coloured applicants; the Faculty of Education at Stellenbosch allocates 25% of all seats to Black, Coloured, and Indian students; and the Faculty of Health Sciences at Wits allocates 20% of the seats to Black and Coloured applicants. UP's Clinical Medical Practice program and the Faculty of Health Sciences at Wits have a quota for applicants from certain provinces. The Faculty of Medicine and Health Sciences at Stellenbosch also determines a quota for applicants with lower SES, while the Faculty of Health Sciences at Wits allocates 40% of the seats to applicants from rural areas and low school quintiles.

– *Step #3*. Students admitted under a disadvantage category are eligible for extended studies programs to support and facilitate their academic career.

The level and scale of implementation of this general approach differ across universities. For example, some institutions have university-wide policies while other allow substantial divergence across faculties or programs of study.

6 Race vs Multidimensional Proxies for Disadvantage

As seen above, many universities use race as a proxy for disadvantage in their algorithms. In some cases, race is used as the only proxy, while in others it is a part of a broader definition. Using race as the only proxy for disadvantage is associated with a number of challenges. First, while race is highly correlated to socioeconomic status in South Africa, by itself it does not necessarily determine belonging to a given social class[43]. Some universities recognize a need for a deeper understanding of the factors associated with race when determining 'disadvantaged classes', and for a gradual transition from reliance on apartheid racial categories to an indicator of disadvantage based on these correlated factors. One suggestion is to focus on factors that characterize the applicants'

43 Zimitri Erasmus, 'Confronting the Categories: Equitable Admissions without Apartheid Race Classification' (2010) 24 *South African Journal of Higher Education* 244; D Benatar, 'Just Admissions: South African Universities and the Question of Racial Preference' (2010) 24 *South African Journal of Higher Education* 258.

school and family backgrounds, such as school quintiles, parental occupation/education, and mother tongue, while also continuing to use race until the association between race and disadvantage weakens[44]. This strategy should not substantially reduce the number of admitted Black applicants, since the data show that the overwhelming majority of disadvantaged applicants would still be from this group. Therefore, admission criteria that include more proxies for disadvantage would help increase the probability that all admitted students are indeed economically disadvantaged[45].

Other challenges arising from using race as the only proxy for disadvantage in South Africa include (i) complications associated with racial self-identification[46], (ii) psychological strains associated to using Apartheid racial categories[47], and (iii) cultivating negative perceptions of Black students as being less capable[48]. The recent transition by the University of Cape Town from using race as the only proxy for disadvantage to more complex socioeconomic criteria was motivated on similar grounds. Specifically, UCT noted the imprecision of race as a proxy for disadvantage, the challenges associated with racial self-identification, and the aspiration to build a non-racial society in the future[49]. Complex socioeconomic disadvantage criteria were introduced in other universities as well, particularly for faculties of Health Sciences, where black students are significantly underrepresented in comparison to the country's racial composition[50].

The rationale behind the use of multiple indicators of socioeconomic status in affirmative action rests in the attempt to reflect the multi-dimensional nature of disadvantage. For instance, at the Faculty of Sciences at Wits, 20% of seats are allocated to best-performing rural learners; another 20% to applicants from Quintile 1 and 2 schools, and another 20% to African and Coloured

44 Erasmus, *supra* fn 43.

45 Benatar, *supra* fn 439.

46 Erasmus, *supra* fn 439.

47 Alexander Neville, 'Affirmative Action and the Perpetuation of Racial Identities in Post-Apartheid South Africa' (2007) 63 *Transformation: Critical Perspectives on Southern Africa* 92.

48 Kanya Adam, 'Affirmative Action and Popular Perceptions: The Case of South Africa' (2000) 37 *Society* 48.

49 University of Cape Town News, 'UCT's New Student Admission Policy Explained' (2014), available at <https://www.news.uct.ac.za/article/-2014-07-03-ucts-new-student-admission-policy-explained> (accessed 19 May 2022).

50 As of 2014, Black students composed 39.2% of all students at South African medical schools, while Blacks composed 79.6% of the country's population (LJ van der Merwe and others, 'South African Medical Schools: Current State of Selection Criteria and Medical Students' Demographic Profile' (2015) 106 *South African Medical Journal* 76).

applicants. Even though this quota-based system is more complex and goes beyond the applicant's race, it still does not represent the complexity of all factors determining disadvantage.

UCT, UP, and Stellenbosch attempt to address this by introducing algorithms that generate different admission scores for applicants with equal academic performance but different SES. All three universities use related proxies for disadvantage, which could be broadly grouped into three categories:

- economic need: measured by receiving state aid or a need-based scholarship;
- family background: measured by the level of educational attainment of family members, parental first language;
- educational background: measured by school quintiles or school fees.

UP's Clinical Medical Practice program does not define a separate category for disadvantaged students, rather it accounts for 'suitability and equity' factors when computing MPS of all applicants. Depending on the maximum and minimum values of the 'suitability and equity' factors, it can have a different impact on the overall MPS.

As we have seen above, UCT and Stellenbosch determine a quota for applicants with disadvantaged backgrounds, and eligible students compete within this pool unless they are accepted as part of the general admission pool. While defining disadvantage, Stellenbosch only considers applicants with a SES of 6 and higher (out of 10); applicants with lower scores compete with other applicants in the general category without any adjustments. UCT's algorithm includes students with all disadvantage scores, allowing students from more disadvantaged backgrounds to have a higher multiplication factor.

There are strengths and weaknesses to both approaches. By allowing applicants with very low disadvantage scores to compete in this special pool, UCT may potentially harm applicants from the *most* disadvantaged backgrounds. This would be relevant for students who do not have high enough scores to compete with stronger applicants with a lower disadvantage score. Stellenbosch restricts access to this special pool by setting a high disadvantage factor, making this pool accessible only for highly disadvantaged students. At the same time, students from less disadvantaged backgrounds might be left behind since they have to compete in a general pool. These are just some examples of the complexities and tradeoffs involved in designing 'equitable' affirmative action admission policies.

In addition to these tradeoffs, there might also be implementation challenges due to mis-measurement of socio-economic status. Students might be unaware of their school quintiles[51]. The data from 2009 show that 33% of UCT applicants from South Africa did not know their school quintile[52]. At the same time, youth might be mis-informed about parental background or household finances. While some of these difficulties may be circumvented by relying on administrative sources (e.g. high schools records, tax transcripts, etc.), it is unclear to what extent these measurement issues impact universities' ability to correctly target disadvantaged youth in their admission policies.

7 Discussion

Historically white universities in South Africa have made progress in facilitating access to previously excluded students. As mentioned in the previous sections, most universities rely on target quota systems and extended programs, and some of them (particularly for Health Sciences) introduced more sophisticated affirmative action criteria, integrating multi-dimensional proxies for disadvantage rather than relying on a single factor. A good example of this change is the new student admission procedure introduced at UCT, which is based on a 3-stage process and accounts for multiple factors to better detect applicant disadvantage with the goal of placing 'similar' applicants into similar pools. To further improve the targeting of disadvantaged students in admission procedures, universities may need to continue refining their admission algorithms. In this regard, machine learning and data mining may be seen as particularly promising tools for facilitating these efforts.

While related, machine learning and data mining use data for different purposes. Data mining is focused on detecting patterns in data, normally through managing and analyzing big datasets. Machine learning focuses instead on the design of models that can help predict outcomes on the basis of past experience[53]. Machine learning and data mining are often used as complements, with the patterns detected though data mining helping to inform model choice in machine learning. For example, both statistical tools have been applied in education to improve student retention. Specifically, data mining and machine learning are used to identify at-risk students and/or predict student

51 Judy Favish and Jane Hendry, 'UCT's Admissions Policies: Is the Playing Field Level?' (2010) 24 *South African Journal of Higher Education* 268.

52 Ibid.

53 Zhi-Hua Zhou, *Machine Learning* (Springer Singapore 2021).

performance, which is crucial for the design and targeting of academic support interventions[54].

Given the complexities in defining 'disadvantage' and in applying appropriate measures to correct for it, there might be a role for machine learning and data mining in the admission processes at South African universities. Data mining can be used to better understand patterns in past admission decisions and identify areas for improvement. Machine learning algorithms are capable of processing information on a large number of applicant features, which can help define a more accurate index of disadvantage. These data-driven innovations could eventually lead to the creation of an all-encompassing admission threshold.

Despite their technical advantage, however, ill-designed statistical algorithms may carry a risk of exacerbating existing inequalities. An interesting example in this regard is the student screening system, called GRADE, which was piloted at the University of Texas-Austin in the United States. GRADE used past admission data to evaluate applicants' academic quality. Using a number of attributes from the applicant's package, the statistical algorithm assigned a score to each student[55]. Using a different set of attributes[56], a second model predicted admission decisions and enrollment based on past admission data[57]. While both models performed relatively well in predicting admission decisions and were only supposed to aid and facilitate the traditional human-reviewed admission process, it was noted that these algorithms could easily become

---

54 Dursun Delen, 'A Comparative Analysis of Machine Learning Techniques for Student Retention Management' (2010) 49 *Decision Support Systems* 498; Carlos Márquez-Vera and others, 'Early Dropout Prediction Using Data Mining: A Case Study with High School Students' (2016) *Expert Systems* 107; Luiz Carlos Barbosa Martins and others, 'Early Prediction of College Attrition Using Data Mining' (2017) *Proceedings – 16th IEEE International Conference on Machine Learning and Applications* 1075; Nguyen Thai Nghe, Paul Janecek, Peter Haddawy, 'A Comparative Analysis of Techniques for Predicting Academic Performance' (2007) *Proceedings – Frontiers in Education Conference* T2G-7; JP Vandamme, N Meskens, JF Superby, 'Education Economics Predicting Academic Performance by Data Mining Methods' (2007) 15 *Education Economics* 405.

55 These attributes include GPA, GRE, applicant's undergraduate institution, research area, preferred faculty advisor, letters of recommendation, and statement of purpose. See Austin Waters and Risto Miikkulainen, 'GRADE: Machine-Learning Support for Graduate Admissions' (2014) 35 *AI Magazine* 64.

56 These attributes include age, gender, SAT score, GPA, decile, number of visits, number of interviews, number of institutional contacts, expected family contribution, AP honors, US citizen, territory, high school state, and high school type.

57 Thomas Lux and others, 'Applications of Supervised Learning Techniques on Undergraduate Admissions Data' (May 2016) *ACM International Conference on Computing Frontiers* 412.

biased, perpetuating existing cycles of inequalities. A likely reason for this was the reliance on the admission profiles of students admitted in the past, where certain groups were either underrepresented or completely excluded[58]. Partly as a result of these risks, the University of Texas at Austin phased out the use of GRADE in their admission process[59].

If South African universities were to adopt advanced statistical tools in admission decisions, it would be necessary to avoid any mechanism that could reinforce past discriminatory patterns. This tradeoff between statistical innovations and risk of bias is the subject of a strand of research that investigates alternative ways to achieve 'algorithmic fairness'. Algorithmic fairness can be broadly viewed as a means to ensure that a machine learning algorithm does not assign a potentially discriminatory outcome to a subject based on her characteristics (attributes). While different (and more narrow) definitions of algorithmic fairness can be found in the literature depending on the subject level – individual vs group – they are generally concerned with achieving an equal probability of a valued outcome at that subject level[60].

Of particular interest to the South African higher education system are algorithms that deliver counterfactual predictions. Such algorithms may be designed to correct for 'historic disadvantage' so that the assigned disadvantage factors can ensure equal probability of acceptance between applicants from groups of varying historical disadvantage[61]. Designing an admission procedure of this type in South Africa would mean that the algorithm should *adjust* an applicant score for the multiple factors that have impacted her academic preparedness up to university-level studies. For example, a Black applicant from a low quintile school could have her APS significantly adjusted if historic data show that her race and school quintile prevented her from attaining a higher APS. The computation of an adjusted APS for all applicants would

58 Quach Katyanna, 'Uni Revealed It Killed off Its PhD-Applicant Screening AI – Just as Its Inventors Gave a Lecture about the Tech', *The Register*, December 2020, available at <https://www.theregister.com/2020/12/08/texas_compsci_phd_ai/> (accessed 20 May 2022).

59 Ibid.

60 These definitions include equalized odds, equal opportunity, demographic parity, fairness through awareness, fairness through unawareness, treatment equality, test fairness, counterfactual fairness, fairness in relational domains, and conditional statistical parity. See Ninareh Mehrabi and others, 'A Survey on Bias and Fairness in Machine Learning' (2021) 54 *ACM Computing Surveys* 115:1.

61 Yixin Wang, Dhanya Sridhar and David M Blei, 'Equal Opportunity and Affirmative Action via Counterfactual Predictions' (2019), available at <http://arxiv.org/abs/1905.10870> (accessed 31 August 2022); Matt Kusner and others, 'Counterfactual Fairness' (2017) *NIPS 2017 – 31st Conference on Neural Information Processing Systems* 4069.

then allow an 'algorithmically fairer' comparative evaluation of students from different backgrounds. In intuitive terms, such adjusted APS would represent the result that an applicant from a disadvantaged background would have achieved if she had enjoyed the same socioeconomic advantages as more privileged applicants.

While theoretically appealing, it is important to note the extraordinary complexity associated with defining a counterfactual score based on incomplete historic data and potentially biased past admission decisions. Additionally, there is a risk that the algorithm might accept students that are not adequately prepared for university level studies, which may lead to negative consequences, such as dropping out or under-performing – i.e. the mismatch hypothesis[62].

To facilitate the design and eventually the implementation of a fair admission algorithm, we encourage further research on (i) the statistical properties of potential algorithms to choose from and on (ii) the availability and quality of different data sources containing information on socioeconomic background and academic success. In this regard, a key advantage of machine learning is the ability to process a large number of variables correlated to disadvantage. This could lead to a more nuanced understanding of the impact that different socio-demographic factors have on applicants' academic preparedness and produce an APS distribution that more accurately controls for disadvantage and thus more effectively levels the playing field.

62 Sigal Alon and Marta Tienda, 'Assessing the "Mismatch" Hypothesis: Differences in College Graduation Rates by Institutional Selectivity' (2005) 78 *Sociology of Education* 294.

CHAPTER 7

Quantification and Parameterisation of Legal Research: The Case of Poland

Andrzej Jakubowski

1 Introduction*

The "quantification of performance" (QP) is a regulatory technique in the field of scientific research. Scientific categories, scientific and academic promotions, and funding depend more and more not only on the Impact Factor (IF), *h*-index, and other statistical data, but also on a wide spectrum of diverse parametric indicators. Measurement techniques also apply to the humanities and social sciences, including legal sciences, which are being gradually quantified[1]. The results obtained in this way are used both for the evaluation of the scientific output of individual researchers and for the overall assessment of academic and higher education institutions (HEIs). Moreover, quantitative techniques increasingly determine the legislative and policy solutions adopted in the fields of research and higher education worldwide. Yet the quantification methodologies used have often been criticised for their lack of consistency, transparency[2], and the hegemony of certain academic centres and languages[3]. Significantly, the 2012 San Francisco Declaration on Research Assessment (DORA)[4] emphasised that "the scientific content of a paper is much more

* The author wishes to acknowledge the support received from the National Science Centre (Poland), No UMO-2019/35/ B/HS5/02084. He would also like to thank Piotr Stec for his valuable comments.

1 For a detailed overview, see Tim C.E. Engels and Emanuel Kulczycki (eds), *Handbook on Research Assessment in the Social Sciences* (Edward Elgar 2022).

2 Marc P. Hauer et al., 'Quantitative analysis of automatic performance evaluation systems based on the *h*-index' (2020) 123 *Scientometrics* 735; also see Colin A. Chapman et al., 'Games Academics Play and their Consequences: How Authorship, *H*-Index and Journal Impact Factors Are Shaping the Future of Academia' (2019) 286 *Proceedings of Royal Society B* 20192047, available at <http://dx.doi.org/10.1098/rspb.2019.2047> (accessed 15 June 2023).

3 For instance, see Franciszek Krawczyk and Emanuel Kulczycki, 'On the geopolitics of academic publishing: The mislocated centers of scholarly communication' (2021) 4(1) *Tapuya: Latin American Science, Technology and Society* 1984641, available at <https://doi.org/10.1080/25729861.2021.1984641> (accessed 15 June 2023).

4 Available at <https://sfdora.org/read> (accessed 15 June 2023).

 | DOI:10.1163/9789004680944_008

important than publication metrics or the identity of the journal in which it was published"[5], and encouraged the use of a combination of "a variety of journal-based metrics"[6]. Moreover, the Agreement on Reforming Research Assessment (2022 Agreement) covers the principles, commitments, and timeframe for reforms and lays out the principles for the Coalition for Advancing Research Assessment (CoARA)[7]. This document requires that assessment be based "on qualitative judgement for which peer review is central, supported by responsibly used quantitative indicators where appropriate"[8].

Considering the ongoing debate over the mechanisms of QP in the field of scientific research, this chapter addresses the mechanisms of quantification, evaluation, and categorisation of legal research in Poland in the context of the new financial perspective for the academic sector (2022–2025). The quantification of academic performance constitutes the core of the recent Polish reform of the higher education and research sector, set up by the 2018 Act "Constitution for Science"[9]. The Act introduced a new legal regime which, among others, concerns the indicator-based evaluation of universities and other academic centres every four years. As a result of the evaluation scientific categories are designated. These categories, awarded within respective research disciplines, essentially determine the possibility of carrying out studies of a general academic profile and awarding academic degrees. The evaluation results may greatly affect the allocation of public funds available to each academic institution in Poland. The first evaluation covered the years 2017–2021, and its results were officially published in July 2022; appeals procedures are still underway.

Against this background, this chapter analyses the methodology of quantification of scientific publications in the field of legal science in Poland. More precisely, it concerns the evaluation algorithm established by the secondary regulations of the Minister of Education and Science (MES) implementing the Constitution for Science and its operation in the practice of public administration.

---

5 Ibid., para. 4.

6 Ibid., para. 6.

7 Agreement on Reforming Research Assessment (20 July 2022), available at <https://coara.eu/app/uploads/2022/09/2022_07_19_rra_agreement_final.pdf> (accessed 14 June 2023).

8 Ibid., at 3 and 5; also see Global Research Council, 'Statement of Principles on Peer/Merit Review' (2018), available at <https://globalresearchcouncil.org/fileadmin/documents/GRC_Publications/Statement_of_Principles_on_Peer-Merit_Review_2018.pdf> (accessed 14 June 2023).

9 Act of 20 July 2018 – Law on Higher Education and Science, consolidated text: [2023] Poland's Journal of Laws issue 742; the official English translation is available at <https://www.gov.pl/attachment/d6975935-4b24-4be3-96f1-09c51589958a> (accessed 14 June 2023).

The analysis proceeds as follows. Firstly, general issues of QP of scientific research and its impact on legal regulation in the field of research and education are examined. Secondly, the chapter outlines the current process of evaluating research and academic performance in Poland, based on the regulatory framework introduced by the Constitution for Science. It discusses the role of the subsequent implementing regulations, which established a list of peer-reviewed monographs and journals and assigned them a score/rank. The methods of evaluation of a journal's IF (and thus its academic value) are scrutinised. Thirdly, the chapter discusses the challenges and shortcomings of the current QP of research in Poland. In fact, before the end of evaluation period the MES retroactively modified the list of scientific journals several times, thus altering the actual indicators of research performance and profoundly affecting the process of implementing the regulatory regime of the Constitution for Science.

Finally, in light of the above discussions the paper is aimed at addressing and substantiating a wider problem, i.e. to what extent the "quantification of performance" (QP) – based on the variety of mechanisms, both low-tech and machine-driven – is today used to shape the regulatory framework of scientific research in the social sciences and humanities. Is it possible to create international, objective standards and indicators in this regard? What are the challenges of such objectivisation of research in the form of numerical data? What should be the role of international scientific communities, such as the International Academy of Comparative Law, in providing support for international standard-setting with respect to the evaluation of scientific research?

2 Quantification of Scientific Performance and Its Regulation: General Remarks

The quantification of academic performance (quality of research results and scientific publications) has been the subject of a wide-ranging academic and societal debate in recent years. As researchers, we are constantly inundated with invitations to take part in quality assessments of universities and departments. Annual rankings set the rhythm of academic life, and their presence in indexing databases has become a priority for journal editors and researchers worldwide[10]. Indeed, since the 1990s many national higher education systems

10 Among a wide range of major international rankings and scientometric indices and indexes, one can list: Academic Ranking of World Universities (ARWU) – Shanghai Ranking Consultancy; World's Best Universities Ranking – US News & World; The World

have introduced legislative solutions that make the principles of funding and the functioning of the scientific world dependent on parametric indicators. Existing performance evaluation models rely on quantification based on performance indicators related to research, innovation and excellence. These indicators are defined according to various policy goals and standards, established by both national and international institutions. In fact, the indicators and their mechanisms of interpretation are produced by both public and private actors at different levels, such as national, international and regional funding authorities and private indexing and ranking bodies[11]. Among other things, impact and innovation assessment tools have also been introduced[12].

In this sense, the quantification of research performance has increasingly become part of a phenomenon that Sally Engle Merry has referred to as an "indicator culture", i.e. "[a] set of techniques and practices of knowledge that has acquired a significant level of public trust and acceptance", while noting that indicators (numbers, rankings, and scores) "seductively promise to provide guidance through a complex world"[13]. In other words, these tools aim to improve transparency, objectivity, and social and economic development[14]. It is thus expected that through a good system and the right indicators the performance measurement and assessment processes can identify gaps between the current state of research and education and the ideal state in order to develop strategies to achieve research and higher education goals[15]. These objectives, annotated by evaluation and quantification methodologies, are often transformed into regulatory instruments. In particular, one can observe

University Ranking and Times Higher Education; Leiden Ranking – Leiden University; Assessment of University-Based Research – European Commission; CHE University Ranking – Centre for Higher Education Development/die Zeit; Performance Rankings of Scientific Papers for World Universities – Taiwan Higher Education Accreditation and Evaluation Council; U-Map – CHEPS, European Multidimensional University Ranking System (U-Multi-rank); Ranking Webometrics.

11 See Gunnar Sivertsen, 'The Use of Bibliometrics in Assessments of Social Scientists', in Engels and Kulczycki (eds), *supra* fn 1, 231.

12 For instance, see Marianne Bauer and Maurice Kogan, 'Evaluation Systems in the UK and Sweden: Successes and Difficulties' (1997) 32(2) *European Journal of Education* 129.

13 Sally Engle Merry, *The Seductions of Quantification: Measuring Human Rights, Gender Violence and Sex Trafficking* (Chicago University Press 2016) 221.

14 See OECD, *Enhancing Public Research Performance through Evaluation, Impact Assessment and Priority Setting* (2009) DSTI/STP/TIP(2009)5, available at <https://www.oecd.org/sti/inno/Enhancing-Public-Research-Performance.pdf> (accessed 14 June 2023).

15 See further Andrea Bonaccorsi and Luca Secondi, 'The Determinants of Research Performance in European Universities: A Large Scale Multilevel Analysis' (2017) 112(3) *Scientometrics* 1147.

the widespread practice of enacting regulatory instruments governing research performance indicators and their use[16].

On the other hand, as already mentioned the academic milieux worldwide has constantly expressed its lack of confidence in the indicator culture[17]. In particular, DORA clearly recommends not to "use journal-based metrics, such as Journal Impact Factors, as a surrogate measure of the quality of individual research articles, to assess an individual scientist's contributions, or in hiring, promotion, or funding decisions"[18]. Moreover, it recommends that researchers, "[w]hen involved in committees making decisions about funding, hiring, tenure, or promotion, make assessments based on scientific content rather than publication metrics"[19]. The 2022 Agreement goes even further, calling to "[a] bandon inappropriate uses in research assessment of journal-and publication-based metrics, in particular inappropriate uses of the Journal Impact Factor (JIF) and h-index"[20], for the sake of reducing "the dominance of a narrow set of quantitative journal-and publication-based metrics"[21]. Accordingly, such "inappropriate uses" comprise: (i) "relying exclusively on author-based metrics (...) to assess quality and/or impact"; (ii) "assessing outputs based on metrics relating to publication venue, format or language", and (iii) "relying on any other metrics that do not properly capture quality and/or impact"[22]. In this regard, "the use of rankings of research organisations in research assessment" should

16 For instance, the system of research evaluation in Slovenia, based on the Research and Development Activity Act ([2006] Slovenia's Official Gazette No. 22/06 – official consolidated text, 61/06 – Societies Act-1, 112/07, 9/11 and 57/12 – Supportive Environment for Entrepreneurship Act (ZPOP-1A)), makes a number of professional qualifications in the academic world conditional on meeting parametric criteria. In this regard, heads of basic research projects are required to demonstrate that they have achieved at least 100 points from scientific publications specified by the secondary regulation of the Public Research Agency of the Republic of Slovenia governing research performance indicators (specific rules apply to various disciplines); they need to have an IF and the minimum score from scientific publications, documented cooperation with other funding agencies in the last five years and the minimum number of pure citations in the last ten years. See Rules on the Criteria for Establishing Compliance with the Conditions for being the Head of a Research Project [2016] Slovenia's Official Gazette No 53/16.

17 For early voices, see e.g. Per O. Seglen, 'Why the impact factor of journals should not be used for evaluating research' (1997) 314 *British Medical Journal* 498, Jerome K. Vanclay, 'Impact factor: outdated artefact or stepping-stone to journal certification?' (2012) 92 *Scientometrics* 211.

18 DORA, *supra* fn 4, para. 1 ("General recommendation").

19 Ibid., para. 15.

20 2022 Agreement, *supra* fn 7, at 6.

21 Ibid.

22 Ibid.

also be avoided as these are deemed "inappropriate for assessing researchers", and limit the research community in its scientific autonomy by abiding to "criteria and methodologies set by external commercial companies"[23]. Hence "[r]esearch organisations should also be mindful that public communication (e.g. the active advertising of an institution's rank) can contribute to the perception that research quality conflates with ranking positions"[24].

While advancing these recommendations, the 2022 Agreement calls for reform of the assessment system for research, researchers, and institutions. The overall goal is to reduce dependence on journal-based metrics, such as journal IF, and try to create an academic culture where importance is placed on the intrinsic value of research. As of 12 June 2023, the 2022 Agreement has been signed by 580 organisations from forty-five countries of the world[25]. Significantly, on 8 November 2022 it was also signed by the European Commission, which also endorsed DORA. According to the CoARA's action plan, the reform of research assessment is scheduled for over the next five years[26].

3 Poland's Constitution for Science and the Quantification of Academic Performance for the Period 2017–2021

All the considerations discussed above are also present in the Polish debate on the QP in the field of scientific research, as already fifty-two Polish institutions have signed the 2022 Agreement[27], while the current model of quantification of research performance, established pursuant to Poland's Constitution for Science, is essentially based on the "culture of indicators". Undoubtedly, this current model is one of the best examples of relying on quantitative indicators.

Works on the reform of Polish science and higher education have been ongoing since the early 2000s. While the Constitution for Science entered into force on 1 October 2018, its adoption was preceded by an extensive, expert diagnosis of the state of science and higher education in Poland, commissioned by the MES (at that time the Ministry of Science and Higher

---

23 Ibid.
24 Ibid.
25 See <https://coara.eu/agreement/signatories/#signatories> (accessed 15 June 2023).
26 See <https://coara.eu/agreement/the-timeframe> (accessed 15 June 2023).
27 See <https://coara.eu/agreement/signatories/?category%5B0%5D=poland#signatories> (accessed 15 June 2023).

Education)[28]. The diagnosis related to the assessment of the level and quality of performance of Polish scientists. It was measured by the number of publications in the most respected scientific journals; the number of prestigious scientific prizes awarded; and/or the volume of funds obtained in European grant competitions. The data contained in the diagnosis indicated a number of problems affecting the development of the science and higher education system in Poland which – in comparing the position of Polish universities in international rankings – have been deepening over the past two decades. This is evidenced, according to experts, by the successive relative declines in international rankings and scientometric indices. Similarly unfavourable, according to the experts, was the picture of Polish science in relation to the success rate in obtaining the European Research Council (ERC) grants. Added to this was the low presence of Polish authors in top-ranked world scientific journals, such as *Nature*, *Science*, or *Cell*. The experts completed their negative picture of Polish science with comments on the very low mobility of Polish researchers.

In light of these findings, the MES reached the conclusion that there was a pressing need to change the academic system in Poland in order to make it more competitive on the global scene[29]. According to the MES, the following objectives of the reform were identified: (i) de-bureaucratizing the Polish system of higher education and science; (ii) increasing the internal autonomy of HEIs in organisational matters; (iii) increasing the quality of scientific research; (iv) intensifying the responsible professional development of researchers; (v) moving away from the so-called 'scientific publication spotlight'; (vi) strengthening the international position of Polish science; (vii) guaranteeing a high quality of education at all levels, including doctoral and vocational education; (viii) broadening the field of linking teaching and scientific research with their practical application (societal and economic impact)[30].

The Constitution for Science established five categories (A+, A, B+, B, and C) to be assigned to institutions of higher education (HEIs) and the science system in respective research disciplines. In this regard, the act introduced a major increase in the importance of the evaluation of scientific activity; the assessment of which will determine the right to confer the doctoral and

---

28 Georg Winckler et al., *Peer Review [of] Poland's Higher Education and Science System. Horizon 2020 Policy Support Facility* (2017), available at <https://ec.europa.eu/research-and-innovation/sites/default/files/rio/report/PSF-Peer_review_Poland__FINAL%2520REPORT.pdf> (accessed 15 June 2023).

29 Barbara Kromolicka, '"Konstytucja dla Nauki – Ustawa 2.0" szansą czy zagrożeniem dla rozwoju nauki i szkolnictwa wyższego?' (2018) 22(2) *Pedagogika Szkoły Wyższej* 77, 78–9.

30 Ibid., at 81.

postdoctoral degrees, i.e. the overall status of a HEI, as well as its level of public funding. These entitlements are reserved only for HEIs that have been awarded an A+ or A category in their respective research disciplines. Firstly, this is a much higher requirement than that for doctoral qualifications (B+), and HEIs which are qualified within categories B and C cannot award doctoral degrees, and subsidies for their research budgets are to be limited). Secondly, it is an example of bridging scientific research and the ability of a HEI to provide high quality education in its status as a research university.

It should be emphasised that the evaluation of scientific activity is undertaken within a given research discipline (such as law, sociology, history, etc.)[31] by the HEI, and not within research activities undertaken by individual administrative units (faculties, institutes, schools, and departments) of this institution. In other words, according to the Constitution for Science the evaluation is to be performed within a discipline, and it covers all academics employed in research and research and teaching positions (and not only selected, most productive, researchers). Thus, in the model adopted by the Constitution for Science, the quantification of the research performance of individual researchers – and not that of respective units within the HEI structure – is crucial. Yet only selected achievements are considered for evaluation: up to four top-ranked publications per researcher. In principle, this is aimed at focusing on ambitious research rather than on "producing" publications. In this regard, the quality of publishing output is the major criterion for evaluating the achievements of a given HEI within a particular discipline. The two other criteria are: (i) financial results of scientific research and development work (e.g. the number of research grants awarded); and (ii) the impact of scientific activity on the functioning of society and the economy (determined through qualitative assessment)[32]. Based on the results of the evaluations so constructed, scientific categories (A+, A, B+, B, and C) are assigned to HEIs[33]. In other words, the category which is awarded to a scientific discipline at a given HEI is crucial, and not only for financial reasons. It has a bearing on the survival of a given centre, as this determines, *inter alia*, the possibility of conferring degrees and titles; the academic nature of the university; the possibility of running doctoral schools/programmes; and even the independence of the establishment of new educational and research programmes. All centres with a category lower than B+ will lose these rights.

---

31 Full list of scientific disciplines is available at <https://www.gov.pl/attachment/77ced6fc-ccdb-44c2-a1f2-7c6531882b6f> (accessed 14 June 2023).

32 Constitution for Science, *supra* fn 9, art 267(1).

33 Ibid., art 268(1).

According to the Constitution of Science, evaluation shall be carried out every four years, and shall cover a period of four years preceding the year in which it is carried out[34]. The results of the first evaluation for the first period (2017–2021)[35] were ready in 2022, and the list of scientific categories awarded to institutions of higher education and the science system in respective research disciplines was published in July 2022[36]. A total of 65 A+ scientific categories, 323 A categories, 582 B+ categories, 139 B categories and 36 C categories were assigned within 48 disciplines.

In terms of legal sciences, the leading centres are: Warsaw University of Technology and the University of Białystok, both with an A+ category. Among 39 institutions with legal science disciplines, none was assigned a C category, while the vast majority of them were awarded a B+ category.

4 Constitution for Science and Publication Indicators

As already explained, one of the main elements of the reforms introduced by the Constitution for Science concerns the quality of research results. The primary means of evaluating the activities of academics therein is scored/ranked publications. Moreover, this system implies measuring the value of publications by the rank of the scientific journal/publisher. According to Article 267(2) of the Constitution for Science, the MES shall specify, by way of a secondary regulation: "(1) the types of scientific and artistic achievements to be considered in the evaluation of the quality of scientific activity, the definitions of a scientific monograph and article, the detailed criteria and manner of assessing achievements, the manner in which the scientific category is defined, as well as the manner in which the evaluation is carried out, given the specificities of conducting scientific activity within the given fields, in particular social sciences, the humanities and theology [...], comparability of results achieved by entities within the disciplines, as well as reliability and transparency of the evaluation"; (2) the way of compiling the list of: (a) publishers and "the manner in which the number of points is determined and allocated, considering the reputation of publishing houses and their classification into groups corresponding to their rank"; and (b) the list of "scientific journals and peer-reviewed material from international conferences [...], and the manner

34 Constitution for Science, *supra* fn 9, art 266.

35 The period of evaluation was extended to five years due to the COVID-19 pandemic.

36 See <https://www.gov.pl/attachment/d5acf6a7-772b-49d3-8054-12969a56b8f9> (accessed 14 June 2023).

in which the number of points is determined and allocated, considering the reputation of the journals and conference materials".

In this regard, while the scientific content of a research outcome (publication) is important, the publication metrics or the identity of the journal (and its parametric standing) in which it was published are crucial for the entire outcome of research assessment.

4.1 *Scientific Monographs' Indicators*

On this basis, a secondary regulation – the Ordinance of 22 February 2019[37] – was adopted, and the list of ranked publishers was compiled. The final, revised version of the list (as of July 2021)[38] includes 815 publishers and assigns points for scientific monographs published by them.

Accordingly, there are 779 publishers at Level I (a monograph equals 80 points), and 36 publishers at Level II (a monograph equals 200 points)[39]. While the first group mostly features Polish publishers, the second one contains exclusively top-ranked international publishers publishing mostly in English and German.

However, in the case of research carried out within scientific disciplines belonging to the humanities, social sciences and theological sciences, the total point value of monographs is increased. In particular, the value of a scientific monograph amounting to 200 points (Level II) or 80 points (Level I) is increased to 300 and 100 points respectively[40], while in the case of the scientific editing of a monograph, if the total point value of the monograph (Level II), the scientific editor shall be awarded 150 points, instead of 100 points in

37 Ordinance of the Minister of Science and Higher Education of 22 February 2019 on the evaluation of the quality of scientific activity, consolidated text: [2022] Poland's Journal of Laws 661.

38 See the MES Communication of 22 July 2021 on the list of publishing houses publishing peer-reviewed scientific monographs, available at <https://www.gov.pl/attachment/1feb29b3-5278-4366-86e9-f7dfa2b1b474> (accessed 15 June 2023).

39 Academic Press, Bloomsbury Publishing, Brepols Publishers, Cambridge University Press, Columbia University Press, Cornell University Press, Duke University Press, Brill, Edward Elgar Publishing, Equinox Publishing, Harrassowitz Verlag, Harvard University Press, Intellect (Bristol, UK), John Benjamins Publishing Company, Johns Hopkins University Press, MIT Press, Mohr Siebeck, Oxford University Press, Peeters Publishers, Princeton University Press, Routledge, SAGE Publications, Stanford University Press, Franz Steiner Verlag, T&T Clark, Taylor & Francis Group, University of California Press, University of British Columbia Press, University of Chicago Press, Edinburgh University Press, University of Michigan Press, University of Minnesota Press, University of North Carolina Press, Vandenhoeck & Ruprecht Verlage, Wiley-Blackwell, Yale University.

40 Ordinance of 22 February 2019, *supra* fn 37, para. 12(5)(1).

other disciplines[41]. In other words, in disciplines belonging to the humanities, social sciences and theology, monographs get an increased score due to the implied importance of book publications in these research areas. It should also be emphasised that the methodology of selecting publishers was purely based on experts' opinions and thus de facto arbitrary, as were the point thresholds set by the MES[42]. The exact criteria for selecting certain publishers selecting (and omitting others) are not known, nor why this list does not reflect the geographical or linguistic diversity of global research[43].

4.2 *Ranked Journals' Indicators*

Much more important from the point of view of the quantification of research performance is the regime for establishing and compiling the list of scientific journals and peer-reviewed materials from international conferences (list of journals). The rules governing this regime were introduced by the Ordinance of 7 November 2018[44]. Accordingly, the legal instrument determines the methods of assigning the number of points (numeric value) to each individual journal, taking into account the journal's recognised reputation. Accordingly, the list of journals includes:

(i) scientific journals that are included in international databases: (a) Scopus; (b) Science Citation Index Expanded; (c) Social Sciences Citation Index; (d) Arts & Humanities Citation Index; and (e) Emerging Sources Citation Index[45];

(ii) peer-reviewed materials from international conferences that are included in the international database DBLP Computer Science Bibliography, in the case of a conference included in the Computing Research and Education Association of Australasia (CORE)[46];

(iii) scientific journals that are the subject of projects financed under Poland's governmental grant scheme[47].

41 Ibid., para. 12(5)(2).

42 Ordinance of the Minister of Science and Higher Education of 7 November 2018 on the compilation of lists of publishers of scientific monographs, scientific journals, and peer-reviewed materials from international conferences, consolidated text: [2020] Poland's Journal of Laws 349, paras. 3–4.

43 However, it should be noted that monographs published by publishers which are not included on the list can (under certain conditions) be subject to expert evaluation, and can be awarded 120 points; see Ordinance of 22 February 2019, *supra* fn 37, paras. 3(3) and 12(6)(1).

44 See *supra* fn 42.

45 Ibid., para. 6(1).

46 Ibid., para. 6(2).

47 Ibid., para. 6(3).

The list of journals may also include foreign scientific journals indexed on the international database European Reference Index for the Humanities and Social Sciences (ERIH+), if this is justified by a journal's academic position. The inclusion of such journals is based on an expert assessment. Yet overall, the value of a research outcome is evaluated according to the journal IF (reflected by inclusion in a prestigious index) in which such research output is published. In other words, what counts is the parametric ranking of a journal where such an output is published. Accordingly, the total point value of a scientific article published in ranked journals included in the list of journals shall be 20, 40, 70, 100, 140 or 200 points, while the total point value of a scientific article published in a journal not included in that list shall be 5 points[48].

The detailed methodology for the evaluation of scientific journals was specified under paragraph 8 of the Ordinance of 7 November 2018. This establishes that the assessment is performed pursuant an analysis including centile values calculated in specific scientific disciplines on the basis of IF values, in accordance with a given international database. Firstly, for journals indexed on Scopus the following centile values (impact indicators) are taken into account: Source Normalized Impact per Paper (SNIP), CiteScore, and Scimago Journal Rank (SJR)[49]. As for journals indexed on the Science Citation Index Expanded, Social Sciences Citation Index, Arts & Humanities Citation Index, and Emerging Sources Citation Index, the following indicators are considered: Journal Impact Factor, Article Influence, and Category Normalized Citation Impact (calculated using scientific articles published within the period of five calendar years ending one year before the year in which the inclusion of scientific journals and peer-reviewed proceedings from international conferences in the databases is established – separately for each indicator)[50]. Based on these indicators (calculated centile values), the Ordinance of 7 November 2018 assigns points to scientific journals, as set forth in Table 7.1 below[51].

However, scientific journals which have been allocated a different number of points in scientific disciplines on the basis of the same IF shall, on the basis of the arithmetic mean of those points, be allocated the number of points that is closest to that mean, in accordance with the values of points laid down in Table 7.1. Where it is not possible to ascertain the number of points that is closest to the calculated mean, scientific journals shall be allocated the higher

48 See Ordinance of 22 February 2019, *supra* fn 37, para. 12(1).

49 Ordinance of 7 November 2018, *supra* fn 42, para. 8(1)(1).

50 Ibid., para. 8(1)(2).

51 Ibid., para. 8(2).

TABLE 7.1 Impact indicators and points assigned. Ordinance of 7 November 2018, para. 8(2)

No	Centile value	Points
1.	at least 97	200
2.	at least 90 but less than 97	140
3.	at least 75 but less than 90	100
4.	at least 50 but less than 75	70
5.	at least 25 but less than 50	40
6.	if the centile value is less than 25	20

number of points[52]. Scientific journals which are indexed on Scopus, Science Citation Index Expanded, Social Sciences Citation Index, Arts & Humanities Citation Index, and Emerging Sources Citation Index, and which do not have a calculated value of a given IF in particular scientific disciplines, shall be assigned 20 points[53].

The evaluation of scientific journals and peer-reviewed proceedings from international conferences takes place in two stages: objectivised percentile value; and expert assessment.

In the first stage, parametric values regarding impact indicators are considered. Scientific journals included in the ERIH+ database, which have an international reputation and have a particular impact on the development of a scientific discipline and meet ethical and scientific standards, may also be included in the list of journals on the basis of expert opinions. These journals shall be assigned 20 points[54]. The same number of points shall be awarded to scientific journals that are the subject of projects financed under Poland's governmental grant scheme[55].

The second stage of the assessment involves an analysis of whether the value of the points attributed to a scientific journal or peer-reviewed materials from an international conference corresponds to the actual impact of that journal or peer-reviewed materials on the development of science, taking into account: (i) the relevance of the scientific journal or the peer-reviewed proceedings of the international conference in the scientific discipline in

52 Ibid., para. 8(3).
53 Ibid., para. 8(4).
54 Ibid., para. 11(1).
55 Ibid., para. 10(3).

comparison to other scientific journals or peer-reviewed proceedings of international conferences; (ii) the specific publication practices and citation patterns of the scientific discipline; (iii) the position of the scientific journal or peer-reviewed proceedings from an international conference in recognised journal databases; and (iv) the value of impact indicators not included in the first stage of evaluation[56].

On the basis of this assessment, a scientific journal, or peer-reviewed proceedings from an international conference, may be awarded a different number of points than would result from the "objective" impact indicators. Such a change may consist in either increasing or decreasing the points by up to two point thresholds in accordance with the values referred to in Table 7.1. A change in points requires detailed justification[57].

5 Legal Journals' Indicators and the Challenges of Quantifying the Performance of Legal Research

As can be seen from the above, the mechanisms for assessing the quality and impact of scientific journals are based on a fairly formalised system of quantification, taking into account "objectified" indicators. It thus should not come a surprise that the list of journals compiled on the basis of these criteria proved difficult in the evaluation of scientific publications published in journals not indexed in international databases. This was particularly true for research outcomes included in scientific journals in fields of the humanities and social sciences published in languages other than English. This is because, based on the parametric criteria, articles published in those journals could not obtain high scores (the vast majority could not get more than 5 or 20 points). Moreover, in the practice of the 2017–2021 evaluation, it turned out that HEIs were required to present the highest-scoring publications, i.e. those awarded 100 points or more in the list. Clearly, the vast majority of Polish scientific journals had no chance of obtaining such high rankings. Understandably, this aroused opposition from the Polish scientific community[58].

For these reasons, the MES modified the list of scientific journals several times (even in the last weeks of the evaluation period), and did so retroactively.

56 Ibid., para. 13(1).

57 Ibid., para. 13(2).

58 Further read Jakub Krzeski, Krystian Szadkowski, Emanuel Kulczycki, 'Creating Evaluative Homogeneity: Experience of Constructing a National Journal Ranking' (2022) 31(3) *Research Evaluation* 410.

In fact the list, containing more than 30,000 scientific journals, was subject to very profound changes, which were not evaluated by any expert body and did not respect the methodology of assigning numeric value to each journal. Instead, their quantification and parametrisation was driven by pure policy considerations. The MES attempted to appreciate the value of Polish journals which were, according to it, of particular societal and cultural significance, stating that: "[t]he essential criterion is the quality of publications and their impact in the relevant area of knowledge. [...] Account is also taken of the journals' impact in their respective fields of research, as well as their connection with national culture and their role in strengthening the civilisational identity of Polish culture"[59].

In this context, it should be stressed that the way in which legal texts and law journals were evaluated was marked by controversy from the beginning. If a journal was not indexed on the international bibliometric databases (Web of Science or Scopus) or had a low citation rate (and law journals often fall into this category), it could get only 20 points, and could only be upgraded to 40 or 70 points through expert assessment. In fact in 2018, when the Constitution for Science entered into force, there was only one Polish law journal, *Journal of Juristic Papyrology*, indexed on Scopus. Hence objective criteria for the actual IF of most Polish law journals could hardly be established. The situation has gradually changed, thanks to major efforts on the part of journals' and publishers' editorial committees. However, as of the end of the evaluation period (2021) only eleven Polish law journals are indexed on Scopus (see Table 7.2)[60]. In practice, this means that Polish legal science, and in particular science published in Polish, does not stand a chance of obtaining a high rank in the process of quantifying research performance under the regime of the Constitution for Science. It is thus argued that basing the parametric evaluation and the evaluation of scientific quality on citations alone may not always reflect the specificities of legal research, where the most specialised and advanced research

59 See Dorota Stelmaszczyk, 'MEiN: zmiany w punktacji czasopism wynikają z troski o właściwy rozwój polskiej nauki' (12 February 2022) <https://naukawpolsce.pl/aktualnosci/news%2C86328%2Cmein-zmiany-w-punktacji-czasopism-wynikaja-z-troski-o-wlasciwy-rozwoj> (accessed 14 June 2023).

60 Please note that the *British Journal of American Legal* (no. 7) is not a Polish law journal. It is based at the Centre for American Legal Studies, Birmingham City School of Law, and published by Sciendo (De Gruyter Open Ltd.); see <https://sciendo.com/journal/BJALS> (accessed 15 June 2023). As of 15 June 2023, there are twelve Polish law journals indexed on Scopus; see <https://www.scimagojr.com/journalrank.php?category=3308&country=PL&year=2022> (accessed 15 June 2023).

publications would not necessarily be those with the highest number of citations[61].

However, the need for an objective system of measuring the impact of legal research in Poland has not widely been contested. In fact, it has been argued that the objective measures are not wrong, but defectively constructed. The system averages data across disciplines, underestimating results in the humanities and social sciences, including legal research. In this regard, much discussion has been devoted to the comparative assessment of existing journals' rankings in other jurisdictions, and their methodologies[62]. In fact, only some national systems provide for an extensive system of indexes, while in others, such as Italy, legal sciences have been placed in the category of "non-bibliometric" sciences, i.e. sciences for which citation analyses based on international bibliometric databases are inadequate. As a result, the evaluation of legal research is carried out through expert evaluation[63]. Taking into account these different national experiences, it has been suggested to broaden the list of impact indicators on the one hand[64], and to enhance the role of expert evaluation in legal sciences on the other[65].

Yet, the system for measuring the impact of law journals remained unchanged in Poland at the end of the 2017–2021 evaluation process. It was also noted that articles written for those dealing with a particular legal system tended to find fewer readers and consequently yield fewer points than those published in journals from other disciplines. Polish law researchers therefore published abroad, but in non-legal journals. Hence, much of this research output supported the ranking position of other disciplines at the expense of law. Meanwhile, a simplified procedure was used which did not provide for expert assessment at all. During the evaluation period, the MES decided to value Polish law journals "*ex gratia*, often awarding them more points than very good foreign journals"[66]. And suddenly it turned out that there were

61 Further read Grzegorz Wierczyński, 'Problemy oceny parametrycznej polskich czasopism naukowych z dziedziny nauk prawnych' (2020) 9 *Państwo i Prawo* 3.

62 Ibid., at 4–12.

63 See <https://www.anvur.it/attivita/classificazione-delle-riviste> (accessed 15 June 2023).

64 Grzegorz Wierczyński, 'Wykaz czasopism naukowychz dziedziny nauk prawnych z perspektywy danych o cytowaniach dostępnych w bazie Google Scholar' (2022) 5 *Państwo i Prawo* 3.

65 Wojciech Dajczak, 'Czasopismo prawnicze 2.0: racjonalna ewolucja czy wymuszona rewolucja?' (2021) 83(2) *Ruch Prawniczy, Ekonomiczny i Socjologiczny* 123.

66 Piotr Stec, 'Ewaluacja nauk prawnych w sumie pozytywna, ale nie bez wątpliwości' (18 August 2022) at <https://www.prawo.pl/student/ewaluacja-nauk-prawnych-prof-piotr-steca,516785.html> (accessed 14 June 2023).

journals which – according to the rules set up by the Ordinance of 7 November 2018 should start with 20 points – which were assigned 100 points or more. Such decisions, affecting the entire system of quantification of legal research performance, both procedurally and substantively, were in breach of the legal regime established by the Constitution of Science. These changes were introduced arbitrarily at the MES level, and were justified by the opinion that many of the journals made a unique, positive – but only in Polish science – contribution to the development of the given fields of knowledge. In doing so, MES's representatives emphasised that "this contribution was a criterion for evaluation"[67]. The solution created enormous chaos and uncertainty. Polish law journals, which were generally awarded very high scores, increased their "production" capacities, accommodating larger numbers of articles. Hence the race for law/legal researchers for high-scoring publications began, even though the legal basis for the evaluation raised legal and policy concerns which were more than justified.

As the results of the entire evaluation were based on such a questionable system of assessment, a number of appeals are currently underway and it is likely that many of these cases will be reviewed by the Polish administrative courts in the future. The results of this judicial review will be relevant to the new evaluation for 2022–2025.

At the moment, the quantification of legal research performance and its methodology for the upcoming years remains rather uncertain. Moreover, it has been argued that the current, defective tools of QP in the field of scientific research will lead to a flawed assessment of the quality of the higher education system in Poland, more generally. This may negatively affect the quality of research, comprising doctoral and post-doctoral programmes[68]. Hence, it seems that the recommendations of the 2022 Agreement need to be taken seriously into consideration when establishing the criteria for qualitative indicators for assessing QP in the field of humanities and social sciences, and in particular legal research.

67 Stelmaszczyk, *supra* fn 59.

68 See Emanuel Kulczycki and Dariusz Jemielniak, 'Nie hukiem ale skomleniem [Not with a bang but with a whimper] (2022) 4 *Nauka* 77.

TABLE 7.2 Scimago journal & country (2021)

1 - 12 of 12 < >

	Title	Type	↓ SJR	H index	Toal Docs. (2021)	Toal Docs. (3 years)	Toal Refs. (2021)	Toal Cities (3 years)	Citable Docs. (3 years)	Cites/Doc. (2 years)	Ref. / Doc. (2021)
1	Santander Art and Culture Law Review	journal	0.224 Q2	5	25	87	1052	18	73	0.18	42.08
2	Studia Iuridica Lublinensia	journal	0.202 Q3	4	136	99	5791	54	97	0.55	42.58
3	Krytyka Prawa	journal	0.141 Q3	1	76	57	1543	15	49	0.26	20.30
4	International and Comparative Law Review	journal	0.137 Q3	3	16	55	599	21	55	0.38	37.44
5	Journal of Juristic Papyrology	journal	0.130 Q4	8	0	8	0	1	1	0.00	0.00
6	Yearbook of Antitrust and Regulatory Studies	journal	0.129 Q4	6	18	71	462	4	65	0.08	25.67
7	British Journal of American Legal Studies	journal	0.122 Q4	4	16	45	469	6	45	0.09	29.31
8	Polish Yearbook of International Law	journal	0.108 Q4	1	0	30	0	1	29	0.03	0.00
9	Comparative Law Review	journal	0.106 Q4	1	20	40	179	7	37	0.23	8.95
10	Decyzje	journal	0.102 Q4	2	5	44	165	2	42	0.07	33.00
11	Comparative Legilinguistics	journal		1	11	0	340	0	0	0.00	30.91
12	Prawo i Wiez	journal		0	51	0	1255	0	0	0.00	24.61

AVAILABLE AT <HTTPS://WWW.SCIMAGOJR.COM/JOURNALRANK.PHP?CATEGORY=3308&COUNTRY=PL&ORDER=SJR&ORD=DESC> (ACCESSED 20 DECEMBER 2022)

6 The Future of the Quantification and Parameterisation of Legal Research in Poland and Beyond

This chapter has identified a number of problems related to the quantification of legal research performance, while considering the Polish legal system established by the 2018 Constitution for Science.

Firstly, it has been shown that flawed evaluation methods, constructed solely on objectified indicators of scientific impact and reputation, can negatively affect the functioning of research, research institutions, and the entire higher education sector. Attempts to correct such flaws through arbitrary decisions by state authorities can – even though often driven by justifiable policy motives of fairness and equity – corrupt the entire system and deprive it of credibility, both in the eyes of the scientific community and in the eyes of the wider public.

Secondly, it has been argued that referring only to the parametric indicators included in international databases may have a detrimental impact on the scientific, linguistic, and cultural diversity of the research conducted. It seems that IF pressure may also influence attempts to falsify these indicators through efforts to increase "citability". In this regard, the operation and results of the evaluation system under the 2018 Constitution for Science appear to confirm the threats and risks already identified by DORA and the 2022 Agreement.

Thirdly, it can be argued that the significant reduction of expert knowledge in favour of objectified parameters may indicate a deep crisis of science in general. This would manifest itself in a loss of trust in the scientific community and the judgments and assessments made within it. Hence the role of qualitative judgments, which in peer review is central, should be enhanced in line with the recommendations by DORA, the Global Research Council[69], and the 2022 Agreement. At the same time however, the "objectivized" indicators should not be abandoned, but rather their use should be tailored to a given discipline and field of research (taking into account its specificities while considering the diversity of global research). Hence, it is important to note the important demands raised in the Polish debate on quantification which relate to a better correlation of existing bibliometric instruments with scientific context and expert assessment. The latter, however, should not be in any way arbitrary. On the contrary, it should be based on clear questionnaires and principles, and the decisions made should be accompanied by clear control mechanisms, including the possibility of effective appeal.

Therefore, it seems necessary to increase the role of comparative research into the impact of methodologies for constructing parametric indicators and their influence on legislation in the area of science and higher education. As for legal sciences, such a role should be fulfilled by international non-governmental organisations of comparative law experts (i.e. the international scientific legal communities), such as the International Academy of Comparative Law, which would then contribute to the development of guidelines and standards for the quantification of legal research performance, while taking into consideration the cultural differences and different legal traditions. In this sense, comparative law research and practice have an important role to fulfil in building standards for assessing QP in legal studies and their outcomes, while considering their societal impact locally, regionally and globally.

69 See Global Research Council, *supra* fn 8.

PART 2

National Policy Making

CHAPTER 8

Algorithmic Decision-Making and Public Sector Accountability in Africa – New Challenges for Law and Policy

Raenette Gottardo

1 Introduction

As Lauritzen has pointed out[1], philosophers such as Aristotle have much to contribute to understanding messy transformations. For leaders across the public and private sectors what has been termed 'agile technologies' and the 'fourth industrial revolution' and 'digital transformation' heralds epochal change worthy of the most ardent analytical frameworks that philosophers such as Aristotle has used to grapple with deep and systemic change.

This era requires those grappling with digital transformation to draw on four quadrants, according to Lauritzen[2]: Science (Episteme), Wisdom (Sophia), Expertise (Techne) and Prudence (Phronesis). As digital transformation poses epistemic, philosophical, political, policy, moral, ethical, legal and sociological questions far beyond the science of big data and code, the questions that arise will raise challenging issues for scholars, politicians, lawyers, street-level bureaucrats (who will find themselves becoming systems bureaucrats) and for anyone engaged in public sector decision-making at a high level. Whilst a fair amount of expertise is involved in algorithmically assisted decision-making, whether in the public or private sectors, this will be wholly inadequate without science, wisdom and prudence guiding the overall strategic direction of any digital transformation. The risk is that accountable governance is sacrificed in the face of the deep systemic changes these technologies will bring to the process of public sector decision-making.

We are living in a world of rapid and dynamic change driven by accelerations in technological evolution with which we struggle to keep pace. Law, likewise, is grappling with the rapid evolution in crafting rule of law, human rights

1 Pia Lauritzen, 'A Philosopher's guide to messy transformations' (19 May 2022) *Strategy + Business – Leadership*, available at <https://www.strategy-business.com/article/A-philosophers-guide-to-messy-transformations> (accessed 21 October 2022).

2 Lauritzen, *supra* fn 1, 3.

 | DOI:10.1163/9789004680944_009

and accountability frameworks that must shift constantly in tandem with the development of algorithms, machine learning systems and, latterly, foundation models that are turbocharging artificial intelligence. Graphcore's 'Good Computer' in the United Kingdom, Frontier in the United States, Google's BERT and its successors such as OpenAI's GPT-3, Europe's Bigscience and China's Wu Dao ('Enlightenment'), a trillion dollar parameter model built by the Beijing Academy of Artificial Intelligence, all point to new and ever greater capabilities their creators did not foresee[3], heralding the fact that AI is moving full steam ahead into its industrial age. Not only does this point to a dramatically altered world with deep and lasting economic impact, but decision makers and their polity will be, and already are, deeply impacted by the unseen filters which these models bring into public and private sector decision making. The focus of AI research is now squarely on foundation models with a dizzying array of parameters that certainly will far exceed human cognitive ability. It is important to understand upfront that foundation models represent a complete phase change for AI. This is an important distinction as the first wave of digital changes in governance relied heavily on pre-labeled datasets that formed the bedrock of the bulk of algorithmically assisted decision-making systems. What foundational models represent is a step change as such models are trained with a different technique called self-supervised learning that runs the risk of moving the human further and further away from the decision-making loop.

This is a crucial differentiating factor as much of the existing systems, as well as the research and analysis that will be traversed in this paper, largely deals with older models of AI and very little research literature exists about this step change in the AI revolution heralded by foundation models. Neither is there deep literature about the implication it may have for existing and crafted decision making structures of AI that currently exist. A far greater understanding of this step change will be required by future research that falls beyond the confines of this current paper and its focus on AI in Africa. Whilst various players, including politicians, may want even more powerful models at their disposal, it is always important that research weighs both the opportunities as well as the overall risks or moral hazards if we are to avoid what has been termed the 'Turing trap' – letting automation do what augmented people processes can also do and perhaps continue to do more effectively.

3 The Economist Briefing, 'The World that BERT built. Huge 'foundation models' are turbocharging AI progress. They can have abilities their creators did not foresee' (2022) *The Economist* (11 June 2022), available at https://economist.com/interactive/briefing/2022/06/11/huge-foundation-models-are-turbo-chrging-ai-progress (accessed 21 October 2022).

2 Algorithmic Decision-Making and the Public Sector: Core Challenges

This paper seeks to grapple with some of the reasons why algorithmically assisted decision-making poses specific challenges to public sector accountability across the board whilst drawing closer attention to how these new challenges to law and the public policy process may be more acute and pronounced in Africa. With at least two World Economic Forum (WEF) Centers for the fourth industrial revolution on the continent, in South Africa and Rwanda respectively, the continent is rapidly becoming a hotbed for experimentation with algorithmic assisted decision making and AI. Whilst there may be positive developments for the continent out of these experimentations, there are associated risks associated with what has been termed by Zuboff 'surveillance capitalism'[4].

Zuboff's work exhaustively shows how humans themselves are no longer mere citizens but data subjects that are themselves the raw material to leverage human experience itself, through algorithms and AI in the hands of the private sector, to hidden commercial activities and purposes such as extraction prediction and sales. According to Zuboff, 'surveillance capitalism' is "an expropriation of critical human rights that is best understood as a coup from above: an overthrow of the people's sovereignty"[5].

The way firms such as Google (Alphabet), Microsoft and Facebook (Meta) capture what Zuboff refers to as 'behavioral surplus' and use it for others or to create other products for genuine market transactions with advertisers is a key part of their profitability – hence the term surveillance capitalism. It seems clear that in a market such as Africa, an untapped market, with a nascent AI, MLS, and algorithmically assisted decision-making market, the scope for surveillance capitalism to take root is considerable. The manner in which the continent itself, and its policy makers, will engage strategically (and hopefully critically) with this technology will therefore be crucial. Whilst the great scope for significant economic development and leapfrogging will be considerable and desirable, the moral hazards for human rights will have to be a focal point of continent-wide thought and critical engagement.

---

4 Soshana Zuboff, *The Age of Surveillance Capitalism. The Fight for a Human Future at the New Frontier of Power* (Profile Books 2019).

5 Zuboff, *supra* fn 4, frontmatter.

As Raji states,

> [a]s firms would be willing to pay for such knowledge to better sell their products, 'surveillance platforms' are thus able to earn 'surveillance revenues' that translates to 'surveillance capital', the logic of which is 'surveillance capitalism', which thus underpins the surveillance economy[6].

What seems clear is that firms such as Amazon (AWS), Alphabet, Meta and Microsoft will realistically be making money from getting to know their African users quite a bit better. Some of the institutional factors in Africa that makes the adoption of these systems far more challenging include, but are not limited to, concerns of human rights, poor underlying data quality, weak rule of law contexts, institutional challenges and weak institutions, corruption and the capture of the state which may see public and private sector roles far too closely aligned, as well as weak procurement systems. These factors and different contextual challenges may pose hurdles in Africa.

What is at stake in this debate both globally and in the broader African Union (AU) context, where the continent will be releasing a continental AI strategy by the end of 2022, are two crucial issues. First, the way these systems constitute a new hybridization of public and private roles and power in the delivery of public services which challenges existing legal and accountability frameworks. Existing accountability frameworks and systems are built for these sectors separately and new developments also challenge the notion that only the public sector has the power to act on the entire population. As Taylor shows[7], when the private sector derives a level of power akin to that enjoyed by the government or public sector, it will require what she terms 'thick legitimacy' in the eyes of the public, as what will be needed is a far more nuanced idea of political power and accountability that can respond not only to the legality of corporate behavior, but to its legitimacy overall when it is exercising powers that would normally fall under public law, constitutional law and administrative law provisions.

Second, is the fact that these systems increasingly adopted by governments all over the world, threaten to replace bureaucrats with technological 'sorcerers', according to Bell[8], if requisite safeguards are not properly crafted and

6 Rafiq Raji, 'Zuboff's surveillance capitalism: Implications for Africa tech policy' (2020) *Business Day* (4 February 2020), available at <https://businessday.ng/columnist/article/zuboffs-surveillance-capitalism-implications-for-africa-tech-policy-1/> (accessed 21 October 2022).

7 Linnet Taylor, 'Public Actors Without Public Values: Legitimacy, Domination and the Regulation of the Technology Sector' (2021) 34 *Philosophy and Technology* 897–922, available at <https://doi.org/10.1007/513347-020-00441-4> (accessed 21 October 2022).

8 Bernard W. Bell, 'Replacing Bureaucrats with Automated Sorcerers?' (2021) 150(3) *Daedalus* 89–103, available at <https://doi.org/10.1162/DAED-9-01861> (accessed 21 October 2022).

created. He argues that, whilst these systems promise to reduce inconsistent decision making by reducing the exercise of official discretion, minimizing the imprecise nature of government rules, and smoothing administration, the very defining characteristics of these systems (opaqueness and non-intuitive correlations) can undermine the very essence of the principles of core administrative law. These core administrative law principles include that all citizens be treated equally according to clear and transparent objective criteria, that regulations be made and based on proper rationality in linking means to ends, and, that all administrative action be fully reviewable by external players and be transparently seen to be so.

As Bell points out with respect to the adoption of these systems by federal agencies in the United States of America, AI impacts all these norms: "the resultant tension, at least for now, will constrain administrative agencies' most ambitious potential uses of artificial intelligence"[9]. It is noteworthy that, in the US, the Biden administration has released in 2022 an AI Bill of Rights that appears to be mindful of these challenges[10].

It is important that we look at these two issues in far greater depth separately: firstly, the level of public and private sector power and the role of hybridization in public sector decision making (Section 2.1); secondly, the effective impact of these systems on public sector decision making and accountability challenges (Section 2.2).

2.1 *A Different Level of Private Sector Power in Public Spaces: Hybridization and Its Challenges*

As Taylor notes[11], the involvement of the private sector in public sector governance leaves citizens bereft of the ability to opt out, and confers considerable new power on the private sector to take steps and act on a scale of the entirety of the population of a country at a level unseen before. This single and simple fact means that private firms are intervening at the population wide level with clear consequences for social and political life requiring not only bureaucracies, policymakers and politicians to respond, but also sociologists, legal scholars and political scientists to respond in their research to these fundamental shifts that challenge some of the assumptions in their discipline about the separation between the public and private sphere as technological advances

9 Bell, *supra* fn 8, 89.

10 The White House, 'Blueprint for an AI Bill of Rights. Making Automated Systems Work for the American People' (2022), available at <https://www.whitehouse.gov/ostp/ai-bill-of-rights/> (accessed 21 October 2022).

11 Taylor, *supra* fn 7.

reshape our world and pose fundamental challenges to accountability across all areas of law. The question of whether law itself will have to hybridize to build a nexus between public and private law that will be a stronger tool for accountability is an important one, and requires proper contemplation. There is a very clear and growing tension between technology adoption, on the one hand, and rights and freedoms, on the other hand. This tension will arise in areas as diverse as health care, migration and arms control.

The private sector led nature of much of the datafication underway places these tensions under an important magnifying glass due to what Taylor calls the "hybrid type"[12] of public private engagements – that is, engagements distinctively different to older style public-private-sector-partnerships (PPPs). This is shaped by the new ubiquitous ability of the private sector to act on entire populations for their data mining activities that are transnational in scale and scope and imply a qualitative difference that is relevant and worthy of far closer attention, study, and legislative reform.

According to Taylor,

> [t]his hybrid type of engagement starts with a commercial investment in capacity that results in a monopoly on data about our core public services or entitlements. In turn, that data serves to enable companies to capture new markets and create new products that lead to lucrative government contracts[13].

She points to an activist probe in the United States of America that found, as an example, that Amazon Web Services had 204 federal authorizations for government data maintenance, Microsoft had 150, Salesforce had 31 and Google (now Alphabet) had 27. This illustrates why questions of technical governance and accountability are now more complex when there is no clear line between commercial and public actions and values any longer or at best a thin dotted line. In countries with weak or hollowed out state capacity, these risks are magnified.

For the African continent, geopolitically and with an eye to their domestic politics, these questions are profound as the role of technology firms speaks directly to questions of domination of populations. These questions simply must be debated and resolved very publicly on the African continent given

12 Taylor, *supra* fn 7, 899.

13 Ibidem.

the possible problems of power, dependence and arbitrariness that could arise through the presence of these firms.

African governments would be correct to be both enthusiastic but also wary with a view to their rule of law, constitutions and public administrative law provisions, many of which have been carefully crafted in post-colonial, post-conflict and transition contexts. Where such systems are not, as yet, securely embedded, the risks will multiply. As Taylor points out, the case of welfare payments and the involvement of a private sector firm in South Africa perfectly illustrates these tensions[14]. It shows that the problems that arise cannot be addressed by data protection laws or data ethics and must instead be addressed as a 'thick legitimacy' concern.

This is in keeping with the European Court of Human Rights' nuanced take on digital surveillance cases. The European Court has started to treat these cases as not merely cases that touch on interference or harm, but as questions that relate to issues of domination and arbitrary exercises of power. The arbitrary exercise of power is an area of great familiarity to administrative law. What will be required will be nothing short of a revolution in how we reimagine democratic and regulatory probing of these private sector entities to ensure that there is no departure from the core underpinnings of key administrative law prescripts.

The notion that there is no difference between public services provided by the public sector and those provided by the private sector, when there is a clear profit motive involved in the latter case, must be confronted carefully despite claims that less transparency must often of necessity prevail when commercial sensitivities are at stake. The question of 'thick legitimacy' shows that the exact opposite is true. Responsibility remains in the hands of the state but the practical difficulties of discharging this where there is deep dependency on a private sector player cannot be denied. The case of South Africa's welfare payments firm Cash Paymaster Services (CPS) perfectly illustrates the impact these factors have on civil and political rights and the rule of law itself.

The firm in question, CPS, was contracted by the South African government, in breach of Section 217 of the country's constitutional provisions on fair and transparent procurement, to conduct welfare grant distribution in South Africa. Even though South Africa has eleven official languages, CPS conducted the distribution process in English and used unfamiliar digital systems for recipients of welfare payments. The cumulative impact marginalized the poorest South Africans further and paved the way for a host of other credit products

14 Taylor, *supra* fn 7.

and services to be offered, on an unsolicited basis, to welfare recipients. This effectively eroded the welfare payment as many individuals opted for other credit products that reduced the effective impact of the welfare payment as a tool of poverty alleviation. South African courts, and the Constitutional Court in the case of CPS, have framed corporate exploitation of the public through their data as questions worthy of considering a firm's standing as an illegitimate or legitimate actor in relation to the public. This is in keeping with Taylor's concept of 'thick legitimacy' highlighted above.

Unfortunately, however, the state's sheer dependence on CPS diluted the impact of the courts' clear moral voice and resulted in a renewal of the contract despite findings that it was corruptly concluded and breached the constitution. According to Taylor, "[i]n formal terms, this legitimized CPS [...], although the courts and the petitioners' statements are clear that this was not the objective"[15].

This is the reason why Taylor argues so strongly that firms that act as quasi-governmental actors, while pretending to merely be doing business, must be subjected to the 'thick legitimacy' standard to address the political legitimacy challenge that can otherwise result as is in evidence in the CPS case in South Africa[16]. She argues that the 'consent' South Africans were required to engage in to become 'users' of the system was tantamount to forced cooperation and hollowed out 'consent' completely with clear rights and civil and political rights implications. For arguments' sake, if those South Africans who did not wish to be served in English or with an electronic system had been properly represented, the ability of CPS to serve the public adequately would have been politically contestable and so too could have been the decision to have moved the provision of such a crucial service online.

The question of accountability for technology firms therefore looms large and will be addressed in greater detail in subsequent sections. What seems clear is that the need to hold states accountable for regulating the behavior of corporate entities at a new scale is an imperative necessity:

> we are in need of institutions that are independent and robust to economic and political pressure, and that can respond to all the stages of a given application of technology – proposed, planned and operational[17].

15 Taylor, *supra* fn 7, 906.
16 Taylor, *supra* fn 7, 907.
17 Taylor, *supra* fn 7, 916.

This independence must be from both the public and the private sector. The core point is that data policy is not merely economic. It is social, and this is where a particularly significant challenge will be present in Africa as it grapples thus far largely with the economic dimension and not with the social or the political dimenstion. For example, South Africa's 4th Industrial Revolution Commission Report is nearly entirely silent on the scale of the legal and constitutional challenges these technologies will pose[18].

Busuioc points to the crucial nature of the accountability questions AI confronts us with and to the specific features that pose challenges to holding algorithms to account[19]. These features include compounded information challenges and the absence of sufficient justifications and of explanations of how algorithms work, which, in turn compounds both the diagnosis of their failure and the possibility for redress for any harm suffered. Algorithms make inferences and, by doing so, strike at the heart of accountability. Transparency is a clear necessity but will prove to be insufficient for robust accountability. Busuioc argues that one of the solutions must be located at the design end of these systems with the need for systems architects to create understandable and interpretable models and for this to become an industry home and the need for those who preside over the procurement of such systems and regulators to demand such clarity.

The use of these systems will be deeply embedding altered decision-making processes that can alienate responsible officials and trigger deep legitimacy questions for bureaucracies. This will be pronounced in transition or post conflict states where part of the core challenge is to build trust in the state and in its new institutions including its bureaucracy and the underpinning tenants of its decision-making processes. Busuioc's work calls attention to the tensions that exist and the importance of scrutinizing whether systems that claim to

18 Department of Communications and Digital Technologies, 'Notice 591 of 2020. Summary Report and Recommendations Presented by the Presidential Commission on the Fourth Industrial Revolution' (January 2020), available at <https://www.itweb.co.za/static/misc/pdf/COMMUNICATIONS-AND-DIGITAL-TECHNOLOGIES-NOTICE-591.pdf> (accessed 21 October 2022). See also Global Partners Digital and Stanford Global Digital Policy Incubator, 'National Artificial Intelligence Strategies and Human Rights: A Review' (April 2021), 2nd edn, 39–40, available at <https://www.gp-digital.org/publication/national-artificial-intelligence-strategies-and-human-rights-a-review-second-edition/> (accessed 21 October 2022).

19 Madalina Busuioc, 'Accountable Artificial Intelligence: Holding Algorithms to Account' (2020) 81(5) *Public Administration Review* 825–836, available at <https://www.doi.org/10.1111/puar.13293> (accessed 21 October 2022).

keep a human in the loop do not in practice see bureaucratic actors losing the ability to understand, scrutinize, and, in effect, exercise meaningful control[20].

Given that the two core foundation stones of bureaucratic legitimacy are bureaucratic expertise and accountability, it seems clear that these systems have the profound ability to diminish these two foundations simultaneously. The consequences of this are potentially devastating especially in fragile states. Clearly accountability mechanisms are needed, such as model certification, third party independent and ongoing testing of model performance, use of models with audit trails of their decision making and such audit trails need to be visible and clearly understandable, and algorithmic impact assessments to be conducted prior to public sector deployment[21].

Yet, whilst these steps will all be quite important at the systemic level, none of them get to the nub of the issue, namely that public sector AI tools need a clear exploration of the reasons for individual decision making as a fundamental tenant of administrative law that is justiciable and administratively reviewable in the courts. For scholars of global comparative law, it is therefore important to develop an entire ethos of scholarship dedicated to keeping track of emerging case law in different jurisdictions that deal with these issues.

Within the African continent the work of the African Commission on Human and Peoples' Rights and the African Court on Human and Peoples' Rights will be of crucial importance, as these systems enter the African continent. Given the similarities that are already emerging between the European Court on Human Rights and the South African Constitutional Court's jurisprudence, the importance of such cross jurisdictional work will become ever more important as AI enters Africa and other national and apex courts on the continent.

A relevant consideration in this regard is whether there ought to be a moratorium on 'black box' models in the public sector as a policy question that will demand higher levels of systems design. This will be a critical policy question for the AU and the African Commission on Human and Peoples' Rights and the African Court in years to come. Regulation is never popular, and is costly, but against the penetration of these tools into every area of life on the continent – the criminal justice system; local government; education; law enforcement; migration; health; social security; housing etc. –, it seems a fundamental non-negotiable necessity, from a civil and political rights and broader human rights perspective, that these policy questions be properly aired and answered at the

20 Busuioc, *supra* fn 19.

21 Busuioc, *supra* fn 19.

very least. These are policy choices, which require careful societal deliberation and consent. The answer may look different in every continental and regional body, given its specific history and the specific challenges it faces. Whilst the systems that are being built may be transnational in their scope and ambition, this does not mean that localization and context is unimportant. In fact, it is of very great importance as the way different legal systems will weigh these issues will also show.

A recent global study by the Ada Lovelace Institute (ADA), AI Now Institute (AI Now), and Open Government Partnership (OGP) of 2021 analyses the initial wave of algorithmic accountability policy for the public sector pointing to the clear need to have algorithmic accountability across countries and contexts, due to the similarity of the issues and the transnational nature of some of the actors[22]. Debates on what form these algorithmic accountability policies should take – from legally binding commitments to higher level principles and voluntary guidelines – is varied and will give an indication to early adopters in Africa of the general direction of the global discourse. Important policy indicators are emerging in the European Union and the United States of America in this regard.

What the report also shows, however, are the limits of legal and policy mechanisms to ensure safe and accountable algorithmic systems, the narrow pool of evidence it is drawing from, the relevant recent evolution of such policies since 2019, and the opportunity for policymakers to adopt some best practices as they monitor and evaluate the experiments of countries as diverse as France, Hungary, Mexico, Singapore, the USA, Australia, Canada, Morocco, the Netherlands, New Zealand, Sweden, the United Arab Emirates, Uruguay, Finland, India and the UK, plus the European Union, that were part of the first wave of policy mechanism scrutinized in the report.

According to the report, some of the base practices to look towards include (but are not limited to): systematic and effective transparency around assumptions and objectives behind policy mechanisms, strategic engagement with sectoral agencies, timely and ongoing engagement with affected communities and civil society, and leveraging peer to peer learning networks and global principles[23].

---

22 Ada Lovelace Institute, AI Now Institute, Open Government Partnership, 'Algorithmic Accountability for the Public Sector' (2021), available at <http://www.opengovpartnership.org/documents/algorithmic-accounability-public-sector/> (accessed 21 October 2022).

23 Ada Lovelace Institute et al., *supra* fn 22, 17.

A different solution was proposed by Wallach and Marchant[24]. As they have pointed out, at the advent of the rise of discourses about algorithmic accountability practices, there is a severe 'pacing problem' seeking to ensure that regulation keeps pace with AI technological evolution. What their work shows is a total mismatch that exists between the prevailing approach taken by governments and what may be required for effective ethical and legal oversight. Such challenges will be more acutely felt in Africa.

To address what they have labeled a 'pacing gap', Wallach and Marchant call for the creation of governance coordinating committees (GCCs) to craft a coordinated oversight mechanism for such transnational technology. Such a GCC is envisaged as a global body enforcing 'soft law' (i.e., institutional controls by insurers, journal publishers, grant funding agencies, courts and governments) which is to be supported by regional bodies that can ensure consistent approaches. Such a GCC can then have relationships with partners such as the WEF, the IEEE, the Partnership in AI and AI research centers and incubators. They see such a GCC as a key 'agile governance' innovation. It seems clear that regional bodies are already taking steps to address these questions regionally.

As will become clear in next sections, the AUDA-NEPAD (African Union Development Agency – New Economic Partnership for African Development) created the African Union High Level Panel on Emerging Technologies (APET) to look at Africa's approach to these questions on a continental level. The APET AI strategy is due for public release soon. Individual African states, such as South Africa, which houses a WEF Fourth Industrial Revolution hub (launched in 2016 at the WEF meeting in Cape Town), have strategic policy documents, such as South Africa's Fourth Industrial Revolution Commission Report which sets out more strategic approaches[25]. Whilst this is a good first step, it is clearly already falling short of the algorithmic accountability standards emerging in policy discussions elsewhere, as will be seen in subsequent analysis. Even for a country as advanced as South Africa, the questions will be significant as the South African state itself emerges from an era of state capture where the lines between the public and the private sector were often blurred indistinguishably as the Zondo Commission Report has shown[26]. Risk of further capture of

24 Wendell Wallach and Gary E. Marchant, 'An Agile Ethical/Legal Model for the International and National Governance of AI and Robotics' (2018), available at <https://www.aies-conference.com/2018/contents/papers/main/AIES_2018_paper_77.pdf> (accessed 21 October 2022).

25 See *supra* fn 18.

26 Judicial Commission of Inquiry into Allegations of State Capture, Corruption and Fraud in the Public Sector including Organs of State, 'Reports', voll. 1–6 (2022), available at <https://www.statecapture.org.za/site/information/reports> (accessed 21 October 2022).

the state would therefore, arguably, be more pronounced with the widespread adoption of new AI systems within the bureaucracy.

At the level of the European Union (EU), the block has been highly proactive on the legislative front, following its regulation on data protection (the so-called GDPR)[27] with the introduction of a proposal for a EU AI act which caters for the regulation of both specific single focused AI system as well as the 'brain' of AI[28]. EU policymakers have stated their express desire to ensure that the AI Act (AIA) sets a global regulatory standard for AI[29], yet some argue that the power of the EU AIA lies in what has been termed the 'Brussels effect'[30]. This refers to the EU's unilateral ability to set rules that can apply and appeal to a market of over 450 million consumers. The AIA's provisions will have a significant impact on categories of AI such as high-risk AI in products, high risk AI in Human Services, and AI that interacts with humans. Some of the aspects covered include AI systems in automotive vehicles, boats, elevators, medical devices, industrial machinery, and more. Products entering the EU market will have to comply with the AIA, which sets out clear transparency obligations and mandates registration in a public database of high-risk AI. The AIA has oversight provisions over EU governments' algorithms and algorithmic systems, and people need to be informed if they are interacting with an AI system formally – which is a boon for transparency. As said, critics have argued that the AIA's global impact will be limited to the 'Brussels effect', and to targeted territorial impact[31]. However, the fact that it will be a policy marker for other jurisdictions, including the African Union, cannot be denied. Indeed one can speculate what role, if any, EU regulatory actions has already had on the United States Artificial Intelligence Bill of Rights and whether it has succumbed to the 'Brussels effect' to ensure continued market access for its technology industry.

Another important EU development, and policy marker for other jurisdictions, is the in-principle adoption of the EU's Digital Services Act (DSA)[32]. The

27 Regulation (EU) 2016/679 on the protection of natural persons with regard to the processing of personal data and on the free movement of such data, and repealing Directive 95/46/EC.

28 European Commission, Proposal for a Regulation of the European Parliament and of the Council Laying Down Harmonised Rules on Artificial Intelligence (Artificial Intelligence Act), COM/2021/206 Final.

29 European Commission, *supra* fn 29, Explanatory memorandum, no. 1.

30 See for instance Alex Engler, 'The limited global impact of the EU AI Act' (2022), *Tech Tank Brookings Institute* (14 June), available at <https://www.brookings.edu/blog/techtank/2022/06/14/the-limited-global-impact-of-the-eu-ai-act/> (accessed 21 October 2022).

31 Engler, *supra* fn 30.

32 Regulation (EU) 2022/2065 on a Single Market For Digital Services (Digital Services Act) and amending Directive 2000/31/EC.

DSA aims at forcing technology companies to adhere to new obligations to remove illegal content and goods rapidly, to give users and researchers explanations of how their algorithms work, and to police misinformation more proactively. Therefore, the act bans targeted advertising, prohibits dark patterns, requires transparency on recommender algorithms, requires the offering of recommender systems that are not profiling based, requires explanations for content removal deemed to be illegal, requires data provision to researchers on how online risks evolve, demands information retention about traders on online marketplace platforms anti bonds clear misinformation strategies. These are significant new requirements. Larger companies such as Amazon (AWS), Meta, Alphabet and Microsoft will face the greatest scrutiny. The EU suite of policies includes its Digital Markets Act (DMA)[33] aimed at creating a level playing field for tech players within the single common European market. The EU suite of legislative instruments will be likely followed by various jurisdictions as policy markers[34].

In the United States of America, a comprehensive report on the use of algorithms in the United States government's federal administrative level, compiled by Stanford Law School and New York University's Law School, represents the first stab at understanding actual AI in use at the 142 most significant federal government departments, agencies and sub agencies[35]. This is important empirical work and consists of three parts: Part 1 deals with AI use in federal government departments, agencies and sub agencies, Part 2 deals with case studies that have specific applications across a diverse array of government and governance tasks, and Part 3 deals with cross cutting institutional, legal and policy polemics, questions and challenges raised by AI use.

The first of its kind, the report weighs up arguments about efficiency gains in governance against questions about whether this cross boundary public action-private contracting raises unique challenges, whether the use of AI is permitted at all, what an optimal algorithmic design end user interface may

33 Regulation (EU) 2022/1925 on contestable and fair markets in the digital sector (Digital Markets Act).

34 James Vincent, 'Google, Meta and others will have to explain their algorithms under new EU legislation. The Digital Services Act will re-shape the online world' (2022) *The Verge* (23 April), available at <https://www.theverge.com/2022/4/23/23036976/eu-digital-services-act-finalized-algorithms-targeted-advertising> (accessed 21 October 2022).

35 David Freeman Engstrom, Daniel Ho, Catherine Sharkey, Mariano-Florentino Cuéllar, 'Government by Algorithm: Artificial Intelligence in Federal Administrative Agencies' (2020), available at <https://law.stanford.edu/press/acus-stanford-law-school-and-nyu-school-of-law-announce-report-on-artificial-intelligence-in-federal-agencies/> (accessed 21 October 2022).

look like, and the scope of human machine interfacing. Compiled for a ACUS (Administrative Conference of the United States), it seems clear from the US case that serious challenges emerge for scholars of administrative law and policy scholars that may not have closely followed the 'algorithmification' of their federal agency level of governance and its expansive use of AI at state and local levels as well. The rights implications are stark and dramatic.

Citron and Calo ask with great insight whether the rise of an 'Automated Administrative State' represents a deep crisis of legitimacy[36]. They argue strongly that administrative agencies must be careful to discard the expertise and nimbleness that is the very reason for their existence and call for a strong consideration of when and how to adopt tools that ought only to enhance, not undermine and compromise, the very foundations of the legitimacy of federal agencies and the state itself. Given that as much as close to 45% (64 agencies) have embraced some dimensions of AI or MLS – with the most common type being used in regulatory resource, analysis and monitoring, enforcement, public services and engagement, internal management and adjudication[37] –, it is clear that these systems are being used across some of the most sensitive dimensions of core tenants of administrative law highlighted by Bell[38].

Importantly, the 'Government by Algorithm: AI in Federal Administrative Agencies' report is comprehensive and makes a strong backdrop case for human in the loop AI processes and not to simply replace humans with systems. It seems the need to retain a degree of street-level-bureaucracy within the broader evolving context of 'systems bureaucrats' in an AI era remains important. We now turn to add more detailed analysis of what challenges 'systems bureaucrats' may face as administrative law comes under pressure in an era of AI. It has already had an impact with the adoption of an Artificial Intelligence Bill of Rights by the White House at the time of writing[39].

2.2 *From 'Street-Level' to 'Systems' Bureaucrats – More than a Culture Change Is at Stake*

In weighing the culture shift that may occur within bureaucracies, it is important to grapple with an understanding of how the introduction of AI systems in public sector decision making may affect the nature of the bureaucracy, and the level of trust that it enjoys from the public in society more generally when

36 Ryan Calo and Danielle K. Citron, 'The Automated Administrative State: A Crisis of Legitimacy' (2021) 70 *Emory Law Journal* 797–845 (2021).

37 Calo and Citron, *supra* fn 36, 801–802.

38 Bell, *supra* fn 8.

39 The White House, *supra* fn 10.

only a thin veil will separate it from powerful private sector players on which it will become entirely dependent.

It is also important to understand that the nature of activities of the bureaucracy is but one relevant aspect, as the body politic, more broadly, will be impacted by the introduction of an expansion of AI. Despite some of the in-principle objections in legal and administrative scholarship on the use of algorithms in the public sector, Kennedy Waggoner and Ward argue that the public appear less concerned about the rise in hybrid decision making[40]. Whilst debates rage amongst policymakers about the level of trust to place in AI, their research, perhaps controversially, argues that people are fairly trusting of algorithms is relative to other sources of advice or wide-ranging discretion:

> We find that people are quite trusting in algorithms relative to other sources of advice, even with minimal information about the algorithm or when they are explicitly told that humans are just as good at the task[41].

Whilst this may be so, we need to unpack the intellectual and in principle concerns that arise from private sector contracting for public action. Bell reminds us that governments have three coercive powers – enforcement, adjudication and rulemaking – that emanate from the *trias politica* which AI and machine learning systems and algorithms will impact. One of the critical challenges that arises, in the case of his research for U.S. federal agencies, is the question whether the decisions of algorithms will be binding or non-binding and the role of humans when the inevitable question of explainability arises that will challenge leaders aiming to retain control of policy: "not even the agency head can reliably discern with precision the policy the AI/ML algorithm applies in producing its decisions"[42].

For such leaders, data and computer processing specialists will be crucial interlocutors for their accountability vis-a-vis their external environment. Similarly, the area of judicial review, a fundamental rights issue is differential but is not perfunctory as the algorithm may be incapable of explaining the result in such a way that it pleases a court's inquiry. Questions arise as to whether courts are to review the process for decision making itself or the outcomes produced by algorithms and how non expert members of the judiciary ought to accomplish such a task. If we accept that explainability is important

40 Ryan Kennedy, Philip Waggoner, Matthew M. Ward, 'Trust in Public Policy Algorithms' (2022) 84(2) *Journal of Politics* 1132–1148.

41 Kennedy, Waggoner, Ward, *supra* fn 40, 1132.

42 Bell, *supra* fn 8, 92.

within the realm of legislative rules, ancillary issues arise including that correlation is not equal to causation and that regulatory limits must be placed on people's conduct, and not on their inherent traits (i.e. their race or their gender which is where much algorithmic bias lurks). The reasons for full correlations must be clear for proper causation to be convincingly argued.

Bell highlights how questions of transparency will be a minefield and shows that proprietary code may be immune to Freedom of Information Act (FOIA) requests raising ever greater hurdles for transparency and accountability: "to the extent that transparency is desirable, it will be more difficult to achieve when the AI/algorithm is proprietary as the FOIA probably allows the agency to withhold such information and the government may feel compelled to do so"[43].

It, therefore, seems sensible for Bell's proposal that federal agencies in the USA must grapple with how to make AI 'black box decisions' both more transparent and intuitive to be followed[44]. If this occurs, the question is whether these systems will be able to engender any form of public trust. Such imperatives will be even more compelling across the African Union where trust levels in government and bureaucracies are low already prior to the introduction of AI systems in public sector decision making. Simply arguing that the latter would solve the former is tantamount to lazy thinking and minimizes the considerable challenges that will be involved. It also trivializes and minimizes the formidable legal questions.

Drawing on concrete experience from the U.S. for illustrative purposes, Hartmann and Wenzelburger look at the use of AI in the criminal justice sector in the United States and seek to show how such a system functions in the decision-making process at local government level in Wisconsin in particular[45]. Their study demonstrates just how the introduction of a risk assessment tool at the local level of government has fundamentally altered the decision-making process in Wisconsin. They show how the algorithm's introduction of a degree of statistical prediction, which was unavailable in the past, transformed decision making:

43 Bell, *supra* fn 8, 99.

44 Ibidem.

45 Kathrin Hartmann and Georg Wenzelburger, 'Uncertainty, risk and the use of algorithms in public decisions: a case study on criminal justice in the USA' (2021) 54 *Policy Sciences* 269–287.

> this is mainly due to the fact that the evidence generated by the algorithm introduces a notion of statistical prediction to a situation that was dominated by fundamental uncertainty about the outcome before[46].

Their study shows just how fallible the risk scoring is that uses a set of categories has altered the decision making where the use of the software practically became the norm. They attributed this to the fact that the tool helps decision makers in contexts of high uncertainty by providing three data points of risk by which to consider the danger of recidivism. The use of these data points as research lead and evidence-based references for decision making within the bureaucracy at local level of policing in Wisconsin is a useful insight as the authors argue that the general context of risk and uncertainty is part of the reason the tool became so popular. Given how many situations of risk and uncertainty hallmark decisions in the public administration more generally, it seems to stand to reason that such systems that leverage data points, will prove to be exceedingly popular.

The same authors also point out that it is of equal importance to judge whether the algorithm's internal rules are indeed ethically defendable and to assess whether the entire system as a whole, and how it has altered the overall decision-making process, can be regarded more broadly as politically legitimate. These are crucial considerations that will arise in each public sector arena and every single public sector decision that will be subjected to AI. As Brand shows, there is a need to create proper frameworks for human and technological interaction to satisfy the needs of society not merely to add regulatory burdens[47]. Such a set of broader ethical and legal principles are arising at U.S. federal agency level and in the European Union, both at the EU level and in specific countries. However, a cross cutting approach may indeed be overdue and required to safeguard the policy process, the rule of law and human rights as we conceive of it. Questions such as whether algorithms need separate legal personality or whether this is entirely unnecessary will also arise and require answers.

A deeper understanding of the profound societal impact of algorithms is needed and sociologists and political scientists need to start urgently grappling with such questions in their theoretical frameworks and in their research. A bare minimum requirement for any set of ethical and legal principles is the

46 Hartmann and Wenzelburger, *supra* fn 45, 269.

47 Dirk J. Brand, 'Algorithmic Decision-making and the Law' (2020) 12(1) *eJournal of eDemocracy and Open Government* 115–132, available at <https://doi.org/10.29379/jedem.v12i1.576> (accessed 21 October 2022).

promotion of accountability, fairness and respect for human rights. This point is strongly underscored by Gottardo in her work that calls for the establishment of a Special structure for Algorithmic Accountability housed within the UN Human Rights Council on a permanent basis[48].

Zalnieriute, Crawford, Boughey, Moses and Logan argue that there are core legal and practical issues at stake in the implementation and supervision of such systems in practice and that these issues go to the very core of fundamental and foundational legal values including the rule of law[49]. They argue further that it is particularly acutely so in the arena of security and law enforcement: "[t]he tensions between increasing automation of government decision making, on the one hand, and the foundational values of public law on the other, are likely to escalate in the future"[50].

This inevitably calls for urgent public discourse across silos of policymakers, governments, and citizenry. When automation effects individuals, their urgent rights to redress calls for effective legal remedies, and for avenues to pursue such legal remedies with a degree of success or at least the prospect of success. This will be ever more urgent if AI systems mean that the future of government decision making may be incompatible with fundamental legal values and norms. Such a situation would be untenable.

De Fine Licht and de Fine Licht seek to emphasize the role of transparency, but with reference to how the public will come to perceive AI decision making and whether it will be viewed most legitimate and worthy of the acquiescence or at the very least their acceptance[51]. They advocate a limited form of transparency (focused on the justification of decisions) as a sufficient ground for what they have termed 'perceived legitimacy'. Whilst they may consider such legitimacy on a narrow basis sufficient, and it may protect commercial sensitivities, it may prove to be inadequate to satisfy a standard of 'thick legitimacy'.

What their argument appears to suggest, however, is that such limited transparency may in practical effect not be different to how public officials

---

48 Raenette Gottardo, 'Building Global Algorithmic Accountability Regimes: A Future-focused Human Rights Agenda Beyond Measurement' (2021) 5(1) *Peace, Human Rights, Governance Journal* 65–96.

49 Monika Zalnieriute, Lisa Burton Crawford, Janina Boughey, Lyria Bennett Moses, Sarah Logan, 'From Rule of Law to Statute Drafting. Legal Issues for Algorithms in Government Decision-Making', in Woodrow Barfield (ed), *The Cambridge Handbook of the Law of Algorithms* (CUP 2020) 251–272.

50 Zalnieriute et al., *supra* fn 49, 272.

51 Karl de Fine Licht and Jenny de Fine Licht, 'AI, Transparency, and public decision-making' (2020) 35 *AI and Society* 917–926, available at <https://doi.org/10.1007/500146-020-00960-w> (accessed 21 October 2022).

currently explain their decisions without full recourse to a full remit of information about how they arrive at these decisions.

Henman identifies four specific public administrative challenges that are relevant in debates about AI deployment[52]. These are: (1) accuracy, bias and discrimination, (2) legality, due process and administrative justice, (3) responsibility, accountability, transparency and explainability, and (4) power, compliance and control.

He argues that the crucial challenges will be to shape and use AI to pursue and enhance clear social and economic objectives, and that this process must be informed by the insights and experiences of what has gone before as governments have deployed algorithms, and to secure policy learning across contexts. In this regard work that is being done at the University of Houston by Professor Ryan Kennedy on how we should hold algorithms accountable in public policy and empirical work being leveraged to craft an algorithmic accountability benchmark, based on proper empirical experience[53], will be of considerable importance to a newly growing field trying to bridge the academic normative debates on algorithms with more empirical work on their actual use and deployment in the field. Such empirical work will prove crucial as other countries and regional bodies increasingly come under pressure to adopt public action and private contracting interfaces as part of their public-sector decision-making processes. Similar empirical work conducted at African universities in an AU context will be crucial.

Coyle elaborates more as to why mere explainability will not be an answer to transparency challenges and what will constitute 'good' policy outcomes where AI is used[54]. She points out that there is a clear tradeoff between performance and explainability and that these systems may be more useful the more 'black box' they are. She argues that policy arises as a compromise between competing goals whereas algorithms need clear goals and not compromises to function optimally. She argues that giving algorithms such precise specific objectives may not always be possible. Whilst the exposure of public policy

52 Paul Henman, 'Improving public services using artificial intelligence: possibilities, pitfalls, governance' (2020) 42(4) *Asia Pacific Journal of Public Administration* 209–221.

53 Sarah Tubbs, 'Holding Algorithms Responsible for Public Policy – University of Houston Researchers Awarded NSF Grant to Develop Technology to 'Improve Local Government'' (23 September 2021), available at <https://www.uh.edu/news-events/stories/2021/september-2021/09232021-holding-algorithms-accountable-in-public-policy.php> (accessed 21 October 2022).

54 Diane Coyle, 'The tensions between explainable AI and good public policy' (15 September 2020) *TECH*, available at <https://www.brookings.edu/techstream/the-tensions-between-explainable-ai-and-good-public-policy/> (accessed 21 October 2022).

tradeoffs may be useful, this is not a technical problem of computer code but a political one. She makes a strong argument that a lot of hard work must be done to restore trust in public institutions and to assure the public of their general trustworthiness before machines are deployed to make decisions.

It is exactly in this area where some of the crucial challenges arise for a country such as South Africa. South Africa faces in particular significant problems with regard to datasets, due to its history of apartheid and discrimination which informed and infected its public databases that contains the bulk of information about its citizenry. We now turn to these discourses to highlight specific challenges based on some empirical examples from a leading African state.

3 South Africa, the Fourth Industrial Revolution and Algorithms in Public Sector Decision-Making: Challenges and Opportunities

At a practical level, South Africa is moving with rapid speed to adopt and leverage new technologies for development. At the World Economic Forum meeting in Cape Town, in 2019, the leader of the World Economic Forum, professor Klaus Schwab, announced that the C4IR South Africa would be hosted at the Council for Scientific and Industrial Research (the CSIR)[55]. In the same year, the President of the Republic, President Cyril Ramaphosa, appointed a Presidential Commission on the Fourth Industrial Revolution[56].

This Commission, chaired by the President, is aimed at identifying relevant policies, strategies and action plans that will position South Africa as a competitive global player in 2019 in the AI space. Whilst the global context of COVID-19 may have diverted attention from the policy, the trajectory of the policy machinery of the states has been set.

The Commission issued its report to the President on the 23rd of October 2020 during the height of the COVID pandemic. The report emphasizes that the activity of the Commission seeks to address South Africa's competitiveness and to address the well-being of her people by addressing the triple challenge

55 World Economic Forum, 'Centre for the Fourth Industrial Revolution, C4IR South Africa' (23 December 2019), available at <https://www.weforum.org/organizations/centre-for-the-fourth-industrial-revolution-south-africa> (accessed 21 October 2022).

56 Presidency of the Republic of South Africa, 'President appoints Commission on Fourth Industrial Revolution' (9 April 2019), available at <https://www.thepresidency.gov.za/press-statements/president-appoints-commission-fourth-industrial-revolution> (accessed 21 October 2022).

of poverty unemployment and inequality. In the context of a timeline of global economic progress, the report seeks to contextualize digital transformation within an African context: "[i]n Africa's development outlook in the fourth IR, we seek to understand the kind of balance that must be struck between science and capital, in order to produce economic competitiveness and societal wellbeing"[57].

The report envisages dramatic change, that will impact both the policy process itself as well as the legal frameworks that would be affected by such change. Change will embrace expansion of fiber broadband, data centers, 5G wireless infrastructure, the states' need for computing and storage facilities, cybersecurity, and institutional and operational capacity. It is crucial to note that the report shows an awareness, at least in principle terms, that such change must take place within a particular constitutional ethos in South Africa:

> [i]n keeping with the ethos of the South African constitution, the 4IR must become a citizens' initiative, rooted in communication among sectors of society, to ensure awareness, inclusive participation and collaborative construction of the desired path forward. There is also a need for youth participation in this revolution and the mandate of the National Youth development agency (NYDA) should be expanded to drive this[58].

But how will this practically happen? What are some of the early signs and signals in one of Africa's most important democracies where these technological changes will be spearheaded? Early signs show that special efforts need to be made to ensure that the positive promise of the four IR technologies are realized. These technologies will need to be sufficiently sensitive to the significant demands of the South African Bill of Rights and particularly mindful of its vertical and horizontal application that will test the public and private sectors' commitment to first-and second-generation human rights.

This balancing act will take place against the rich textured map of jurisprudence on rights matters in South Africa's Constitutional Court, and against the questions that arise in the newly evolving context of the fourth IR where public action and private contracting will have to be held to the same rigorous standards in a context of the new hybridized forms of decision making this will generate. In the case of South Africa, at least, the horizontal and vertical application of the Bill of Rights will mean that neither the public nor the private

57 Department of Communications and Digital Technologies, *supra* fn 18, 13.
58 Department of Communications and Digital Technologies, *supra* fn 18, 172.

sector will be able to move away from any of the commitments in the Bill of Rights due to algorithmically inspired decision-making processes. In fact, the South African Constitution's Bill of Rights may prove to be the biggest test of hybrid public and private power in an African context.

A couple of examples are necessary to illustrate how important it will be for the deployment, and development, of these nascent technologies and algorithmically assisted decision making in the South African context to be subjected to rigorous standards of transparency and robust tests of their claims to be 'neutral' and 'bias-free' if the constitutional imperative a rights-based constitutional state is to be adhered to.

This is more pertinent in a country that is slowly recovering from a period of devastatingly ravaging state capture that has compromised and weakened all state institutions. Two examples, one from the public and one from the private sector, serve to illustrate the point. The first example, from the public sector, is the case of the algorithm deployed by the South African Revenue Service (Section 3.1). The second example, from the private sector, is the case of Vumatel and Vumacam, deployed within the broader private security industry within South Africa where CCTV cameras are blanketing SA suburbs under permanent surveillance using facial recognition software and algorithmically assisted profiling (Section 3.2).

3.1 *The Public Sector: SARS and Its Risk-Based Algorithm*

In an appearance before the South African parliament in early March 2022, the South African Revenue Service's Commissioner, its titular head the SARS Commissioner, defended the agency's adoption of a 'risk' based algorithm drawing powerfully on the assumed neutrality of the algorithm. In an appearance before the committees of parliament, he implied that a risk-based algorithm that selects taxpayers at random for tax return verification based on risk indemnifies the tax collector from accusations that it is acting in an arbitrary fashion or as a 'bully':

> The claim that we bully the little man and we allow the bigger entities to go it's not borne out by the evidence. Our risk engine is agnostic as to who the taxpayer is and responds only to the risk rules and the algorithms that we write. You are selected for verification not because you are a little guy or a big guy but because you are a risk to the fiscus, potentially non-compliant and even criminal[59].

59 Edward Kieswetter, as reported by Marianne Merten, 'Is the South African Revenue Service's risk algorithm the glitch in the tax collectors' matrix' (8 March 2022) *Daily*

Whilst this assertion was made with respect to value added tax returns in South Africa, it is indicative of an approach that will also inform individual personal tax returns. The Commissioner made the point before Parliament that 66% of the cases picked up by the risk-based algorithm would be habitual non compliers, and 20% of personal tax return cases would be selected by the risk-based engine. The extent to which he opted to depersonalize the process by continuing to emphasize that the process of risk selection is done by the algorithm, not by the formal public sector decision makers in their formal roles, is perhaps, arguably, a step too far given the country's well developed tax case law, its Bill of Rights, and its taxpayers charter and the presence of a dedicated Tax Ombud regulatory authority tasked with overseeing the South African Revenue Service.

The Tax Ombud is a regulatory structure aimed at functioning as a special administrative protective structure given the special status that the South African Revenue Service enjoys as a special entity outside of the normal strictures of the South African public service. Assertions by the Commissioner that there is no source code 'opinion' here as to who is selected is therefore not acceptable in the context of constitutional protections that exist in the South African constitution against arbitrary exercises of administrative powers and strong constitutional and national law protections mitigating for administrative review rights and information provision (enshrined in sections 32 and 33 of the South African Constitution) in particular. These rights are further buttressed by a strong data protection system embracing both the Protection of Personal Information Act (POPIA)[60] as well as the Promotion of Access to Information Act (PAIA)[61] and the administrative justice provisions contained in South Africa's Promotion of Administrative Justice Act (PAJA)[62]. The level of personal concerns about SARS continues to grow as is evidenced by more complaints and greater levels of activity on the part of the dedicated Tax Ombud. Given the new level of algorithmically assisted decision making that has been adopted in a specialised agency of the South African state, it will become an important testing terrain for the trade-offs that will be made in

---

Maverick, available at <https://www.dailymaverick.co.za/article/2022-03-08-is-the-sa-revenue-services-risk-algorithm-the-glitch-in-the-tax-collectors-matrix/> (accessed 21 October 2022).

60 Protection of Personal Information Act 4 of 2013, available at <https://www.gov.za/documents/protection-personal-information-act> (accessed 21 October 2022).

61 Promotion of Access to Information Act 2 of 2000, available at <https://www.gov.za/documents/promotion-access-information-act> (accessed 21 October 2022).

62 Promotion of Administrative Justice Act 3 of 2000, available at <https://www.justice.gov.za/legislation/acts/2000-003.pdf> (accessed 21 October 2022).

adopting such a system within the South African public sector more generally. Having been a critical arena of state capture in South Africa, the rebuilding of the revenue authority must be extra sensitive to the rule of law context in which it operates and rebuilds. The Tax Ombud is grappling with growing complaints, having addressed 1340 out of 2967 complaints in the 2020/2021 financial year, according to its annual report, and promising to finalize a compendium of Taxpayers' Rights – which has trended on South African social media as #TaxPayersRightsMatter[63].

Beyond the SARS risk algorithm, some municipalities in South Africa are using algorithms as a mechanism to manage their indigent register. In the case of the South African Revenue Authority as well as the Drakenstein Municipality local authority, this is placed on the level to which the decision is placed further away from the politics as a distinctive positive development. This is in stark contrast to growing literature that reveals the extent to which such algorithmic decision making is not in fact neutral and may not be for a host of reasons related to buyers or actual policy decisions that influence the bias in coding terms. As Razzano has emphasized, one of the glaring challenges in South Africa – one of Africa's states with more datasets readily available – is that there are biases in data sets or even just profound inaccuracies and underlying data that inhibit predictive tools and algorithms from functioning soundly[64].

Given the countries' dramatically complex past of racial segregation and efforts at transformative policies and politics in its politics and policy, datasets may be deeply compromised and problematic, certainly with any deeper longitudinal base in mind. The extent to which the data protection legislation can assist is limited and future focused. It cannot address past data problems or longitudinal statistical glitches in datasets that are underlying. In a context such as this, which is highly complex, reliance on 'black box' data set arguments will run into a wall of transparency requests accentuated as it will be by the country's history of a quest for equal rights for all its citizens. Demands for transparency by design will be considerable and, it is in fact, what the 4IR Commission envisages as a guiding principle in any event.

63 Office of the Tax Ombud, 'Tax Ombud's Annual Report 2021/22' (2022), 2, 27, 39, available at <https://www.taxombud.gov.za/wp-content/uploads/2022/09/Tax-Ombud-Annual-Report-202122.pdf> (accessed 21 October 2022).

64 Gabriella Razzano, 'Transparency and accountability are fundamental for the use of algorithms in the public sector' (9 March 2022) *Daily Maverick*, available at <https://www.dailymaverick.co.za/opinionista/2022-03-09-transparency-and-accountability-are-fundamental-for-the-use-of-algorithms-in-the-public-sector/> (accessed 21 October 2022).

A racially segregated history of exclusion from crucial public services, the sheer risk of any form of exclusion due to an algorithm or an algorithmically assisted decision-making process that falls foul of constitutional provisions and progressive realization of human rights will be a profound and existential moral hazard in a country as complex as South Africa. Engendering trust in such systems, were they to be adopted across different segments of the public sector, will be crucial. This rings true for both the public and private sectors that will be involved in such processes of the South African body politic more generally. This is ever more so where there are public private sector partnerships that have already entrenched a degree of cross sectoral collaboration in the country.

Whilst the rights of citizens (or 'data subjects'), protected as they are in POPIA will be crucial, the need for proper transparency and more accountability will be more pronounced than ever in the aftermath of what was termed to have been the capture of the South African state by private interests as evidenced in the findings and recommendations for reform of the state in the report of the Zondo Commission of inquiry[65].

The collection of and quality of data which the South African state has on its population will be a mission critical factor for any notion of algorithmically assisted decision making in the public sector. This is a profound challenge for a state that has traditionally had fragmented data sets and that is trying to conduct its latest iteration of its South African national census.

The adoption of algorithmically assisted systems and AI systems, under the broader banner of 4IR, are aimed at leveraging technology to address poverty unemployment and inequality in South Africa and the broader continent. This will have clear budgetary and procurement implications not only within the South African state but across the African continent. South Africa's 4IR Commission envisages exactly such procurement:

> This consumptive power is an opportunity for the state to determine the forms of four IR production it is willing to reward/incentivize through procurement. In so doing, the state, as procurer, can directly determine the emergence of 4IR industries that respond to its consumption appetite as well as the national economic development objectives[66].

65 Judicial Commission of Inquiry into Allegations of State Capture, Corruption and Fraud in the Public Sector including Organs of State, *supra* fn 26.

66 Department of Communications and Digital Technologies, *supra* fn 18, 37.

The report emphasizes the education, health, social and economic infrastructure and policing services areas as ripe for such technology procurements. These are exactly the areas of policy and public services where a host of other countries have already invested in what has been termed the first wave of algorithmically assisted decision-making processes within the public sector reviewed by the ADA Lovelace Institute report cited above[67].

It is with the crime and policing sector in mind that we now turn to another area where algorithmic decision making, and a level of profiling, is already visible in South Africa. In this instance, it is present in the private sector given the level of involvement and role of the private sector within the private security space in South Africa – which has supplemented the work of the South African Police Service (SAPS) and the South African National Defence Force (SANDF) since the early years of the transition to democracy in the early 1990s in the country.

What makes this application of technology within the private sector slightly more unusual is that it is not the private sector being contracted by the public sector formally but an entirely private sector entity playing a disproportionate role given the significant role which the private security industry plays in the South African security space.

3.2 *The Private Sector: Vumatel and Vumacam, CCTV Surveillance and Algorithms and Security*

Before focusing on the South African material, however, it is important to point to a similar development highlighted within the United States for comparative purposes, and to contextualize the South African case.

In the United States of America, Amazon ring cameras are ubiquitous in American private neighborhoods with what already amounts to the company's privatized surveillance system[68]. This may be falling foul of pro-privacy legislative prescripts drawing the attention of some senators such as senator Edward Markey. Amazon has encouraged formal partnering between camera owners, law enforcement and other departments creating a current of data which police can scan, without any warrants, using and leveraging the consent of residential private camera owners. There is therefore a pattern emerging of invasive data collection and private sector collaboration with police departments without the private sector being bound by the strictures, checks, and

67 Ada Lovelace Institute et al., *supra* fn 22.

68 Sam Biddle, 'Sen. Ed Markey Calls on Ring to Make Itself Less Cop-Friendly' (14 June 2022) *The Intercept*, available at <https://theintercept.com/2022/06/14/amazon-ring-camera-police-privacy-ed-markey/> (accessed 21 October 2022).

balances that apply to policing powers that are formally being exercised by the state – which, theoretically, has the monopoly on the use of force and coercive instruments. Such datasets can then be mixed and used to enhance facial recognition systems and profiling systems outside of the remit of the public sector and its oversight systems. It is necessary to point out that ring video doorbells can also record audio and that this is therefore a formidable surveillance system. The police ought not to be able to monitor the public through entirely private means. This falls outside of the remit of rights protections citizens enjoy and is entirely illegal. Doorbell cameras ought not to aid an unchecked proliferation of surveillance capacities without the requisite oversight of the state.

Within South Africa, this exact scenario is playing out where a private companies' smart CCTV network systems are being accused, by some more critical authors, of driving what has been termed 'AI powered apartheid' in South African suburbs[69]. The CCTV systems in question, Vumacam, have video analytics abilities to track individual faces, behaviors, objects and patterns it could all of Johannesburg with 15,000 cameras. What is resulting in practice is an AI driven rollout of a nationwide CCTV network in a still deeply racially divided country, which finds itself in the hands of a private sector entity not subject to the same human rights base checks and balances as the state. The efforts by two South African fiber companies, Fibrehoods and Vumatel, to bring fiber to people's front door and with it, the backbone for a nationwide Vumacam AI-powered CCTV network is akin to that of Amazon Ring in the United States of America where this has already proven to be controversial.

Given that the South African private security sector is bigger than the formal police and military sectors combined, and outguns the formal forces at a ratio of three to one, this is a powerful surveillance backbone for an inadequately regulated industry in private hands despite the best efforts of the sectoral regulator the private security industry regulatory authority (PSIRA). Some of the Vumacams are now equipped with modern video analytics, along with infrared and thermal imaging. According to Kwet, Vumacam uses Australia's iSentry – software developed for Australia's military to detect unusual behavior – and Israeli Briefcam – software developed and used to summarise video action for post-incident reports and probes –[70]. Whilst Briefcam has the capacity to do so, Vumacam claims not to be using its facial recognition capabilities, but only

69 Michael Kwet, 'Smart CCTV Networks are Driving an AI Powered Apartheid in South Africa' (22 November 2019) *Motherboard Tech by Vice*, available at <https://www.vice.com/en/article/pa7nek/smart-cctv-networks-are-driving-an-ai-powered-apartheid-in-south-africa> (accessed 21 October 2022).

70 Kwet, *supra* fn 69.

to use automatic license plate recognition technology (ALPR) in South African suburbs where its services are present.

According to Kwet, "what constitutes 'abnormal behavior detection' appears to be racially biased in a region where security officers disproportionately target people of color"[71].

The rise of systems reflecting all the underlying possible racial assumptions a culture might make as part of the DNA of the system, with dire human rights consequences, is more pronounced in the private sphere. At least the South African Bill of Rights has a horizontal and vertical application and holds the private sector to as high as standard as the public in this regard.

South Africa cannot afford to have the pass laws of its past reincarnated as the AI powered closed circuit television footage of the present. Such systems pave the way for massive violence in a country with a fragile history and young constitution and Bill of Rights. Whilst Vumacam engages with the South African Police Service (SAPS), it claims that police require a subpoena before they release any footage. Such wall-to-wall surveillance enables pattern-of-life-analysis by algorithms for both government and corporate analysis and are replete with moral hazard as has been seen from drone strikes elsewhere in a different military context.

Given the constitutional architecture, and South Arica's POPIA data protection provisions akin to the European Union's General Data Protection Regulation (GDPR), it stands to reason that Vumacam and Vumatel may be in breach of these provisions despite the political support such systems appear to enjoy from the dominant political parties within the country given its fragile security situation.

A higher standard of rights protections and respect ought to be expected from the country that only a few decades back opted to dismantle the shackles of an oppressive rights denying system. One of the core test cases will be to see whether the data protection laws that exist permit massive surveillance in the name of security regardless of broader rights implications for the private and public sector alike. As can be clearly seen, the analogies between Amazon Ring and Vumacam in the United States and South Africa, respectively, are deeply troubling as they bring AI systems into human rights spaces without proper checks and balances normally associated with instances where the state exercises its surveillance powers subject to legal restraints. The hybridization of public and private power requires proper and robust legal and regulatory responses that protect human rights and administrative law.

---

71 Ibidem.

South Africa's Bill of Rights and constitutional architecture overall, as well as its clear provisions for access to information and just administrative action provisions set out in the constitution and in national legislation, clearly demarcate the terrain of transparency and accountability as cornerstones for the South African public sector. This implies that any administrative action, including administrative action that is incorporating AI, machine learning systems and any form of algorithmically assisted decision making, must adhere to those sets of interlocking human rights and legal provisions and would therefore be reviewable in South African courts. Any form of digital transformation within the South African public sector, and state, including any decisions to procure such systems, with a globally sourced or localized versions of globally sourced technology, will be reviewable in South African courts.

Such review will also be possible under the Public Finance Management Act[72] and section 217 of the South African Constitution that will require proper competitive bidding as well as due process provisions that ensure all prospective suppliers are treated equally. What will be required however will be a set of public sector leaders that understand these systems and the importance of maintaining meaningful human control over them in a complex country such as South Africa, and a bureaucracy that can digest the shift from street level bureaucrats to what Plantinga refers to as 'system-level-bureaucrats' that merely 'steer' public sector decisions through algorithms[73].

In a public management context where AI, machine learning systems and algorithmically assisted decision-making systems becomes mainstream, the real challenge of epistemic dependence and policy alienation of public officials becomes a real risk. Local understanding of context, reliability of data sets, inclusive decision making, and algorithmic accountability, will be crucial aspects of any deployment of these systems in South Africa and on the African continent more broadly. While such systems carry the promise of leapfrogging for developmental outcomes, they cannot leapfrog localized rule of law and constitutional systems which in some contexts may be fragile transitional post conflict settings where the public sector is only slowly building up levels of trust. This will also be true in states where the state has been hollowed out due to any form of capture or regulatory capture and trust levels are consequently low.

---

72 Public Finance Management Act 1 of 1999, available at <http://www.treasury.gov.za/legislation/pfma/act.pdf> (accessed 21 October 2022).

73 Paul Plantinga, 'Digital discretion and public administration in Africa: Implications for the use of AI' (2022) *Information Development*, available at <https://doi.org/10.1177/02666669221117526> (accessed 21 October 2022).

Beyond the Bill of Rights in South Africa, its citizens ('data subjects' from an AI perspective), enjoy a degree of protection in the Protection of Personal Information Act which is a data protection provision. Protections include inoculations against breaches, theft and discrimination. South Africa, furthermore, has its Cyber-Crime Act aimed at preventing unlawful access to computer systems or computer data storage, and the illegal interception of data as well as the processing of unlawfully intercepted data[74], as well as the Communications Technology Act, which regulates the electronic filing of documents with government agencies and statutory corporations, while also promoting efficient delivery through reliable electronic records[75].

Globally, technology is developing faster than the laws, regulations and case law, and it can expose citizens, data subjects, to a host of risks. As South Africa embarks on implementing key recommendations of its 4IR Commission Report, questions may arise about amending its laws as the country moves into a new era of technology which could determine its success in a global digital economy.

Gottardo addressed the rights-based implications of these new technological decision-making tools, and suggested an algorithmic accountability regime and structure, to be expressly created and based within the UN Human Rights Council[76]. In a similar vein, previous work proposed that the South African Human Rights Commission, a constitutional and statutory Chapter 9 State Institution Supporting Constitutional Democracy (SISCD), ought to be given the role and an expressly adapted mandate which could be achieved by legislative amendment, of being expressly consulted in weighing the rights-based implications of public sector systems that are procured that incorporate AI decision making systems[77].

Under current South African constitutional law, the South African parliament may refer any legislative matter to the constitutional court for a review of its constitutionality[78]. In the same vein, the South African Human Rights

74 Cybercrimes Act 19 of 2020, available at <https://www.gov.za/documents/cybercrimes-act-19-2020-1-jun-2021-0000> (accessed 21 October 2022).

75 Electronic Communications and Transactions Act 25 of 2002, available at <https://www.gov.za/sites/default/files/gcis_document/201409/a25-02.pdf> (accessed 21 October 2022).

76 Gottardo, *supra* fn 48.

77 Raenette Gottardo, 'Algorithmically assisted decision-making in the Public Sector and Constitutional Rights: Beyond Digital Transformation' (2021), paper presented at the 2nd Postdoctoral Research Conference of Southern Africa at Stellenbosch University (on file with the author).

78 South African Constitution, Article 80, available at <https://www.gov.za/documents/constitution-republic-south-africa-1996> (accessed 21 October 2022).

Commission may be given express new powers to bolster its role in terms of the legislative and executive authority[79], as the recommendations of the Fourth IR Commission report finds its way into the policymaking process and onto the legislative agenda[80]. Such a role could contribute to ensuring that policies adopted and enacted by the executive and legislature, the two arms of the South African state, may ensure algorithmically assisted decision-making processes are infused with the rights-based ethos of the South African constitution.

What is currently at stake globally, as these systems are adopted within the public service, is a sea change in how civil servants make decisions and exercise discretion. This implies court challenges for data governance. As McMillan has pointed out in a discussion paper prepared for the Industrial Development Think Tank (IDTT) at the Center for Competition, Regulation and Economic Development at the University of Johannesburg[81], these challenges of data governance must be comprehensively addressed if South Africa is to realize its desire to be a country with the requisite levels of protections, such as the POPIA, that warrants the trust of its citizens ('data subjects') to enable it to enhance the South African brand as the country pursues the realistic opportunity to become a regional and even international hub for data centric services for the African continent and further afield[82].

As McMillan points out[83], South Africa's POPIA's section 17 provides that a person may only be subjected to automated processing under certain conditions if it results in a decision with legal consequences or affects him or her to a substantial degree based solely on automated processing of information for profiling purposes. Such processing is allowed if it is carried out for the conclusion of a contract or alternatively if there is a law or a code of conduct in existence that provides information to the person allowing him or her to make representations as part of the decision-making process.

Whilst section 17 is in keeping with global best practice, such as the EU GDPR, it may prove inadequate as these systems evolve and are adopted making not only the role of the statutory Information Regulator more important

79 South African Constitution, Article 184, available at <https://www.gov.za/documents/constitution-republic-south-africa-1996> (accessed 21 October 2022).

80 Department of Communications and Digital Technologies, *supra* fn 18.

81 Rory McMillan, 'Data Governance: Towards a Policy Framework. Discussion Paper prepared for Expert Panel on Regulating Digital Platforms for Economic Development' (April 2020), available at <https://www.competition.org.za/ccred-blog-digital-industrial-policy/2020/7/6/data-governance-towards-a-policy-framework> (accessed 21 October 2022).

82 McMillan, *supra* fn 81.

83 McMillan, *supra* fn 81, 22.

but also the role of the South African Human Rights Commission and the courts under judicial review.

As the POPIA covers the public and private sector, and the South African ITC sector proliferates, these provisions also enjoy both horizontal and vertical application that binds the public and private sector. The scope for justiciable human rights that can be affected by these systems is clear. McMillan rightly observes that "[f]urther efforts will be needed to determine how much further law and regulation should stretch into setting norms rather than leaving such steps to industry bodies, standards and ethics"[84].

It is the contention of this author that the South African Human Rights Commission will have a significant role to play in such a process as a norm developer that will have global reach due to its close connection to the jurisprudence of the South African Constitutional Court which has its own policy influencer role to play internationally.

Amongst the areas that McMillan flags for possible future policy and legal attention are transparency, the risk of algorithmic bias and the availability of rights and mechanisms to contest decisions and the overall ethics of AI.

On the transparency front, he notes that the POPIA provisions do cater for the provision of sufficient information about the underlying logic of the automated processing to enable a citizen (or 'data subject') to make representations about the decision. As has been noted, the fact that access to information rights and just administrative action rights are contained in the South African Bill of Rights with both vertical and horizontal application, means that those systems can always be subjected to review on constitutional grounds if all else fails. This also holds true with respect to the burning issue of algorithmic bias where race religion and ethnicity in a country like South Africa will bring additional moral hazard mindful of the history and legacy issues that will demand that any and all algorithms all machine learning systems or algorithmically assisted decision making systems or AI deployed in the country will need to prevent unfair discrimination as the constitution prohibits it.

According to McMillan,

> [t]his will involve working out how existing laws should apply to such technologies, and potentially regulating to mitigate the risk of discriminatory outcomes. This might be through a strict liability for disparate impact of decisions or requiring organisations to introduce technical measures that reduce discrimination[85].

84 Ibidem.

85 McMillan, *supra* fn 81, 23.

With respect to rights and mechanisms to contest decisions, McMillan notes that the POPIA only envisages the right to make representations in the case of automated decision making whereas the global trend is moving towards having recourse to a human appeal where an AI system may not be nuanced about detailed circumstances[86]. This is therefore an area of the POPIA that may require attention as it may fall short of constitutionally enshrined rights of review.

On the ethics in AI front, McMillan notes the importance of ethics development as a process along the full life cycle and product life cycle of any system from development through to sale[87]. This is an area where the South African Human Rights Commission can evaluate and elevate a rights-based ethos as a Code of Good Practice ethical norm for both the South African public and private sector – mindful of the country's past and of some of the more recent illustrative examples of SARS and Vumacam that have already been cited above.

The questions of ethical standards, drawing on lessons from the first generation of the development of such systems globally, straddle the ethics and accountability remit and should include internal authorities in organisations approving decisions, recording explicitly designed choices made, accountability for models and their functionality that are deployed and proactive awareness at the levels of brands, channels for inquiries, appeals and any reviews of the implications of systems chosen. South Africa has a set of targets in its 4IR Commission's recommendations and aspires to grow its digital services sector and to stimulate demand from abroad, including under the provision of the new African Continental Free Trade Agreement (AfCTA). To do this successfully, it will need to keep a close watch on global trends and particularly the evolution of debates on ethics and human rights standards if it wishes to secure a localized industry with a possible African market in its list of priorities. In such considerations the human rights question must remain of paramount importance and represents a moral imperative given the country's own past.

McMillan proposes a key a set of measures aimed at bolstering the POPIA to ensure it has the requisite protections to build trust. These include:

> embracing privacy by design and default [rather than allowing privacy to be consented away], required use of data protection impact assessments, adoption of substantive privacy requirements based on the reasonable expectations of consumers and requirements that data be used for a

86 Ibidem.

87 Ibidem.

> legitimate purpose that benefits the individual concerned. Novel mechanisms can be tried, such as legal frameworks for fiduciary responsibility, encouragement of data intermediaries, and personal data management services providers[88].

It seems clear that South Africa's POPIA is but only one step on the long path. Much more will need to be in place on the legislative front if the requisite trust levels to build a localized algorithmically able state with export potential is desired.

Putzier (2017) echoes this sentiment and believes that more would be required on the policy front as the current 4IR Commission Report falls short in some key respects[89]. Whilst the report is viewed as a step in the right direction for greater policy clarity, it seems clear that its contents calls for far deeper societal conversations in the policy space and proper public consultation. Given that the report was released at the height of the COVID-19 pandemic in 2020, its content has not been scrutinized nor debated from a constitutionalist or broader societal vantage point. More concerning still, any debate on its merits will have to address the concerns about state capture highlighted by the Zondo Commission and its clear proposals for reforms of the South African state machinery[90].

The South African state is confronting these challenges and similar challenges confront the African continent, the AU as a regional organization and individual African states. It is therefore important to briefly consider this dimension, if only for the sake of completeness.

4 Africa, AI, MLS and Algorithmic Decision-Making: Quo Vadis?

In 2016 the NEPAD AU Development Agency was tasked by the African Union Heads of State and Government to create a system to source expert opinion on the interrelated questions of technological development, acquisition and its

88 McMillan, *supra* fn 81, 25.

89 Mark Ludwig Putzier, 'The Readiness of the South African Private and Public Sector for the Fourth Industrial Revolution' (2017), Research proposal submitted in partial fulfilment of the requirements for the degree of Masters of Business Administration (MBA) in the Faculty of Business and Economic Sciences in the Graduate School of Business at the Nelson Mandela University, available at <https://core.ac.uk/download/pdf/158296133.pdf> (accessed 21 October 2022).

90 Judicial Commission of Inquiry into Allegations of State Capture, Corruption and Fraud in the Public Sector including Organs of State, *supra* fn 26.

deployment for economic development in Africa. This was a clear continental priority against growing concerns expressed under phrases such as 'cyber colonialism' that invoke images of extractive entities – in this case data as the new commodity – and data mining firms as a new form of 'colonialism'.

This gave rise to growing debates about localization and leveraging technology as a leapfrogging device for African development. These discourses and narratives, in turn, created strong support for the founding of the African Union's 10 member African Union High Level Panel on Emerging Technologies (APET), aimed at advising the African Union on how the continent is to harness innovations and emerging technology for socio economic development[91]. In this sense APET is fulfilling a strong think tank type role to African Union member States, and relies on a set of focus areas to guide its work. Whilst the mandate is quite broad, embracing the adoption of AI machine learning systems and of algorithmically assisted decision making in the African public sector will fall under its mandate squarely as it arises under the prioritized ten emerging technologies for the continent's socio-economic development. The ten priorities are: gene drives, microgrids, drones for precision agriculture, next Gen medicine, artificial intelligence, urban agriculture, synthetic biology, gene editing, 3D printing, next Gen batteries, water purification.

The first three of these focus areas have received the bulk of the thinktanks' attention, and reports and recommendations were launched at the African Union summit in Kigali on 8 June 2018. Currently, APET is dealing with AI, blockchain, next generation batteries and gene editing. There is therefore a fair degree of complementarity between APET's immediate priorities and South Africa's 4IR Commission report priorities. This is not surprising given the policy advocacy role the country plays continentally.

What seems inevitable, coming up beyond law, politics, policy and regulatory frameworks, is that a considerable narrative contestation will unfold on the African continent as far as digital technology and digital transformation is concerned.

Proponents will favor the narrative strands of leapfrogging and economic development to favor and advocate for the fourth industrial revolution, whilst opponents will point to the concerns of data extraction and cyber colonialism and cyber colonization.

What seems certain is that the debate will be had. What also seems certain is that it will play out in a global context of heightened great power competition

91 See <https://www.nepad.org/microsite/african-union-high-level-panel-emerging-technologies-apet> (accessed 21 October 2022).

and tensions that play out as they always have on the African continent where the stark reality is that the African Union's AI race is shaped in many ways by the United States and China. Where the United states dominates the architectural levels (with multinational companies such as Alphabet, Microsoft and Amazon all having opened artificial intelligence labs or innovation hubs in Africa), the counterveiling reality is that China has a strong dominant position on the infrastructure front through a plethora of more affordable mobile devices (such as Huawei and ZTE).

The AI ecosystem in Africa is only in its infant stages and, despite countries like South Africa seeking to establish itself as an AI hub with strategies for localization and continental trade ambitions, the road ahead will be complex. Geopolitics, financing and access to financing and weak rule of law and weak institutions will make this road appear longer and more winding still.

Emphasizing the role played by the Fourth Industrial Revolution in presenting Africa with considerable opportunity, South African president Cyril Ramaphosa – in his capacity as Chairman of the African Union at the 33rd Ordinary Session of the Assembly of Heads of State and Government in Addis Ababa in Ethiopia – called for the creation of an Africa Artificial Intelligence Forum (AAIF)[92]. Emphasizing the need for an African voice in the AI discourse and development, the Next Einstein Forum Report draws on the fact that initiatives such as Black in AI, Alliance for AI and others working with Zindi and Data Science for Africa seek to bring this African voice to the fore.

The possible role of a properly constituted African AI Forum (AAIF), APET, and the African Commission on Human and People's Rights (ACHPR) to see to the human rights dimensions of the evolution of these discourses on the continent will be pertinent. Greater debate will also be necessary to ensure legislative frameworks at a regional level and national level can keep pace. For example, the AU convention on cyber security and personal data protection, adopted in 2014, has only had five states ratifying it[93]. This is a poor legal bedrock on which to roll out systems with such deep and far reaching potential human rights consequences. As far as data protection laws for security and privacy concerns go, only marginally above 50% of African countries, amongst them Kenya and South Africa, have passed such laws.

92 Admire Moyo, 'Africa must establish AI forum, says Ramaphosa' (11 February 2020) *ITWeb*, available at <https://www.itweb.co.za/content/LPwQ5MlyVpzqNgkj> (accessed 21 October 2022).

93 African Union Convention on Cyber Security and Personal Data Protection, adopted on 27 June 2014, available at <https://au.int/en/treaties/african-union-convention-cyber-security-and-personal-data-protection> (accessed 21 October 2022).

If one returns to the cyber colonialism narrative strand, it is easy to see why it has carried such currency, considering that what is at stake is the extraction of personal data at continental level, contestation about the continent's digital architecture, populations that have yet to be connected to technology, international trade laws that could favor and be skewed towards western States and China despite any AfCFTA progress and localization strategies that are, equally, in their infancy. It is no exaggeration from this narrative strand perspective of cyber colonialism to claim that states societies and individuals are facing insurmountable threats to sovereignty, personal freedom, and privacy.

The AU working group on AI met in Cairo on 6 December 2019 where it had its first workshop that identified the need to reach its objective of crafting an African strategy for AI and for the continent to reach a unified position on AI[94]. This group was formed by way of a Ministerial Meeting resolution of the AU's Specialised Technical Committee on Communication and ICT in October 2019. The APEC has specifically recommended a continental AI strategic framework and its forthcoming report 'AI for Africa harnessing artificial intelligence for Africa socioeconomic development' is due for release soon.

Such a strategy will in all likelihood embrace AI economic goals and targets for the African Union, stipulate what frameworks on economic investments and growth will be required, and what the value will be to be gained from such activities for the continent from adopting AI. The adoption and release of the report will see two countervailing narrative strands of cyber colonialism, on the one hand, and economic development through technological leapfrogging, on the other, take center stage.

Other components which such an AU AI continental strategy using the convening power of the AUDA – NEPAD and APET will embrace are as follows: financial investments for AI, venture capital for AI, the role of trade and AFCTA in continental AI, commercialization of AI in Africa, the creation of an AI fund, revisions of regulations and crafting of new regulations and policies conducive to African AI companies and their creation, growth and expansion.

This process will evolve rapidly and the Calestous Juma Executive Dialogue on Innovation and Emerging Technologies (CJED) will undoubtedly play a role in the narrative discourse to address views on AI through policy briefs, working papers and other documents. At a legacy level, consequently, his work 'The New Harvest: Agricultural Innovation and Its Enemies' (2011) and 'Innovation

94 Egyptian Ministry of Communications and Information Technology, 'Egypt Hosts AU Working Group on AI First Session' (6 December 2019), available at <https://mcit.gov.eg/en/Media_Center/Press_Room/Press_Releases/40507> (accessed 21 October 2022).

and Its Enemies: Why People Resist New Technologies' (2016) will remain highly influential in cyber colonialism discourses[95].

In terms of narrative strands, it is important to note that the draft Digital Transformation Strategy for Africa (2020 to 2013 DTS) is being drafted by the AU[96]. The Strategy mentions AI specifically as the leapfrogging opportunity. In the document, AI is mentioned in the context of digital innovation entrepreneurship, digital industry, emerging technologies, as a policy recommendation to be adopted by the public and private sectors, and as an area for which a digital single market must be created. The DTS expressly calls for a Digital Single Market (DSM) drawing its inspiration from the EU's DSM announced in 2015 which aims to create such an EU wide market for access to online products and services, to foster market conditions favoring the growth of digital networks and services, and the overall growth of the EU digital economy. The AU DTS document envisages and sets as its objective a digital single market in Africa by 2030. The prospect of such a market will influence the use of AI in Africa in the future.

What is lacking in the equation is the realization of exactly how dramatically AI will reconfigure our society and the economy, and how the public and private sectors across the African continent will operate and be reshaped by these forces for change.

Whilst the possible gains cannot be naysaid, proper thought needs to be given to the impact this will have on ethics, governance and society more generally. The deeper impact on human rights in societies where the rule of law and state institutions may be weak, requires deeper consideration not only rhetorical gloss or starkly contrasting narrative positions for practical or utilitarian persuasive purposes.

Whilst an AU's AI continental strategy will be a big step forward, the human rights component must be taken cognizance of as an emergency. The continental, regional and national AI innovation ecosystems and AI institutes that may be established must have a human rights component to secure the overall well-being of the people of the continent if they ought to be regarded as more

95 Calestous Juma, *The New Harvest: Agricultural Innovation and Its Enemies* (OUP 2011); Calestous Juma, *Innovation and Its Enemies: Why People Resist New Technologies* (OUP 2016).

96 African Union, 'The Digital Transformation Strategy for Africa (2020–2030)' (2020), available at <https://au.int/sites/default/files/documents/38507-doc-dts-english.pdf> (accessed 21 October 2022). A proper analysis of the AU Strategy on AI, as well as a proper benchmarking against the strategies of other regional bodies is not possible at the time of writing as its release is pending.

than mere 'data subjects' to be harvested and commercially harnessed. The people of the AU will need to be seen as crucial co-creators of leapfrogging and development.

In this regard, it is important to take sufficient cognizance of the African Commission on Human and People's Rights' resolution number 473 on the need to undertake a study on human and people's rights and artificial intelligence (AI), robotics and other new and emerging technologies in Africa, passed in February of 2019[97].

The resolution called to the opportunities and perils of artificial intelligence in Africa and its impact on human rights, specifically in the context of the AU science, technology and innovation strategy for Africa in the context of the fourth industrial revolution. The resolution properly places special emphasis on the need to infuse any AI discourse in Africa with the continent's own norms:

> Emphasizing the need for sufficient consideration of African norms, ethics, values such as Ubuntu, communitarian ethos, freedom from domination of one people by another, freedom from racial and other forms of discrimination in framing of global AI governance frameworks[98].

The resolution calls for the need to undertake a proper study on the impact of AI robotics and other new and emerging technologies on human and people's rights in Africa. It urges that any AI developments be compatible with the rights and duties states have in the African Charter and that AI be made applicable to the African continent and properly localized and governed bearing in mind the continental norms and values that have to prevail in any governance frameworks. The resolution is cognizant of the need for transparent use of such systems and calls for them to be made easily understandable by those that will be affected by their decisions and decisions made by such systems. The resolution calls expressly for a comprehensive legal and ethical governance framework for AI to ensure compliance with the EU charter, and other regional treaties, and urges the EU and regional bodies to prioritize developing regional regulatory frameworks for AI and new technologies.

The resolution appeals to all state parties to the convention to ensure proper meaningful human control in any systems or AI or technology that is adopted

97 African Commission on Human and People's Rights, 'Resolution Resolution on the need to undertake a Study on human and peoples' rights and artificial intelligence (AI), robotics and other new and emerging technologies in Africa. ACHPR/Res. 473' (2021), available at <https://www.achpr.org/sessions/resolutions?id=504> (accessed 21 October 2022).

98 African Commission on Human and People's Rights, *supra* fn 97.

in their countries to safeguard fundamental human rights and commits itself to undertake a study in order to further develop guidelines and norms that address issues relating to AI technologies, robotics and other new and emerging technologies and their impact on human rights in Africa working together with an African group of experts on AI and new technologies.

There is therefore a need to build an immediate, strong, and enduring bridge between the work of APET and the work of the African Commission on Human and People's Rights as enunciated in resolution 473 of February 2021 to ensure that Africa's citizens remain her full citizens and do not become only 'data subjects' in a new digital age.

CHAPTER 9

Governance and Quantification of Performance in China

Ivan Cardillo

1 Introduction

China's impressive development over the last four decades has been possible thanks to a strong emphasis on results and performances. Fundamentally, in a country that practices a planned economy, it is important to develop a system to guarantee that the right people are appointed for the right jobs, and that results are not only obtained but also obtained at the expected time. China's state governance approach is based on the following steps: planning, organizing, staffing, leading, controlling the work quality, and timing. Thus, all social actors are subject to a system of assessment of performances. For the Chinese leadership, it is a matter of fighting against laziness (懒 *lan*) and a lazy government (懒政 *lanzheng*)[1], and, most importantly, to manage the difficulties in effective governance and balance centralized policies with local needs, especially in remote areas and in a country like China, geographically big and with a centralized government.

The chapter intends to present the numerous assessment systems designed and applied in the country, especially those in relation to state-administered justice, state administration, assessment of Party's members, public education, and society in general, thus providing an overall picture of how metrics work in China.

What emerges is a comprehensive system of state's management and governance of the society deeply based on performances, where systems of assessment dictate punishments and awards based on principles of morality, trust, and compliance with the law. Chinese society governance is based on the *san jia ma che* (三驾马车, a two-wheeled chariot drawn by a team of three horses),

1 See 宋小宁， 佟健， "懒政"、综合政绩考核与政府机构改革，《经济社会体制比较》(Xiaoning Song and Jian Tong, '"Lazy Administration", Comprehensive Performance Evaluation and Government Organization Reform' (2019) 2 *Comparative Economic & Social Systems*) 127–133 at <http://www.aisixiang.com/data/119612.html> (accessed 11 February 2023).

 | DOI:10.1163/9789004680944_010

the three horses being the legal system, the system of social credit, and the system of the culture of morality, implemented by the binding force of the law, of credit rules and moral rules. The current challenge for the leadership is to find the best way to combine together[2].

2 State-Administered Justice

A system of appraisal of judges' work was already part of the Judges Law when adopted for the first time in 1995[3]. Recently revised in 2019, the law dedicates to the matter the entire Chapter 6, emblematically titled "Evaluation of, Rewards for and Disciplinary Actions against Judges". The examination and evaluation of judges, carried out by a special committee established within the court, evaluate the judge's performance in judicial work, professional ethics, professional level, working ability, and style of judgment, but the emphasis should be on judicial work[4]. Results fall into four grades: excellent, competent, basically competent, and incompetent, and they constitute the basis for the adjustment of salary, award, punishment, removal, demotion, and dismissal[5]. Performances worthy of reward are:

(1) having made remarkable achievements in realizing impartial justice;
(2) having made outstanding achievements in summarizing experience in judicial practice that may serve as a guide in judicial work;
(3) having made significant achievements and contributions in handling major cases, handling emergencies and undertaking special important work;
(4) having made proposals for the reform of judicial work that have been adopted and have produced remarkable results;
(5) having made judicial proposals that have been adopted, and having achieved remarkable results in publicizing the importance of the

2 See吴晶妹， 信用立法思考：未来我国三大信用法,《法学杂志》 (Jingmei Wu, 'Thoughts on Credit Legislation: China's Three Future Credit Laws' (2022) 3 *Law Science Magazine*) 85–98.

3 Judges Law of the People's Republic of China (2019 Revision). This paragraph focuses on the assessment system for judges, but it is due to mention that a parallel system has been designed for prosecutors and people's procuratorates too.

4 Judge Law article 41.

5 Judge Law article 42.

legal system and guiding mediation organizations in the mediation of all kinds of disputes;

(6) having performed other meritorious deeds.

In 2008, the Supreme People's Court issued a guiding opinion[6] launching the trial period of a scientific and unified case quality evaluation system (CQES) as part of the 'Outline of the Second Five-Year Reform of the People's Courts'[7]. In March 2011, in light of the successful results of the trial implementation period, the Supreme Court gave final approval to the CQES and published a decisive guiding opinion to launch a national system of "case quality" assessment of China's courts and judges[8], and the 'Guiding Opinions to Improve Case Quality Evaluation'[9].

The CQES means to "design various indices to judge the fairness, efficiency and effects of the trial work of the people's courts, use all available judicial statistical data, apply multi-indicator evaluation technology, establish a quantified model for case quality evaluation, and calculate the composite indices of case quality to make overall judgment and analysis on the quality of cases handled by the people's courts at all levels of the whole nation"[10], in line with the purposes, functions and characteristics of the trial work of the people's courts.

The CQES is not simply a practical tool for the administration of justice, but it fulfills key functions of the constitutional architecture of the legal system too. It is functional to the constitutional principle of democratic centralism, according to which all administrative, supervisory, judicial and procuratorial organs of the State are created by the people's congresses, to which they are responsible and by which there are overseen, and the National People's Congress and the local people's congresses at various levels are responsible to the people and subject to their supervision[11]. Furthermore, local people's

6 Supreme People's Court, 'Notice of the Supreme People's Court on Issuing the Guiding Opinion of the Supreme People's Court on Carrying out the Case Quality Evaluation Work (for Trial Implementation)' ('最高人民法院印发《最高人民法院关于开展案件质量评估工作的指导意见(试行)》的通知') (2008).

7 Original title '人民法院第二个五年改革纲要'.

8 See Supreme People's Court, "The Supreme People's Court Officially Issues Guiding Opinions on Case Quality Evaluation" ('最高人民法院正式发布案件质量评估工作指导意见') (2011) at <https://www.court.gov.cn/zixun-xiangqing-2298.html> (accessed February 11, 2023).

9 Original title '最高人民法院发布指导意见完善案件质量评估'.

10 Supreme People's Court, *supra* fn 6, paragraph 1.

11 Article 3 of the Constitution. Ultimately courts are subject to the supervision of the people. Scholars have argued that people's supervision would lead to a populist administration of justice. See Benjamin L. Liebman, 'A Populist Threat to China's Courts?', in

courts at various levels are responsible to the organs of the state power which created them[12]. Thus, the CQES is presented as an objective, scientific and fair system to supervise judicial work and realize democratic centralism. The scientific character is declared to be found in the metric logic of indices.

The CQES is based upon modularized methods to design indices and elaborate their combination and evaluation. The evaluation index system is composed of three grade II indices, namely justice, efficiency, and effects of trial work. The grade II indices are composed of thirty-three grade III indices.

The index of justice in trial work is composed of eleven grade III indices, namely, the ratio of cases the jurisdiction over which is changed, the ratio of cases under trial by jury in the first instance, the ratio of cases whose first judgment is changed in appeal, ratio of cases remanded by the appeal court to the court of the first instance for new trial, ratio of cases whose effective judgment is changed, ratio of effective cases remanded for new trial, ratio of cases subject to the second instance, ratio of cases with discontinuation or termination of enforcement, ratio of cases under illegal trial, ratio of cases under illegal enforcement, and ruling paper quality index.

The index of efficiency in trial work is composed of eleven grade III indices, namely, the ratio of cases placed on file within the statutory time limit, the per capita number of concluded cases in the people's courts, the annual per capita number of cases concluded by judges, ratio of cases concluded against cases placed on file, case conclusion equilibrium level, ratio of cases for which the summary procedure is applied in the first instance, ratio of cases for which judgment is made in court, ratio of the average trial time against the time limit for concluding trial, ratio of the average enforcement time against the time limit for enforcement, ratio of the average duration when cases are not concluded against the time limit for concluding trial, and ratio of the average duration when enforcement is not concluded against the time limit for enforcement.

The index of effects in trial work is composed of eleven grade III indices, namely, the ratio of appeal cases, the ratio of petition cases, the ratio of cases concluded through mediation, the ratio of cases withdrawn, the ratio of complaints by letters and visits, the ratio of repeated complaints by letters and visits, the ratio of cases actually enforced, the ratio of cases whose execution objects are realized, the ratio of cases whose judgment is voluntarily executed,

---

Margaret Y.K. Woo and Mary E. Gallagher (eds), *Chinese Justice: Civil Dispute Resolution in Contemporary China* (Cambridge University Press 2011) 269–313.

12 Article 133 of the Constitution. See also article 9 of the Organic Law of the People's Courts of the People's Republic of China.

the ratio of cases whose complaints are settled by the first judgment, and index of public satisfaction level.

The Supreme People's Court determines the weight number of each evaluation index in order to reflect its importance.

Evaluation index data are social, political, economic, and cultural information collected from several sources and channels such as trial process administration, legal papers, statistical ledger, judicial statistical statements, discipline inspection statistical statements, questionnaire from National People's Congress' deputies, Chinese people's Political Consultative Conference's members, supervisors over honest and clean government, the parties concerned and their attorneys and the general public, non-governmental investigation agencies, and the Statistical Yearbook of the government. All data should be verified and stored in a specific computer database within a judicial statistical system[13].

The actual calculation method of the indexing and the proportion between indicators and indexes, including the mathematic formula, was adopted by the Supreme People's Court in 2013 with the 'Measures for the Indexing of Case Quality Evaluation of the People's Courts (for Trial Implementation)'[14].

In 2021, the system of assessment of judges' work was updated by including additional indicators in order to "adhere to the guidance of Xi Jinping Thought on Socialism with Chinese Characteristics in a New Era, thoroughly implement Xi Jinping Thought on the Rule of Law, follow the organizational line of the Party and the guidelines and policies for work on officials in a new era, focus on building a more scientific and reasonable assessment mechanism that is in better line with judicial laws, put political standards in the first place, highlight the actual effects of assessing the trial and enforcement work of judges, maximize the leading or guiding role of the assessment, and strive to build a team of high-quality professional judges tested competence in politics, business, responsibilities, discipline, and conduct"[15]. With this Notice, the Supreme People's Court set forward indicators related to morality, capability, diligence, performance, and integrity. "Morality" is defined as the implementation of the political ideology of the country, improvement of the capacity for political

13 On the issue of judicial database see Ivan Cardillo, 'Disciplina dell'intelligenza artificiale e intelligentizzazione della giustizia in Cina' (2022) 3 *BioLaw Journal – Rivista di BioDiritto* 139–167.

14 Original title '人民法院案件质量评估指数编制办法(试行)'.

15 See the Supreme People's Court, 'Notice by the Supreme People's Court of Issuing the Guiding Opinions on Strengthening and Improving the Assessment of Judges' ('最高人民法院印发《关于加强和完善法官考核工作的指导意见》的通知') (2021).

judgment, and abiding by political discipline and rules[16]. The assessment of the political quality of judges shall be recorded in specific political quality files. "Capability" refers to legal expertise and work capabilities, including but not limited to laws' and policies' application, risk control, technology use, and public opinion guidance. "Diligence" refers to work style. "Performance" is the main assessment content and includes the number of cases handled, the case-handling quality, the case-handling efficiency, and the case-handling effects. In doing so, judges are expected to safeguard national security and social stability based on the political, legal, and social effects of the cases. Lastly, "integrity" refers to discipline and implementation of the guiding principles of the Eight-Point Frugality Code of the CPC Central Committee[17].

Assessments can be of two types: routine assessment, whose results are divided into four grades, very good, good, fair, and poor, and annual assessment, whose results are divided into four grades, outstanding, competent, basically competent, and incompetent. The assessment results of judges are taken as the basis for the promotion and demotion of judges, the removal of judge quotas, and the distribution of performance bonuses.

The CQES has a deeper impact on judges' work and life if considered in light of the judicial responsibility system. According to such principle, judges, collegial bench, president of the court, judge's assistants, clerks, and judicial police officers, should bear responsibility for their fulfillment of duties[18]. The 'Several Opinions of the Supreme People's Court on Improving the Judicial Accountability System of People's Courts'[19] enacted in 2015, indicates the performance evaluation system as a core tool to evaluate judicial responsibility. Often judges, in order to reduce their responsibility, try to decide similar cases in a similar way[20]. In doing so, they do not simply reduce personal responsibility but also boost the time for handling cases, resulting in better performances. The use of technology is thus fundamental. It allows to publish decisions

16 Supreme People's Court, *supra* fn 15, paragraph II point 8.

17 Available at <http://jtgl.beijing.gov.cn/jgj/jgxx/94246/mtlj/163739/index.html> (accessed February 11, 2023).

18 See articles 33, 39, 41, 48, 49, 50, Organic Law of the People's Courts of the People's Republic of China.

19 Original title '最高人民法院关于完善人民法院司法责任制的若干意见'.

20 This duty is also prescribed by the Supreme People's Court, 'Opinions of the Supreme People's Court on Improving the Working Mechanism for Unifying the Application of Law' '最高人民法院关于完善统一法律适用标准工作机制的意见' (2020).

online, be transparent and fulfill the duty of people's oversight, but also to create a database to find previous decisions[21].

Alongside judges' assessment, the Supreme People's Court, jointly with the Ministry of Justice, adopted in 2019 the 'Measures for the Training, Appraisal, Rewards and Punishments for People's Assessors'[22], for the purpose of regulating the training, appraisal, rewards, and punishments for people's assessors. Basic people's courts and justice administrative agencies at the same level should appraise the performances of the trial duties of people's assessors on a routine base and year-end base. A year-end appraisal shall rate the performances of people's assessors into the grades as excellent, competent, basically competent, and incompetent. The appraisal of people's assessors shall include their ideological level and moral character, work performance as assessors, working attitude, trial discipline, style of judgment and participation in training, and other aspects. The appraisal results serve as a basis for commending and rewarding people's assessors. Of particular importance for a positive evaluation are those behaviors addressed to the maintenance of social stability[23].

Scholars argued that the CQES has a distortive effect on judges' work, resulting in a 'conducting baton'. Judges begin to look for subterfuges to keep good statistics[24]. Typically, near the end of the year, courts may arbitrarily refuse to take cases just to make statistics on the case clearance rate look better or cases that would certainly be appealed by one of the parties[25]. Furthermore, the quality of data collection and the comparison methodology between courts (often the comparison is between courts significantly different from one

21 See Supreme People's Court, 'Provisions of the Supreme People's Court on the Publication of Judgments on the Internet by the People's Courts (2016 amendment)' ('最高人民法院关于人民法院在互联网公布裁判文书的规定 (2016 修订))' (2016); Supreme People's Court, 'Provisions of the Supreme People's Court on the Disclosure of Trial Process Information on the Internet by People's Courts' ('最高人民法院关于人民法院通过互联网公开审判流程信息的规定') (2018). For a comprehensive analysis on the role of technology in the administration of justice, see Cardillo, *supra* fn 13.

22 Original title '最高人民法院、司法部关于印发《人民陪审员培训、考核、奖惩工作办法》的通知'.

23 Ibid., article 24.

24 See Jonathan J. Kinkel and William J. Hurst, 'The Judicial Cadre Evaluation System in China: From Quantification to Intra-state Legibility' (2015) 224 *The China Quarterly* 933–954.

25 See Hangping Chen, 'Doing Justice: Chinese Civil Procedure and Its Reform' (2019) *Civil Procedure Review* 153–170.

another in terms of load of work, type of controversies, and level of difficulty) turn the use of CQES into a case of metric fixation[26].

The strong impact CQES has on judicial activities justifies doubt on its legitimacy in light of the article 131 of the Constitution, which establishes the principle of independence of the judicial power from any interference by any administrative organ, public organization, or individual[27].

3 State Administration, Cadres' Evaluation and Party Evaluation

In the Chinese system, state administration and Party leadership are strictly connected. The scholarly debate defined China's state administration as a "party government system"[28], based on a politics-administration dichotomy model[29], where the party has a superior role. After the constitutional reform of 2018, the leadership of the Communist Party is officially recognized as a constitutional principle[30]. In that same year, the Civil Servant Law was reviewed, and the amended version of article 4 explicitly states that civil servants shall adhere to the leadership of the Chinese Communist Party. In addition, it is important to note that civil servants are also party members. Thus, they are subject to the Party member evaluation system too. So, the Party affects the country management in two different ways, at the constitutional level as a fundamental principle of the legal system and also through the assessment system of its member. For this reason, we discuss the two systems of assessment for civil servants and for party members together.

The first attempt to create a performance appraisal system dates back to the very foundation of the People's Republic of China. In November 1949, the Organization Department of the Central Committee of the Communist

26 Kwai Hang Ng and Peter C.H. Chan, '"What Gets Measured Gets Done": Metric Fixation and China's Experiment in Quantified Judging' (2021) *Asian Journal of Law and Society* 255–281.

27 For a discussion on the issue of the legality of judges' performance appraisal system, see 杨铜铜, 法官绩效考核制度的非司法化困境及其调试《法制与社会发展》(Tongtong Yang, 'The dilemma of non-judicialization of judges' performance appraisal system and its debugging' (2022) *Law and Social Development*) 85–104.

28 陈明明, 在革命与现代化之间:关于党治国家的一个观察与讨论 (Mingming Chen, *Between Revolution and Modernization: An Observation and Discussion about the Rule of the Party*) (Fudan University Press 2015) 31.

29 林弋, 公务员法立法思想研究，林弋主编, 公务员法立法研究 (Yi Lin 'Research on Legislative Thought of Civil Servant Law', in Yi Lin (ed), *Research on the Civil Servant Law* (China Personnel Publishing House 2006)) 15.

30 Article 1, paragraph 2 of the Constitution.

Party of China promulgated the 'Regulations on the Work of Appraisal of Cadre'[31], requiring that the appraisal of cadres should focus on aspects such as positions, viewpoints, styles, policies mastering, observing discipline, contacting the masses, and learning attitude. In January 1951, the Organization Department of the Central Committee proposed to use 'political quality' and 'professional ability' as the criteria for evaluating cadres. 'Quality' and 'ability' became the two keywords for the cadre's evaluation. In December 1953, the Organization Department of the Central Committee issued the 'Notice on How to Conduct the 1953 Year Cadre Appraisal'[32], which stipulated the methods of cadre appraisal, namely: individual review, group discussion, and leadership review[33]. Furthermore, the annual year-end appraisal was changed into the time when cadres were transferred or summarized special work. For cadres who had not been transferred for a long time, the assessment should take place every three years to five years for an appraisal[34].

After the cultural revolution, in 1979, the Organization Department of the Central Committee issued the 'Opinions on Implementing the Cadre Evaluation System'[35] and restored the assessment system as a regular mechanism based on the key principles of morality, ability, diligence, and performance[36].

Deng Xiaoping formulated the principle of "combining political integrity with professional competence" (德才兼备*decai jianbei*)[37]. Since then, "integrity" and "ability" have been the two pillars of officials' selection[38]. Recently,

31 Original title '关于干部鉴定工作的规定'.

32 Original title '关于如何进行 1953 年年终干部鉴定的通知'.

33 For a comprehensive and detailed account of the evolution of the appraisal system in the early decades of PRC, see 孙彩红, 公务员考核的内容与标准 – 历史、现状与未来,《地方政府管理》(Caihong Sun, 'Contents and Standards of Civil Servant Examination – History, Current Situation and Future' (2001) *Local Government Management*) 32–33.

34 The change took place in November 1956 with the 'Notice of the Central Committee on the Year-end Appraisal of Cadres'. See 张铁网, 领导干部考核制度改革与创新, (Tiewang Zhang, *Reform and Innovation of the Examination System for Leading Cadres*, CPC Central Party School Press 2003) 34.

35 Original title '关于实行干部考核制度的意见'.

36 For more information on the evolution of the appraisal system see 戴晓曙, 中国特色干部考核评价制度变迁研究,《社会治理》(Xiaoshu Dai 'Research on the Changes of Cadre Examination and Evaluation System with Chinese Characteristics' (2020) *Social Governance Review*) 24–35.

37 'Resolution on Certain Questions in the History of Our Party since the Founding of the People's Republic of China adopted in 1981', English translation available at <https://digitalarchive.wilsoncenter.org/document/resolution-certain-questions-history-our-party-founding-peoples-republic-china> (accessed February 11, 2023).

38 The decision was also confirmed during the "Resolution of the CPC Central Committee on the Major Achievements and Historical Experience of the Party over the Past Century

the principle has been further elaborated into the formula "possess both ability and political integrity, put morality first and appoint people on their merits" (德才兼备、以德为先，五湖四海、任人唯贤, *de cai jian bei, yi de wei xian, wu hu si hai, ren ren wei xien*)[39]. The assessment system's function is to guarantee that party members remain eligible[40].

If "integrity" stresses political virtue as conformity to ideological ideals, "ability" means good economic performances, and officials are promoted or demoted according to them[41]. "Integrity" and "ability" go hand in hand with the dichotomy of "rule of law" and "rule of virtue", and together constitute two principles of Xi Jinping Thought on the Rule of Law[42]. Xi Jinping Thought on Rule of Law requires: "Fostering a high-quality team of professionals with both integrity and ability for legal work" and "Ensuring that leading officials at various levels faithfully implement major decisions and plans made by the CPC Central Committee on overall law-based governance"[43]. The current five-year development plan reiterates the importance of improving the incentive-oriented performance evaluation mechanism that suits the requirements of high-quality development[44], thus emphasizing concrete results.

---

in 2021", English translation available at <https://english.www.gov.cn/policies/latestreleases/202111/16/content_WS6193a935c6d0df57f98e50b0.html> (accessed February 11, 2023).

39 See 戴晓曙, 中国党政领导干部选拔与考核制度的构成与特点,《中国浦东干部学院学报》 (Xiaoshu Dai, 'Selection and Appraisal System of Talents for Party and Government' (2009) *Journal of China Executive Leadership Academy Pudong*) 38–41. For a historical perspective, see Jérôme Doyon and Long Yang, 'Shades of Red: Changing Understandings of Political Loyalty in the Chinese Communist Party, 1921–2021' (2022) 51 *Journal of Current Chinese Affairs* 386–410.

40 See the 'Regulations on the Selection and Appointment of Party and Government Leading Cadres' ('党政领导干部选拔任用工作条例') issued by the Central Committee of the Communist Party of China.

41 See Zhiyue Bo, 'Economic performance and political mobility: Chinese provincial leaders' (1996) 5 *Journal of Contemporary China* 135–154. See also Hongbin Li and Li-An Zhou, 'Political turnover and economic performance: the incentive role of personnel control in China' (2005) 89 *Journal of Public Economics* 1743–1762. For a discussion on the relationship between political values and performances as the basis of the meritocratic system, see Daniel Bell, *The China Model: Political Meritocracy and the Limits of Democracy* (Princeton University Press 2018).

42 See <http://www.moj.gov.cn/pub/sfbgw/jgsz/jgszjgtj/jgtjzyyfzgbmsj/zyyfzgbmsjtjxw/202203/t20220324_451360.html> (accessed February 11, 2023). Xi Jinping Thought on Rule of Law is an example of deglobalization of the rule of law concept. See Mauro Bussani, 'Deglobalizing Rule of Law and Democracy: Hunting Down Rhetoric Through Comparative Law' (2019) 67 *American Journal of Comparative Law* 701–744.

43 See <http://en.qstheory.cn/2020-12/11/c_571383.htm> (accessed February 11, 2023).

44 See article 63 of the '14th Five-Year Plan for National Economic and Social Development and Long-Range Objectives for 2035', English translation available at

In November 2013, during the Third Plenary Session of the 18th Chinese Communist Party (CPC) Central Committee, the Party adopted the decision of 'Decision of the Central Committee of the Communist Party of China on Several Major Issues Concerning Comprehensively Deepening Reform'[45], which set the goal of improving the modernization of China's system and capacity for governance. Accordingly, the assessment system for development achievements is reformed in order to: "correct the bias in assessing political performance based solely on the rate of economic growth, increase the weight of indicators such as resource consumption, environmental damage, ecological benefits, overcapacity, technological innovation, safe production, and new debts, and pay more attention to labor and employment, residents' income, social security, and people's health status"[46]. According to the Decision the establishment of a scientific system of indicators and assessment standards is essential for the construction of the rule of law[47].

The Central Committee divided officials into three different categories (三支队伍 *sanzhi duiwui*)[48]: officials in Party and government institutions, staff of public institutions, management personnel of state-owned enterprises, and made further efforts to realize the "five differences" (五个区别 *wuge qubie*) or "differentiation" based on the nature of the job, appointment methods, administrative hierarchy, differences in different regions and different stages of development, job responsibilities.

In the same year, the Organizing Department of the Central Committee of the Communist Party of China (CCCPC) issued the 'Notice on improving the performance appraisal of local Party and government leading bodies and leading cadres'[49] in order to reform the evaluation system according to the new guidelines of the Central Committee. Supervision and evaluation became strictly connected, and the level of professionalism has increased. Achievements should be evaluated by adopting an overall appraisal of economic, political,

---

<https://cset.georgetown.edu/wp-content/uploads/t0284_14th_Five_Year_Plan_EN.pdf> (accessed February 11, 2023).

45 Original title '中共中央关于全面深化改革若干重大问题的决定'.

46 Ibid.

47 Ibid., paragraph 30. The development of assessment standards as part of the rule of law reform is further explained in the 'Decision of the CPC Central Committee on several major issues concerning Comprehensively advancing the rule of law' ('中共中央关于全面推进依法治国若干重大问题的决定') adopted in 2014.

48 The concept of '三支队伍' (*sanzhi duiwui*) is a complex concept without a fixed definition. In different contexts, such as party construction or party management, or party in rural areas etc., it refers to different categories.

49 Original title '关于改进地方党政领导班子和领导干部政绩考核工作的通知'.

cultural, social, and ecological impact. Political and personal integrity remain criteria to evaluate officials' abilities. The Notice became now a platform for sharing relevant news, training purposes, tests[50].

3.1 *Civil Servants' Assessment*

Civil servants' work is regulated by the Civil Servant Law of the People's Republic of China[51], lastly revised in 2018. According to this law, civil servants should be appointed on the basis of both integrity and ability, with priority given to integrity, on the basis of merit regardless of origin, on the basis of dedication and impartiality, by highlighting political standards and attaching importance to practical work achievements[52]; consequently, their work is evaluated according to these specific qualities[53]. Assessments are divided into assessments in usual days, special assessments, and assessments on a regular basis. Results can be of four types outstanding, competent, basically competent, and incompetent. The regular assessment result constitutes the basis for adjusting posts, functions, ranks, levels, wages, rewards, training, and dismissal of civil servants. Are considered "good behaviors", among others: active work, having achievements, playing an outstanding exemplary role, maintenance of social stability, saving state assets and property, fighting against acts in violation of disciplines and law, winning honors and interests for the state in foreign exchange and cooperation[54]. Civil servants assessed as "incompetent" in the annual assessment for two consecutive years should be dismissed[55].

In 2020 the Organization Department of the CPC Central Committee revised the "Provisions on the Assessment of Civil Servants"[56], adopted in 2006. The Provisions specify that in assessing civil servants, their morality, capability, diligence, performance and integrity should be assessed comprehensively. "Morality" is referred to political quality and moral character, to be understood as respect for the political ideology; "capability" is referred to political identification ability, learning, investigation, and research capability, the ability of administration by law, and ability to engage with the people, communicate and coordinate, implement, reform and innovate, and respond to

50 See <http://cpc.people.com.cn/GB/67481/94156/372307/?ivk_sa=1024320u> (accessed February 11, 2023).

51 Original title '中华人民共和国公务员法'.

52 Civil Servant Law, article 7.

53 Ibid., article 35.

54 Ibid., article 52.

55 Ibid., article 88.

56 Original title '公务员考核规定'.

emergencies; “diligence” is referred to devotion for work, discipline, dedication; “performance” is referred to quantity, quality, and efficiency of the completed work and the benefits therefrom; “integrity” is referred to the respect for the Eight-Point Frugality Code of the CPC Central Committee.

Local governments, such as people’s governments of all provinces, autonomous regions, and municipalities directly under the Central Government, are subject to a specific system of performance evaluation. In accordance with the ‘Notice of the State Council on Issuing the Quality Development Outline (2011–2012)’[57], the State Council approved, in 2013, the ‘Measures for Quality work Evaluation’[58], for the purpose of evaluating and guiding local governments in further strengthening the quality work, intensifying quality safety responsibilities, and improving the overall quality level. The evaluation year is set to begin on July 1 of each year until June 30. The work is led by the General Administration of Quality Supervision, Inspection and Quarantine, and performed together with the member entities of the Inter-ministerial Joint Meeting for the National Quality Work and experts in the relevant fields.

The evaluation focuses on two aspects: quality safety and quality development in such fields as product quality, project quality, and service quality, and the content of the evaluation includes the completion of quality objectives and the implementation of quality measures.

Points of evaluation are distributed in the following way: forty points for quality goal, based on quantitative indicators of product quality, related to manufacturing product quality and agricultural products quality and safety, and quantitative indicators of engineering quality related to the rate of construction projects; sixty points are assigned for quality measures, based on quality macro management (such as quality development plan formulation and implementation, establishment and operation of quality work coordination mechanism, implementation of brand development strategy, establishment and development of quality statistical analysis system, quality input mechanism operation, industry access and industrial policy implementation), quality and safety supervision (such as Quality Supervision Capability and System Construction, crack down on counterfeiting and shoddy products and special rectification, Quality Integrity Construction, Construction of Quality and Safety Risk Management Mechanism, Construction of Consumer Rights Protection Mechanism, Product Quality Supervision, Engineering Quality Supervision, Service Quality Supervision), quality infrastructure

57 Original title ‘国务院关于印发质量发展纲要（2011–2020年）的通知’.

58 Original title ‘国务院办公厅关于印发质量工作考核办法的通知’.

(such as Standards, metrology, certification and accreditation infrastructure, Inspection and testing technology capacity building, Comprehensive Capacity Building for Port Inspection and Quarantine, Quality Talent Team Construction)[59].

After the evaluation, a final score is assigned, corresponding to four classes, namely, Class A (90 and above), Class B (80–89), Class C (60–79), and Class D (59 and below). Only people's government with a Class A result will have priority in the arrangement of relevant projects. Those getting a Class D should file a report to the State Council and put forward correction measures within a prescribed time limit. The evaluation results shall be delivered to the cadre's administrative departments and the disciplinary inspection and supervision organs to serve as an important basis for the comprehensive evaluation and appraisal, and accountability of the leading groups and leading cadres of the people's governments of the provinces[60].

Finally, special assessment systems have been established for specific purposes, such as the system of the "food basket" (菜篮子*cailanzi*), with the specific purpose of guaranteeing a high-quality agricultural product[61], and the system for the protection of arable land[62], or special categories of workers such as the migrant worker[63].

59 See the annex of the Measures.

60 On the impact of the assessment system of local cadres on the overall administration of the country, see Susan H. Whiting, 'The Cadre Evaluation System at the Grass Roots: The Paradox of Party Rule', in Barry J. Naughton and Dali L. Yang (eds), *Holding China Together. Diversity and National Integration in the Post-Deng Era* (Cambridge University Press 2004) 101–119.

61 See the 'Notice of the General Office of the State Council on the issuance of the methods for the 'food basket' assessment system for mayor's responsibility' ('国务院办公厅关于印发"菜篮子"市长负责制考核办法的通知') (2017), and the recent 'Opinions of the Central Committee of the Communist Party of China and the State Council on Doing a Good Job in Comprehensively Promoting the Key Work of Rural Revitalization in 2022' ('中共中央 国务院关于做好2022年全面推进乡村振兴重点工作的意见') (2022).

62 See the Notice of the General Office of the State Council on the 'Measures for the assessment of cultivated land protection responsibility targets for provincial governments' ('省级政府耕地保护责任目标考核办法') (2018).

63 'Notice of the General Office of the State Council on the issuance of the assessment methods to ensure the payment of wages to migrant workers' ('国务院办公厅关于印发保障农民工工资支付工作考核办法的通知') (2017).

4 Public Education

According to the Teachers Law of the People's Republic of China[64] (adopted in 1993 and revised in 2009) schools or other institutions of education shall conduct an assessment of teachers' political awareness and ideological level[65], professional qualifications, attitude toward work, and performances[66]. In the process of assessment, opinions from teachers themselves, their colleagues, and students shall be taken into full consideration.

Since 2011, a similar system has been established for teachers in kindergartens, primary schools, ordinary middle schools, and secondary vocational schools[67].

The assessment system went through further development in 2016 with the adoption of the 'Guiding Opinions of the Ministry of Education on Deepening the Reform of the Evaluation System for Teachers in Colleges and Universities'[68], which clarified the overall requirements of the assessment: "Put teacher's morality first, teaching as the key, scientific research as the basis, and development as the basic requirements, adhere to the direction of running a socialist school, adhere to both ability and political integrity, pay attention to evaluating teachers based on ability, performance and contribution, and overcome only academic qualifications, professional titles, and only academic qualifications".

The assessment focuses on morality[69], quality, classroom teaching discipline, the orientation of scientific research (i.e. to serve the needs of the

64 Original title '中华人民共和国教师法'.

65 The Teachers Law defines teachers as professionals working for the socialist cause (article 3). Periodical training courses should be taken by all the teachers of the country. The most recent one was on Xi Jinping's Thought on Rule of Law.

66 See article 22 of the Teachers Law.

67 See 'Opinions of the National Education Commission on continuing to do a good job in the trial work of primary and secondary school teacher assessment certificates' ('国家教育委员会关于继续做好中小学教师考核合格证书试行工作的意见') (2011). In 2017 the system was also extended to primary and secondary school teachers, and leaders, see 'Interim Measures for the Administration of Leaders in Primary and Secondary Schools' ('中小学校领导人员管理暂行办法') (2017). In 2019, the 'Policy of Reducing the Burden on Primary and Secondary School Teachers' ('中小学教师减负政策') was introduced, as part of the special work of rectifying formalism, and the supervision, inspection, evaluation, and assessment items that affect teacher education and teaching were cleaned up in a centralized manner, so as to create a good environment for teachers to devote themselves to teaching and educating people.

68 Original title '教育部关于深化高校教师考核评价制度改革的指导意见'.

69 According to the 'Guiding Opinions of Six Departments including the Ministry of Education on Strengthening the Reform of College Teacher Team Construction in the New Era' ('教育部等六部门关于加强新时代高校教师队伍建设改革的指导意见')

country, to serve the national innovation-driven development strategy and local economic and social development)[70].

There are several kinds of assessments: annual assessment, employment period assessment, promotion assessment, etc. Generally speaking, there are two main assessment systems: the annual assessment and the comprehensive assessment, usually every three years. The first is mainly devoted to the assessment of teaching duties. The general requirement is to obtain 208 points (课时 *keshi*). Usually, one teaching hour corresponds to one point, but it can change according to the curricula of students. Supervision of the thesis and participation in the graduation committee is also quantified in points.

The comprehensive assessment evaluates publications (academic journals are ranked in different ways. Publications in 'A plus' journals give more points than those on average Social Sciences Citation Index or Chinese Social Sciences Citation Index, Arts & Humanities Citation Index, SCI), social services (activities for the community connected with science popularization, or consultation for government policy), conferences, research projects (national grants are essential for career development and more prestigious if compared to provincial grants), international cooperation, application of scientific research results.

Evaluation has three possible results: outstanding, qualified (up to standard), or not qualified. The assessment results shall be the basis for teachers' appointment and pay rise as well as rewards, usually cash prizes, punishments, and career development.

For teachers enrolled within the annual salary system (年薪制 *nianxin zhi*), the university withholds 30% of the annual salary. It pays 10% after successfully

---

(2020), and the 'Opinions of the Ministry of Education and Other Six Departments on Strengthening the Construction of Rural Teachers in the New Era' ('教育部等六部门关于加强新时代乡村教师队伍建设的意见') (2020), both adopted in 2020, teacher morality is the primary requirement and first standard for teacher recruitment, professional title review, job employment, tutor selection, evaluation rewards, appointment period assessment, project declaration. All newly recruited teachers in colleges and universities must receive special training on teachers' morality and ethics before starting their jobs. In my case, I had to watch a movie selected by the competent department and write and submit a commentary. Moral cultivation was reiterated as a priority also in 2021 by the State Council in the 'Report of the State Council on the construction of the teaching staff and the implementation of the Teacher Law' ('国务院关于教师队伍建设和教师法实施情况的报告') (2021).

70 This pragmatic approach to research leaves little space in academic journals for those areas not strictly connected with practical needs, such as history. I witnessed many debates of legal historians complaining about the few opportunities they have to publish in top academic journals and, consequently, fewer possibilities for carrier growth.

passing the annual assessment and the remaining 20% after passing the comprehensive assessment.

Besides, the school can award special prizes for particular skills, such as clarity of teaching, students' positive feedback etc.

The assessment is carried out by the scientific committee of the school. Despite the rigid metric of the appraisal procedure previewed by the law, it is not unusual to find decisions merely based on the "spirit of the law".

A dishonest behavior in scientific research integrity should be shared with the national credit information sharing platform and punished in accordance with the law of the state[71].

5 Society in General

For society at large, the Chinese government developed the Social Credit System (SCS), which affects individuals and corporations (Corporate Social Credit System)[72], not only of Chinese nationality but also foreign citizens and companies. The SCS embeds one of the twelve core values of socialism: "honesty" and addresses the issue of a "low trust", morality, and lack of civic virtues in China[73], and constitute one of the tools developed to boost "honesty" within the society[74].

In 2014, the Chinese State Council released the 'Planning Guidelines of Social Credit System Construction (2014–2020)'[75] outlining the goal of establishing a basic social credit system by 2020. In 2018, the National People's

---

71 Article 33 of the 'Regulation on National Science and Technology Awards' ('国家科学技术奖励条例') (2020).

72 Lauren Yu-Hsin Lin and Curtis J. Milhaupt 'China's Corporate Social Credit System: The Dawn of Surveillance State Capitalism?' (2023) 253 *The China Quarterly*.

73 See孟融, 社会信用体系建设中的美德缺失及其填补 – 关于信用法治构建的政治与法律哲学思考, 《浙江学刊》(Rong Meng, 'The Lack of Virtue in the Construction of Social Credit System and its Filling – Political and Legal Philosophical Reflections on the Construction of Credit Rule of Law' (2022) *Zhejiang Academic Journal*) 88–97.

74 The phenomenon of lack of trust, also known as lack of solidarity, is very complex and includes several behaviors. The most representative one is called the 碰瓷 *pengci* scam, and it is also the root also of the article 184 of the Civil Code, also known as the 'good Samaritan rule', where a virtuous behavior needs to be encouraged by the law and not punished. The article states that "[a] person who voluntarily provides emergency assistance and causes harm to the recipient of assistant shall not assume civil liability". See 陈丹妮, 从彭宇案谈中国的"好人法", 《法制与社会》 (Danni Chen, 'Talking about China's "Good Man Law" from the Peng Yu Case' (2021) 24, *Legal System and Society*) 13–14.

75 Original title '社会信用体系建设规划纲要 (2014–2020年)'.

Congress formulated the People's Republic of China Social Credit Law, as part of the Plan for the Rule of Law Construction (2020–2025)[76].

In 2019 the General Office of the State Council published the 'Guiding Opinions of the General Office of the State Council on Accelerating the Construction of a Social Credit System and Constructing a New Credit-based Supervision Mechanism'[77]. The aim is to maximize further the role of credit in innovating the supervision mechanism and improving the supervision capacity and level, as functional to the stimulation of the market participants and advancement of high-quality development. The Opinions set forth an ex-ante credit supervision (in handling administrative licensing, exploring integrity education and good faith before implementing operators' access to the market, and use of credit reports issued by public credit service agencies), an interim credit supervision (establishment of catalogue of credit reports for market participants, of a unified social credit code[78] for incorporated and unincorporated organizations, and of a voluntary credit information registration mechanism), and ex-post credit supervision (for recognizing objects subject to joint punishment for dishonesty, urging dishonest market participants to take corrective action within the prescribed time limit, constructing a cross-regional, cross-industry and cross-field joint punishment for dishonesty mechanisms between, investigating the violation of laws).

In 2021, the National Development and Reform Commission issued the 'Public Credit Information Reporting Standards'[79] based on the principles of legality, authenticity, scientificity, readability, and safety. The establishment and improvement of the SCS are considered to be one of the important signs that China's socialist market economy continues to develop. The rapid development of information technology provides excellent support for the

76 For a discussion of SCS and its role in the Chinese definition of Rule of Law see 谭波, 刘昭辰, 习近平法治思想对社会信用体系的理论支撑及指引,《河南财经政法大学学报》 (Bo Tan, Zhaochen Liu, 'Theoretical Support and Guidance of Xi Jinping Thought on the Rule of Law to the Social Credit System' (2021) *Journal of Henan University of Economics and Law*) 7–16. See also Yu-Jie Chen, Ching-Fu Lin, Han-Wei Liu, 'Rule of Trust: The Power and Perils of China's Social Credit Megaproject' (2018) 32 *Columbia Journal of Asian Law* 1.

77 Original title '国务院办公厅关于加快推进社会信用体系建设构建以信用为基础的新型监管机制的指导意见.

78 See 'Notice of the State Council on Approving and Forwarding the General Plan of the National Development and Reform Commission and Other Departments on the Development of a Unified Social Credit Code System for Legal Persons and Other Organizations' ('国务院关于批转发展改革委等部门法人和其他组织统一社会信用代码制度建设总体方案的通知') (2015).

79 Original title '公共信用信息报告标准'.

construction of the SCS and the sharing of relevant information among different platforms[80]. The system focuses on four main areas: honesty in government affairs, business integrity, social integrity, and judicial credibility. It lists compliant behaviors in red lists and non-compliant behaviors in black lists[81]. Being listed means being subject to restrictions or expansions of personal rights and duties, as well as rewards or punishments. The system also uses public shaming mechanisms to encourage compliant behaviors[82].

The joint punishment mechanism is the main deterrent of the SCS. The mechanism is based on the general principle: "one shall be limited everywhere upon credit failure in one place"[83]. In this way, it is possible to maximize the effect of the SCS, its role in warning and educating society, and jointly support the government and the market[84]. The 'Opinions of the General Office of the CPC Central Committee and the General Office of the State Council on Accelerating the Advancement of the Development of a Credit Supervision, Warning and Punishment System of Dishonest Persons Subject to Enforcement'[85] adopted in 2016, clearly state that "imposing credit supervision, warning and punishment on dishonest persons subject to enforcement

---

80 See the 'Notice by the General Office of the State Council of Issuing the Implementation Plan for Strengthening the Sharing and Application of Credit Information to Promote Financing of Micro, Small and Medium-sized Enterprises' ('国务院办公厅关于印发加强信用信息共享应用促进中小微企业融资实施方案的通知') (2021).

81 The blacklist system was already used before the implementation of the SCS, see Alexander Trauth-Goik and Chuncheng Liu, 'Black or Fifty Shades of Grey? The Power and Limits of the Social Credit Blacklist System in China' (2022) *Journal of Contemporary China* 1–17.

82 See, for example, article 262 of the Civil Procedure Law, stating that: "Where the party against whom enforcement is sought fails to perform obligations determined in a legal instrument, the people's court may take or notify a relevant entity to assist in taking the measure of restricting exit from China, the measure of recording the failure in the credit system, the measure of publishing information on the failure on media and other measures prescribed by law".

83 See the 'Notice of the Supreme People's Court, the National Development and Reform Commission, the Ministry of Industry and Information Technology, and Other Departments on Taking Joint Disciplinary Actions against Dishonest Persons subject to Enforcement in Tendering and Bidding Activities' ('最高人民法院、国家发展改革委员会、工业和信息化部、住房和城乡建设部、交通运输部、水利部、商务部、国家铁路局、中国民用航空局关于在招标投标活动中对失信被执行人实施联合惩戒的通知') (2016).

84 See 吴晶妹, 社会信用立法要解决的根本问题 (Jingmei Wu, Fundamental Problems to be Solved by Social Credit Legislation) available at <https://mp.weixin.qq.com/s/2sEYCNQxmZUdUSm233czoA> (accessed February 11, 2023).

85 Original title '中共中央办公厅、国务院办公厅关于加快推进失信被执行人信用监督、警示和惩戒机制建设的意见'.

is helpful to promote such persons in voluntarily performing the obligation as specified in the effective legal instruments, improve judicial credibility and advance the development of the social credit system". As for the main goal of the joint punishment the Opinions clarify that "all regions and all departments shall attend to their respective duties, join forces, and build a credit supervision, warning, and punishment system so that those losing faith in one area shall be restricted everywhere". Main punishments include several restraints on qualifications for posts, access qualifications, honor and credit, special market transactions, high consumption and relevant consumption, strengthening routine supervision and examination, and strengthening criminal punishment. Additional tools are public disclosure of information on dishonesty and sharing credit information.

The system today is not yet a unified, standardized one. What is established today is a policy framework and regulations that encompass a large number of initiatives. Forty-seven institutions are involved in shaping the system. These include the State Council as cross-ministerial coordinator, the National Development and Reform Commission (NDRC), and the People's Bank of China in the lead. Many of these institutions are also responsible for implementing the system by establishing and managing platforms to track "social credit" in their respective policy fields[86]. Regional and local authorities are also closely involved[87]. However, there is no central, structured depository of related documents. Thousands of documents can be found on ministry websites, and those run by provincial and municipal governments[88].

The construction of the legal framework of the SCS is far from complete. The draft of the Social Credit Law[89] has not been approved yet. The core issue is how to define the subject and object of the credit legal relationship[90]. An additional challenge is how to combine economic credit and public credit and to

86 Information on individual credits is made public and transparent through the unified national platform "Credit China" at <https://www.creditchina.gov.cn> (accessed February 11, 2023).

87 See Marta Infantino and Weiwei Wang, 'Challenging Western Legal Orientalism: A Comparative Analysis of Chinese Municipal Social Credit Systems' (2021) 8 *Journal of European and Comparative Law and Governance* 46–85.

88 For a general analysis of the SCS functioning until 2018, both at the national and local level, including private social credit systems, see Rogier Creemers, 'China's Social Credit System: An Evolving Practice of Control' (2018), at <https://papers.ssrn.com/sol3/papers.cfm?abstract_id=3175792> (accessed 11 February 2023).

89 Original title '社会信用法'.

90 See Jingmei Wu, *supra* fn 84.

compromise between legal requirements of good faith for public power based on unified values with the pragmatic need for comprehensive legislation[91].

On the general public side, the SCS seems to receive support from Chinese citizens[92].

5.1 *Worker's Assessment Mechanism*

A special assessment mechanism is the worker's assessment, set forth by the 'Regulations on Assessment of Workers'[93] adopted in 1990. The Regulations are formulated to assess workers' ideological and political achievements as well as performances in production and work, determine their real technical and professional levels, bring into play their initiative in productive labor and in studying politics and technical know-how, and raise the quality of the contingent of workers in an all-round way, so as to meet the needs of the socialist modernization in our country[94]. Regulations apply to enterprises and institutions owned by the whole people and State organs.

The assessment of workers is divided into recruitment examination, examination for becoming regular workers and determining their grades at the end of the period of probation, examination before taking up a post and in expectation of a transfer, examination at the present grade, examination for promotion, and appraisal to see if they qualify for the post of technician or senior technician. After passing the examinations at the present grades, workers can apply for examinations for a promotion, which is generally held once every two to three years. With the recommendation of their teams and groups and the approval of workers' assessment organizations, those who have made special contributions can apply to take part in examinations for a promotion or in examinations for being promoted more than one grade. Those who have passed the examinations will be granted corresponding certificates of "technical grades", which will serve as a basis for job assignment and the readjustment of wages[95].

The subjects of examination consist of ideological, and political achievements, performances in production or work and technical and vocational

91 See 王伟, 论社会信用法的立法模式选择,《中国法学》(Wang Wei, 'On the Choice of Legislative Model of Social Credit Law' (2021) *China Legal Science*) 228–248.

92 See Genia Kostka, 'China's social credit systems and public opinion: Explaining high levels of approval' (2019) 21 *New Media & Society* 1565–1593. The way the SCS is presented does shape public opinion. See Xu Xu, Genia Kostka, Xun Cao, 'Information Control and Public Support for Social Credit Systems in China' (2022) 84 *The Journal of Politics* 2230–2245.

93 Original title '工人考核条例' enacted in 1990.

94 See article 1 of the Regulations.

95 See article 10 of the Regulations.

levels. Assessment of workers' ideological and political achievements mainly includes respect for the Constitution, law, and State policies as well as the rules and regulations of their own units and good professional ethics, and a fine attitude towards labor[96]. Assessment of workers' performance in production and work mainly consists of the quantity and quality in fulfilling production tasks, their capability to solve technical and vocational problems in production and work, their willingness to pass on skills and experience to others as well as their record in safe production[97]. A system of granting one hundred marks to the best worker is used in the appraisal of technical and vocational levels, with sixty marks given to those who just passed the examination[98]. When a worker succeeds in all three fields of ideological and political achievements, performances in production and work, as well as technical and vocational levels, it means he has passed the examinations.

6 Conclusions

Chinese culture of quantification is a complex phenomenon, resulting from the combination of several elements related to state administration, socialist political ideology, and traditional culture.

At the administrative level, the quantification process helps to address the need to coordinate the dual organizational structure and the dual decentralized structure of China's state governance model.

From a political perspective, in Socialist ideology, we find principles like "those who do not work should not eat"[99], a paraphrase of an older Paulian precept *Qui non lavorat non manducet*[100], mentioned in the Soviet Constitution[101]. Deng Xiaoping's interpretation says: "Work more, get more, work less, get less, don't work, don't get anything"[102]; another translation says "to each according to his work"[103].

96 See article 13 of the Regulations.

97 See article 14 of the Regulations.

98 See article 17 of the Regulations.

99 In Chinese '不劳动者不得食'.

100 Paul, Second Epistle to the Thessalonians 3:10.

101 For an interpretation of the principle in the Soviet context, see Alicja Ornowska, 'He Who Will Not Work Shall Not Eat: The Penalty of Compulsory Labour in Early Soviet Law and Its Impact upon Other Criminal Legislations' (2014) 55 *Annales Universitatis Scientiarum Budapestinensis de Rolando Eötvös Eotvos Nominatae – Sectio Iuridica* 297–322.

102 In Chinese 多劳多得，少劳少得，不劳不得. See 邓小平,《邓小平文选（1975–1982年）》(Deng Xiaoping, *Selected Works of Deng Xiaoping (1975–1982)*, People's Publishing House 1983) 48.

103 In Chinese '各尽所能 按劳分配'.

In Chinese traditional culture, there are many references to the importance of good performance. For Confucius, it is related to having faith in the ruler: "Zi Gong asked about government. The Master said, 'The requisites of government are that there be sufficiency of food, sufficiency of military equipment, and the confidence of the people in their ruler'. Zi Gong said, 'If it cannot be helped, and one of these must be dispensed with, which of the three should be foregone first?' 'The military equipment', said the Master. Zi Gong again asked, 'If it cannot be helped, and one of the remaining two must be dispensed with, which of them should be foregone?' The Master answered, 'Part with the food. From of old, death has been the lot of all men; but if the people have no faith in their rulers, there is no standing for the state'"[104].

On the other hand, Legalism emphasizes rewards and punishments. In "The Book of Lord Shang", there is an entire chapter discussing rewards and punishments. In the chapter on "Making Orders Strict", we can find: "Following upon this comes the condition where people will do it because they are encouraged by means of rewards and restrained by means of punishment"[105].

Finally, from the practical perspective of officials' daily work, we find written in the handbooks for magistrates that: "Having successfully completed the tour of duty without mishap, the magistrate must congratulate himself if he gets a promotion or a transfer as reward for his administrative competence and integrity"[106].

104 See Analects 12.7, translated by James Legge.

105 See Jan J.-L. Duyvendak, *The book of Lord Shang* (Éditions Arthur Probsthain 1928) 255.

106 See Huang Liu-hung, *A Complete Book Concerning Happiness and Benevolence. A Manual for Local Magistrates in Seventeenth-Century China* (edited and translated by Djang Chu, The University of Arizona Press 1984) 617.

CHAPTER 10

Use and Abuse of Quantitative Methodology for Policymaking in Japan

Tatsuhiko Inatani and Masahiko Kinoshita

1 Introduction

Quantitative methodologies including econometrics and EBPM (Evidence-Based Policy Making) have not, in general, been used effectively in policymaking in Japan. However, in recent years the Japanese government has gradually changed its attitude toward quantitative methodology in several policy areas and has adopted a more sophisticated approach for policymaking. In particular, the Japanese Digital Agency was established in 2021 and has been promoting a digital transformation of the Japanese governance system, indicating a new data-driven experimental policy approach.

To describe the situation hitherto, we choose criminal justice as a typical example of the employment of quantitative methods by Japanese bureaucrats (Section 2). Criminal justice notably features massive amounts of existing statistics, although they may not be effectively used. After this analysis, we explore the structural factors that may have influenced attitudes among Japanese policy makers (Section 3). The overview is followed by a brief introduction to the policy of the newly established Japanese Digital Agency, which could change the entire picture of Japanese attitudes toward quantitative methods for policymaking (Section 4). The conclusions follow (Section 5).

2 Criminal Justice

Massive, nationwide statistical data exist for criminal justice. The National Police Agency and the Ministry of Justice of Japan annually publish white papers on crime and punishment[1]. However, despite these seemingly

1 See the website of the Japanese National Police Agency at <https://www.npa.go.jp/publications/whitepaper/index_keisatsu.html> (accessed 21 October 2022) and of the Japanese Ministry of Justice at <https://www.moj.go.jp/housouken/houso_hakusho2.html> (accessed 21 October 2022).

 | DOI:10.1163/9789004680944_011

desirable conditions for quantitative analysis, Japanese criminal policy tends to be created in response to shocking episodes, not as the result of careful consideration of the data. Japanese criminal policy is a good example of a story-driven style of policymaking rather than a data-driven one[2]. A story-driven style of policymaking refers to a method of policy-making in which policy decisions are based on memorable incidents or episodes rather than on facts and data.

The treatment of car accidents may be a good illustration of this tendency. The fatality rate for car accidents in Japan decreased over the course of the 1970s (from 16.33 to 7.35 per 100,000 persons) and then slightly increased in the 1980s (from 7.54 to 9.03 per 100,000 persons), decreasing again in the 1990s (from 9.11 to 7.12 per 100,000 persons)[3]. However, legal responses became more punitive in legislation passed in 2001, which reformed the Penal Code by inserting the new crime of 'dangerous driving causing fatal injuries' (危険運転致死傷罪). This law was passed in response to shocking car accidents that attracted public notice and convinced observers that harsher penalties were necessary. More legislation followed, leading to even harsher punishment, as a result of a set of shocking car accidents. It may be that these severe threats have deterred car accidents, as fatality rates did dramatically decrease during the first two decades of this century (from 7.16 to 3.90 and then to 2.54 per 100,000 persons). However, given that younger people in Japan own fewer cars than their seniors[4] and the number of fatal car accidents due to speeding have correspondingly decreased in that group, when considered together with the enhancements of safety equipment (e.g., the rate of air bag installation dramatically increased beginning in 1997)[5] and improved road conditions[6], the effects of the punishment should be carefully evaluated.

---

2 See Rachel E. Barkow, 'Criminal Law as Regulation' (2014) 8 NYU *Journal of Law & Liberty* 316, 323.

3 See the 'Statistics about Road Traffic' on the portal site for website of Japanese Government Statistics at <https://www.e-stat.go.jp/en/stat-search/files?page=1&layout=datalist&toukei=00130002&tstat=000001027457&cycle=7&year=20210&month=0> (accessed 21 October 2022).

4 See Wataru Sugiyama and Tetsuto Ishigami, *Possession and Usage of Car* (「自動車の保有と利用」) (August 2019) 62 *Finance* 48 (ファイナンス 2019年8月号 62頁), available at <https://www.mof.go.jp/public_relations/finance/201908/201908k.pdf> (accessed 21 October 2022).

5 See the website of the Japanese Ministry of Environment at <https://www.env.go.jp/info/iken/h150407a/a-3-5.pdf> (accessed 21 October 2022).

6 See Shinichi Kodera, Kyosuke Hirasawa, Motoki Asano, A *Study of Factors Contributing to the Decline in Traffic Accident Fatalities* (「交通事故死者数の減少要因に関する一考察」) (2013), available at <https://thesis.ceri.go.jp/db/files/GR0002300278.pdf> (accessed 21 October 2022).

Juvenile justice provides another example of "story-driven" penal policy. Japanese juvenile policy began to increase in severity in 2000[7], although the number of juvenile delinquencies was in the middle of an almost continuous decline[8]. A striking amendment to the Japanese juvenile law occurred in 2014, which enabled harsher sentences to be imposed in selected juvenile cases, although, again, this was a period when the rate of juvenile delinquencies was historically low. However, the Japanese legislature reacted as if the number of juvenile crimes was continuously increasing. A recent study has found that a child's image is not stable and often formed through broadcast media concentrating on some exceptional cases of juvenile criminality[9], which influences the tendency to support a severe punishment orientation[10].

Thus, a sort of penal populism tends to dominate Japanese policymaking in the criminal justice context, which impedes effective employment of quantitative methodology.

If this penal populism leads to ineffective use of quantitative evidence, there might likewise be cases of abusive of data in Japanese criminal policymaking. For example, the number of Japanese police officers shows a steady increase[11]. Japanese police agencies, both nationally and locally, tend to justify their expansion through contradictory and perhaps incorrect interpretations of the number of crimes.

One prefectural police department sought to justify its expansion in the face of a decreasing number of crimes because, on its interpretation, crime was falling due to the effective work of the police officers[12]. At the same time, another

---

7 See Ministry of Justice, *The History of Amendment of Juvenile Law* (「少年法改正の経過」) (without date), available at <https://www.moj.go.jp/content/001216449.pdf> (accessed 21 October 2022).

8 See the website of the Japanese Ministry of Justice at <https://hakusyo1.moj.go.jp/jp/66/nfm/n66_2_2_2_1_1.html#h2-2-1-01> (accessed 21 October 2022).

9 See Kouichi Hamai, 'Imprisonment for 2 yen but Probation for 500 million yen' (『二円で刑務所、5億で執行猶予』) (Kobunsha 2009).

10 Tomoya Mukai and Kyoko Fujino, 'The relationship among severe punishment orientation, fear of crime, and the perceived risk of juvenile crime: The role of the child image as incomprehensible as an antecedent factor' (「少年犯罪に対する厳罰志向性と犯罪不安及び被害リスク知覚の関連–先行要因としての子供イメージに着目して–」) (2021) 60 *Journal of Experimental Psychology* 100 (実験心理学研究60巻2号100頁(2021年)).

11 See Japanese National Police Agency, 'White Paper' (2021), available at <https://www.npa.go.jp/hakusyo/r03/pdf/13_dai6sho.pdf> (accessed 21 October 2022).

12 See the website of the Mie Prefectural Police Agency at <https://www.police.pref.mie.jp/pdf/zouin.pdf> (accessed 21 October 2022).

department sought to justify its own expansion in the face of an increasing number of crimes because of the need for more officers to deter these crimes[13].

It is interesting to note here that both interpretations could be wrong. For example, one study has found that decreasing crime may be rooted in improved welfare policies[14]. Another study has shown that increasing crime rates may be influenced by changes in police policy. That is, beginning in 1999, police began to identify concealed violent crimes to respond to them proactively. The change of course, naturally increased the crime statistics in comparison with the numbers available before[15].

We conclude that criminal justice provides a typical reflection of the Japanese government's attitude toward quantitative approach, which proves to be an ineffective or abusive use of statistics. We suspect that this trend has structural causes. For example, the legislation council committee (「法制審議会」) of the Japanese Ministry of Justice, which has a significant influence on policymaking in criminal justice and almost exclusively consists of legal specialists, might lead to ineffective or abusive tendencies, as it is not clear whether members of this committee have any background in econometrics or EBPM.

3 Structural Factors Impeding EBPM Deployment

We surmise that there are several structural reasons for the weak use of quantitative methods in Japanese legislative policy. Before exploring these, it is necessary to provide some details about the complex Japanese legislative process.

In Japan, the legislative process is governed not only by the Constitution and statutes but also by various de facto practices[16]. According to the Constitution, the Diet whose members are elected by the people is the sole legislative body. However, based on the prevailing interpretation of the Constitution, the Cabinet is also entitled to submit bills to the Diet. In practical terms,

13 See Tottori Prefectural Assembly at <https://www.pref.tottori.lg.jp/90088.htm> (accessed 21 October 2022).

14 See Hiroaki Enoki, Yoko Hosoi, Takafumi Koizumi, Kiyohiko Katahira, 'Statistical Examination of Crime Deterrence Variables' (「犯罪の抑止変数に関する統計的検討」) (2011) 4 *Toyo University Social Welfare Research* 31–38 (東洋大学社会福祉研究)第4号 31頁 (2011年).

15 See Hamai, *supra* fn 9.

16 For an overview of the Japanese legislative process, see Oshima Toshihiko, *Legislation: Theory and Practice* (立法学: 理論と実務) (Daiichi Hoki 2013); Makoto Nakajima, *Legislation* (立法学) (Horitsu Bunka Sya 2020, 4th edn).

the Cabinet has a more significant role than the members of the Diet with respect to submitting bills. Approximately 80% of the legislation passed in the Diet each year is Cabinet bills. Moreover, based on the parliamentary system, the Cabinet is organized with the support of the ruling coalition in the Diet, which means that Cabinet bills are rarely rejected or amended by the Diet. Therefore, the reality is that a large part of the substantive and meaningful legislative work is done before the bill reaches the Diet. Before the cabinet submits bills, various stakeholders are involved in the process. Especially, three groups play a very important role: bureaucrats, councils, and politicians.

Among them, the most essential players are the bureaucrats in administrative organizations, such as the Ministry of Justice, Ministry of Internal Affairs and Communications, and Ministry of Health, Labor, and Welfare (MHLW). They are actually in charge of drafting the Cabinet bills. Sometimes, drafting may begin with direct directions from the Cabinet or ministers, but in many cases, the bureaucrats themselves initiate the legislative process by proposing to the Cabinet or ministers the need for legislation. In addition to writing drafts, bureaucrats also gather and prepare the materials and data they use to support the need and rationale for the legislation. Therefore, the intentions and personal capacities of the bureaucrats can substantially influence the way legislation is prepared.

Second, the councils established in each administrative body also play a significant role in the legislative process. Currently, it is estimated that about 110 councils exist within the administration of the central government. Typical councils are composed of experts, such as university professors, representatives of industry and civic organizations. These councils meet to discuss the necessity of legislation, the legislative framework, and matters to be addressed in legislation. Council reports are not legally binding on the Cabinet or ministers. However, for important legislation, a process involving the council is always adopted: 1) the minister consults the council on the legislation, 2) the council publishes their report, and 3) the bill is drafted based on that report. Bureaucrats take the lead appointing council members, and the majority of council reports are actually written by bureaucrats. Critics assert that the council is simply a shield for bureaucrats to use to avoid criticism that the legislative process is bureaucracy centered. However, the councils are not always bureaucrates' puppets; sometimes legislations are cancelled, or their contents are significantly changed as a result of discussions in the councils.

Politicians themselves are of course important actors in the legislative process. Japanese political practices have developed a unique system called the ruling party review, in which members of the ruling party examine bills before they are submitted to the Diet[17]. The ruling party review is a system that is not grounded in the Constitution or statutes but formed primarily by practice within the Liberal Democratic Party (LDP). The LDP, which has dominated the Diet for many decades, has an institution called the "Political Affairs Investigation Committee." That committee is further divided into several subcommittees for each specific political issue. Each subcommittee is composed of party-affiliated legislatures with expertise in the political issues that the subcommittee deals with. Those politicians often have strong support from certain industries and interested organizations. In practice, before the Cabinet submits a bill, it must be approved by the Political Affairs Investigation Committee, and before that, it must be approved by a subcommittee of that committee. Resolutions of the subcommittee generally must be unanimous, and the legislative process will not move forward if even one legislator strongly opposes the bill. In a manner of speaking, each ruling party member may be said to have a substantial veto power over the bill. The bureaucrats, therefore, carefully lobby the politicians in advance to ensure that their bills are not rejected by the subcommittee. However, the politicians, by implying the use of their veto power, sometimes request the bureaucrats to revise the bills.

We surmise that within the framework of the Japanese legislative process just described, the following three structural factors are responsible for the insufficient use of quantitative methods in policymaking in Japan.

First, the bureaucrats who play the central role in the legislative process lack sufficient expertise in quantitative methods. Japanese bureaucrats, particularly those who are candidates for senior management positions, are appointed through a rigorous competitive examination process. The examinations are performed according to job category, the four most important of which are: the legal professions, the economic professions, the administrative professions, and the science and engineering professions. Recruitment of bureaucrats is done on a ministry-by-ministry basis, and the number of bureaucrats hired overall and for which positions varies by ministry. Overall, 40% to 50% of the bureaucrats actually hired have passed the exam for the legal professions[18]. The examination subjects in this category mainly relate to legal studies such as constitutional law, civil law, and administrative law, and the expertise in statistics and mathematics necessary for quantitative analysis is not considered. In addition, many of the applicants for the law profession examination

17 For detailed information on the reality and function of the ruling party examination, see Nakajima, *supra* fn 16, 103–139.

18 See Kengo Soga, *Contemporary Japanese Bureaucracy* (現代日本の官僚制) (University of Tokyo Press 2016) 207–214.

are senior law undergraduates. Japanese universities are highly specialized at the undergraduate stage into law, economics, science, and engineering disciplines. Statistics and political science are not required for the law curricula of the universities that have produced many bureaucrats, such as the University of Tokyo and Kyoto University. As a result, many students enter the bureaucracy without having learned the minimum knowledge and concepts of statistics and political science at university[19]. The revelation of serious fallacies in statistical data published by the MHLW in 2018 sparked a major controversy. Among the contributing factors to that incident was that there are few experts in statistics within the administration[20]. Nevertheless, the situation that many of the bureaucrats are legal experts and not experts in statistics also stems from some structural factors, so this cannot be easily improved. Japanese legislation requires systematic consistency among statutes, and there are detailed rules for how they are written and worded[21]. Therefore, it is impossible to engage in drafting without a high degree of expertise in law, so legal experts are always needed. However, Japan's public finances are running a severe account deficit, and the government has little financial resources to hire new statistics specialists.

The second structural factor is the lack of reliable statistical data available to implement quantitative policies. A thought-provoking description of this problem has been provided by Akira Morita, one of Japan's most prominent professors of public administration[22]. Morita was the chairman of the Central Social Insurance Medical Council (CSIMC) of the MHLW, which oversees the health insurance system and medical reimbursement. Morita notes that at the CSIMC, data were certainly submitted at meetings, they were never fully reflected in policymaking. Morita suspects that one of the reasons for such a situation is that the reliability of the data can easily be upset through council discussions[23]. Morita points out that, for example, with respect to the data collected through questionnaires, various problems were identified

---

19 In 2018, the MEXT revised the high school curriculum so that statistics became a required subject for graduation from high school. Therefore, the situation where bureaucrats do not have even a minimal knowledge of statistics will be remedied in the near future.

20 MIC answering questions to the Diet, The 198th National Diet Session (14 March 2019), 4 *House of Councillors General Affairs Committee Meeting Records* 11.

21 On one part of the various legislative rules, see Masahiko Kinoshita, 'The Form of Constitutional Amendment in Japan', in Richard Albert (ed), *The Architecture of Constitutional Amendments: History, Law, Politics* (Hart Publishing 2023).

22 Akira Morita, *The Politics of the Government Councils III* (会議の政治学 III) (Jigakusya 2016).

23 Morita, *supra* fn 22, 137.

during discussions, such as (1) a sample volume biased towards certain groups, (2) a low questionnaire collection rate, and (3) problems with tabulation and analysis methods[24]. The reliability of the data was shaken, and the data were eventually not used. In the end, policies are formed based on the personal experiences and sensitivities of the council members. Morita describes this situation as policy-biased evidence rather than evidence-based policymaking[25]. Morita notes the public's negative feelings toward government's collection of personal information as one of the factors contributing to a situation in which the government can only collect data whose reliability is easily challenged. Without an increase in the response rate to surveys, the data cannot dispel suspicions of bias[26]. Additionally, as the first structural factor indicates, lack of expertise among bureaucrats may be part of the reason for the inability to construct reliable statistical data.

A third structural reason is the unpredictability of statistical surveys. As noted above, the reliability of statistical data can be investigated from a variety of perspectives. Nevertheless, once salient data on the existence of correlations are available, questioning the results and excluding the data itself from policy making decisions has a commensurate cost. While the ideal bureaucrat would try to make policies based on reliable data, politicians may not want to do so, and correspondingly, bureaucrats are not always faithful to their ideal in reality. For example, it is currently being debated whether the sale of pharmaceuticals via the Internet should be banned. Pharmacies that sell drugs in their stores may support this measure. Politicians who are supported by pharmacy groups will instruct bureaucrats to move forward with the ban. The bureaucrats must then come up with a reason for the ban. They will propose the legislative reason that the sale of drugs via the Internet leads to misuse and abuse of drugs, which would be more convincing to the public than the protection of traditional pharmacies. But what if the data show that Internet drug sales featured lower risk than face-to-face sales regarding the misuse and abuse of drugs? Companies selling pharmaceuticals via the Internet would use this statistical results to campaign against the sales ban. Also, there might be significant opposition to the legislation in the council. This might prevent bureaucrats from drafting legislation in line with the wishes of politicians. In other words, data that are too compelling have the effect of weakening the bureaucrats' and politicians' control over the legislative process. The reluctance of bureaucrats and politicians

24 Morita, *supra* fn 22, 138.
25 Morita, *supra* fn 22, 137.
26 Morita, *supra* fn 22, 206.

who want to keep the legislative process under their own control to adopt statistical methods is a rational course of action.

4 Digital Agency: New Trends

While the structures that hinder the deployment of EBPM continue to exist, we can see a transformation in the policies of the Digital Agency, a new administrative organization established in recent years.

To achieve Society 5.0, the ideal imagined future of Japanese society, where the integration of cyber and physical systems (CPS) allows people to overcome present-day challenges, including the aging society and the shrinking labor force, an innovative business can be launched that utilizes cutting-edge technologies, like AI and other emerging technologies[27]. In this perspective, the Japanese Digital Agency, established in September 2021[28], is now strongly promoting the digital transformation of the entire structure of the Japanese regulatory system[29].

To promote digital transformation, the agency adopts five fundamental principles: the digital completion and automation principle, the agile governance principle, the public-private partnership principle, the interoperability principle, and the principle for using common infrastructure[30]. The first two principles in particular are very important to understand new trends in Japanese policymaking, including a deeper and more consistent use of quantitative methods.

In particular, the digital completion and automation principle seeks to modify all statutes and regulatory rules that hinder the digital transformation of the Japanese regulatory structure. The statutes targeted are, for example,

---

27 The Cabinet of Japan, 'Basic Plan for Science, Technology and Innovation' (March 2021), available at <https://www8.cao.go.jp/cstp/kihonkeikaku/6honbun.pdf> (accessed 21 October 2022).

28 See the Digital Agency website at <https://www.digital.go.jp/about/> (accessed 21 October 2022).

29 Japanese Digital Agency, 'Meeting of the extraordinary administrative research committee' (November 2021), available at <https://www.digital.go.jp/assets/contents/node/basic_page/field_ref_resources/658916e5-76ce-4d02-9377-1273577ffc88/20211109_meeting_extraordinary_administrative_research_committee_01.pdf> (accessed 21 October 2022).

30 Japanese Digital Agency, 'Structural Reform in the Digital Age and the Direction of Digital Principles' (December 2022), available at <https://www.digital.go.jp/assets/contents/node/basic_page/field_ref_resources/c98d7d7a-24f2-45fe-a3b9-14c635966105/20211222_meeting_extraordinary_administrative_research_committee_01.pdf> (accessed 21 October 2022).

those that obligate human activities where humans can be replaced by robots, AI, or other emerging technologies (e.g., tasks including inspection, surveillance, and routine maintenance) as well as those that require certain technologies for communication or recording (e.g., FD, CD or paper) and thus are not technology neutral.

The Japanese Digital Agency decided to recommend changing over 10,000 statutes and numerous regulatory rules within 2 years, and the process is currently proceeding rapidly. However, to achieve this goal, it will be necessary to interpret or change the legal texts that define the goal of the statute and the rules in a qualitative manner, with terms like "appropriate" or "safe". Because these terms are difficult or impossible for AI to understand, most Japanese regulatory bodies that have jurisdiction over these laws and regulations are pressed to transform these qualitative terms into quantitative standards. To accomplish this transformation, Japanese regulators are forced to employ quantitative methodologies for the identification and clarification of the risks controlled by their previous regulations and to calculate the influence of replacement by digital technologies.

For example, existing quality control regulations for important infrastructures, including bridges and tunnels, oblige local public officers and/or private companies to inspect the infrastructure for appropriateness and safety. For these inspections, experienced workers check the quality of the infrastructure using their own sophisticated approach. However, these inspections are costly and time-consuming; as the labor force shrinks, this problem is exacerbated. Japanese regulators now seek to replace these human practices with sensors and AI. To accomplish this, the qualitative term of "appropriateness" must be transformed into a quantitative standard formed through machine learning based on data from human practices. To assure the safety of the given infrastructure, the regulators seek to calculate the consequences and probabilities of accidents caused by deteriorating infrastructures and how effectively and efficiently replacements can control the risk.

This presents a good illustration of the change of mindset of Japanese regulators. The Japanese Digital Agency is now pushing them in this direction by articulating means of implementing trials, mapping available technologies, and encouraging experimentation, although this may result in failure (failure was once the most hated outcome in Japanese bureaucratic organizations).

The second principle, agile governance, is related to this experiment-friendly trend. Agile governance was originally proposed to respond to situations filled with uncertainty. Society 5.0 will inevitably be fluid, dynamic, and complex, as many complex systems must be connected to form the huge complex system termed the System of Systems. For example, an autonomous drone system is considered a promising system for resolving social problems, like the shrinking labor force. To realize an autonomous drone system, however, it is necessary to connect at least four complex systems to each other: AI in drones, air traffic control for unmanned aircraft, manned aircraft, and air traffic control for manned aircraft. Complex systems can sometimes reveal unexpected risk, or systemic risk, where risk appears through the interaction of various system components. Because the consequences of this interaction are independent of the components' behavior, like the operation of a clock is independent from the behavior of each bolts or gears, it is extremely difficult to foresee such risk.

In addition to the uniquely complex character of its systems, Society 5.0 also has a fluid and dynamic character, thanks to AI, which optimizes its behavior, based on experience and learning from data constantly generated by widespread Internet of Things (IoT).

These characteristics of Society 5.0 actually mean that it will be impossible to control the risk generated by the huge complex system with rules and regulations set in advance, as no one can know the whole system in advance.

An accident involving a Tesla driver assistance system can be used to illustrate such a system. Let us imagine that a driver using Tesla's driver assistance system in Japan falls asleep while driving in heavy traffic, resulting in a fatal accident. In the following criminal trial, the accident was judged to be a violation of the driver's duty to maintain diligence while traveling, although there were arguments to the contrary that the system malfunctioned.

What is the problem in this case? It has previously been observed that cooperative behavior between highly automated machines and humans causes a decline in attention level and loss of a sense of agency in humans[31]. It is undeniable that this undesirable state of mind may have been caused by the automated machine in this case rather than by the individual.

Furthermore, research suggests that even trained professionals may not be able to respond appropriately to events that occur only at low frequencies[32]. In other words, if the performance of Tesla's driver assistance system is good, it may prevent drivers from preventing accidents.

Thus, holding the driver liable for the Tesla accident does not reduce the risk of future accidents, and at the same time, may not lead to proper risk

31 See, e.g., Sukhvinder S. Obhi & Preston Hall, 'Sense of Agency in Joint Action: Influence of Human and Computer Co-Actors' (2011) 211 *Experimental Brain Research* 663; Wayne D. Gray et al., 'The Soft Constraints Hypothesis: A Rational Analysis Approach to Resource Allocation for Interactive Behavior' (2006) 113 *Psychological Review* 461.

32 See, e.g., Jeremy M. Wolfe et al., 'Low Target Prevalence is a Stubborn Source of Errors in Visual Search Tasks' (2007) 136 *Journal of Experimental Psychology: General* 623.

management if Tesla is not obliged to redesign its interface. Here arises the systemic risk, created through the cooperation between the driver and the driver assistance system.

Conversely, it goes too far to say that Tesla should have designed and developed its products and services with the effects of human-machine interaction in mind and that it should be held responsible for the accidents caused by the systemic risks posed by human-machine interaction. There are still too many unknowns about what kind of interface is to be used for an automated machine and what kind of effects these interfaces can have on humans. If we impose regulations that make people responsible for these unknowns as well, it could increase danger and atrophy in the sense mentioned earlier. No one has the right answer.

It is at least clear that it is difficult to control risks to the system by imposing in advance a clear duty of conduct on the part of the driver or on the part of Tesla in advance.

To respond to the fluid, dynamic, and complex situation of Society 5.0, the Japanese government is promoting a new style of governance system, termed "agile governance". This approach is a system designed to respond quickly to a changing situation to control unexpected risks by changing its own structure. Within this new governance system, the emphasis appears to be on collective learning and knowledge creation. To continue to appropriately address risk and uncertainty, it is necessary to learn from unexpected events, including failures, and to continue to address uncertain and fluid conditions brought about by Society 5.0. It is also necessary to consolidate knowledge and information and engage people in collective learning and knowledge creation[33].

In agile governance, all stakeholders must evaluate the value and risks of their activities, obtain feedback from actual operations, and reevaluate their activities, collaborating with other stakeholders where necessary. Through this governance practice, governance systems themselves and the CPS may continuously evolve to address risk and uncertainty in Society 5.0.

However, to promote this new style of governance, regulators and other stakeholders must adopt quantitative methods to evaluate governance tools based on massive data acquired through IoT.

33 See The Ministry of Economy, Trade, and Industry, 'Governance Innovation version 2: A Guide to Designing and Implementing Agile Governance' (2021), available at <https://www.meti.go.jp/press/2021/07/20210730005/20210730005-2.pdf> (accessed 21 October 2022); Tatsuhiko Inatani, 'The New Governance Model in the Society 5.0 and Its Sanctioning System' (「Society 5.0における新たなガバナンスシステムと制裁の役割」) (2022) 94–3 *Houritsu Jiho* 98.

In sum, a digital transformation of the Japanese government like that promoted by the Digital Agency may dramatically change the existing mindset of Japanese bureaucrats and policy makers and push them to adopt more seriously quantitative methodology.

Interestingly, many people employed in the Digital Agency have studied economics, informatics, and computer sciences and have been working in the private sector. These individuals are now actively participating in policymaking. Therefore, the structural factors that could impede EBPM deployment in the criminal justice sector and, more generally, in the regulatory process, are reduced in this agency, because these factors are generated by the higher education system and law-centralized education system at play for Japanese bureaucrats.

5 Conclusion

The Japanese government generally does not effectively employ quantitative methodology, especially in traditional legal areas, for structural reasons. However after the establishment of the Digital Agency and adoption of fundamental principles for digital transformation, this picture has been dramatically changing. The influence of this changing trend is now gradually reaching traditional legal areas including criminal justice.

Of course, it remains to be seen what will happen in the future, and it is too early to draw a decisive conclusion, but the Japanese policymaking system has been gradually changing and quantitative methods like EBPM are becoming more popular in Japanese governance systems. It is striking that the expertise of Japanese bureaucrats is becoming more diverse than it was in the previous law-dominated situation.

We hope that our rough sketch of the Japanese situation may contribute to developing an understanding of the methodologies in play in the policymaking changes underway in Japan.

CHAPTER 11

Measuring Human Rights Performance in the UK: Liberalism, Communitarianism, and the Equality and Human Rights Commission's 'Drunkard's Search'

David McGrogan

1 Introduction

Human rights, often still thought of by the layperson as the justifications for legal claims made by individuals against the state, are now better described as being both a method for declaring the conditions of the good, and the legal mechanism for deploying public and private power in order to achieve those conditions[1]. This has given rise to an emphasis on the activities of duty-bearers (the state, international organisations, and businesses) and the extent to which they are fulfilling their obligations to bring about the utilitarian ends that human rights laws are interpreted to embody[2]. But how this new emphasis on human rights as a mechanism for achieving the general good can be reconciled with the respect for individual autonomy on which human rights are still often rhetorically based has never been adequately theorised. And it is, indeed, increasingly apparent that there has developed a fault-line at the heart of the entire human rights project, with concern being expressed that respect for the rights of the individual cannot be 'made adequately secure against being trumped by the general utility'[3].

1 'By bringing States, civil society, business actors and many others together behind the universal commitment to rights, we can address the root causes of the crises that challenge our societies [and] foster peaceful societies and sustainable development', as the former UN High Commissioner for Human Rights, Michelle Bachelet, once put it. See OHCHR, *United Nations Human Rights Appeal 2020* (OHCHR 2020) 4.

2 See e.g. Sakiko Fukuda-Parr et al., 'An Index of Economic and Social Rights Fulfilment: Concept and Methodology' (2009) 8(3) *Journal of Human Rights* 195; Hannah Miller & Robin Redhead, 'Beyond "Rights-Based Approaches"? Employing a Process and Outcomes Framework' (2019) 23(5) *The International Journal of Human Rights* 699.

3 John Charvet & Elisa Kaczynska-Nay, *The Liberal Project and Human Rights: The Theory and Practice of a New World Order* (CUP 2008) 16.

 | DOI:10.1163/9789004680944_012

The activities of the UK's Equality and Human Rights Commission (EHRC) neatly exemplify the tension between these two imperatives. On the one hand, when it was created, the Commission was given the statutory mandate of fostering in society 'respect for and protection of each individual's human rights' and 'respect for the dignity and worth of each individual'[4]. This, as we shall see, was rooted in an essentially liberal understanding of equality, in which all individuals are understood to be of equal value to others in the sense that they are all self-directing moral agents. By extension, the understanding of the role of human rights which the EHRC was created to embody was essentially deontological (discrimination being wrong simply by dint of individuals possessing equal moral worth), and the vision of justice which was supposed to imbue its activities was essentially corrective (if an individual is wronged by being discriminated against, there must be a remedy).

But on the other hand, the EHRC's work has become increasingly focused on 'measuring' equality and human rights within the jurisdiction, the flagship being its regular, three-yearly reports on the question of 'Is Britain fairer?' – a compendium of data on educational attainment, employment, living standards, health, and so on, aimed at deriving useful inferences about where progress is being made, and identifying areas where it is not[5]. This reveals its day-to-day priorities to be distinctly utilitarian, and, I will argue, communitarian rather than liberal. The EHRC, that is, has become chiefly interested in eliminating statistical inequalities between categories of people across various 'domains' (education, work, living standards, health, justice and personal security, and participation)[6]. Thus, in asking 'Is Britain fairer?', the Commission is really concerned primarily with quantitative equality of outcomes between groups. Its understanding of 'fairness', by extension, is essentially redistributive, and located at the level not of the individual but at the average of all individuals possessing a certain characteristic or set of characteristics (race, sex, sexuality, etc.). This, in turn, means that its understanding of the role of human rights is fundamentally teleological (focused on the elimination of 'systemic' differences of outcome between groups) and its vision of justice distributive, rather than corrective (i.e., concerned chiefly with distributional equality, again between groups).

4 Equality Act 2006, s. 3.

5 The most recent report, Equality and Human Rights Commission, *Is Britain Fairer? The State of Equality and Human Rights 2018*, is available at <https://www.equalityhumanrights.com/sites/default/files/is-britain-fairer-accessible.pdf> (accessed 15 December 2022). The report for 2021 has been delayed but will apparently be published in due course.

6 Equality and Human Rights Commission, *supra* fn 5, 2–3.

The disjuncture between the EHRC's statutory mandate and its everyday practice undoubtedly reflects particular biases and predispositions among the EHRC's Board of Commissioners and staff. But those biases and predispositions are also clearly reinforced by the way in which measurement takes place. Whether Britain is substantively 'fairer' on the basis of average group outcomes is a question which is (purportedly at least) much more readily answered in quantitative terms than the question of whether there is genuine equality between all individuals in society. This, in turn, makes it a much less resource-intensive question to answer, as well – a consideration which, for the perennially cash-poor EHRC, is not insignificant. In other words, while the Board of Commissioners is clearly interested in the issue of substantive equality between groups *per se*, it is also driven to focus on that issue because of the comparative ease of doing so.

This chapter argues that the EHRC's increasing focus on distributive justice at the group level is therefore an example of a particular observational bias, well-known to economists as the 'streetlight effect' or 'drunkard's search'[7]. A policeman, seeing a drunken man on his hands and knees searching the floor around a streetlight, stops and asks the man what he has lost. 'My keys', says the drunkard, and the policeman spends some minutes helping him look. Eventually, having not been able to find the keys, the policeman asks the man whether he is sure that this is where he lost them. 'No', the man responds. 'But the light's much better here'. The EHRC, in other words, is looking at issues concerning substantive equality between groups partially just because that is where it is easiest to look.

The chapter thus poses a critique of the EHRC's measurement framework, but it also asks a question of broader interest. It is often observed that public measurements represent the political priorities of those doing the measuring, and that this can serve to provide an objective veneer to what are in fact profoundly political decisions[8]. What is less well often observed is that what gets publicly measured may simply be a result of its ease of measurement. In other words, it is not necessarily political priorities that inform the exercise of measurement, but practical ones: it is easier to measure some things than others. Since, as is well known, public measurements have a tendency to transmogrify

7 The joke is of early 20th century vintage but the first use in respect of the social sciences seems to have been in Abraham Kaplan, *The Conduct of Inquiry: Methodology for Behavioural Science* (Transaction Publishers 1964) 11.

8 See, for example, the papers collected in Kevin Davis et al., *Governance by Indicators: Global Power through Quantification and Rankings* (OUP 2012).

into public targets and thus political priorities[9], we must then ask the question: are many of our political priorities (such as the EHRC's concern with substantive equality of outcomes between groups) the result not of a political process or even of the prior holding of certain values, but simply of the amenability of the underlying phenomena to quantitative assessment?

In Section 2 of this chapter, I examine the projects undertaken by the EHRC, and locate them within a wider movement in contemporary human rights practice which has as its focus the measurement of what might be called human rights performance. I demonstrate that, by examining what is being measured in these reports, we can relatively easily identify the Commission's priorities. In Section 3, I show that this suggests that the EHRC adopts an essentially substantive, outcomes-based understanding of the meaning of 'equality', and that it therefore conceptualises fairness as being measurable at the level of the group, rather than the individual. This, in turn, marks its understanding of justice as being basically distributive, and its guiding philosophy communitarian rather than liberal. In Sections 4 and 5, I draw on the literature on the sociology of quantification to suggest that, while the Commission's priorities are clearly dictated by a wide range of factors, they can at least in part be explained by describing them as a classic example of a drunkard's search – influenced not by pre-existing values, but simply by what is most easily measurable. In Section 6, I use this observation to open up the use of quantitative performance measurement, particularly by the EHRC, to critical reflection. Section 7 concludes with some wider observations.

2 Measuring Human Rights Performance

In March 2022 the UK EHRC released a preparatory report to provide information to the UN Human Rights Council with regard to the UK's upcoming assessment under the Universal Periodic Review (UPR)[10]. The UPR is a process of 'peer review', in which each UN member issues a report on what it has done to improve its human rights record in the previous five years, which is then subject to comment by other UN members. As the EHRC is the UK's National Human Rights Institution, this report provides an important reference point

9 Alain Desrosières, *The Politics of Large Numbers: A History of Statistical Reasoning* (translated by Camille Naish, Harvard University Press 1998).

10 EHRC, *Universal Periodic Review in Great Britain* (2022), available at <https://www.equalityhumanrights.com/sites/default/files/our-work-human-rights-universal-periodic-review-2022.pdf> (accessed 15 December 2022).

for the entire review, and is supposed in effect to provide an independent perspective as a counterpoint to the UK government's official statements[11]. The report is therefore highly instructive in understanding the opinions and priorities of the Commission itself when it comes to the question of what 'good practice' in relation to human rights really means – and, in turn therefore, what is meant by the phrase 'improving the human rights situation'[12].

The EHRC's report, in common with most of its data-gathering projects, is grouped into seven themes, together with a set of recommendations for each. The themes are 'general measures of implementation', which refers to the actual legislative framework for human rights protection in the UK, followed by 'living standards', 'health', 'education', 'work', 'justice, liberty and personal security' and 'participation'. Each of these is then broken down into sub-themes, so that, for example, 'living standards' is further sub-divided into 'poverty' and 'social care', although most in fact have only one sub-theme[13].

Three things can be instantly observed about these themes, how they are described, and the recommendations attached to them. The first is that they almost exclusively both assume, and produce, a distinctly interventionist model for the relationship between state and society. This is itself indicated merely in the choice of themes alone, the preponderance of which suggest a strongly paternalistic understanding of the role of the state in improving living standards, health, education, working conditions, and so on. But it is further borne out by the choices of sub-theme. Of the eleven sub-themes contained in the report, perhaps two ('policing' and 'immigration'), both of which fall under 'Justice, liberty and personal security', could be said to align with protecting the corpus of individual liberties with which human rights are still most frequently associated in the popular vernacular – the rights to personal security, due process, freedom of association, and so on. The rest of the sub-themes, and the recommendations appended to them, are much more illustrative of a redistributive, communitarian model for human rights, in which they provide the justification for the state taking a significantly interventionist role – providing access to high quality mental health services[14], ensuring that all children reach their full potential through education[15], increasing access to sick pay[16], funding specialist services for victims of domestic

11 Ibid., 5.

12 OHCHR website, 'Universal Periodic Review', available at <https://www.ohchr.org/en/hr-bodies/upr/upr-main> (accessed 15 December 2022).

13 EHRC, *supra* fn 10, 2–3.

14 Ibid., 11.

15 Ibid., 12.

16 Ibid., 14.

violence[17], developing a 'holistic welfare-based system' for dealing with youth offenders[18], and so on. The picture that emerges is of a Tocquevillian 'tutelary power [...] absolute, minute, regular, provident and mild'[19].

The second noticeable characteristic of these themes is their emphasis on the importance of achieving equality of outcomes between groups. It is striking that, for instance, the report does not recommend that the UK government develop a strategy to reduce poverty *per se* but rather to address disproportionate poverty rates between certain groups[20]; that it does not make specific recommendations about improving healthcare in the round but rather about removing barriers and improving access to healthcare for certain groups[21]; that the weight of its concerns with respect to working conditions revolve around the reduction of pay gaps[22]; and that the emphasis of its 'participation' theme is largely on increasing diversity and representation of women, ethnic minorities and disabled people in political parties and the Cabinet[23]. The overall impression created is that improving human rights performance is largely, if not exclusively, a matter of treating people 'fairly', as the report's foreword puts it[24], with the word 'fairly' interpreted to mean treating people in such a way that different groups experience broadly equal outcomes in the aggregate.

And the third and final noticeable feature of the report is its preoccupation with the gathering of data. All of the sub-themes are framed in statistical terms ('in 2019/20 there were 14.5 million people in the UK in relative poverty'[25]; 'waiting times for treatment [at hospital] were already increasing in the decade before the pandemic'[26]; 'ethnic minority workers are more likely than white workers to be on zero-hours contracts'[27]; 'data from the year ending March 2020 show that an estimated 1.6 million women in England and Wales had experienced domestic abuse in the preceding year'[28]; etc.). Many of the recommendations in the report also have a statistical component – whether

17 Ibid., 16.

18 Ibid., 18.

19 Alexis de Tocqueville, *Democracy in America, Volume II* [1840] (translated by James T. Schleifer, Liberty Fund 2012) 1252.

20 EHRC, *supra* fn 10, 9.

21 Ibid., 11.

22 Ibid., 13.

23 Ibid., 20.

24 Ibid., 4.

25 Ibid., 9.

26 Ibid., 11.

27 Ibid., 13.

28 Ibid., 15.

explicit or implicit – which typically functions as a method of measuring success: reforms to social care policy, for example, must have a 'measurable impact'[29]; 'gaps in educational attainment' must be tackled[30]; the government must 'take steps to [...] address the causes of disproportionate numbers of people from ethnic minorities being in prisons and youth custody', and so on[31]. And, characteristically, the report returns time and again to the importance of gathering statistical information as an end in itself – recommending that the government obtain 'robust data' on the impact of the pandemic on education[32], that it 'improve transparency on recruitment, retention, progression and pay'[33], that it improve 'police-recorded crime and outcome data' so as to include information about victims' characteristics[34], and that it require political parties to publish 'diversity data' about their candidates[35]. The report adopts the clear view that the human rights record of the UK can be measured, assessed, and improved through the deployment of statistics, and, indeed, that making available larger amounts of data will itself necessarily be beneficial in those objectives.

In summary, then, the EHRC's report is illustrative of a particular and distinctive understanding of what 'improving the human rights situation' really means. First, it requires the state to take an active role in the project of 'improvement'; second, it interprets improvement not necessarily as the achievement of measurable progress alone but chiefly as eliminating measurable inequalities at the level of the aggregate across different groups; and third, it requires 'the human rights situation' to be ever more carefully measured and assessed through quantitative means – the implication being that 'improvement' can itself also be measured quantitatively in order to determine whether it is in fact taking place.

The EHRC's perspective is hardly novel in contemporary human rights practice – indeed, it might be said to exemplify a general trend. The United Nations human rights organs (from which the EHRC, as the UN-accredited National Human Rights Institution, largely takes its cues) have for the past several decades taken a markedly statistical approach to the task of monitoring the implementation of human rights obligations, and often, like the EHRC, seems

29 Ibid., 10.
30 Ibid., 12.
31 Ibid., 18.
32 Ibid., 12.
33 Ibid., 14.
34 Ibid., 16.
35 Ibid., 20.

to imply that the gathering of data will itself necessarily result in better human rights-related policymaking. The *Management Plan 2022–2023* of the Office of the High Commissioner for Human Rights (OHCHR), for example, puts 'leveraging data for human rights' at the centre of its strategic priorities, describing it as a way to 'improve analysis and decision-making across the full spectrum of human rights'[36]. In this vision, 'recognising the power of data and its application to human rights challenges' will open the door to understanding 'the human rights dimensions of inequality' and therefore 'reinforce advocacy and programming' and 'bolster accountability'[37]. Doing so will require the OHCHR to focus on 'supporting national statistical systems to produce fit-for-purpose data and statistics', and to integrate its activities into a wider agenda across the United Nations which seeks to put data 'at the centre of all strategies [...] across United Nations ecosystems [*sic*]' so as to 'deliver optimal value for the Organisation, people and the planet'[38]. And while it would be something of an exaggeration to say that this approach has become totalising, the notion that monitoring state compliance with human rights obligations should largely be a data-driven exercise filters down to actual practice: when states issue periodic reports on their efforts to protect human rights within their jurisdictions to the UN human rights treaty bodies, as they are required to do[39], they almost exclusively produce lengthy catalogues of statistical measurements of 'improvement' across various metrics, which the relevant treaty body responds to with suggestions on how those metrics can be improved and requests for yet more data[40].

As is the case with the EHRC, a distinct picture of human rights is painted by the attitude adopted to the use of statistics by the OHCHR and other UN human rights organs. First, of course, it implies that there exists such a thing as a state's 'human rights performance' as a measurable phenomenon in its own right – that one can, for example, identify, define and measure quantitatively whether or not a state is performing well (or badly) with regard to each and every human right – to health, to food, to housing, to freedom of association, and so on. And in turn, this implies a picture of the relationship between state

36 OHCHR, *Management Plan 2022–2023* (2022) 9, available at <https://www.ohchr.org/sites/default/files/2022-05/OMP-2022-2023.pdf> (accessed 15 December 2022).

37 Ibid.

38 Ibid.

39 OHCHR website, 'What the Treaty Bodies Do', available at <https://www.ohchr.org/en/treaty-bodies/what-treaty-bodies-do> (accessed 15 December 2022).

40 See, for instance, the UK's 8th periodic report submitted to the Committee on the Elimination of Discrimination Against Women, UN Doc. CEDAW/C/GBR/8, 18th December 2017.

and population in which it is both desirable and possible for the former to simply act so as to improve the circumstances of the latter. Second, it suggests that the priority in deploying statistics is generally not merely to reveal social phenomena in numerical form, but chiefly to identify disparities between groups and thus bring to awareness inequalities of outcome across characteristics such as 'age, ethnicity, income, disability, geographic location, migration status, race, gender and sex', which can then ideally be eliminated[41]. It clearly, in other words, identifies good human rights performance with the elimination of measured average inequalities between particular groups. And third, it is explicit in advocating for an approach to statistics holding that more is always necessarily better: more data will 'improve analysis and decision-making', 'reinforce advocacy and programming', 'bolster accountability', and ultimately deliver 'optimal value' – provided only that it is correctly 'leveraged'[42]. The OHCHR's understanding of human rights, in other words, has a similar flavour to that of the EHCR: human rights are understood as reified real-world phenomena which it is for the state to act to improve, with improvement understood to be the elimination of inequality, measured primarily in quantitative form in the aggregate across the population.

3 Liberalism and Communitarian Visions of Equality

The EHRC's understanding of what 'improving the human rights situation' means, then, is strongly influenced by what has come to be referred to as 'substantive equality' or 'equality of outcome/result'. There is of course a vast literature on the meaning of 'equality' and how it is to be achieved, and in particular on the meaning of 'substantive' versus 'formal' equality[43], which it is not necessary to survey in detail here (not least because there is considerable disagreement when it comes to even the most basic claims about what 'substantive equality' really means)[44]. Instead, I adopt the distinction offered by Michael Foran, though using terminology of my own, between 'liberal' and

41 OHCHR, *supra* fn 36, 9.

42 Ibid.

43 For a succinct summary, see Paul Stancil, 'Substantive Equality and Procedural Justice' (2017) 102 *Iowa Law Review* 1633, 1640–1659.

44 See, for a vivid illustration, Sandra Fredman, 'Substantive Equality Revisited' (2016) 14(3) *International Journal of Constitutional Law* (2016) 712 and Catharine A. MacKinnon, 'Substantive Equality Revisited: A Reply to Sandra Fredman' (2016) 14(3) *International Journal of Constitutional Law* 739.

'communitarian' understandings of equality: whereas the former concerns itself with the deontological principle that no individual should be discriminated against on the grounds of immutable characteristics, the latter concerns itself with the teleological framework of redistribution, wherein the state should ensure that broad parity is achieved between different groups[45]. In the former case, in other words, the emphasis is on corrective justice at the individual level, based on the protection of individual rights. In the latter, the emphasis is on transforming social structures in order to attain distributive justice between categories of people[46]. To take an example which neatly illustrates the cleavage between these two positions, if an employer were to discriminate against two female employees, the personification of the liberal position would acknowledge that those individual employees had been wronged, but would have no particular interest in the question of how this affected women as a group. The personification of the communitarian position, on the other hand, would also be concerned with how this act of discrimination itself wrongs women as a whole. In the former case the principle is deontological and the locus of wrong is located strictly at the level of the individual; in the latter the principle is teleological and the locus of wrong is located at the level of the group – the act of discrimination is not only a wrong in its own right, but as part of a society-wide structure of disadvantage. It is 'systemic'[47]. By the same token, in the former view, injustice is predicated on the existence of a perpetrator – an individual wrong can only occur through the wrongful act of another individual. For the latter, a wrong can simply be 'embedded in the structure of society' and unattributable to a single actor[48]. This means that whereas for the liberal concept of equality the proper focus is providing individuals with redress if they have been discriminated against, and on ameliorating or ending practices that can be evidenced to have discriminatory effects (whether direct or indirect), for the communitarian the project of equality only ends when there is measured parity between all categories of people.

One advantage of describing equality in this way is that it allows us to avoid the thorny subject of whether 'equality of opportunity' is more closely aligned

45 Michael P. Foran, 'Discrimination as an Individual Wrong' (2019) 39(4) *Oxford Journal of Legal Studies* (2019) 901, 902–904.

46 Ibid., 917. On 'corrective' or 'commutative' versus 'redistributive' justice, see Allan Beever, *Forgotten Justice: Forms of Justice in the History of Legal and Political Theory* (OUP 2013).

47 For a typical example of this view, see Tarunabh Khaitan & Sandy Steel, 'Wrongs, Group Disadvantage and the Legitimacy of Indirect Discrimination Law' in Hugh Collins & Tarunabh Khaitan (eds) *Foundations of Indirect Discrimination Law* (Hart 2018) 197–221.

48 Fredman, *supra* fn 44, 720.

with formal or substantive equality[49]. The truth is that the phrase is something of a floating signifier, and can in different contexts be made to mean one or the other: on the one hand, it is suggestive only of the removal of discriminatory barriers (whether direct or indirect) that have the effect of preventing individual members of certain groups succeeding in their chosen activities; on the other, it suggests that there must be what is inevitably referred to as a 'level playing field', wherein 'opportunities' can only be equal where the starting position of everybody in society is broadly the same materially as well as formally[50]. It can in other words be a procedural principle or a substantive one[51]. This flexibility is why there is so little consensus on what the phrase can really be said to mean. But once we describe the cleavage between positions on equality as being one of liberalism versus communitarianism, it becomes straightforward to place equality of opportunity in whatever guise under the umbrella of the former. Equality of opportunity is predicated, that is, on the principle that individual self-direction is a value, and an end, in itself. In the formal sense, this means of course that discriminatory barriers, which act as barriers to individual self-direction, should be removed. In the substantive sense, it means that 'the adequate development in each person of their capacity for self-direction standardly requires a certain level of educational opportunity and social welfare' and that this 'constitutes a crucial aspect of their rights to be recognised as an equally valuable self-directing being'[52]. Whether, that is, equality of opportunity is only formal or requires the creation of an initial 'level playing field', its purpose is the same: to maximise the sphere in which individual self-direction is possible.

The second advantage of thinking of equality in this way is that it allows us to clearly identify the central philosophical distinction which is at the heart of discussions concerning equality and human rights, between those for whom discrimination is wrong in itself because it always harms a given individual (or individuals), and those for whom discrimination is only wrong

49 The literature is extensively surveyed in Christine Sypnowich, 'What's Wrong with Equality of Opportunity' (2020) 48(2) *Philosophical Topics* (2020) 223, 223–233.

50 On the term's extreme 'malleability', see Ben Jackson, *Equality and the British Left: A Study in Progressive Political Thought 1900–1964* (Manchester University Press 2008) 28. Symptomatically, two of the most prominent contemporary legal theorists of equality, Fredman and MacKinnon, cannot themselves agree whether equality of opportunity is to be understood to be a doctrine of substantive equality or not. See MacKinnon, *supra* fn 44, 740.

51 Bernard Williams, 'The Idea of Equality' in Bernard Williams, *The Problem of the Self* (CUP 1973) 230.

52 Charvet & Kaczynska-Nay, *supra* fn 3, 6.

consequentially because of the negative impact it has on group equality. This is most relevant, of course, with respect for 'affirmative action' or other forms of positive discrimination. For the liberal perspective, 'affirmative action' is wrong because every act of affirmation involves an implicit act of discrimination against an individual member of an advantaged group[53]. For every all-woman Parliamentary candidate shortlist, for instance, there are a number of men who are denied selection through no fault of their own[54]. For the communitarian, affirmative action is to be pursued because it furthers the interests of group equality, and 'positive discrimination' is justified in achieving that aim; all-woman Parliamentary candidate shortlists are therefore to be welcomed in correcting a 'systemic' wrong. Whether affirmative action is favoured, in other words, depends on where the emphasis is placed – on the individual or the group. But the distinction is also of wider relevance, of course, simply in terms of allocation of resources. A strategy for improving the human rights situation looks very different, in this regard, simply based on whether that strategy emphasises liberal or communitarian approaches to what constitutes progress vis-à-vis human rights.

The difference between these two ideals of 'equality' is therefore highly significant and consequential, and as a result it clearly matters which framework the EHRC adopts. And as will by now be clear, it is difficult to argue, based on our mapping of its priorities above, that it has anything other than a primarily substantive, distributive and, ultimately therefore, a communitarian conceptualisation of equality. It emphasises the state's role as being to bring about the goal of equality, as measured statistically, and achieved through redistribution, and understands equality as being measurable through the analysis and numeration of results or outcomes. Most importantly, its interest in equality does not result in merely a formal interest in eliminating discrimination against individuals perpetrated by other individuals, but in a substantive interest in achieving measured, aggregate parity between groups in society.

53 There have of course been attempts to square that particular circle, the most prominent example being Ronald Dworkin, 'Reverse Discrimination', in Ronald Dworkin, *Taking Rights Seriously* [1977] (Bloomberg 2013) 319.

54 Richard Kelly & Isobel White, *All-Women Shortlists*, House of Commons Briefing Paper 5057, 7th March 2016, available at <https://researchbriefings.files.parliament.uk/documents/SN05057/SN05057.pdf> (accessed 15 December 2022).

4 The Sociology of Quantification and the 'Drunkard's Search'

It would be straightforward to conclude from these observations that the vision of human rights which is revealed in the practice of the EHRC and OHCHR is a product simply of the priorities of the people working at those organisations. And indeed it is one of the most elementary observations of the sociology of quantification that public measurements tend to reveal the (sometimes implicit or unstated) values of those doing the measuring – in fact, aligning the behaviour of the subject with the priorities of the measurer is usually the whole point of the exercise[55]. Hence, to take an obvious and familiar example, university rankings in the UK now almost universally include the metric of 'graduate prospects', usually measured as a percentage of graduates who are in professional jobs or 'graduate employment' within a certain time period after graduation. This, it goes without saying, reveals an increasingly instrumentalised view of university education, emphasising getting a good job as being one of its main purposes – and also, of course, showing that value for money with regard to education is an increasingly important concern.

At the same time, however, one should never suppose that the relationship between values and measurement is unidirectional. Indeed, the potential for measures themselves to transmogrify into values or 'recreate social worlds' is well known[56]. Once something is measured, it instantly takes on a concrete existence of its own, becoming a 'thing which holds together in the imaginations of politicians, government officials, and the general public'[57] where hitherto the underlying reality was amorphous, abstract, unknown, or accepted uncritically. This, in turn, then causes people to alter not merely their behaviour but also their attitudes in response to what has now been rendered 'real', because human beings are always, and inescapably, reflexive and reactive – and much more so when what is being reacted to has been reified through the use of statistics. This is partly, of course, because numbers have

55 See, e.g., Nikolas Rose, 'Governing "Advanced" Liberal Democracies', reproduced in Peter Miller & Nikolas Rose, *Governing the Present: Administering Economic, Social and Personal Life* (Polity 2008) 199, 212–213; Margaret L. Satterthwaite, 'Indicators in Crisis: Rights-Based Humanitarian Indicators in Post-Earthquake Haiti' (2010) 43 *New York University Journal of International Law and Politics* 865.

56 Wendy N. Espeland & Michael Sauder, 'Rankings and Reactivity: How Public Measures Recreate Social Worlds' (2007) 113(1) *American Journal of Sociology* 1.

57 Wendy N. Espeland & Mitchell L. Stevens, 'A Sociology of Quantification' (2008) 49(3) *European Journal of Sociology* 401, 412.

an inherent authority and 'trustworthiness'[58]. But it is also because they possess what Porter calls 'mechanical objectivity'[59] – emphasising that as well as being purportedly neutral methods of communicating meaning, requiring no specialist expertise, they also suggest that reality itself can be manipulated[60]. Once a phenomenon has been quantified and hence made into a 'thing', attention quickly turns to how the numbers can be changed. Simply put, numerical measurements (apparently, at least), render the world transparent to human actors and therefore open to improvement by human action[61]. And once this has happened, attention tends to accrue to such measures, partly simply because numbers are more easily remembered and more succinctly communicated that non-numerical information[62], and partly because, once a way of expressing phenomena becomes normalised, things that cannot be expressed in that form begin to seem less significant or real[63].

The relationship between measurements and values, in other words, can just as readily flow from the former to the latter than vice-versa, and there are many prominent examples that illustrate that point – from contemporary concerns about climate change, which very clearly derive in part from the capacity for scientists to measure and model temperature changes and amounts of carbon in the atmosphere across time, to the history of the welfare state, which was given much of its impetus by newly-invented statistical tools in the Victorian era which gave the concept of 'poverty' a concrete reality and concomitantly suggested it could be ameliorated or improved[64]. It would be a mistake, of course, to overcorrect by suggesting that this process is itself unidirectional, and that people derive their values merely from what they statistically observe, just as it would be a mistake to suggest that what is measured merely reflects the values of those doing the measuring. The truth is almost certainly somewhere in the middle, and that the relationship between measurement and values is a Humean admixture of causes that is difficult to separate, and which is probably mutually reinforcing.

58 Desrosières, *supra* fn 9; the classic observation is of course that of Max Weber, *Economy and Society* [1921] (translated by Günther Roth, Bedminster Press 1968).

59 Theodore M. Porter, *Trust in Numbers: The Pursuit of Objectivity in Science and Public Life* (Princeton University Press 1995) 4.

60 Espeland & Stevens, *supra* fn 57, 419.

61 Ian Hacking, *The Taming of Chance* (Cambridge University Press 1990).

62 Espeland & Sauder, *supra* fn 56, 18.

63 Georg Simmel, *The Philosophy of Money* (translated by Tom Bottomore and David Frisby, Routledge 1978) 443–45.

64 Gertrude Himmelfarb, *Poverty and Compassion: The Moral Imagination of the Late Victorians* (Knopf 1991).

It is important at least, then, to consider how measurability itself can affect and, in particular, accentuate the adoption within an organisation of certain values or priorities – and how it can divert attention away from unmeasurable or difficult-to-quantify phenomena which may in fact be more important. This is, in essence, the insight encapsulated in the 'drunkard's search' or 'streetlight effect', summarised in the parable set out in the introduction to this chapter. The drunkard's attention is diverted merely by the fact that the streetlight sheds light on an area of pavement; obsessed with what he can see, he ignores what he cannot, even though he is – or ought to be – fully aware in the abstract that he will not find what he is looking for. Eventually, looking 'where the light is' begins to dictate the ends of the organisation itself.

The paradigmatic case in the field of the sociology of quantification has become law school rankings, thanks to the work of Espeland and Sauder in the early 2000s, which elucidated how such rankings, deriving in part from a mixture of specific metrics such as class sizes, staff-student ratios, and the like, affect the priorities and behaviours of law school administrators and managers[65]. Perhaps the most vivid examples concern admissions, where administrators describe sacrificing professional judgment or concerns about diversity, access or good 'fit' in the name of admitting students with good LSAT (Law School Admission Test) scores – the median LSAT score being one of the statistics taken account of in the major law school ranking system[66]. Here, attention is drawn away from what is not, or cannot be, measured – which remains in the dark – towards what is illuminated by the streetlight of mere statistics: the median LSAT score. Similarly, career advisors report advising students to take job offers irrespective of whether they think that the student would flourish in that particular role, because, again, placement statistics – the number of students employed nine months after graduation – are taken into account in rankings, whereas the much more nebulous phenomenon of whether graduates are in suitable jobs based on their own character, experiences, and abilities goes ignored and cannot be quantified[67].

Although it is not made explicit in Espeland and Sauder's work, what is most relevant about these observations is how they transform the values and priorities of the organisation (that is, the law school) almost irrespective of the values of the staff. Regardless of what the members of the law school – academic staff, administrators, career advisors and so on – initially might think is the purpose of their organisation and their personal role, this becomes supplanted in

65 Espeland & Sauder, *supra* fn 56.

66 Ibid., 28–29.

67 Ibid., 27.

practice by whatever values are implicit in what is being measured[68]. Because median LSAT scores matter, this means that students with high LSAT scores are to be admitted by default, and the school itself therefore by necessity takes on the goal of honing the skills of already academically-excellent students. And because employability statistics matter, the school takes on a much more instrumental character than it might otherwise have – causing it to focus on the metric of jobs *per se* to the exclusion of other goals.

This transformation in institutional values is, of course, accentuated when measurements are made public, because they then readily become tied to the concept of 'performance' and thereby become a proxy for whether an organisation is doing well or not and hence whether it garners prestige and, perhaps more importantly, funding[69]. If the percentage of graduates of a law school who find work within nine months is made public, for example, then it is quickly identified as something which should be improved, especially in comparison to its competitors. If it increases, those in charge of the law school are deemed to have performed well and may achieve pay rises or promotions or be eligible for 'better' jobs elsewhere. If it decreases, they are deemed to have performed badly, with predictable consequences – and, of course, those funding the school begin to question whether they should be[70]. This is a feature of human behaviour found not only in market conditions, but in any kind of complex environment[71], and readers will undoubtedly be familiar with its consequences in their own working lives given the 'tsunami' of public measurement that has been unleashed across the developed world since the 1990s[72].

In summary, then, there is a tendency for measurements themselves to become institutional values, almost irrespective of the underlying motives and desires of an institution's personnel, because of the way statistics render their subject concrete and purportedly manipulable, and because of the way they garner attention and divert it away from other phenomena. Much as the members of the institution might be aware at some level that this is happening, and even feel resistant to it, the 'tyranny' of quantification appears almost inescapable[73]. And indeed, as the use of statistical measurements

---

68 Ibid., esp. 22–23 and 28–32.

69 Ibid.

70 Ibid., 23.

71 Andrew B. Kipnis, 'Audit Cultures: Neoliberal Governmentality, Socialist Legacy, or Technologies of Governing?' (2008) 35(2) *American Ethnologist* 275.

72 Paul L. Caron & Richard Gely, 'What Law Schools Can Learn from Billy Beane and the Oakland Athletics' (2004) 82 *Texas Law Review* 1483, 1553.

73 Haridimos Tsoukas, 'The Tyranny of Light' (1997) 29(9) *Futures* 827.

of performance proliferates it becomes impossible to even imagine alternatives[74].

The relationship, then, between what is being measured and the priorities of an organisation is a complicated one. The choice of what to measure undoubtedly often reflects, at least in part, the values of those making the decision. But if those deciding what to measure – for instance, *US News*, the magazine which produces the main law school ranking system in the US – are outside of the organisation, then the decision alone can very quickly cause the organisation itself to align itself with the values of the external decision-makers and radically change its behaviour as a consequence[75]. And at this point it also becomes important to consider whether this process can happen in a more accidental fashion, simply as a result of certain phenomena being more easily rendered into numerical form than others. Once, in other words, it has become widely accepted that statistical methods should be used in order to help improve performance, it may very well simply become natural for attention to be drawn to those aspects of an organisation's interests that are most readily quantified, and for the organisation's priorities to thereby become drawn ever more closely to those aspects to the detriment of others. The UK EHRC's activities, I will argue, give at least an indication that this could be the case, in that they demonstrate how an attachment to the concept of quantification in itself leads quickly to a search for phenomena to quantify, and that this is accompanied by a consequential shift in what is prioritised – not necessarily because the values of the personnel at the organisation in question are initially closely aligned with what is being measured, but simply because of the way in which what is measured affects an organisation's values.

5 Realigning the EHRC's Values

The EHRC was established by a statute, the Equality Act 2006, which sets out its general duty as:

> (a) encouraging and supporting the development of a society in which people's ability to achieve their potential is not limited by prejudice or discrimination,

---

74 José Ossandon, Wendy N. Espeland, Michael Sauder, '"Islands of Qualities in an Ocean of Quantification": A Conversation with Wendy Espeland and Michael Sauder' (2021) 8(2) *Valuation Studies* 103, 109.

75 Michael Power, *The Audit Society: Rituals of Verification* (OUP 1997) 100–121.

(b) there is respect for and protection of each individual's human rights,
(c) there is respect for the dignity and worth of each individual,
(d) each individual has an equal opportunity to participate in society, and
(e) there is mutual respect between groups based on understanding and valuing of diversity and on shared respect for equality and human rights[76].

These priorities are, of course, very broad and nebulous, but they have three features that are significant for the purposes of this chapter. The first is that the emphasis is on the *individual*. While the Commission's general duties under the Act do include fostering 'mutual respect between groups', their main focus is on the individual as rights-holder – a person with dignity and worth, whose human rights must be respected and protected, and who must have an equal opportunity to participate in society with other individuals. The second is that the general duties do not specify that the Commission must encourage a society in which people achieve their potential *per se*. Its focus is only on making sure that prejudice and discrimination do not stand in the way of people's doing so – which is, of course, a different matter. And third is that, when the Act says anything about equality, at least insofar as the general duties of the Commission are concerned, it only does so in relation to the concept of 'equality of opportunity'. It does not suggest that the Commission ought to strive for a society in which there is substantive equality of outcomes or in which everybody is equal overall – or even in which there is aggregate equality between groups. Indeed, the explanatory notes to the Act are quite clear that, as far as different groups are concerned, the aim of the Commission is to make sure there are 'good relations' between them, rather than measured equality[77].

This is borne out by the other substantive provisions of the Act. Section 8, for instance, which sets out the duties of the Commission with regard to equality and diversity, specifies that its powers should be exercised to achieve 'equality of opportunity', and goes on to make clear that 'equality means equality between individuals'[78]. Where the Commission issues codes of practice pursuant to s. 14 this, again, is to be done in order to promote 'equality of opportunity'[79]. There is no express mention of any duty to achieve average substantive

76 Equality Act 2006, s. 3.
77 Equality Act 2006, Explanatory note to s. 3.
78 Equality Act 2006, s. 8, (1) and (2).
79 Equality Act 2006, Explanatory note to s. 14.

equality between groups, or even substantive equality of outcomes between individuals, in the text of the Act itself, and indeed in the original text (in a section now repealed) there was only one major provision concerning groups. Its focus was on reducing crime affecting specific groups and conducting various recreational or educational activities involving them – in keeping with the general duty to effect 'good relations'[80].

This in turn means that the preponderance of the Commission's activities were clearly envisaged to have hinged around enforcement at the individual level and the creation of a regulatory framework of formal equality in which discriminatory practices were made unlawful – as well as a general project of promoting what was often referred to in the period leading up to the enactment of the Human Rights Act 1998 as a 'culture of rights'[81]. The Parliamentary Joint Commission on Human Rights (JCHR), having conducted a wide-ranging consultation with voluntary equalities-and human rights-related groups in its report on the Case for a [Equality and Human Rights] Commission, concluded that there were two categories of unmet need which the EHRC should address: 'the establishment of reactive arrangements' to provide 'redress or relief for those whose rights have been violated or are threatened'; and the 'active nurturing of a culture in which violations of rights [...] are to be avoided' such that public bodies 'respect the rights of individuals and recognises their rights to equal consideration and dignity'[82]. This meant in its view that the EHRC's functions should revolve around education and research; holding inquiries into human rights abuses, making submissions to UN human rights mechanisms, scrutinising existing and proposed legislation, and 'legal enforcement' – i.e. carrying out test cases, third party interventions, and submission of amicus briefs[83]. In its later, more detailed comments on the powers of the new Commission, the emphasis of the JCHR essentially remained this bifold focus on legal enforcement and cultural human rights promotion. It advocated a 'strategic approach' hinging around 'the development of human rights awareness' in public bodies, the third sector, and within the legal profession[84], and made numerous observations about the role that the ECHR should take

80 Equality Act 2006, s. 19 and Explanatory note.

81 See for example the statement of the then Home Secretary, the Rt Hon Jack Straw MP to the JCHR, in JCHR, minutes of evidence, Mar. 14, 2001, HL. 66-I, HC. 332-I, at question 17.

82 JCHR, Sixth Report 2002–2003, paras. 102–103, available at <https://publications.parliament.uk/pa/jt200203/jtselect/jtrights/67/6708.htm> (accessed 15 December 2022).

83 Ibid., para. 105.

84 JCHR, Eleventh Report 2003–4, paras. 25–27, available at <https://publications.parliament.uk/pa/jt200304/jtselect/jtrights/78/7805.htm> (accessed 15 December 2022).

in respect of litigation and dispute resolution[85]. Again, in respect of groups, the JCHR's primary concern was good relations – the promotion of 'community cohesion' and 'dialogue' rather than substantive equality across different metrics[86].

And this both reflected and reinforced the government's approach. The original government white paper proposing the establishment of the EHRC was clearly centred around the promotion of equality of opportunity as distinct from substantive equality, and the removal of discriminatory barriers at the individual level. It set out among the core aims of the Commission the promotion of 'equality of opportunity between people in [...] different groups' – the wording undoubtedly having been chosen to avoid the implication that this would mean equality of outcomes or redistribution between groups as such – alongside eliminating 'unlawful discrimination and harassment' through 'supporting individuals' and strategic litigation, and again emphasised not measured average equality between groups but 'good relations' between them and 'community cohesion'[87]. The Commission would be a 'guarantor for individuals who experience unlawful discrimination' with a clear emphasis on dispute resolution and legal representation[88]. Nowhere does the white paper make the case that the purpose of the EHRC, or indeed of equality and human rights law in general, is to ensure that different groups have similar substantive aggregate outcomes – and, indeed, when a question was raised during a Parliamentary debate over the subsequent Equality Bill regarding under-representation of Protestants in public sector jobs in Northern Ireland, the Minister of State for Northern Ireland's response was to the effect that he wished to see a situation in which 'all individuals are treated as equals and on their merits' – not one in which there was equality of outcome between groups[89].

When the EHRC was established, in other words, the nature of its envisaged role was to promote equality and human rights based on rather different understandings of those terms than those under which the EHRC currently operates. 'Equality' was, during that period, understood to mean that everybody should

---

85 JCHR, Sixteenth Report 2003–4, paras. 29–40, available at <https://publications.parliament.uk/pa/jt200304/jtselect/jtrights/156/15606.htm> (accessed 15 December 2022).

86 JCHR, *supra* fn 84, para. 41.

87 UK Department for Trade and Industry, *Fairness for All: A New Commission for Equality and Human Rights* (DTI 2004) 102–103, available at <https://www.equalrightstrust.org/ertdocumentbank/Fairness%20for%20all.pdf> (accessed 15 December 2022).

88 Ibid., 19–20.

89 Mr David Hanson MP, Hansard HC vol. 450 col. 288, 11th October 2006, available at <https://hansard.parliament.uk/Commons/2006-10-11/debates/06101166000022/EqualityBill> (accessed 15 December 2022).

have, in the words of the Prime Minister at the time, 'the chance to contribute'[90]. This chiefly meant acting to remove discriminatory barriers (whether through legislative review, strategic litigation, dispute resolution, and so on) and undertaking educational and advisory functions so as to promote human rights awareness among public bodies in particular. By extension, the establishment of the EHRC was predicated on the understanding that 'equality' essentially functioned between individuals rather than between groups as such. While an individual's membership of a particular group (or, to use the language of equality law, an individual's possession of protected characteristics) would always be relevant in the sense that discriminatory practices would ordinarily be founded on that status, the essence of equality was all individuals being treated, in the words of the Northern Ireland Secretary, 'as equals and on their merits'. The EHRC's remit was, in essence, to foster in society 'a culture of respect based on equal value, the dignity and worth of every individual'[91].

In this regard, the approach adopted by government of the time, as well as the JCHR, to the subject of 'equality' can be broadly said to have influenced by what I earlier called a liberal, rather than a communitarian, understanding of that concept. It emphasised that equality was a comparator between individuals rather than groups, and was at pains to make clear that it understood 'equality' itself to mean equality of opportunity between individuals (it is also worth observing that this has not changed significantly: the government minister with oversight of the EHRC, currently the Minister for Women and Equalities, has the explicit responsibilities of 'developing an equalities policy that is based on individual autonomy and dignity' and 'promoting equality of opportunity for everyone')[92]. And the work that the EHRC was envisaged to perform was essentially dedicated to realising that vision of how 'equality' would find effect in society – through advocating for legal change, inquiries, litigation and case work, codes of conduct with employers, and general educational work. By extension, we might say that its underlying philosophy was essentially deontological and concerned with the elimination of discrimination as an individual (corrective) injustice or wrong.

---

90 UK DTI, *supra* fn 87, 1.

91 Ms Patricia Hewitt MP, Hansard HC vol 421, cols. 20WS–23WS (12th May, 2004) available at <https://hansard.parliament.uk/Commons/2004-05-12/debates/9149bc66-cb66-4c25-a535-5794b96e9fbe/CommissionForEqualityAndHumanRights?highlight=equality%20bill#contribution-02a56a8f-11c9-49c8-8567-d1b1e83725d5> (accessed 15 December 2022).

92 See 'Ministerial Role: Minister for Women and Equalities', available at <https://www.gov.uk/government/ministers/minister-for-women-and-equalities--3> (accessed 15 December 2022).

The 15 years (at the time of writing) since the EHRC first began its operations have therefore seen a rather radical shift. As we have seen, where once the locus of its interest could be said to be the individual and his or her relationship to other individuals, that locus is now firmly on the 'group' understood as the members of the population possessing a certain protected characteristic. Where once it might have been said that the EHRC's work would be focused on ensuring that individuals do not themselves suffer discrimination and receive a remedy if they do, it now could be said that its main emphasis is on measuring substantive equality of outcomes, in the aggregate, between groups and advocating for methods to bring this about. And where once the preponderance of its activities were intended to be placed on what one might call 'leg work' – the practicalities of enforcement of equality law and providing education and training – it has now become preoccupied with technical projects, and chiefly the gathering and interpretation of statistics. How did this transformation take place?

The truth is that the Equality Act 2006 did contain what, in hindsight, may be seen as a precursor of the current preoccupation with statistical measurement. This was s. 12 of the Act and the duty it imposed on the Commission to 'monitor progress'[93]. 'From time to time', the Act stipulates, the EHRC is to identify 'changes in society', 'results at which to aim for the purpose of encouraging and support' such changes (i.e. 'outcomes'), and indicators for measuring progress towards such outcomes[94]. And the Act also stipulates that the Commissions should monitor such progress and report on it periodically to the relevant government minister – which is the origin of its regular 'Is Britain Fairer?' reports.

This, on the face of it, relatively minor aspect of the EHRC's duties has since become a central part of its work – 'using data and evidence to understand equality and human rights problems' is listed as the very first of its functions in its most recent strategic plan[95], and it now bills its own reports as being 'the most comprehensive review of how we, as a nation, are performing on equality and human rights' – not to mention a 'complete picture of people's life chances in Britain today'[96]. Undoubtedly this shift towards prioritising statistical measurement of progress towards outcomes is part of the same phenomenon earlier identified – the 'tsunami' of public measurement that now takes place across almost all aspects of modern life. And it also presumably reflects

93 Equality Act 2006, s. 12.

94 Ibid.

95 EHRC, *Strategic Plan 2022–2025* (2022) 9, available at <https://www.equalityhumanrights.com/sites/default/files/about-us-strategic-plan-2022-2025.pdf> (accessed 15 December 2022).

96 EHRC, *supra* fn 5, 6.

financial priorities – the EHRC's budget declined from £62 million in 2010 to around £18 million in 2022, and it is certainly the case that gathering of statistics is less resource-intensive than other aspects of the Commission's work, such as supporting litigation, conducting inquiries and so on. And, finally, of course, both of these factors have influenced human rights practice at the UN level[97], which in turn has exerted pressure on the EHRC itself. We have already seen how the OHCHR has taken to emphasising the production of data itself as a strategic priority, and this tendency has only become more pronounced since the Commission was established – with NHRIs like the EHRC being continually encouraged to generate more, and more granular, data on the basis that '[i]f you don't count it, it won't count'[98].

It is hard therefore, given what the insights of the sociology of quantification tell us, to escape the conclusion that the EHRC's 'substantive turn' is at least partly the result of the sheer power of quantitative measurement to dominate attention. Once a phenomenon is measured statistically, as we have seen, it begins to seem more 'real' and hence also manipulable – amenable to change. And, especially once it is shared publicly, it begins also to take on increased significance as a measure of performance: attention is drawn not only to the figure itself, but also to methods for improving it as a way of demonstrating success. The result is that the act of statistical measurement itself begins to drive institutional values, rather than vice versa.

Considered in this light, the EHRC's shift from liberal to communitarian conceptualisations of 'equality' begins to seem not so much the result of a deliberate strategy but a kind of epiphenomenon of the impulse to measure. Put another way, if one were to examine the work of the EHRC in the abstract over the course of its existence, and its increasing preoccupation with measuring the realisation of substantive equality of outcomes between groups, one might be tempted to say that the chain of causation runs from value to action, so that the members of the organisation begin with an interest in substantive equality which drives them to an interest in measuring it, and hence to the act of measurement itself. But it might just as likely be the case that the chain of causation flows in the other direction, from action to values, and that the Commission's interest in substantive equality derives from the fact that it its

97 The OHCHR's budget has been falling in real terms for years. See OHCHR, *United Nations Human Rights Appeal 2022* (OHCHR 2022) 40–41.

98 The then-UN Deputy High Commissioner for Human Rights, Flavia Pansieri, made this statement at a Human Rights Council event in 2014: see <https://www.ohchr.org/en/stories/2014/07/best-seller-users-manual-implementation-human-rights-indicators> (accessed 15 December 2022).

data-centric approach – in which, as we have seen, it is strongly encouraged by the UN human rights apparatus in general – drives its attention towards what can be readily measured quantitatively ('where the light is') and away from what cannot. And since indicators of substantive equality between groups are much more easily generated and assessed than the more diffuse question of whether there is formal equality of opportunity between all individuals in society, the drunkard's attention, so to speak, is naturally drawn to the former than the latter – with a change in institutional values being the inevitable result. It is much more straightforward, for example, to gather data on the number of women MPs in Parliament (an indicator of substantive equality between groups) than it is to identify individual instances of women who have been denied the opportunity to become an MP due to discrimination and provide them with a remedy. It is much easier, by the same token, to gather statistics on the proportion of people from particular groups among the prison population and compare between groups, for example, than it is to identify individual circumstances in which imprisonment has been the result of discrimination and apply a remedy. The fact that the EHRC increasingly prioritises the achievement of substantive equality between groups may therefore very well be a result simply of the features of measurement itself.

6 The Consequences of Measurement

If this is true, of course, then it opens up the EHRC's activities to critical reflection in the round. In the first place, it would indicate that the Commission's preoccupation with the gathering of data needs in itself to be re-examined. It is by now well-established that the act of measuring is not a value-free exercise, and this is not merely true in the sense that what one chooses to measure reflects one's priorities and assumptions. It is also true, as we have seen, in the sense that measurement itself affects – and indeed has the potential to warp – the behaviour of the measurer as it reacts to what is measured. At the very least, this needs to be acknowledged and reflected upon. In the document detailed its measurement framework, the EHRC does outline some critiques of its 'indicator-based approach' (without responding substantively)[99]. But while it acknowledges that focusing on quantifiable information causes a neglect of qualitative aspects of a phenomenon (for instance, the number of teachers

99 EHRC, *Measurement Framework for Human Rights* (2017) 43, available at <https://www.equalityhumanrights.com/sites/default/files/measurement-framework-interactive_pdf.pdf> (accessed 15 December 2022).

versus the substance of what is being taught)[100], it does not consider the possibility that quantification itself may act to subvert or change its own priorities in the way in which this chapter suggests. This is not, it should go without saying, a triviality or quibble. The EHRC was established by statute as a result of the manifesto commitment of the Labour government of 2005[101]. Its mandate therefore derived from the democratically elected government of the day, and it did not include working to achieve measured median equality of substantive outcomes between groups. Yet this is what the Commission increasingly views as its mission – and, indeed, it is quite open about its desire to 'more than [fulfil] [its] statutory obligation to monitor progress' and '[shape] policy and political agendas and [drive] social change'[102]. This should at the very least give the EHRC and its supervising Minister (currently the Minister for Women and Equalities) cause to consider whether has been led astray from what it was established to do. To be clear, whether or not pursuing a communitarian vision of equality is a laudable goal or otherwise is immaterial; the salient point is that if the EHRC is to pursue such a vision, then it must be done on the basis of a democratic mandate in the form of a statutory requirement.

On a related note, but more broadly, there is also of course a tension between the imperative of achieving measured equality of outcomes between groups and the EHRC's core purposes – particularly the emphasis that was placed by the Equality Act 2006 on the 'dignity and worth of each individual'[103]. Where individuals are only perceived as relevant insofar as they are counted in an aggregate figure such as the 'poverty rate', the 'pay gap', figures for 'access to healthcare', and so on, then their 'dignity and worth' is intuitively undermined. This is especially so given the implications of substantive equality when carefully examined: if all that matters is whether aggregate outcomes are broadly similar between groups, then the consequences of public policy for individual outliers are ultimately irrelevant – it is, for example, of no consequence that one member of an 'advantaged' group is treated unfairly on the basis of group characteristics provided that such treatment produces statistical equality across a given metric[104]. This may or may not be desirable, but how it is reconciled to the imperative of protecting 'the dignity and worth of each individual' has never been adequately theorised – and certainly not by the EHRC. The tendency for rationalistic quantitative measurement of value to suppress

100 Ibid.

101 The Labour Party, *Britain Forward Not Back* (The Labour Party 2005) 110.

102 EHRC, *supra* fn 99, 14.

103 Equality Act 2006, s. 3.

104 On this point, see e.g. Christopher J. Peters, 'Equality Revisited' (1997) 110 *Harvard Law Review* 1210, 1212.

and subsume individual distinctiveness is an observation that is of course as old as Aristotle, but it is no less important for that[105].

Thirdly, and perhaps most radically, the question must be raised as to whether the EHRC's own assertion, that ever-more detailed and disaggregated data is necessarily beneficial, is correct. The Commission has a statutory duty to monitor progress. And clearly statistical data has its uses – particularly in identifying patterns of discrimination. Defenders of a quantitative approach would also undoubtedly make the case that, even taking into consideration the pitfalls of data-driven projects, it is better to have more information rather than less. The counterintuitive lesson of the drunkard's search is that sometimes it is actually preferable to have no light at all, because that would force the searcher to make the effort to look in the dark – and ultimately therefore have a better chance of finding his keys. The emphasis on statistics, in other words, not only has an (often unacknowledged) opportunity cost in terms of time, energy and resources, but it also comes associated with the risk that it will distract an organisation from its core functions by examining only what is amenable to measurement. That may very well have consequences that go entirely unobserved, and this also should be cause for further reflection.

7 Conclusion

We have seen, then, that the EHRC has departed considerably from its original mandate. While the Equality Act 2006 and the impulse behind it was clearly based on what we have identified as a liberal understanding of equality, focused on achieving the removal of direct or indirect discriminatory barriers faced by individuals, it is now chiefly concerned with the communitarian achievement of substantive equality of outcomes between groups. This in turn, indeed, has led it to focus on the 'group' as the locus of discrimination in society, and hence to lose sight of the emphasis on individual dignity that its statutory mandate contained. And this, we have seen, could very well be attributed not so much to a change in the prior values of the EHRC's Board and staff, but rather to the imperatives of the act of measurement itself, which draws attention to certain factors at the expense of others and alters organisational priorities accordingly.

The wider lessons of the EHRC's 'substantive turn' are twofold. The first is that, while there is by now a sizeable literature on the sociology of

105 The best modern statement of the Aristotelian position is Martha Nussbaum, *The Fragility of Goodness: Luck and Ethics in Greek Tragedy and Philosophy* (Cambridge University Press 1986).

quantification and its effects, it remains very rare for organisations engaged in public measurement to interrogate the practice in any rigour or depth. While it is sometimes acknowledged that such measures may serve as a purportedly neutral 'cloak' for political choice-making[106], or even that they foster an undesirable increase in the power of technocrats or managers[107], it is much rarer for those conducting public measurement to consider the question as to whether the measurement activities they carry out might actually impact on their own priorities and values in unintended ways. The EHRC is a case in point; while it seems well aware that there are many objections to a data-driven approach[108], it does not appear to have considered whether its own goals may be being dictated simply by what is measurable as opposed to what is not.

The second is that while we are used to thinking of public policy as being the product either of incentives, or of a political process, or of the values of those who design and implement it, more attention should be paid to the question of whether it is simply the result of some features of economic and social life being more measurable than others. When statistics are widely treated as being the preferred way to ascertain whether 'progress' is being made, and when therefore statistical measures become widely available, it is natural that they will drive changes in what is being prioritised – as the example of law school rankings neatly demonstrates. This can, as we have seen, result in public bodies in particular being driven quite far from their original mandates, and often unintentionally. This requires further elucidation, especially through empirical study.

More generally, the story of the drunkard's search ought in the end to spur reflection not merely on the consequences of measurement, but on the goals and priorities of an organisation. The drunkard has an aim in mind – to find his keys. But his search is disconnected from it and will not, no matter how much effort he puts in, achieve it. This speaks to an inalienable feature of human experience, which is the tendency to 'favour the visible' and to 'scorn the abstract'[109], often to the detriment of one's real values. From time to time, it is important to reflect on whether one is actually working towards one's goals or being caught up in a distraction, and this is as true of an organisation as it is true of an individual. The EHRC's substantive turn, in which at times it seems to be working orthogonally or even in opposition to its original mandate, serves as a warning in this regard.

---

106 Sally E. Merry, 'Measuring the World: Indicators, Human Rights and Global Governance' (2011) 52(3) *Current Anthropology* (2011) S83.

107 Hartley Dean, *Human Rights and Social Welfare* (Routledge 2015).

108 EHRC, *supra* fn 99.

109 Nassim N. Taleb, *Fooled by Randomness: The Hidden Role of Chance in Life and in the Markets* (Random House 2001) 262.

PART 3

Transnational and International Market-Related Activities

CHAPTER 12

Profiling in Algorithm-Based Decisions: An African Perspective

Salvatore Mancuso and Livio Corselli[1]

1 AI, Algorithms and Automated Decision-Making – a Legal Issue

The entire world is pervaded by algorithms and much of our daily life deal with virtual mathematical representations of reality. It has been a long time since terms such as 'artificial intelligence', 'machine learning', 'predictive algorithms' and alike, have become part of the common vocabulary, although there are still no shared and accepted definitions for them. This gap therefore makes it necessary to understand what is meant by artificial intelligence (hereinafter AI), a concept very often assimilated and brought back to the idea of algorithm despite the two having a different meaning.

While the algorithm, in fact, represents the codification of a process in a logical sense, a set of rules that must be followed to get to the solution of problems, AI goes beyond, pointing at "machines which are capable of analyzing situation and learning from themselves and then generating answers which may not even be foreseen or controlled by their programmers"[2]. This confusion is justified by the steps forward taken by the most modern algorithms, which are actually nothing but mathematical functions generating a digital copy of reality and, on that ground, creating predictive models in order to ease the decision-making tasks in different fields. Ultimately, AI represents a step further because "it arises from algorithmic programming but, due to the complexity of the process it carries out, the outcome of the programming cannot be predicted by humans, however well informed"[3]. Thus we understand why AI is defined by the Oxford dictionary as "the theory and development of computer systems able to perform tasks normally requiring human intelligence, such

1 Salvatore Mancuso is the author of sections 4 and 5; Livio Corselli of sections 1, 2 and 3.

2 Lord Philip Sales, *Algorithms, artificial intelligence and the law*, Speech, November 12, 2019, at 4, available at <https://www.supremecourt.uk/docs/speech-191112.pdf> (accessed June 2023).

3 Sales, *supra* fn 1, 4.

 | DOI:10.1163/9789004680944_013

as visual perspection, speech recognition, decision-making, and translation between languages"[4].

Setting aside the issue of definitions, which in any case has its obvious importance and which perhaps will find answers only as time goes by, with the ever wider diffusion of new autonomous technologies, there is no doubt that algorithms play a central role in modern Western societies. An algorithm constitutes, in layman's terms, a step by step process to reach the solution of a problem[5]. But the exponential increase in computing capacity has made it possible to work on complex mathematical functions featuring a huge number of variables, thus turning algorithms into tools providing quick solutions to extremely complicated problems. This is demonstrated by the use of algorithms in the field of dynamic programming, an area of study focused on finding solutions to multi-objective dynamic problems, seen as problems involving conflicting objectives that change over time[6].

Machine learning, self-learning algorithms, probabilistic algorithms and so on, are just some of the most recent technological applications we have to deal with and which allow, through a not explicitly pre-programmed machine activity, to provide probabilistic reasoning for decision-making more efficiently than humans. Scholars, at this point, agree that "[t]he use of algorithms in artificial intelligence is essentially about automated decision-making, which can and does influence human decision-making"[7].

The use of algorithms in a variety of different fields (medicine, public administration, management of markets – including financial ones –, provision and assistance in decision-making activities, among others) is nowadays a daily practice, to the point that algorithms are shaping our future and our lives. The huge diffusion of new technologies makes it necessary to tackle the problem also from a legal point of view, trying to find solutions to the questions that the massive use of algorithms is generating in modern societies.

The algorithmic analysis of large amounts of data carried out in order to simplify decision-making tasks creates risks in term of privacy violations, discrimination and non-compliance with fundamental rights, which are recognized

---

4 See <https://www.oxfordreference.com/view/10.1093/oi/authority.20110803095426960> (accessed June 2023).

5 George M. Bodner, 'The Role of Algorithms in Teaching Problem Solving' (1987) 64 *Journal of Chemical Education* 513–514.

6 Radhia Azzouz, Slim Bechikh, Lamjed Ben Said, 'Dynamic Multi-objective Optimization Using Evolutionary Algorithms: A Survey', in Slim Bechikh, Rituparna Datta, Abhishek Gupta (eds), *Recent advances in evolutionary multi-objective optimisation* (Springer 2016) 31–70.

7 Dirk Brand, 'Algorithmic Decision-making and the Law' (2020) 12 *eJournal of eDemocracy and Open Government* 115–132, at 119.

by scholarly literature as "key issues when regulation of algorithmic decision making is concerned"[8]. These risks are heightened by the opaqueness of the operations performed by algorithms, in the sense that it is almost impossible to be fully aware of the process followed by an AI-driven algorithm to achieve a particular outcome. A first problem, therefore, is to understand how the idea of accountability can be applied to algorithms, in particular in cases involving adaptive systems which learn and change over time. Last but not least, algorithms can incorporate the original biases of their creators: just as a building would collapse if the bricks placed on its foundation were defective, so the results of an algorithm can be highly discriminatory if the algorithm is fed or trained on a wrong, unrepresentative, or even deficient data-set.

As said, the use of decision-making algorithms does not only concern issues of data protection, but can also have direct implications in the field of fundamental rights. While turning the light on the African continent, this paper will demonstrate that the degree of adaptation of the software to the context is essential to ensure its efficient application, so as not to amplify the risk of violating rights. In other words, the idea will emerge that a proper functioning of decision algorithms depends on how well their design and databases are tailored to the context to which they are applied.

2 Data Collection, Profiling, Data Exploitation

As a disruptive technology[9], AI has great potential and could allow human beings to achieve unprecedented results. On the one hand, algorithms can perform tasks with less time and effort than a human brain; they can carry out efficient data analysis in order to give back highly accurate forecasts worthy of being a basis for a decision. On the other hand, however, technology is not without risks. The reason is to be found in the data, an essential element for the proper functioning of the algorithm. Without data, the algorithm would remain an empty shell, incapable of any operation due to the lack of a clear starting point.

Since data are a necessary requirement for algorithms, mining, processing, and profiling data activities have become essential to realize an efficient data collection. Considering this, clearly "the larger the database, the better

8 Brand, *supra* fn 6, 127.

9 McKinsey Global Institute, *Disruptive technologies: Advances that will transform life, business, and the global economy* (2013), available at <https://www.mckinsey.com/~/media/McKinsey/Business%20Functions/McKinsey%20Digital/Our%20Insights/Disruptive%20technologies/MGI_Disruptive_technologies_Full_report_May2013.pdf> (accessed June 2023).

the chances of detecting patterns that reveal correlations between individual characteristics and consumer behaviour – allowing for target advertising, custom-tailored services, and individual offers"[10]. The correct functioning of the algorithmic model and the fairness of the results it offers depends on this preliminary, human-driven activity.

Together with data mining and data collection, profiling therefore becomes very important. It consists in identifying and classifying the behavioral characteristics of individuals and social groups within the widest possible datasets; this task is performed through the skills of experts (traditional profiling) or algorithmic analysis (data-driven profiling), in such a way as to be able to trace the behavioral characteristics to well-defined patterns and profiles. From a market point of view, data profiling is the process of examining and analyzing different datasets across the business activity to inform business decisions.

The claim to be able to reduce at least a large part of reality into mathematical data has led to a great confidence in the ability of algorithms to predict future events and behaviors, as long as calculations and analysis are executed on the ground of a sufficient amount of data[11]. Profiling aims to increase the accuracy of these results, trying to contextualize the data: the profile is nothing more than a virtual representation of the subject (individual or social group) created in order to frame her or him in a category and thus identify her or his future behavioral trends. In this regard, it should be stressed that the European Data Protection Regulation (GDPR), which will be further mentioned below, provides a definition of profiling that refers to data-driven profiling, emphasizing its decision-making and predictive purposes. Under article 4 of the GDPR, "profiling means any form of automated processing of personal data consisting of the use of personal data to evaluate certain personal aspects relating to a natural person, in particular to analyze or predict aspects concerning that natural person's performance at work, economic situation, health, personal preferences, interests, reliability, behavior, location or movements"[12].

In any case, data-driven profiling is not an activity totally unrelated to human control. Even in the case of the most probabilistic algorithms, it is possible

10 Matthias Leese, 'The New Profiling: Algorithms, Black Boxes, and the Failure of Anti-discriminatory Safeguards in the European Union' (2014) 45 *Security Dialogue* 494–511, at 502.

11 Colleen McCue, *Data Mining and Predictive Analysis: Intelligence Gathering and Crime Analysis* (2nd edn, Butterworth-Heinemann 2015).

12 Regulation (EU) 2016/679 of the European Parliament and of the Council of 27 April 2016 on the protection of natural persons with regard to the processing of personal data and on the free movement of such data, and repealing Directive 95/46/EC (General Data Protection Regulation), article 4, no 4.

to trace a form of human influence in all their functions, from their inner and outer architecture, to the processes for selecting the data and the methods to perform an analisys on them. This influence becomes extremely relevant when legal implications of algorithmic decision-making are considered. We easily find human influence in case of deterministic algorithms, but there is a human contribution even in the case of self-learning systems, which "requires a certain level of training by a human operator, at least until a bayesian network (i.e. a probabilistic mathematical model) is set up and updates in the database may be analyzed and incorporated automatically"[13]. This means that data-driven profiling generates only temporary hypotheses or momentary groupings that could disappear as the reference database changes. In other words, "citizens are faced with profiling practices that make it possible to control and steer individuals without a need to identify them"[14], in a process of decomposition that makes the individual 'liquid', considered only as a set of data exposed to constant variations.

States and big transnational corporations have the means to algorithmically exploit the data they collect and, consequently, all the interest in obtaining as much information as possible. Data has therefore become an asset and a currency at the same time; online tracking and, even more so, the use of biometric sensors allows the collection of various data (including, but not limited to, ad clicks, device specific information, face scan, internet service provider (ISP), phone numbers, search queries, time, date, browser history, email addresses, internet protocol (IP) addresses, location, operating system, profile information). All this data "creates an anonymous digital profile of millions of users that is ultimately used to integrate multiple accounts to produce personalized content for location services and notification, and, most importantly, to be sold to data brokers, used as a means for selling access to users for targeted advertising by third party corporations, or collected and stored for future predictive analytic use"[15].

Profiling therefore does not look at data as an expression of the personality of individual human beings or of the culture of a social group; quite the contrary. The collection and exploitation of data through technical means amplify

13 Leese, *supra* fn 9, 503.

14 Mireille Hildebrandt and Serge Gutwirth, 'Concise Conclusions: Citizens out of Control', in Mireille Hildebrandt and Serge Gutwirth (eds), *Profiling the European citizens: cross-disciplinary perspectives* (Springer 2008) 365, 368.

15 Danielle Coleman, 'Digital Colonialism: The 21st Century Scramble for Africa through the Extraction and Control of User Data and the Limitations of Data Protection Laws' (2019) 24 *Michigan Journal of Race and Law* 417–439, at 425.

the dehumanization of the human being. Complex cultural, moral, and political problems intimately linked to the contexts in which people live are thus reduced to measurable and quantifiable entities, which can be algorithmically manipulated[16]. The decomposition of the human being into data annihilates human identity, also insofar as it makes it easier to influence and manipulate the behavior of individuals. The exploitation of data, in the end, may represent a new form of human exploitation. As we will see, the more sensitive the data is, the greater the intrusion into the private sphere of the individual.

Things get even more complicated when the use of algorithms is not limited to reveal the habits and behaviors of consumers in the digital world, but rather involves fields such as those of security, justice and public administration management. An example can be provided by the Passenger Name Record System enacted by the European Union, a tool that, while allowing the detection of suspicious travel routes and the identification of criminals and terrorists, to a certain extent also weakens the EU legal framework on fundamental rights and data protection[17].

As the case of the Passenger Name Record System makes clear, the exploitation of data is less and less linked to the condition of the consent of the data subject: technological improvements make it possible to obtain and collect data through increasingly 'subtle' procedures such as, for example, the aforementioned online tracking activity, which often happens without the user's knowledge and has only recently started to come under legislative consideration. Similarly, biometric and facial recognition technologies store data regarding the physical and somatic characteristics of a large sections of the population, often indiscriminately and without people's knowledge or consent. This is also true for the use of satellite technologies, of which most citizens are simply not aware.

In order to react to these problems, many countries, and most conspicuously the European Union, are working to regulate the use of algorithmic applications in all their aspects, from data collection to data processing. Hopefully, the enactment of specific rules addressing the practice of algorithmic decision-making might constrain or avoid the use of algorithms that are particularly intrusive in the private sphere and likely to give back or induce errors to the point of compromising the effectiveness of several fundamental rights.

---

16 Abeba Birhane, 'Algorithmic colonization of Africa' (2020) 17 *Scripted* 389–409, at 397.

17 Leese, *supra* fn 9, 503.

3 Data and Context

What has been said so far describes the growing importance and diffusion of data-driven profiling and algorithmic decision-making practices. It is now necessary to focus the analysis by looking more closely at the African context.

In the most developed countries of the world, where digital technology first spread, the use of machine learning algorithms has already generated several problems. An example is to be found in the study published in 2018 by the National Institute of Standards and Technology of the United States which, after highlighting the huge progress made by facial recognition algorithms, compared the outcomes returned by more than 90 different software. Among other things, the study found out that "Asian and African American people were up to 100 times more likely to be misidentified than white men, depending on the particular algorithm and type of search"[18]. Similarly, "many algorithms developed in China do not give the elevated false positive rates on Chinese faces that algorithms developed elsewhere do. […] This suggests that training data, or perhaps some other factor intrinsic to the development, can be effective at reducing particular false positive differentials. Thus, the longer-term mitigation would be for developers to investigate the utility of more diverse, globally derived, training data"[19]. It had also already happened in 2018 that the 'Rekognition' software, developed by Amazon, returned wrong results when applied to the faces of some members of the United States Congress[20].

However, once it is highlighted that the proper functioning of an algorithm and the return of accurate results depends on the quality and representativeness of the data which the algorithm is fed or trained with, it must be concluded that to use in a given context data collected elsewhere could give back absolutely erroneous and misleading outcomes. In other words, the data

18 Drew Harwell, 'Federal study confirms racial bias of many facial-recognition systems, casts doubt on their expanding use', *Washington Post*, December 19, 2019, available at <https://www.washingtonpost.com/technology/2019/12/19/federal-study-confirms-racial-bias-many-facial-recognition-systems-casts-doubt-their-expanding-use/> (accessed June 2023).

19 Patrick Grother, Mei Ngan, Kayee Hanaoka, *Face Recognition Vendor Test* (*FRVT*), *Part 3: Demographic Effects* (National Institute of Standards and Technology (NIST) 2019), available at <https://nvlpubs.nist.gov/nistpubs/ir/2019/NIST.IR.8280.pdf> (accessed June 2023).

20 Jacob Snow, 'Amazon's Face Recognition Falsely Matched 28 Members of Congress With Mugshots, in American Civil Liberties Union', *ACLU blog*, July 26, 2018, available at <https://www.aclu.org/blog/privacy-technology/surveillance-technologies/amazons-face-recognition-falsely-matched-28> (accessed June 2023).

collected in a given geographical area, which reflect the behaviors and the culture of the population living in that area, should not be used for algorithmic calculations that are going to be applied in completely different places, populated by people with different cultures and customs. One might even go as far as to claim that, besides data, also the algorithm itself, its basic design and the way in which it operates must respect the features of the context on which the algorithm is called to act. In other words, algorithms should be conceived, programmed and linked to the society in which they will work.

This does not happen when algorithms intended to be applied in specific geographical areas are exported without any amendment to be used in different African contexts. The transplant of Western-made technologies in Africa is a classic example of what has been called 'digital colonialism'. Some have defined digital colonialism as "the decentralized extraction and control of data from citizens with or without their explicit consent through communication networks developed and owned by Western tech companies"[21], placing the emphasis on the exploitation of data by Western corporations. Actually, digital colonialism is also affected by the spheres of political influence that have been emerging in Africa in recent years, especially after the fall of the Soviet Union. This is why it is probably more correct to define the digital colonialism as a sort of algorithmic neo-colonization. Thanks to globalization, which has lifted new players on the international scene, algorithmic neo-colonization is brought by a wide variety of actors that use algorithmic data analysis for predictive and decision-making purposes, including Global North states and big tech corporations.

The African context already knows experiences of external intrusion. The colonial history of the continent is (in)famous, and it is well know that the law was often used by the countries of the Global North as an instrument of hegemony and economic subordination. However, after the end of the cold war, the number of the actors involved in African geopolitics have substantially increased. In this period, relations between Western and African countries have been transformed from political to economic ones[22]. In this historical moment, transnational corporations and big international financial organizations have asserted themselves, together with the states, as partners for development. The approach adopted by this plethora of Western actors has been largely based on conditional aid, that is, on the disbursement of aid to countries that agreed to implement structural reform packages (including, e.g., the creation

21 Coleman, *supra* fn 14, 422.

22 Salvatore Mancuso, 'Geopolitiche africane e dinamiche giuridiche' (2020) 26(2) *Gnosis* 58–69, at 61.

of a democratic and multi-party system, the privatization of state economic activities, the constitutional protection of human rights). This explains why, in recent times, there has been an increasing Chinese influence on the African continent, especially in the Eastern regions. Joining Chinese cooperation programs does not require particular efforts, since the Chinese policy is based on the principle of non-interference in the internal affairs of the States. However, it also involves the establishment of economic and political relationships between Chinese institutions and African countries at the highest political level.

Currently, Chinese cooperation policy is included in the broader framework of the Belt and Road Initiative (BRI), of which the African continent represents a crucial part. In March 2020, 138 countries joined the BRI, including 38 countries from sub-Saharan Africa, making Africa the most present continent within the program. This is highly relevant for algorithmic governance too, since China is a major player in AI surveillance all around the world[23], and supplies several countries with next-generation technologies through national companies – notably Huawei, Hikvision, Dahua and ZTE. The purchase of these technology products by African countries is often realized through the provision of subsidized loans in order to encourage governments to purchase them, especially in countries that otherwise would not have access to such technologies, such as Kenya and Uganda.

As part of the BRI, the Chinese government launched in 2015 the Digital Silk Road (DSR). Through investments in digital infrastructure and advanced technologies (in particular AI, quantum computing and global satellite technology), the DSR seeks to improve connectivity in the world while also ensuring to China a leading role as a global technological superpower. The DSR, therefore, adds political goals to economic ones, increasing China's soft power on the international stage. Africa has a great development potential in the digital economy. In the field of facial recognition, a technology already discussed with concern, the role of major exporter of China and its transnational corporations should be particularly emphasized. Zimbabwe, for example, reached an agreement with Guangzhou CloudWalk company in 2018 – the same company involved in the practice of AI surveillance of the Uighur population – to purchase facial recognition software and monitoring systems in order to identify and suppress threats to public order. The data was a large part of the sale price, having been permanently acquired by Cloudwalk and allowing the Chinese

23 Steven Feldstein, 'The Global Expansion of AI Surveillance' (2019) *Carnegie Endowment for International Peace Working Paper*, at <https://carnegieendowment.org/files/WP-Feldstein-AISurveillance_final1.pdf> (accessed June 2023).

company to improve the detection rate in recognizing faces with darker skin color[24].

Through this policy, China reaches several results, such as the economic and political control of a large slice of the African continent on the one hand, and the possibility to expand databases and the availability of data, on the other hand. As a result, China can now produce more performant algorithms allowing quicker and increasingly precise automatic decisions, thus realizing a sort of technological exploitation of the population.

Regardless of the cooperation model applied by a particular state or organization, external interventions have in common a tendency to offer solutions without amendments and adaptations. "The Achilles heel of these packages lies in the fact that they are prepackaged, standard, offered without variations in the different countries that accessed the aid programs, and completely decontextualized from the reality they were intended for"[25]. To give an example, it has been shown in the medical field that the use of Western proven and effective methodologies may not yield the same result if applied without changes on the African continent: in the sub-Saharan context, for instance, it is extremely complex to successfully use mammography to prevent breast cancer, a tool that works very well in the countries of the Global North[26].

The same happens today in the technological field. For example, in Nigeria, one of the most technically advanced countries in Africa, the software industry has not been so much supported by institutions and policymakers. "As a result, the country became heavily dependent on foreign software, which accounts for more than 90 per cent of all software used in Nigeria"[27]. Today, however, the State is turning to China, which has recently worked to establish strong economic and diplomatic relationships with the country. To date, China is the leading exporter to Nigeria, and has over 200 companies operating in the

24 Irene Spadaro, 'Intelligenza artificiale, l'asso della Cina nella partita con l'Africa. La "roccaforte" Nigeria', *Agenda Digitale*, January 19, 2021, available at <https://www.agendadigitale.eu/cultura-digitale/intelligenza-artificiale-lasso-della-cina-nella-partita-con-lafrica-la-roccaforte-nigeria/> (accessed June 2023).

25 Mancuso, *supra* fn 21, 62.

26 Eleanor Black and Robyn Richmond, 'Improving early detection of breast cancer in sub-Saharan Africa: why mammography may not be the way forward' (2019) 15(3) *Globalization and Health*, at <https://globalizationandhealth.biomedcentral.com/track/pdf/10.1186/s12992-018-0446-6.pdf> (accessed June 2023).

27 United Nations Conference on Trade and Development (UNCTAD), *Information Economy Report 2012. The Software Industry and Developing Countries* (United Nations 2012), available at <https://unctad.org/system/files/official-document/ier2012_en.pdf> (accessed June 2023), at 5.

country and managing many vital infrastructures, especially in the sectors of rail transport and the exploitation of oil resources.

As already explained, algorithmic decision-making is capable of a significant impact on reality. While the reliance on algorithm might favor advancements, it also raises risks that cannot be underestimated. It is unlikely that a continent, which has been trying to get out of poverty for a long time, will choose to renounce the benefits offered by current predictive technologies. However, it widely emerged that data is essential for the functioning and effectiveness of algorithms and that data collection activities, including the most recent forms of profiling based on biometric identification, allow an intrusion into the individual sphere. This means, again and again, that the processing of sensitive data can led to new forms of exploitation of human beings, with virtual chains replacing the real ones.

For this reason, some actions taken by Western tech companies are viewed with great disfavor and cause concern. A striking case regards Facebook (now Meta), which in 2016 began mapping a large part of the African territory according to criteria related to population density, using data collected from the population itself, high resolution satellite images and artificial vision techniques. In doing so, the company did not consider it necessary to inquire about the availability of personal data or to obtain people's consent to their transfer, but simply justified the operation on humanitarian grounds. This shows the development of a technological rhetoric, that follows a path similar to the one which, in the past, characterized colonial rhetoric[28].

Other, more recent examples seem to confirm this line of development. A study by American and European researchers tried to demonstrate that using machine learning on data collected from the mobile phone network may improve the targeting of humanitarian aid. It is worth to mention the existence of a study evaluating a social assistance program implemented in Togo that used algorithms to distribute economic resources against the negative effects of the Covid-19 pandemic. The researchers first identified through machine learning software and satellite images several areas of 2.4 km by 2.4 km in the territory of Togo with the respective degree of relative well-being of inhabitants, and then estimated "the average daily consumption of each mobile phone subscriber by applying machine-learning algorithms to mobile phone metadata provided by Togo's two mobile phone operators"[29]. In doing

28 Birhane, *supra* fn 15, 392.

29 Emily Aiken, Suzanne Bellue, Dean Karlan, Chris Udry, Joshua E. Blumenstock, 'Machine learning and phone data can improve targeting of humanitarian aid' (2022) 603 *Nature* 864–870, at 865.

so, they claimed they were able to obtain information and allocate humanitarian aid more precisely. While aware that "this novel approach to targeting requires careful consideration of the ways in which individuals can be incorrectly excluded from receiving programmed benefits"[30], the authors concludes by stating that "our analysis shows how non-traditional big data and machine learning can improve the targeting of humanitarian assistance"[31]. However, the same researchers seem not to realize that inferring the overall degree of well-being of a country's population through data collected from mobile phones is a highly intrusive practice capable of generating harmful consequences (especially, but not only, in case of mistakes) – a practice that should be socially acceptable only if justified by superior reasons. To what extent is it necessary to balance, on the one hand, the massive exploitation of data gathered from mobile telephones and, on the other, the need to identify more precisely the individuals to whom more humanitarian aid is to be allocated?

This is not the place to answer such question. The point here is that mitigating the risks deriving from data collection, profiling and automated decision-making is absolutely necessary so that Africa does not have to give up an important development tool. When adapted to the context and made by and for local people, algorithms and AI have a great beneficial potential. The following two illustrations, one concerning agriculture apps and one on facial recognition software, show the potential of such technology.

The African continent has recently experienced several examples of data-driven agriculture, which are expected to increase agricultural production and help farmers in different ways. One interesting experiment regards the app eGranary, developed by Leonida Mutuku, a young Kenyan researcher: "[f]armers log the metrics of their production into the platform, including the size of their farm, the crops grown and how much they pay their workers. Based on this information, and using advanced analytics, the app works out what inputs they need to maximise their yield, such as quality seed and fertiliser, and these are made available to them in the form of credits disbursed by the credit provider"[32]. In the last years, Africa has seen an increase in digital start-ups dealing with precision farming which are profiling as many farms as possible to optimize results through data-driven decisions.

30 Aiken, Bellue, Karlan, Udry, Blumenstock, *supra* fn 28, 869.

31 Aiken, Bellue, Karlan, Udry, Blumenstock, *supra* fn 28, 870.

32 Sophie Reeve, 'Data4Ag: Profiling presents opportunities for smallholders' (2018) 190 *Spore* 18–22, at 20.

It has been said that biometric profiling raises several concerns, and that facial recognition is a major example. In this field, young African researchers are trying to develop more appropriate solutions for the context. The racial prejudice suffered by the Western facial recognition algorithms prevent the technology from being successfully applied to the African continent. In 2018 four software engineers set up a company in Ghana to address the limitation by which Western algorithms are affected; once they expanded the database, including a large sample of faces from sub-Saharan African people, they were able to build up the BACE API algorithm, which is very important due to its unique features. BACE API verifies identities remotely and instantaneously using AI and facial recognition by matching the live picture of the user to the image on their official documents. The use of live images and video rather than only images is unique to BACE API and improves the success rate in matching faces, verifying that the images are of real people instead of preexisting photo. It is interesting to quote the words of the young Ivorian researcher Charlette N'Guessan who, as the mastermind of the project, is worried about the implications of an uncontrolled importation of 'external' algorithms. "I think Africa needs more local AI solutions because that's where the challenge is now. Most of the solutions are coming from outside. We need to develop these skills early by generating interest in AI among young people"[33]. In doing so, N'Guessan is aware that "it's very important to be responsible and ethical with AI"[34] – in other words, data protection policies are badly needed.

4 Fundamental Rights and Data Protection

As said, automated decision-making procedures may not be perfect. A wrong software decision may have harmful consequences, to the point of jeopardizing fundamental rights. One of the main problems coming out from the use of algorithms is the possible discrimination against individuals on a variety of grounds, for example on race, gender or age. In this sense, a damage could

33 Audrey Donkor, 'The race to build facial recognition tech for Africa is being led by this award-winning engineer' (2020) *Quartzafrica*, available at <https://qz.com/africa/1905079/facial-recognition-tech-in-africa-boosted-by-ghana-ai-startup/> (accessed June 2023).

34 Frank Hersey, 'Biometric BACE API founder plans to bring AI problem-solving approach to all aspects of life', *Biometricupdate*, 2021, available at <https://www.biometricupdate.com/202103/biometric-bace-api-founder-plans-to-bring-ai-problem-solving-approach-to-all-aspects-of-life> (accessed June 2023).

derive from a wrong software design, but also from biases attached to data, as the algorithm could learn from data collected by humans and adopt the biases of humans attached to that data[35]. Consequently, the design of the algorithm and the creation of databases must be carried out with particular care, in light of the technological advances characterized bythe use of highly intrusive biometric techniques. As has rightly been stated, "with the automation of the social comes the automation and perpetuation of historical bias, discrimination and injustice"[36]. What is happening in Kenya offers a good example: the more the government pushes to implement a system of national biometric identity documents for its citizens, the more problems are arising for those minorities which have historically faced challenges in acquiring such identity documents. This means that racial, ethnic and religious minorities face the risk to be excluded and discriminated.

In addition, several other problems arise in the field of data protection, which is a matter of utmost importance in the digital era. This interest in both anti-discrimination and data protection in not surprising as "the issue at stake here is the discriminatory consequences of data processing operations"[37]. Among others questions, what legal framework should be adopted for algorithmic activities, especially in the field of automated decision-making? To be precise, there are already some applicable legal tools; therefore, it seems appropriate to look at what is happening in terms of data protection legislations in the world, and in particular in the area of our interest.

The European Union was the first institution to deal with the matter comprehensively. A Data Protection Directive was already adopted in 1995[38], but technological advances forced a reform to fill the gaps of what has rapidly become an obsolete legislation. Today the General Data Protection Regulation, already mentioned above, represents the main piece of legislation on data protection in Europe and, probably, in the whole world. Even if the GDPR legally binds only the EU member States, it also applies to the processing of data wholly or partly by automated means (art. 2) in "the context of the activities of an establishment of a controller or a processor in the Union, regardless of

35 Brand, *supra* fn 6.

36 Birhane, *supra* fn 15, 400.

37 Raphaël Gellert, Katja de Vries, Paul de Hert, Serge Gurtwith, 'A Comparative Analysis of Anti-Discrimination and Data Protection Legislations', in Bart Custers, Toon Calders, Bart Schermer, Tal Zarsky (eds), *Discrimination and Privacy in the Information Society: Data Mining and Profiling in Large Databases* (Springer 2013) 61–89, at 63.

38 James R. Maxeiner, 'Freedom of information and the EU data protection directive' (1995) 48 *Federal Communication Law Journal* 93–104.

whether the processing takes place in the Union or not" (art. 3). This so-called external relevance of the GDPR is the main reason for its influence beyond the European territorial borders[39]. In addition, the GDPR establishes some guidelines and principles that have been transposed into many other world legislations, especially (but not only) those of the sub-Saharan region.

The GDPR provides some rights related to data in the digital environment. Among others, GDPR-based rights include the right: i) to be informed about the processing of personal data, which must take place in a lawful, fair and transparent manner (art. 5, 13, 15); ii) to receive an explanation about the logic involved in the processing of data (art. 14); iii) to obtain access to personal data hold by controllers (art. 15); iv) to ask for the correction of incorrect data (art. 16); v) to be forgotten (art. 17); vi) to request that decision based on automated processing or profiling and based on personal data are made by natural persons, not only by computers (art. 22).

As already pointed out, the influence of the GDPR to other geographical areas has been inevitable. Even if, in the African environment, life is basically communal, and people traditionally believe in the philosophy of Ubuntu (which means "I am because we are"), the idea of privacy, fueled by the spread of capitalism and globalization, has turned out into one of the individual rights whose protection is most often sought. The GDPR represents, nowadays, a model and an inspiration for several national legislations, including some recent African legal texts.

While data protection legislations are still generally missing in Africa – which is not good in the light of the significant increase in internet penetration –, many transnational organizations and states have in recent times tried to bridge the gap both at the continental and single country level.

In 2014 the African Union, the successor to the Organisation of African Unity (OAU), adopted the African Union Convention on Cybersecurity and Personal Data Protection, also known as the Malabo Protocol. This act, however, is not yet effective because it has not been ratified by the minimum number of states required. Among the countries of East Africa, only Rwanda has ratified it by the end of 2019[40]. The text is made up of 38 articles as well as an introductory part dedicated to definitions; it represents one of the most complex convention in the field of cybersecurity. In particular, article 13 identifies the following six

39 Matúš Mesarčík, 'Apply or not to apply? A Comparative View on Territorial Application of CCPA and GDPR' (2020) 4(2) *Bratislava Law Review* 81–94, at 84, available at <https://blr.flaw.uniba.sk/index.php/BLR/article/view/171/173> (accessed June 2023).

40 Victoria Nyawira Gitau and Louisa Ochilo, 'Data Protection in East Africa' (2021) *Pavia and Ansaldo Newsletter*, available at <https://www.pavia-ansaldo.it/wp-content/uploads/2021/01/Data-Protection-in-East-Africa.pdf> (accessed June 2023).

principles relating to data protection, which are similar to those provided by the GDPR, namely: i) consent and legitimacy; ii) lawful and fair processing; iii) purpose, relevance and retention of data; iv) accuracy of data over its lifespan; v) transparency of processing; vi) confidentiality and security of personal data.

Meanwhile, some African States are enacting their local legislations on data protection. Even if these national laws are focused on protection of personal data, the issue of automated decision-making is included in such legislations due to the relation between the rights of individual data subjects and algorithmic decision-making activities[41]. Yet, it is often hard to enforce such legal texts. This is basically due to the significant cultural and legal diversity across the continent and the differences in access to technology and online services among African countries[42]. An example is the South Africa Protection of Personal Information Act (so-called POPI Act). The POPI Act was passed in 2013, but it took three years to establish an effective data protection authority and many more years to make it work; the law only became effective in July 2021. Considering that the city of Johannesburg has plenty of CCTV cameras around the streets and that several private companies are expanding in the AI-powered surveillance field (as said by Birhane, who informs us of the existence of companies specialized in the creation of facial recognition software such as Vumacam)[43], a clear regulatory framework is more than necessary.

Another example is provided by Zimbabwe. The strong Chinese influence in that territory, especially in the field of digital technologies, has prompted to accelerate the enactment of data protection laws, but it is only recently (namely, on December 3, 2021) that the country has equipped itself with such a tool. Prior to this, the Draft Data Protection Bill had been under consideration by the government since 2015. The Zimbabwe Data Protection Act tries to set a framework for the protection of privacy and personal data rights, undoubtedly representing a commendable step forward in the enforcement of privacy rights and the protection of personal data in the country. Yet, it is also beyond doubt that some time will be needed before its impact could be gauged.

A further, and telling, illustration is offered by the already mentioned Kenya experience, which is very important to point out again. Biometric identification and surveillance are becoming important topics on the political agenda of the Kenyan government, as it is evidenced by the existence of the National

41 Brand, *supra* fn 6, 127.

42 Internet Society and African Union, *Personal Data Protection Guidelines for Africa* (2018), available at <https://www.internetsociety.org/wp-content/uploads/2018/05/AUCPrivacyGuidelines_2018508_EN.pdf> (accessed June 2023).

43 Birhane, *supra* fn 15, 405.

Integrated Identity Management System (NIIMS) program. In the Kenyan electoral system voters are identified through biometric data (fingerprints). In 2018 it emerged that the (in)famed data mining company Cambridge Analityca may have played a role in the ruling party's victory, influencing voters' behaviour[44]. Furthermore, in an attempt to counter the increasingly frequent acts of terrorism, the government has mandated Safaricom – the main telecommunication service provider in Kenya – to reach an agreement with Huawei to install 1800 CCTV cameras around Nairobi and to provide the necessary AI software[45]. All this shows that legislation is needed. Nowadays, data protection in Kenya is regulated by the Data Protection Act No. 24 of 2019 – heavily inspired by the GDPR – which came into effect on November 25, 2019. The Data Protection Act, however, only establishes a basic framework. In this regard, the High Court of Kenya had the chance in 2020 to issue a constitutional judgment on the NIIMS, stating that its implementation cannot go further until there is an appropriate and comprehensive regulatory framework governing its implementation. The Court held "[a] declaration that the collection of DNA and GPS co-ordinates for purposes of identification is intrusive and unnecessary, and to the extent that it is not authorised and specifically anchored in empowering legislation, it is unconstitutional and a violation of Article 31 of the Constitution"[46].

That being said, the Kenyan experience shows well how much a country wishing to use a data-driven approach in governing people's behavior must provide clear safeguards anchored in legislation. These rules must not be limited to the issue of data protection, but must address the specific issues coming from the use of different technologies, including data collection and exploitation for predictive and decision-making purposes. As the High Court of Kenya argued, the existence of a data protection law might not be enough when the issue at stake is that of biometric identification for electoral purposes. Rather, there is the need of a specific internal legislation on biometric identification.

This is the more so since new problems are looming on the horizon. According to recent news, China has reportedly created an AI system that can assess the loyalty of Communist Party members. Such system should be able

44 Duncan Miriri, 'Kenya's ruling party says hired firm linked to data breach', *Reuters*, March 20, 2018, available at <https://www.reuters.com/article/facebook-cambridgeanalytica-kenya-idUSL8N1R24G2> (accessed June 2023).

45 N.D. Francois, 'Huawei's Surveillance Tech in Kenya: A Safe Bet?', *Africa Times*, December 18, 2019, available at <https://africatimes.com/2019/12/18/huaweis-surveillance-tech-in-kenya-a-safe-bet/> (accessed June 2023).

46 A copy of the judgment can be found at <http://kenyalaw.org/caselaw/cases/view/189189/> (accessed June 2023).

to analyze facial expressions and brain waves of Communist Party members to determine how receptive they are to 'thought education'. In particular, on the one hand the system can judge how party members have accepted thought and political education, while on the other hand it can provide real data for thought and political education to be improved and enriched[47].

This step follows the development by Alibaba Group of the app called 'Xuexi Qiangguo' or 'Study to make China strong', designed to teach Xi Jinping's ideology. Once the app is downloaded, it gains access to the users' ID card number, real name, 'bio-data' gleaned from the annual health check, shopping history, phone number, location data and deleted content. The app permits users to earn points by reading articles, watching videos, and answering quizzes on Communist heroes. At the same time, it tracks the amount of time users spend browsing inspirational quotes from President Jinping and watching short videos of his speeches and travels. Members can redeem their scores for gifts such as pastries and tablets[48].

Clearly, a system like this can have disruptive effects if exported into Africa. Power management in Africa follow dynamics that are different from those of Global North societies. These dynamics often lead to situations that are considered as pathologic from the Western point of view, in which countries are run by a single person who intends to stay in power for life[49]. In a situation like this, and having considered the number of African leaders closely linked with China, a system like the one that is allegedly being developed in China might serve to certain African leaders to scan the loyalty of the citizens and to eliminate from the beginning any attempt to build up an opposition.

China has also developed an AI prosecutor that can charge people with crimes with more than 97 per cent accuracy. This system, which was tested at the Shanghai Pudong People's Procuratorate (the biggest and busiest district prosecution office in China) using 17,000 real life cases from 2015 to 2020, can identify 'dissent' against the state and suggest sentences for supposed

---

47 Jonathan Chadwick, 'China claims to have developed an AI that can read the minds of Communist Party members', *Daily Mail online* (July 4, 2022), available at <https://www.dailymail.co.uk/sciencetech/article-10980343/Chinas-AI-check-loyalty-party-members.html> (accessed June 2023).

48 Nina Ludviksen Thorsen, 'Xuexi Qiangguo – Digitalization of Chinese propaganda', University of Oslo, Department of Culture Studies and Oriental Languages, February 6, 2020, available at <https://www.hf.uio.no/ikos/english/studies/voices-middle-east-asia/voices-from-east-asia/xuexi-qiangguo-–-digitalization-of-chinese-propaga.html> (accessed June 2023).

49 Salvatore Mancuso, 'Rule of law with African characteristics', in Muna Ndulo and Cosmas Emeziem (eds), *The Routledge Handbook of African Law* (Routledge 2022) 278–290.

criminals, removing people from the prosecution process. The AI prosecutor is able to identify and press charges for the eight most common crimes in Shanghai. These are crimes 'provoking trouble', like credit card fraud, gambling crimes, dangerous driving, theft, fraud, intentional injury and obstructing official duties[50].

Again, this system is potentially exportable to Africa and – at the same time – also potentially disruptive in the African context. Being a system that can identify 'dissent' against the state and suggest sentences against the defendant, it could be designed to identify dissent against the leader and sentence the opponents, becoming therefore an instrument to eliminate the opposition and people belonging to rival clans and ethnic groups that the establishment considers an obstacle to the preservation of power.

Ultimately, the negative implications that may arise from the use of AI technologies in the African context – and that therefore shall be prevented with the utmost urgency – involve the possibility to reach undesirable outcomes that, while being not explicitly unlawful, might nonetheless circumvent aspects of the law that are poorly equipped to regulate AI technology, thereby limiting the proper application of the rule of law principle.

5 Conclusions

It is clear that the growing diffusion of automated decision-making practices around the world requires the development of an adequate legal framework to ensure protection at all stages of the process – from data collection, to profiling, to the design of the algorithm itself and its application. Western countries are quite aware of this, so they have equipped themselves with legal tools that, more or less directly, try to fill the void. Scholars know that "ethical basis that includes respect for human rights should be the key guiding approach for any future developments"[51]. This paper demonstrates, first of all, that the matter cannot be regulated by aiming exclusively at data protection: any future regulatory framework must provide specific safeguards for individual fundamental rights other than privacy, as all of them are at risk in the algorithmic decision-making process.

---

50 Jack Newman, 'China develops AI "prosecutor" that can identify "dissent" and press charges for common crimes "with 97% accuracy"', *Daily Mail online*, December 27, 2021, available at <https://www.dailymail.co.uk/news/article-10346933/China-develops-AI-prosecutor-press-charges-97-accuracy.html> (accessed June 2023).

51 Brand, *supra* fn 6, 130.

Secondly, it clearly emerged that the correct functioning of decision-making algorithms depends on the fact that algorithmic data collection, profiling and design are suitable for their application within the context. Importing Western or Chinese algorithms to the African continent is a failure due to the non-representativeness of the data used to feed them. This practice is spreading the technological influence on Africa, togheter with the collection from African countries of masses of data by foreign states and transnational corporations and the application (often without consent) of non-domestic softwares on the entire African territory or in a single African country. Algorithms in Africa must serve local communities and must not be blindly imported from other countries, in order to make AI a worthy resource to realize the continent's cultural and traditional communitarian values.

Thirdly, from an African point of view, it is important to take all the benefits deriving from data-driven decision-making technologies without, at the same time, running into the typical risks stemming from their operation. African countries should enjoy the benefits of innovation while avoiding the perpetuation of the well-known dynamics of influence that was typical of the colonial policies of the last century which, it is feared, might today reappear in a digital and technological shape. Digital colonialism could be even more pervasive and dangerous than historical colonialism, insofar as it reaches domination not through weapons but through pervading and intrusive technological tools. At the same time, the strong ties existing between China and African countries could bring some African leaders to take advantage of the AI tools developed in China to eliminate rivals and silence opposition.

Actually, interesting prospects are opening up for Africa through technological advances and the use of decision-making algorithms, and this is not only from an economic and social perspective. Technologically speaking, the need to find digital in-house solutions for Africa has led, as it has been pointed out, to the flourishing of start-ups launched by young African researchers, who try to free the continent from the foreign digital umbrella. This is a quiet revolution, that starts from the technical adequacy of data collection and profiling with respect to context, and that might lead to the creation of software able to provide reliable forecasts so as to allow efficient decisions to be made. Through technical progress, and thanks to the work of its experts, Africa may therefore have a real chance of emancipation from external controls.

It is interesting to note that, perhaps for the first time in history, African countries have the opportunity to use the law as a tool for emancipation. The law, which for a long time allowed colonial powers to expand their influence on the continent and to impose their own cultural traits could, paradoxically, be a means of affirming their independence. The need for a context-sensitive, specific legislation on algorithmic decision-making practices has already been underlined, especially for rules that go beyond data protection. What should now be stressed is that African States have the chance and the opportunity to issue innovative and targeted regulations, suitable to their territory and eventually different from foreign rules. However, to date, it seems that African countries are focusing almost exclusively on data protection laws, similarly to what happened in Europe, featuring provisions directly inspired by Western principles. African data protection laws may probably be more effective if they were not limited to a passive imitation of the GDPR but were adapted to the needs of the African context.

Ultimately, the global algorithmic revolution requires both general and contextualized analysis. African countries must make an effort to ensure that this opportunity to grow will not turn to a new form of exploitation, while at the same time elaborating digital solutions based on the continent's traditional values – a land where the individual is nothing if placed outside the social group and where no one is discriminated against.

CHAPTER 13

Trust in an 'Omnimetric Society'? Reputational Systems in Platforms as Tools for Assessing Contractual Performance and Applying Remedies

Teresa Rodríguez de las Heras Ballell

1 Setting the Scene

In an overinformed, extremely complex, and highly changing society, decision-making is a demanding, time-consuming, uncertain, and, very frequently, frustrating process. An informed, well-founded decision requires an onerous, and rather complicated series of steps to gather, compare, select, and finally trust relevant information and a significant amount of data collected, often, from different sources, and not always readily available. Considering the costs and the complexities of such an overwhelming process, users strive to enhance the effectiveness of their decision-making by taking various routes. Sometimes, decisions are purely intuitive, others are irrational or (unintentionally, or at times, intendedly) driven essentially by emotions; many times, decisions are indeed rather effective as a result of a wise balance of available information, time, and resources, on the one hand, and the ultimate purpose, on the other. To that end, trust is instrumental. In ensuring effective decision-making processes, or, simply, in enabling decisions in a complex society progressing at an unstoppable pace, trust is crucial. Trust is the catalyst for social interaction and relations of cooperation and exchange in the market. Users adopt decisions based on that information that is perceived as reliable, or trusting a prescription or a recommendation given by a trusted third party, or relying on other peers' advices and experience in the absence of (or the mistrust in) authoritative sources.

Thus, users may decide to invest in the investment funds AAA rated by accredited credit rating agencies, to buy the product sponsored by an influencer they follow, to rent the apartment with the highest rating in AirBnB despite no previous personal experience with the counterparty, to select a hotel on the basis of a high number of positive comments by other previous travelers, or to rely on and even forward and publish (fake) news simply because it has become crushingly popular in terms of likes and retweets. Wrong or right, decisions are easier if they are enabled by reliable recommendations, advices, prescriptions,

 | DOI:10.1163/9789004680944_014

positive reviews, high ranking, and other forms of 'peer-determined truth' (rating, opinions, likes, or top popularity).

This is the rationale behind the rise of reputational systems implemented by platforms as a trust-generating tool in the platform economy[1]. Platforms have become the most prominent organizational model for a variety of social and economic activities in the digital economy[2]. With a number of conspicuous benefits and efficiencies – economies of scale, network effects, data aggregation – they leverage to grow and expand in the market, platforms have indeed transformed the digital economy into a platform economy.

Besides becoming key economic actors in the global economy, platforms emerge as powerful 'regulators' in the digital society[3]. That provides an enticing approach to the role of platforms in the exercise of rights and liberties, the prevention and control of illicit content, the conformation of public speech, and the dispute resolution. Platforms aspire to replicate and emulate legal systems, creating 'private legal systems', on the basis of a fabric of contractual terms and conditions, internal policies, and contract-based mechanisms for content curation, dispute resolution or complaint-handling. Thus, platforms regulate users' activities, supervise compliance and performance, sanction and penalize infringement, and handle complaints and provide dispute resolution mechanisms[4].

Platforms' regulatory power includes the assessment of users' performances, carried out through algorithm-driven rating, ranking, reviews and recommender systems. The metrics developed to assess performance may have

---

1 Teresa Rodríguez de las Heras Ballell, 'The Emergence of Digital Communities: Generating Trust, Managing Conflicts, and Regulating Globality … Digitality', in Carol J. Greenhouse and Christina L. Davis (eds), *Landscapes of Law: Practicing Sovereignty in Transnational Terrain* (University of Pennsylvania Press 2020) 250–277.

2 Teresa Rodríguez de las Heras Ballell, 'The background of the Digital Services Act: looking towards a platform economy' (2021) 22(1) *ERA Forum* 75–86.

3 Teresa Rodríguez de las Heras Ballell, 'Las plataformas: nuevos actores (y reguladores) de la actividad económica', in Beatriz Gregoraci Fernández and Francisco Velasco Caballero (eds), *Anuario de la Facultad de Derecho de la Universidad Autónoma de Madrid. Derecho y política ante la pandemia: Reacciones y transformaciones. Tomo II. Reacciones y transformaciones en el Derecho Privado* (Universidad Autónoma de Madrid and Agencia Estatal Boletín Oficial del Estado 2021) 403–417, available at <https://www.boe.es/biblioteca_juridica/abrir_pdf.php?id=PUB-DH-2021-207> (accessed 21 December 2022).

4 Teresa Rodríguez de las Heras Ballell, 'Rules for a Platform Economy: A Case for Harmonization to Counter «Platform shopping» in the Digital Economy', in Ilaria Pretelli (ed), *Conflict of Laws in the Maze of Digital Platforms – Le droit international privé dans le labyrinthe des plateformes digitales – Actes de la 30e Journée de droit international privé du 28 juin 2018 à Lausanne* (Schulthess 2018) 55–79.

fundamental legal implications in the exercise of rights and liberties. Suffice it to think that sanctions for bad ratings are applied immediately and automatically, with forceful efficacy and limited (or no) possibility for internal or external scrutiny.

Against this context, after setting the scene in Section 2, the chapter elaborates on the significance of trust (Section 3) and on how trust is generated and perceived in an 'omnimetric society' (Section 4). Within this context, Sections 5–6 reflects on possible solutions, principles and embryonic rules to balance the interests at stake in the use of algorithmic reputational system in assessing performance and applying remedies in the platform economy. Section 7 summarizes the main findings and conclusions.

2 Informed Decision-Making in an Overinformed, Complex Society

In assessing users' performance, algorithm-driven rating, ranking, review or recommender systems play a critical role. Drivers, riders, sellers, tenants, users are rated, ranked or recommended on the basis of selected criteria. These reputational systems can be fueled by other users' ratings, as P2P models, and/or a variety of provided, inferred or observed data (time, location, transactional experience, activity, preferences, followers, number of likes) by the platform operator. A number of consequences are linked to the obtained rating, the position in the rankings or the received reviews, as well as stemming from being downrated, demoted or non-recommended: penalties, suspension of service, closing of the account, restriction of access to certain services, change of labor conditions, loss of visibility, or other remedies provided for by the penalties policy of the platform.

Several court decisions[5] related to work platforms (majorly, on-demand delivery platforms) have given evidence of the use of reputational systems to allocate orders, distribute work, calculate wages or bonuses, or even trigger the firing of the 'unreliable' rider. Although many of these decisions were intended to mainly tackle the question of the labor nature of the relationship between the platforms and the workers[6], in their reasoning, courts have explored and

5 As a mere illustration, see for instance the Spanish Supreme Court's decision of 25 September 2020 (STS 2924/2020, ECLI:ES:TS:2020:2924) and the Italian decision by the Tribunal of Bologna (labour chamber) of 31 December 2020 (General number 2949/2019), both of which do explicitly refer to the role of the 'reputational score' in the algorithmic management.

6 Some rulings have been in favour of the employment nature of the working relationship such as the decisions of the French Court of Cassation on Uber (Cour de cassation, *chambre sociale*, decision no. 374 of 4 March 2020), of the Spanish Superior Court of Madrid on

unpacked the 'legal anatomy'[7] of platforms and delved deep into the platforms' internal policies and algorithmic governance[8].

The concerns aroused by work platforms related to the working conditions, including "more limited access to social protection and social security coverage, health and safety risks, insecure work, fragmented working hours and inadequate levels of income and difficulties in ensuring the recognition of collective rights"[9] spotlighted the legislative attention with a set of measures proposed by the European Commission aimed to improve the working conditions in platform work[10]. But the algorithmic logic does equally underlie the

---

Deliveroo (Tribunal Superior de Justicia de Madrid, Sala de lo Social, decision no. 40/2020 of 17 January 2020), and of the Barcelona Court on Roofoods Spain (Juzgado de lo Social n° 24 of Barcelona, decision no. 259/2020 of November 18, 2020), which acknowledged the employment nature of the employment relationship of as many as 748 riders. Belgian, Italian and Dutch courts have ruled out that the work relationship is self-employment on the basis of riders' alleged freedom in the performance of the service: see the references in Delphine Defossez, 'The employment status of food delivery riders in Europe and the UK: Self-employed or worker?' (2022) 29(1) *Maastricht Journal of European and Comparative Law* 25–46.

7 Teresa Rodríguez de las Heras Ballell, 'The Legal Anatomy of Electronic Platforms: A Prior Study to Assess the Need of a Law of Platforms in the EU' (2017) 3(1) *Italian Law Journal* 149–176.

8 European Commission, 'Study to support the impact assessment of an EU initiative to improve the working conditions in platform work, Final Report' (22 October 2021), available at <https://op.europa.eu/en/publication-detail/-/publication/454966ce-6dd6-11ec-9136-01aa75ed71a1/language-en> (accessed 21 December 2022), revealing the extensive use of algorithms in determining aspects of works. As per the conducted survey, algorithmic management is employed at workplaces, other than work platforms, in particular, for the following purposes: 6.2% for work schedules, shifts or working hours; 18.4% for pay; 8.6% for working locations or routes; 13.4% for the content of work or tasks; 9.4% for the pace of work; 10.2% – for the assessment of performance; 10.8% for specific clients with whom they work; 10.3% for the collection of client or customer feedback about their work.

9 European Economic and Social Committee, 'Opinion on the Working conditions package – platform work' (SOC/709) (23 March 2022), available at <https://www.eesc.europa.eu/en/our-work/opinions-information-reports/opinions/working-conditions-package> (accessed 21 December 2022).

10 The package proposed by the European Commission includes: a communication setting out the EU approach and measures on platform work, draft guidelines clarifying the application of EU competition law to collective agreements of solo self-employed people seeking to improve their working conditions, and a proposal for a Directive on improving working conditions in platform work (see in particular European Commission, Proposal for a Directive of the European Parliament and of the Council on improving working conditions in platform work (COM/2021/762 final), at <https://eur-lex.europa.eu/legal-content/en/ALL/?uri=CELEX:52021PC0762> (accessed 21 December 2022)). On the Commission's package, see <https://ec.europa.eu/commission/presscorner/detail/en/ip_21_6605> (accessed 21 December 2022).

performance assessment in other platforms. Traders may be demoted, downrated or subject to limiting conditions or higher fees on the basis of their reputational score in a marketplace. User accounts may be closed or their content systematically removed on grounds of their peer-to-peer unreliability score. News or videos may be displayed more or less prominently as per the number of likes they gain. Trustworthy project promoters, as described and scored by other peers or previous investors, may be eligible to access to credit in better conditions in a crowdfunding platform. Bus drivers may be penalized in their salaries or even dismissed if the automated reputational systems fed by data collected from sensors installed in their vehicles (and scores given by other drivers) classified them as imprudent or reckless.

Certainly, it cannot be ignored that reliability is also a key factor guiding our decisions in a non-digital context. We buy at the local shop we trust, the product we have already tested, and where we have had a previous good experience. We do also tend to rely on recommendations and advices given by trusted third parties in order to adopt a decision in a complex situation when information is too abundant, too technical, or uncertain. Yet, we blindly rely on 'peer-determined truth' in those cases where we let ourselves be swept away by factors such as popularity, virality or visibility as perceived indicia of credibility.

Thus, as in the non-digital society, trust is instrumental to the development of the digital society. Nonetheless, the overwhelming informative nature of the digital society has flooded decision-making processes with unmanageable amounts of data whose accuracy cannot be verified and obfuscated the ability to adopt informed, free decisions. Digital society has transferred to trust one of its most critical vulnerabilities: the tyranny of quantification. Popularity and virality have filled the unsatisfied perception of reliability. Reputational systems as a tool to assess performance and apply remedies in the platform economy are testimonial of such a trend. The digital society is an 'omnimetric society', where everything must be measured and only what can be measured matters. A perfect and synergetic combination of (algorithmic and Artificial Intelligence-driven) automation, a flourishing data economy and a burgeoning platform economy has settled a conducive environment for our 'omnimetric society' to thrive.

What follows puts forward, and pivots on, our fundamental thesis of an 'omnimetric society', aiming to unveil some of its consequences.

3 Defining the Context: The Significance of Trust

Trust is a broad and multifaceted concept that different scientific disciplines look at from different perspectives[11]. It is therefore not easy to articulate a concept of trust that is operational in different contexts, and it is even more complex to try to formulate it as a legal concept. While it is clear that the roots of trust lie in modern information markets, the abundance of information, however, not only leads to 'poverty of attention' but also affects the pillars of credibility. Hence, recent studies reveal that accurate information is not always enough to disprove or correct errors, so that other factors must be considered to ensure that more than informing, persuading is achieved[12]. In short, trust depends not only on whether all correct and relevant information is available, but is essentially determined by how it is accessed, how it is perceived, and how it is processed to generate a perception of credibility.

This observation allows us to articulate in this chapter a working concept of trust, which is made up of two parts.

First, an objective component that emphasizes the truthfulness, correctness, sufficiency and availability of the information necessary to make a rational decision.

Second, a subjective component that determines the perception of credibility on which trust is based. This perception is positively reinforced by factors and indications of credibility based on reputation, experience, popularity, attribution of recognized functions (regulated credit rating agencies[13], professional doctors, prescribers). The digital society has made it more difficult to ascertain and verify the objective dimension, while at the same time multiplying the factors and cues that can reinforce the perception of credibility and altering its effects. Moreover, the subjective component of perception has

---

11 Brian O'Neill, 'Trust in the information society' (2012) 28 *Computer Law & Security Review* 551–559.

12 See R. Kelly Garrett and Brian E. Weeks, 'The Promise and Peril of Real-Time Corrections to Political Misperceptions' (2013) *CSCW '13: Proceedings of the 2013 conference on Computer supported cooperative work* 1047–1058, available at <https://dl.acm.org/doi/10.1145/2441776.2441895> (accessed 21 December 2022), which questions the effectiveness of devices and programs that instantly warn users of false information published online or controversial data.

13 On the relevant role of information in the markets and the function of trust in the protection of traffic safety, see, extensively, Manuel Alba Fernández and Teresa Rodríguez de las Heras Ballell, 'Las agencias de rating como terceros de confianza: responsabilidad civil extracontractual y protección de la seguridad del tráfico' (2010) 29(120) *Revista de Derecho Bancario y Bursátil* 141–177.

gained such prominence in determining trust that it has pushed the objective component into second place, rending it almost irrelevant. Faced with the difficulty of verifying the veracity and correctness of information, and as a result of a progressive deterioration of references to authority and reliability, the digital society relies on credibility factors based on popularity, virality, relevance, or visibility, as opposed to objective criteria of veracity and correctness that are increasingly imperceptible.

Uncertainty heightens the perception of risk, which in turn affects decision-making. All decisions with economic content are, to a large extent, determined by risk assessment. This risk assessment is mainly based on the information that can be acquired about the different elements of the transaction and their interpretation. Information, abundant and widely available in modern markets and, overwhelmingly, in the digital market, should serve to generate and reinforce trust, the effect of which is, in turn, to reduce risk and thus facilitate trade[14]. However, in these over-informed markets, effective accessibility to information, its visibility and, above all, its credibility must be guaranteed. Indeed, in the digital market, trust is nowadays the scarcest asset.

The generation and retention of trust is therefore essential to support the proper functioning of the digital marketplace and the digital society, to stimulate cooperative and exchange relationships and even, in the medium term, to ensure its subsistence and viability[15].

Trust reduces complexity and enables people to deal with the uncertainty and complexity because it reduces the alternatives and thus allows to focus attention only on certain available options[16], facilitating decision making[17].

---

14 Tamar Frankel, 'Trusting and Non-Trusting on the Internet' (2001) 81 *Boston University Law Review* 457–458, in reference to commercial relationships entered into over the Internet.

15 The impossibility of identifying and evaluating trustworthy providers and content could lead to the *breakdown of* the digital market. Intermediaries, as we will argue later in the text and in relation to other functions and means, contribute to the efficiency and operability of the digital market by adding value to electronic transactions through five possible means: information search, selection of relevant information, management of industrial and intellectual property rights, authentication of information and data processing. P.K. Kannan, Ai-Mei Chang, Andrew B. Whinston, 'The Internet Information Market: The Emerging Role of Intermediaries', in Michael J. Shaw, Robert Blanning, Troy Strader, Andrew Whinston (eds), *Handbook on Electronic Commerce* (Springer 2000) 569–590, at 573–578.

16 Niklas Luhman, 'Familiarity, confidence, trust: problems and alternatives', in Diego G. Gambetta (ed), *Trust: Making and Breaking Cooperative Relations* (Basil Blackwell 1988) 94–107.

17 Claire A. Hill and Erin A. O'Hara, 'A Cognitive Theory of Trust' (2006) 84 *Washington University Law Review* 1717–1796, at 1724.

Trust is therefore a mechanism for reducing uncertainty in complex organizations with unpredictable circumstances[18]. It is certainly not the only tool for uncertainty containment and complexity management. Rules, in all their manifestations and from the various sources of production and control – the law, the market, social norms – fulfil this function primarily and highly effectively. However, trust reinforces this role and acquires greater prominence in transactional or social interaction contexts where the effectiveness of norms may be weakened. In the digital society, less predictability about the applicable law or about the effectiveness of decisions in conflict resolution, uncertainty in the identification of parties, or the decentralized operation of the digital economy make trust the most important mechanism for reducing the complexity of social interactions and commercial transactions.

Information thus determines the level of trust. Lack of information will normally lead to a lack of trust, not necessarily distrust and, from the point of view of a rational decision, an incentive not to contract or at least a tendency not to cooperate due to risk aversion. It may therefore be presumed that the prejudice of a missed opportunity will always produce less harm than a misplaced overconfidence that will surely lead to a loss-making decision[19]. Similarly, the quality of relevant information determines the efficiency and stability of business relationships. Having complete, accurate and truthful information will usually mean the correct placement of trust or mistrust, and thus determine an efficient decision-making process. In the medium and long term, well-placed trust also reduces transaction and verification costs[20]. Likewise, false, inaccurate, biased or partial information will typically lead to excessive and misplaced trust or mistrust, and thus to inefficient decision making involving missed opportunities or frustration of expectations, expected conflicts and potential losses.

If truthful and relevant information feeds the objective component of trust, the perception of credibility, marked by factors and indications of trustworthiness, supports the subjective component that is increasingly decisive in the consolidation of trust in the digital society.

---

18 In the literature on the concept and function of trust in social behaviour, see in particular Francis Fukuyama, *Trust: The Social Virtues and the Creation of Prosperity* (The Free Press 1995); J. David Lewis and Andrew Weigert, 'Trust as a social reality' (1985) 63(4) *Social Forces* 967–985; Luhmann, *supra* fn 16.

19 Russell Hardin, 'Distrust' (2001) 81 *Boston University Law Review* 495–522, at 496; Hill and O'Hara, *supra* fn 17, 1737.

20 Frankel, *supra* fn 14.

Experience is essentially the vector of trust. We place our trust on the basis of our previous experiences[21] in successive transactions[22]. But in the first contact, when the exchange or the relationship is initiated for the first time and we have no past experience, trust has to be based on other factors and we look for indications of trustworthiness. Reputation[23] is the main indication of trustworthiness when past experience is lacking[24]. In short, reputation is really a reflection of the experiences of others.

Trust as a catalyst for social interaction and relations of cooperation and exchange has several dimensions that have to do with the type and origin of the information that is incorporated in the judgement of the degree of trustworthiness in each situation. In this chapter, the concept of 'aggregate trust' from the taxonomy of trust dimensions previously elaborated[25] is picked.

'Aggregate trust' would reflect a kind of community or self-regulatory response to create systemic trust when the market or the social environment lacks formal tools to endorse trustworthiness criteria. It is a reaction of the

21 In this sense, the focus so far has essentially been on assessing trust in the Internet as a measure of trustworthiness of the environment, so that the Internet is described as an "experience technology" which means that as users gain more experience in the digital space, they gain more trust in the transactions and social interaction they carry out in this environment. See William H. Dutton and Adrian Shepherd, *Trust in the Internet: the social dynamics of an experience technology* (Oxford Internet Institute 2003).

22 This would broadly respond to what Luhman defines as *familiarity* in his conceptual scheme familiarity-credibility-trust: Luhmann, *supra* fn 16.

23 Applying Luhman's conceptual toolkit that distinguishes between familiarity, which is basically based on knowledge resulting from past experiences, and trust, which reflects reasonable expectations about future behaviour, the empirical study by Gefen (David Gefen, 'E-commerce: the role of familiarity and trust' (2000) 28 *Omega*, 725–737) has confirmed the importance of both factors in the purchasing behaviour of users in e-commerce (online bookstores).

24 In turn, the use of an intermediary is conditioned by a series of direct and indirect variables that determine the degree of adoption of their services. In addition to *trust*, the need for experience or *expertise* is the most important determinant. Through an econometric study, Chircu, Davis and Kauffman have confirmed that trust and expertise are relevant variables in determining the degree of intervention of intermediaries in the framework of electronic transactions. Alina M. Chircu, Gordon B. Davis, Robert J. Kaufmann, 'The Role of Trust and Expertise in the Adoption of Electronic Commerce Intermediaries' (2000) 405 *AMCIS 2000 Proceedings* 710–716, available at <http://aisel.aisnet.org/amcis2000/405> (accessed 21 December 2022). This explains why new intermediaries resort to loyalty strategies and transfer their reputational factors from the traditional environment to the electronic context, in the face of the threat of 're-intermediation' by traditional intermediaries who retain the potential of their specialized knowledge.

25 This proposal was already put forward in Alba Fernández and Rodríguez de las Heras Ballell, *supra* fn 13.

market itself to generate trustworthy environments through collective actions by operators, outside of regulatory measures, with the aim of preserving and increasing the quality and reliability of services and the perception that the public may have of the industry in general (codes of conduct generated and adopted by the industry itself), of the reliability of information (collective and decentralized drafting and review phenomena through wiki techniques), or of users' credentials to interact (reputational systems, complaint and notification mechanisms).

Hence, the increasing relevance of 'aggregate trust' feedbacks the transformation of our society in an 'omnimetric society'.

4 Trust in an 'Omnimetric Society'

Our digital society has transferred to trust one of its most critical vulnerabilities: the tyranny of quantification. As the digital revolution drastically reduced the costs of quantifying, counting, sorting, and ranking, the digital society has become increasingly exposed to the tyranny of quantification[26]. Lists, rankings, ratings, numbers, and percentages now seem to offer the surest and most effective instruments for understanding a complex and highly uncertain world. Certainly, quantification helps decision-making. But the obsession with reducing every variable, every human behavior, every argument to the measure of numbers has intensified a blind confidence in the value of quantification to order the world, to measure quality, to quantify reliability, in short, to objectify any attribute and to measure, (arguably) without the threat of subjectivism, any aspect of society.

The digital society is an 'omnimetric society', where everything must be measured and only what can be measured matters. The dominance of quantification, as a triumph of *dataism*, suggests objectivity, evokes neutrality, and facilitates decision-making through a simple comparison of attributes according to their order and priority.

The perception of this pervasive quantification of the world in the digital society is essential to understanding the new coordinates of trust. In an omnimetric society, the perception of credibility is associated with criteria of popularity, virality and relevance. Thus, the veracity of information is relegated if it is not supported, amplified and reinforced by indices of popularity and

26 Bruno S. Frey, 'Omnimetrics and Awards' (2017) *CESifo Working Paper* no. 6582, 3, available at <https://www.crema-research.ch/wp-content/uploads/2022/01/omnimetrics-and-awards.pdf> (accessed 21 December 2022).

relevance. The perverse effect of this dominance of quantification is that popularity has come to replace veracity. In short, in our concept of trust, the subjective component of perception has overridden the objective component of truthfulness. Thus, one cannot effectively combat false information without the amplifying effect of popularity.

The most visible and alarming evidence of this vulnerability of the omnimetric society is the worrying phenomenon of disinformation reflected in the uncontrolled growth of *fake news*[27]. This problem has become extraordinarily relevant on the international political scene and has aroused deep concern about its destabilizing effects on our societies. The gravity of this situation reflects, on the one hand, the collapse of the role of trusted third parties and authority references, and is exacerbated, on the other, by an expansive movement towards decentralized systems of trust (*peer-determined truth*).

Decentralization has pervaded the digital society in all its dimensions. On the one hand, with the emergence and overwhelming expansion of distributed ledger technologies (DLT), which herald a profound transformation of markets, organization, communities, and processes, under decentralized schemes. On the other hand, with the growing popularity of social and economic models of cooperation, exchange or interaction based on *peer-to-peer* schemes, generating distributed trust and inspired by the economic rationale of sharing. These trends have materialized in the flourishing collaborative economy sector in its multiple forms, in the growing recourse of users to recommendation systems based on the opinion of other users, and in the widespread penetration of reputational, review or opinion mechanisms. These models are a response to a progressive deterioration of authority reference points, a loss of confidence in centralized control, and a widespread inclination to value as neutral and respect as impartial the opinion, recommendation or action of peers (*peer-determined truth, like-minded people opinion*). The concurrence of these technological, social and business factors has, in our view, shaped a second generation of the digital society.

In the shaping of these decentralized and reputational models, the features of an omnimetric society can also be observed. The value of opinion is conferred by numbers, popularity, relevance in quantitative terms. This is essentially how reputational and opinion systems work. The greater the number of opinions, the greater the credibility of the rating awarded; the positioning in

27 Teresa Rodríguez de las Heras Ballell and Jorge Feliu Rey, 'Digital Intermediary Liability or Greater Responsability: A Remedy for Fake News?', in Russell L. Weaver, Steven Friedland, Laetitia Tranchant, Guilhem Gil (eds), *Twenty-First Century Remedies: Comparative Perspectives* (Carolina Academic Press 2019) 91–114.

the first position of the ranking by the public is perceived as more impartial and reliable than the opinion of a critic; the reputation of a user depends on the opinion of others who interact with him or her as opposed to the merits, references or accreditations of third parties; the virality of a news item (repeated, forwarded, shared, retweeted) gives it visibility and greater credibility as opposed to expert opinions or public rectifications which are viewed with suspicion and distrust.

The reputational, distributed trust and decentralized models that we describe have an impact on two dimensions of trust. On the one hand, they present themselves as a clear and obvious exponent of aggregate trust generators. On the other hand, however, they also operate on the dimension of systematic trust. Indeed, they replace or reinforce traditional systems of systematic trust, such as the normative or institutional framework. In short, a decentralized system tries to create its own 'system' capable of generating trust, and reputational mechanisms on a platform replace social models of interaction and trust and bypass the need for centralized normative, institutional or trust systems.

5 Fairness and Transparency in Reputational Systems

Our omnimetric society is fueled by automation. In this light, reputational systems may be seen as automated decision-making (ADM) processes as defined by the 'Guiding Principles on ADM in Europe' published by the European Law Institute, under the responsibility of the author of this chapter, in 2022[28]:

> ADM is a (computational) process, including AI techniques and approaches, that, fed by inputs and data received or collected from the environment, can generate, given a set of pre-defined objectives, outputs in a wide variety of forms (content, ratings, recommendations, decisions, predictions, etc)[29].

28 European Law Institute, 'Guiding Principles on Automated Decision Making in Europe' (2022), prepared by Teresa Rodríguez de las Heras Ballell, available at <https://www.europeanlawinstitute.eu/fileadmin/user_upload/p_eli/Publications/ELI_Innovation_Paper_on_Guiding_Principles_for_ADM_in_the_EU.pdf> (accessed 21 December 2022).

29 The definition of ADM is largely aligned with the definition of algorithmic decision-making proposed by Article 2 of the ELI's 'Model Rules on Impact Assessment of Algorithmic Decision-Making Systems Used by Public Administration'. See European Law Institute, 'Model Rules on Impact Assessment of Algorithmic Decision-Making Systems Used by Public Administration', at <https://www.europeanlawinstitute.eu/fileadmin/user_upload/p_eli/Publications/ELI_Model_Rules_on_Impact_Assessment_of_ADMSs_Used_by_Public_Administration.pdf> (accessed 21 December 2022).

This definition is largely based on the (ongoing) definition of 'AI systems'[30] elaborated by the European Commission for the purposes of its draft Regulation on artificial intelligence (AI Act)[31]. Under that definition, the following key elements are deemed as necessary for qualifying a process as ADM: (1) inputs (these can be human-based inputs, machine-generated data, or interactions with the environment); (2) pre-defined objectives; (3) techniques and approaches to achieve those objectives; and (4) outputs (deliver, enable or support content moderation; ratings, rankings, predictions or recommendations; online advertising; complaint handling and dispute resolution; traceable traders (Know Your Business User approach); algorithmic management in platforms; credit scoring; pricing, trading and investing, or compliance).

ADM can produce or deliver a myriad of outputs from a rating to a credit granting decision, from a product recommendation to the allocation of work assignments, from a recruitment decision to the flagging or the removal of illegal digital content. Insofar as the variety of outputs is immense, the resultant legal consequences and the applicable legal regimes to ADM differ and are potentially multiple and varied.

Against such a backdrop, this chapter assumes that reputational systems are ADM systems that either generate outputs that will be employed as inputs of subsequent decision-making (feeding ADM or supporting human decisions), or produce a final decision that have direct effect on the legal or the

30 Article 3(1) of the European Commission, 'Proposal for a Regulation of the European Parliament and of the Council laying down harmonized rules on Artificial Intelligence (Artificial Intelligence Act) and amending certain Union legislative acts' (COM/2021/206 final), at <https://eur-lex.europa.eu/legal-content/EN/TXT/?uri=celex%3A52021PC0206> (accessed 21 December 2022): 'Artificial intelligence system (AI system) means software that is developed with one or more of the techniques and approaches listed in Annex I and can, for a given set of human-defined objectives, generate outputs such as content, predictions, recommendations, or decisions influencing the environments they interact with'. As the legislative process has not concluded yet, the definition is evolving. On 16 May 2023, the Draft compromise text was published incuding an amended definition of AI system in Article 3: 'a machine-based system that is designed to operate with varying levels of autonomy and that can, for explicit or implicit objectives, generate outputs such as predictions, recommendations, or decisions that influence physical or virtual environments.'

31 A similar definition was adopted by the European Parliament in its 'Resolution with recommendations to the Commission on a civil liability regime for artificial intelligence' ((2020/2014(INL)), at <https://www.europarl.europa.eu/doceo/document/TA-9-2020-0276_EN.html> (accessed 21 December 2022): "AI-system means a system that is either software-based or embedded in hardware devices, and that displays behavior simulating intelligence by, *inter alia*, collecting and processing data, analyzing and interpreting its environment, and by taking action, with some degree of autonomy, to achieve specific goals".

contractual status of the affected person (the end user). In the former case, the classification of a worker as unreliable by the reputational system will support the subsequent (automated or human) decision to dismiss him/her. In the latter case, the reputational system demotes a trader in a platform, or classifies an applicant as ineligible, or flags a post as false, and, consequently, it directly impacts on the competitive position of the trader, the contractual status of the applicant, and the free speech of the author of the flagged, removed or demoted post.

The potential, as well as the inherent risks, of automation have not gone unnoticed in the European Union (EU) and, indeed, there are multiple references scattered in EU pieces of legislation and in-process initiatives. On the contrary, the principles of transparency, explainability, risk assessment, and human oversight of algorithm-driven systems are crystallising in the EU legislative initiatives adopted in the last few years and in those proposed more recently.

However, even if important guiding principles can be inferred from the legislative scene and useful rules on algorithm-based systems and automated means can already be found in Union legislation, they do not form a consistent, coherent, and all-embracing body of principles/rules governing automated decision-making systems. Provisions dealing with ADM in Union legislation are scattered, apply to different extents and scopes, sometimes overlap and other times clash, thus forming a fragmented and inevitably incomplete, legal framework for ADM in the Union. A small selection of existing provisions on ADM will suffice to illustrate the lack of coherence of the EU regulatory approach.

Article 22 GDPR[32] on decisions based solely on automated processing, including profiling, has long been the centerpiece of the EU's legal approach to ADM and embodies its main policy goals. But it is not its goal to set out a complete legal framework for the use of automated processing. Neither the natural scope of the Regulation, nor the content of the provision itself invite such high expectations. It is not indeed a legal regime for ADM.

The Platform-to-Business Regulation (P2B Regulation)[33] confirms that policy by laying down transparency requirements in the provision of ranking

32 Regulation (EU) 2016/679 of the European Parliament and of the Council of 27 April 2016 on the protection of natural persons with regard to the processing of personal data and on the free movement of such data, and repealing Directive 95/46/EC (General Data Protection Regulation).

33 Regulation (EU) 2019/1150 of the European Parliament and of the Council of 20 June 2019 on promoting fairness and transparency for business users of online intermediation services.

services. Likewise, algorithmic accountability, and transparency do also cross-cut some obligations laid down in the Digital Services Act (DSA)[34] – recommender systems, terms and conditions, content moderation. Risks arising from algorithmic decisions (automated decision-making) are acknowledged throughout the DSA and are accordingly subject to risk assessment and risk-mitigating measures as applied to very large online platforms. The interplay between the P2B Regulation and the DSA raises multiple issues that require further and careful consideration.

Besides, the proposed Artificial Intelligence Act (AI Act)[35] represents a risk-based approach to AI systems and the consolidation of certain principles aimed at guiding the placing on the market and the use of AI on the basis of the intended purpose of the system concerned.

Finally, the recent Proposal for a Directive on improving working conditions in platform work[36] (Directive on Platform Work) devotes its Chapter 3 to algorithmic management under the principles of transparency, human monitoring, and human review of significant decisions.

All the references above show that automated decision-making systems are attracting regulatory attention in the EU agenda. Nevertheless, rules related to automated processes are scattered in different pieces of legislation, partial in their scope, and unharmonised. Some rules are sector-specific, while others apply solely to certain types of automated systems (rating, recommender systems, algorithmic management). Besides, despite the fact that the main policy goals are enshrined in a number of legal provisions (transparency, explainability, human monitoring), their implementation in practice is still uncertain, may be unfeasible or too costly, or become significantly complex.

Uncertainties about the applicability of existing rules on ADM or the principles guiding a systemic use of algorithms and AI systems for commercial purposes and in economic activities make predictability difficult and allow neither to control nor to unleash ADM potential. A sound, clearer legal framework for ADM is highly needed.

34 Regulation of the European Parliament and the Council on a Single Market for Digital Services (Digital Services Act) and amending Directive 2000/31/EC.

35 European Commission, *supra* fn 30.

36 European Commission, *supra* fn 10.

6 The European Law Institute's Guiding Principles on Algorithmic Decision Making

With the aim of contributing to this exercise, ELI adopted 12 Guiding Principles on ADM that aim at providing further guidance on establishing a legal framework for automated decision-making (ADM) in the EU.

In this chapter, it is advocated that these principles can also help to mitigate the risks raised by the use of reputational systems as a tool to assess performance and apply sanctions. All principles do naturally apply to reputational systems insofar as they are ADM. But focus should be directed towards, in particular, some of them.

First, as per Principle 1, "[a]n operator that decides to use ADM for a particular purpose shall ensure that the design and the operation of the ADM are compliant with the laws applicable to an equivalent non-automated decision-making system"[37]. Far from being regarded as an obvious and evident principle, its role is fundamental, and much more enabling that it may be initially perceived. The principle that ADMs have to be law-compliant provides a benchmark to assess against for each and every use of ADM, including reputational systems. It determines which are the legal parameters the ADM should be followed. In fact, this principle signals the applicable law that the ADM should be subject to. Thus, if the reputational system, as previously discussed, is employed to assess the work performance of an employee, to distribute tasks, or to calculate bonuses, the pertinent labour legislation (including collective agreements)[38] will provide for the rules, limits, and prohibitions. While if the reputational system would be used (in case of being authorised) to assess creditworthiness of applicants to financial products and services, banking and financial regulations would apply.

Second, in conformity with Principle 6, "[t]he complexity, the opacity or the unpredictability of ADM is not a valid ground for rendering an unreasoned, unfounded or arbitrary decision"[39]. This principle is crucial as it ensures that

37 European Law Institute, *supra* fn 28, 12.

38 Aida Ponce del Castillo and Diego Naranjo, 'Regulating algorithmic management: An assessment of the EC's draft Directive on improving working conditions in platform work' (2022) *ETUI Policy Brief* no. 08, available at <http://dx.doi.org/10.2139/ssrn.4243530> (accessed 21 December 2022).

39 European Law Institute, *supra* fn 28, 10. The Proposal for a Directive on Platform Work also stipulates that: "(d)igital labour platforms shall provide the platform worker with a written statement of the reasons for any decision taken or supported by an automated decision-making system to restrict, suspend or terminate the platform worker's account, any decision to refuse the remuneration for work performed by the platform worker, any decision on the platform worker's contractual status or any decision with similar effects"

any decision made or assisted by the ADM (triggered by the reputational system, in our case) and employed for the intended purpose can be explained. Complex, opaque or unpredictable features should not be brought forward as excuses not to give reasons or to refuse to account for the decisions made by the ADM. The fact that the 'score' results from gathering opinions of customers, data collected by sensors installed in the vehicle, likes received, or ratings gained cannot mean that the resultant decision is on that sole ground inexplicable, arbitrary, discriminatory or unreasoned. Otherwise, in the absence of a statement of reasons supporting a decision, the affected person is not in a position to assess the correctness of the decision and is deprived of the right to challenge a decision affecting them.

Third, pursuant to Principle 8, "[a]utomation shall not prevent, limit, or render unfeasible the exercise of rights and access to justice by affected persons. An alternative human-based route to exercise rights should be available"[40]. As a specific application of the principle of law-compliance, this Principle spotlights the risk that the exercise of rights by the affected person and effective access to justice may be prevented, hampered or limited by the inadequate, excessive, abusive, or manipulative use of automation. There are two types of concerns. On the one hand, where the user affected by the decision can only exercise a right by resorting to an algorithmic process. For instance, resorting to a complaint-handling system implemented in the same platform and fully (or partially) automated that it does not enable to explain the reasons to challenge the decision other than choosing from a limited list of pre-selected situations. On the other hand, where the user affected by the ADM is deprived of the possibility of exercising a right or access to justice solely on the grounds that the contested decision was made by ADM. For example, if the decision has been to close the user account without prior notice and therefore the user does not have access to the statement of reasons, the relevant data to use as evidence, or simply the dispute resolution mechanisms available in case of disagreements as they depend upon being a registered user in the platform.

(European Commission, *supra* fn 10, article 8(1)). Yet, articles 13(2)(f), 14(2)(g) and 15(1)(h) GDPR expressly require that the controller provide the data subject with "meaningful information about the logic" involved in automated decision-making, and "the significance and envisaged consequences of such" automated processing. DSA does also require a "statement of reasons" supporting content moderation.

40 European Law Institute, *supra* fn 28, 21.

7 Conclusions

This chapter explores how the need to generate reputation in the digital economy has fostered the rise of a variety of reputational mechanisms that rely on the concept of 'peer-determined truth'. This model fuels, and at the same time is stoked by, the fundamental thesis that our digital society is an omnimetric society, where everything is measured and only what can be measured matters. Under the same logic, reputational systems are employed, in the platform economy, as tools to assess performance and apply sanctions in a myriad of contractual contexts, quantifying and controlling the behavior of riders, traders, tenants, creators, project promoters, and so on and so forth. It is the tyranny of quantification. Only the number matters, and numbers rule.

The developed metrics to assess performance have then fundamental legal implications in the exercise of rights and liberties. Consequences of bad rating or demotion are applied automatically, without scrutiny and with the strong effectiveness and forceful efficacy of technology-enabled remedies (deactivated passwords, closed accounts, suspended services, removed content). Metrics developed to assess performance may be based on irrelevant criteria, biased patterns, stereotypes, or discriminatory parameters. On top of that, algorithmic opacity, lack of explainability, risk of bias, absence of monitoring, or right to object decisions can in practice leave users defenceless, unprotected and, to a certain extent, deprived from their rights to appeal and access to justice.

The chapter elaborates the thesis of an 'omnimetric society' and explores the legal and social implications of a metrics-based performance measurement in platforms, be they social networks, sharing-economy platforms, electronic marketplaces, or crowdfunding platforms, among others. Beyond the principles of transparency and explainability, the chapter proposes some possible solutions, relying upon the 'Guiding Principles on Automated Decision-Making' recently elaborated by the author of this chapter and approved and published by the ELI. Although drafted for the European context, the Principles may provide useful answers to the global challenge of unleashing the full potential of automation without compromising the protection of individual and collective rights and liberties.

CHAPTER 14

Performance Measurements in Compliance with Corporate Social Responsibility Obligations

Lukas Heckendorn Urscheler

1 Introduction

In the 20th century, the corporate world developed the concept of Corporate Social Responsibility (CSR) as a response to popular dissatisfaction and public regulatory pressure[1]. Originally a managerial and ethical concept, it became part of a more legal discussion in the end of the 20th and beginning of the 21st century. In this debate, CSR has for a long time been understood as a voluntary mechanism, expressing the commitment of corporations to the society at large, i.e. their efforts to have a positive impact on a variety of stakeholders[2].

The Business and Human Rights movement changed this perspective considerably. In fact, since the late 1970s, there has been a long struggle to find a way to integrate multinational corporations in the international human rights landscape; especially advocacy groups were calling for ways to hold these increasingly powerful actors accountable for their potentially negative impacts on human beings and the environment. This seemed necessary, as their financial power started to exceed the power of some states. More importantly, a range of disasters, starting with the tragic Bhopal chemical accident, showed the consequences of corporate carelessness. However, several attempts to find ways to bring international corporations into international law did not bring any results. Only in the early 2000, the 'Protect, Respect and Remedy' framework developed by John Ruggie in his role as the UN Secretary General's Special Representative on Business and Human Rights offered a solution. This framework found its way into the UN Guiding Principles on Business and Human Rights, unanimously endorsed by the UN Human Rights Council in 2011. The UN Guiding Principles on Business and Human Rights had

1 Cf. Krista Nadakavukaren Schefer, 'Social Powers, Social Responsibilities and Corporations: From CSR to Business and Human Rights' (2020) 139 *Zeitschrift für schweizerisches Recht* II 5; Birgit Spießhofer, *Unternehmerische Verantwortung. Zur Entstehung einer globalen Wirtschaftsordnung* (Nomos 2017) 27 and 54 ff.

2 See Spießhofer, *supra* fn 1.

 | DOI:10.1163/9789004680944_015

an important effect on the revision of the OECD Guidelines for Multinational Enterprises and triggered developments in regional and in national law.

An important reason for the success of the framework was a change in the discourse. Previous discussions essentially focused on legal arguments. The main point of debate was the issue whether and to what extent (international) corporations could have duties (and rights) under international law. In a contrast to this legal debate, the new framework was first of all conceptual[3]. While reflecting the current state of international law, it introduced concepts that businesses were familiar with (from other areas), and it applied them to the way corporations deal with human rights issues. The concept of due diligence is one of them. The idea of reporting about human rights issues also fits well with existing reporting obligations of corporations towards shareholders. Translating issues of human rights into previously existing concepts made them accessible – and also acceptable – for corporations. In other words, the 'Protect, Respect and Remedy' framework was successful because rather than introducing something completely new, it only added the human rights dimension to tools already familiar to the corporate world.

In this contribution, I will look at one tool that was taken from the corporate world and filled with human rights content. Performance measurements are typically linked to the world of business and economics. In the 1990s, however, they started to find their way into the field of human rights, first as a tool to keep track (and possibly compare) how States respect human rights[4]. Their use in the context of corporate sustainability could be seen as 're-export': the business tool (performance measurement) that was adapted to the human rights context moves back to the corporate world: to measure corporate human rights compliance.

---

3 John Gerard Ruggie, *Just Business: Multinational Corporations and Human Rights* (Norton & Co. 2013) 78. See further John Ruggie, 'Business and Human rights: Further Steps toward the Operationalization of the 'Protect, Respect and Remedy' Framework: Report of the Special Representative of the Secretary-General on the Issue of Human Rights and Transnational Corporations and Other Business Enterprises, John Ruggie' (2010), available at <https: //www2.ohchr.org/english/issues/trans_corporations/docs/A-HRC-14-27.pdf> (accessed 11 March 2023).

4 David McGrogan, 'Human Rights Indicators and the Sovereignty of Technique' (2016) 27 *European Journal of International Law* 385 at 388; for law and measurement generally, see Mathias Siems, 'Measuring the immeasurable: how to turn law into numbers', in Michael Faure and Jan M. Smits (eds), *Does Law Matter? On Law and Economic Growth* (Intersentia 2011) 115.

While human rights indicators have been widely discussed in academic literature[5], the writing on sustainability indicators for corporations seems less developed[6], though it is exponentially growing. The aim of this contribution is to analyse what role tools of measurement play for corporations in the area of business and human rights, from a legal point of view, and what the implications are, especially for compliance of corporations with obligations in this area. Referring to existing literature in the field, I will therefore first briefly describe several commonly used measurement tools (Section 2), before evaluating how the international (Section 3) and the European legal framework (Section 4) deal with them. Section 5 will conclude.

2 Measuring the Impact of Corporations on the Environment and the Society

As indicated above, the term Corporate Social Responsibility (CSR) can be traced at least to the middle of the 20th century. Today, a concept that focuses on measurement is becoming increasingly important: ESG (Environment, Social, Governance) is the key term[7]. It was developed in 2005 in the context of the formulation of the Principles of Responsible Investment (PRI) with the involvement of the UN and especially the UN Environment Programme (UNEP)[8]. Its purpose is to integrate economic, social and governance factors into investment strategies and risk management decisions[9]. It is more

5 Gauthier de Beco, *Non-Judicial Mechanisms for the Implementation of Human Rights in European States* (Bruylant 2009) 169 ff., with further references; Kevin Davis, Angelina Fisher, Benedict Kingsbury, Sally Engle Merry (eds), *Governance by Indicators: Global Power through Quantification and Ranking* (OUP 2012); for a discussion of the anthropological dimension, see Sally Engly Merry, 'Human Rights Monitoring and the Question of Indicators', in Mark Goodale (ed), *Human Rights at the Crossroads* (OUP 2013) 140–150.

6 One of the exceptions is Ronen Shamir and Dana Weiss, 'Semiotics of Indicators: The Case of Corporate Human Rights Responsibility' in Davis et al. (eds), *supra* fn 5, 110–131, which does not take a legal approach (at 110).

7 Anne-Christin Mittwoch, Leah Wetenkamp, Annika Bleier, 'Unternehmensrechtliche Nachhaltigkeit und ESG' (2022) *Neue Juristische Wochenschrift* 3601 at N 5.

8 See Federica Doni and Lara Johannsdottir, 'Environmental, Social and Governance (ESG) Ratings', in Water Leal Filho, Anabela Marisa Azul, Luciana Brandli, Pinar Gökcin Özuyar, Tony Wall (eds), *Climate Action. Encyclopedia of SDG* (Springer 2020) 435; for an explanation, see Cynthia A. Williams, 'Comparative and transnational developments in corporate social responsibility', in Afra Afsharipour and Martin Gelter (eds), *Comparative Corporate Governance* (Elgar 2021) 92 at 97 ff.

9 Ibid.

concrete and specific than CSR, as it aims at making sustainability considerations operational: developed at the same time than the 'Protect, Respect and Remedy' framework discussed above, it follows a similar approach in the sense that it integrates the sustainability considerations into the logic of business and investment. This logic attaches particular importance to measuring. Compared to CSR, it has a strong focus on quantification and reporting[10]. As CSR, ESG covers sustainability generally and is therefore broader than the 'Protect, Respect and Remedy' framework that is essentially linked to human rights.

The terminological evaluation – from CSR to ESG – reflects the growing importance of measurement in the area: there is a big number and wide range of initiatives that measure sustainability performance. The already mentioned Principles of Responsible Investment for instance provide an overview and list (under the heading of "Social issues") about 20 "Key human rights benchmarks"[11]. In the last years, the number of measurement tools like the PRI – be it indicators, ratings or indices – has dramatically increased[12], reflecting the involvement of different stakeholders and interests[13]. International organizations such as the UN, but also human rights and civil society organizations such as the Danish Institute of Human Rights, are promoting this development, hoping that the indicators will push corporations to take into account sustainability issues, or at least facilitate it[14]. The corporate world is (also) interested in indicators as a tool of marketing and communication to investors and consumers, being aware that sustainability has become an important topic in the public discourse. In addition, as will be shown below (Section 3), the regulatory framework increasingly requires the use of indicators. And last but not least, a whole industry specialized in sustainability reporting has developed.

10 See, e.g., Sean O'Neill, 'What is the difference between CSR and ESG?' (2023), available at <https://www.thecorporategovernanceinstitute.com/insights/lexicon/what-is-the-difference-between-csr-and-esg/> (accessed 11 March 2023); see also <https://socialgoodconnect.org/what-is-esg/> (accessed 11 March 2023).

11 See <https://www.unpri.org/human-rights/human-rights-benchmarks-for-investors-an-overview/10375.article> (accessed 11 March 2023).

12 Damiano de Felice, 'Business and Human Rights Indicators to Measure the Corporate Responsibility to Respect: Challenges and Opportunities' (2015) 37 *Human Rights Quarterly* 511, at 513–514 and (for an overview) at 521 ff.

13 See for an overview on transnational standards more generally, Williams, *supra* fn 8, 100 ff.

14 See de Beco, *supra* fn 5, who treats indicators as a non-judicial mechanisms for the implementation of human rights.

The big number of indicators and stakeholders implies that indicators can have different functions. They can be seen as a tool for marketing[15] and promotion of a corporation, an incentive for promoting sustainability issues, a way to indicate compliance with the legal framework or a management tool that allows measuring progress. The different functions are sometimes contradictory, and this is probably one reason for the big number of existing indicators.

It is therefore important to look at who has developed and who uses these indicators. Some indicators are developed by corporations in their process of self-reporting, others by third parties who can be independent from the industry (what would typically be the case for the regulator) or who represent the industry and/or other stakeholders, and some of them in collaborative processes by multiple actors. The author of an indicator is important when assessing its purpose, though it is only one of the elements that matter when assessing its validity[16].

Literature on human rights indicators distinguishes between structural indicators (reflecting the ratification of legal instruments/policies), process indicators (measuring the procedures to implement), and indicators focusing on the outcome[17]. The UN Office of the High Commissioner for Human Rights (OHCHR) also refers to these three categories[18]. The underlying idea is "to measure the commitment of the duty-bearer to the relevant human rights standards, the efforts that were undertaken to make that commitment a reality and results of those efforts over time"[19]. This distinction (originally created to assess the quality of care in health care services)[20] might be helpful when assessing the indicators that corporations use.

15 See (with a focus on Unilever and Nestle) Maria Eugenia Trombini and Markus Pohlmann, 'Self-Regulation and human rights: the contested terrain of corporate actors in the food and beverage industry' (2023) 122 *Zeitschrift für Vergleichende Rechtswissenschaft* 4, at 13.

16 For a critical approach, see Shamir and Weiss, *supra* fn 6, 129.

17 De Felice, *supra* fn 12, 532 ff.

18 OHCHR, *Human Rights Indicators. A Guide to Measurement and Implementation* (OHCHR 2012) 34 ff., available at <https://previous.ohchr.org/Documents/Publications/Human_rights_indicators_en.pdf> (accessed 11 March 2023).

19 OHCHR, 'Report on Indicators for Promoting and Monitoring the Implementation of Human Rights' (HRI/MC/2008/3), 6 June 2008, para 8 (and see also para 17), available at <https://www.ohchr.org/en/documents/reports/report-indicators-promoting-and-monitoring-implementation-human-rights-hrimc20083> (accessed 11 March 2023).

20 McGrogan, *supra* fn 4, 389, with further references.

3 Measurement in International Legal Instruments Relating to Corporate Social Responsibility (Business and Human Rights)

Two main instruments have shaped the development of corporate social responsibility considerations in the last twenty years: the UN Guiding Principles on Business and Human Rights, unanimously endorsed by the UN Human Rights Council in June 2011 (Section 3.1), and the OECD Guidelines for Multinational Enterprises that gave rise to a recommendation in May 2011 of the governments of the OECD member states as well as other adhering governments (Section 3.2). In spite of their soft-law nature, they both have a considerable impact[21] and will therefore be presented more in detail below.

It is important to underline the existence of several international standards and standard setting initiatives dealing with ESG reporting. The Global Reporting Initiative[22] and the Task Force on Climate-related Financial Disclosures (TCFD) linked to the G20 are two examples. In recent years, however, a consolidation took place. Several organizations were consolidated into the IFRS Foundation[23]. In the wake of this consolidation, the IFRS Foundation, a not-for-profit, public interest organisation that is at the origin (through the International Accounting Standards Board) of the influential International Accounting Standards[24], created a new standard-setting board – the International Sustainability Standards Board (ISSB) in 2021[25]. The ISSB published a first draft on "General Requirements for Disclosure of Sustainability-related Financial Information" in 2022 and is currently finalizing this standard[26]. The ISSB standards deal with measuring as 'metrics and target' in a detailed way.

21 See, e.g. Barnahli Choudhuri, 'Hardening Soft Law Instruments in Business and Human Rights', in Jean Jacques du Plessis and Chee Keong Low (eds), *Corporate Governance Codes for the 21st Century. International Perspectives and Critical Analysis* (Springer 2017) 189.

22 An independent non-profit institution established in Amsterdam with roots in a non-profit organization; its standards are apparently used by more than 10.000 companies. See <https://www.globalreporting.org/about-gri/> (accessed 11 March 2023).

23 For example the Climate Disclosure Standards Board (see <https://www.ifrs.org/sustainability/climate-disclosure-standards-board/> (accessed 11 March 2023)) or the International Integrated Reporting Council (see <https://www.integratedreporting.org/the-iirc-2/council/> (accessed 11 March 2023)).

24 See Flurin Riederer, *The impact of IFRS on domestic accounting rules: The case of Switzerland* (Helbing 2019).

25 See <https://www.ifrs.org/groups/international-sustainability-standards-board/> (accessed 11 March 2023).

26 See the website of the ISSB for current developments, at <https://www.ifrs.org/projects/work-plan/general-sustainability-related-disclosures/#current-stage> (accessed 11 March 2023).

However, given that this contribution focuses on the way law deals with indicators, the following considerations will not deal with those or other existing standards, in spite of their potential normative value and impact on national law. The European law on sustainability reporting (see below, Section 4, especially at 4.3) provides an illustrative example of both how such standards deal with performance measurement and of how they can achieve normative force. For the international standards, especially the ISSB standards, once adopted, it is likely that they will achieve legal relevance through practice and/or reference in national legal instruments[27].

3.1 *The UN Guiding Principles*

The UN Guiding Principles on Business and Human Rights (UNGP) explicitly refer to the use of measurement (only) in Principle 20. Principle 20 is an operational principle relating to the responsibility of corporations to protect human rights. It explains how "business enterprises should address adverse human rights impacts with which they are involved"[28]. According to Principle 20, "[i]n order to verify whether adverse human rights impacts are addressed, businesses should track the effectiveness of their responses" by using "qualitative and quantitative indicators". The indicator here is not a tool to measure the impact of the corporate activity, but to evaluate corporate responses.

While the Guiding Principles themselves do not mention indicators elsewhere, the official Guide does so in its comment on Principle 21. Principle 21 deals with communication of business enterprises. According to the guide, "the reporting should cover topics and indicators concerning how enterprises identify and address adverse impacts on human rights. Independent verification of human rights reporting can strengthen its content and credibility. Sector-specific indicators can provide helpful additional detail".

In the context of UNGP, the normative framework establishes two ways to use indicators: to evaluate a corporation's response, but they are also a useful tool in the process of reporting. The two uses fulfill two different functions. In the process of reporting (that might also have an impact on the process within the corporation itself), indicators can provide a reference point for corporations to identify their adverse impact on human rights. In that sense, they are a tool to measure adverse human rights impacts as such. In the process of evaluating the responses, the reference to indicators and measurement has a

27 On the politics of accounting standards, see Tim Büthe and Walter Mattli, *The New Global Rulers. The Privatization of Regulation in the World Economy* (Princeton University Press 2011) at 44 ff and 99 ff.

28 Foundational principle 11.

different function: it aims at forcing the corporation to follow up and evaluate its responses and therefore to counter the risk of the corporation not addressing its adverse impacts, or not doing so effectively.

3.2 *The OECD Guidelines*

The OECD Guidelines for Multinational Enterprises are recommendations addressed by governments to multinational corporations. They are not legally binding, but they nevertheless provide "principles and standards for responsible business conduct in a global context consistent with applicable laws and internationally recognised standards"[29].

The OECD guidelines themselves do not deal with indicators in sustainability reporting[30]. They do, however, refer to measurement in the chapter on the environment: enterprises should "provide the public and workers with [...] measurable and verifiable and timely information on the potential environment, health and safety impacts of the activities of the enterprise, which could include reporting on progress in improving environmental performance"[31]. The measurement does refer to the potential environmental and health and safety impacts. Differently than what is the case under the UNGP, the requirement to measure under the OECD guidelines does not necessarily apply to the way in which the corporation is dealing with the above-mentioned impacts; it could be limited to the impacts alone.

It appears, therefore, that the OECD guidelines refer less to indicators than the UNGP. They take up the mechanisms and terminology of the UNGP without providing more detail relating to measurement. They do refer, however, to some of the reporting initiatives mentioned above.

The silence of the OECD Guidelines on measuring and indicators does not mean that the OECD are not aware of the topic or not promoting indicators. It is rather a consequence of the level of detail in the Guidelines, and it might also reflect the state of general consensus at the time the Guidelines were adopted. In the meantime, the OECD has developed several so-called 'Due Diligence Guidances': one for responsible business conduct generally, one for minerals from conflict-affected and high-risk areas, one for extractive industries, and one for the garment and footwear sector[32]. An OECD-FAO Guidance deals with

29 OECD, *OECD Guidelines for Multinational Enterprises* (OECD 2011), Foreword, available at <https://www.oecd.org/daf/inv/mne/48004323.pdf> (accessed 11 March 2023).

30 The term indicators is only used in Chapter 5 on employment and industrial relationswhen refering to the indicators on the existence of an employment relationship developed by the ILO (ILO Recommendation 198 of 2006).

31 OECD, *supra* fn 29, 42.

32 See <https://mneguidelines.oecd.org/duediligence/> (accessed 11 March 2023).

agricultural supply chains. The OECD Council adopted formal recommendations for each specific guidance, and other governments can adhere to them; they can therefore be regarded as international soft-law or at least claim some normative value[33]. Each guide deals with indicators and measurement in a more detailed way, as the two examples below show.

The General Due Diligence Guidance published in 2018 talks about indicators at several stages of the due diligence process. First, and in line with the UN Guiding Principles, indicators are seen as a tool "to define and measure improvement" in the prevention and mitigation of adverse impacts[34]. The more detailed annexes refer to indicators more often: first, in the context of prioritisation, i.e. for assessing whether scale, scope and irremediable character of an adverse impact requires dealing with it[35]; second, when assessing whether adverse impacts have been responded to effectively[36].

The OECD Due Diligence Guidance for Responsible Supply Chains of Minerals from Conflict-Affected and High-Risk Areas[37] published in 2016 is of particular interest, because it was a model for several regional instruments such as a regional certification mechanism approved by the Heads of State and Government of the African Great Lakes Region or the European Regulation 2017/821 (so-called Conflict Minerals Regulation)[38]. More significantly, the European Conflict Minerals Regulation refers to the OECD Conflict Minerals Due Diligence Guidance repeatedly, particularly (but not only) when referring to measures and indicators[39]. As its

33 Other OECD documents (on institutional investors and child labour) have not gone through the same formal process.

34 OECD, *OECD Due Diligence Guidance for Responsible Business Conduct* (OECD 2018) 30, at b), available at <https://mneguidelines.oecd.org/OECD-Due-Diligence-Guidance-for-Responsible-Business-Conduct.pdf> (accessed 11 March 2023).

35 OECD, *supra* fn 34, Annex, 42, with numerous examples on what indicators can be used to identify the scale, scope and irremdiable character of adverse impact in table 3 (such as extent of impact on health and frequency at which bribes are paid).

36 OECD, *supra* fn 34, Annex, 82; examples are the "percentage of impacted stakeholders engaged who feel impacts have been adequately addressed" or the "number of implemented action points".

37 OECD, *OECD Due Diligence Guidance for Responsible Supply Chains of Minerals from Conflict-Affected and High-Risk Areas* (OECD 2016, 3rd edn), available at <http://dx.doi.org/10.1787/9789264252479-en> (accessed 11 March 2023).

38 Regulation (EU) 2017/821 of the European Parliament and of the Council of 17 May 2017 laying down supply chain due diligence obligations for Union importers of tin, tantalum and tungsten, their ores, and gold originating from conflict-affected and high-risk areas; see preamble 5 and 6.

39 Article 5(3) Regulation (EU) 2017/821.

title[40] illustrates, Annex III of the OECD Conflict Minerals Due Diligence Guidance deals with indicators for measuring improvement. It identifies a range of issues the supply chain policy should address (e.g. security and related issues, exposure of artisanal miners to adverse impacts, money laundering) and proposes measures to address them as well as indicators for measuring improvement. Indicators – often taken from international standards – include the "number and percentage of operating sites where artisanal and small-scale mining takes place", the "percentage of security personnel trained in [...] policies or procedures concerning [relevant] aspects of human rights", but also structural qualitative indicators that do not involve numerical measurement such as "the supply chain policy" or "the nature and form of risk assessments". Even though there is a big number of indicators, many of them leave doubts either with regards to the feasibility of their use (e.g., "percentage of minerals or money illegally taxed or extorted from upstream actors by public or private security forces") or their ability to actually reflect improvement, especially in the case of structural indicators. Indeed, finding appropriate indicators is particularly difficult in this area. The importance the OECD gives to the issue is probably a result of the companies' need to show concrete progress, responding to public pressure; and the easiest way to show progress is by 'proving' it through measurement.

4 Regulating Measurement at the Regional Level: The Use of Indicators in EU Law on Sustainability

The European Union has adopted an increasing number of instruments in the area of sustainability. Interestingly, the use of measurement and indicators is most prominently regulated in instruments dealing with reporting and disclosure. Therefore, the following considerations focus on the three main instruments that deal with sustainability reporting: the Non-financial Reporting Directive (Section 4.1), the European instruments relating to sustainable finance (Section 4.2), and the Sustainability Reporting Directive (Section 4.3).

I will not discuss sector-specific rules such as the European Timber Regulation 995/2010[41] or the Conflict Minerals Regulation 2017/821. The

40 Annex III: Suggested Measures for Risk Mitigation and Indicators for Measuring Improvement.

41 Regulation (EU) 995/2010 of the European Parliament and of the Council of 20 October 2010 laying down the obligations of operators who place timber and timber products on the market.

European Timber Regulation does not refer to indicators or measurement in a detailed way, and it will soon be replaced by a Regulation on deforestation-free supply chains[42]. The Conflict Minerals Regulation simply refers to the OECD framework when it comes to measurement and indicators[43].

4.1 *A First Step: The Non-Financial Reporting Directive*

The oldest general European instrument currently in force in the area of sustainability is Directive 2014/95 on non-financial reporting. It introduced a reporting obligation for certain large undertakings, requiring them to include in their management report a non-financial statement "relating to, as a minimum, environmental, social and employee matters, respect for human rights, anti-corruption and bribery matters", at least "to the extent necessary for an understanding of the undertaking's development, performance, position and impact of its activity"[44]. This statement should include "non-financial key performance indicators relevant to the particular business".

In its guideline on the Directive, published in 2017, the European Commission first observes that the non-financial statement should not be limited to key performance indicators (KPI), but should include narrative-based disclosures and indicator-based disclosures. This first statement makes it clear that indicators are not seen as the only way to report. Other considerations focus on key performance indicators: according to the European Commission, the KPI should on the one hand be consistent with what the company uses

42 The European Commission published its proposal for a new regulation in 2021 (see European Commission, Proposal for a Regulation of the European Parliament and of the Council on the making available on the Union market as well as export from the Union of certain commodities and products associated with deforestation and forest degradation and repealing Regulation (EU) No 995/2010, COM(2021) 706 final). The European Parliament and the Council reached a (provisional) agreement in December 2022 (see the Press release by the European Commission of 6 December 2022, available at <https://ec.europa.eu/commission/presscorner/detail/en/ip_22_7444> (accessed 11 March 2023)); the European Parliament is currently debating the proposal (see <https://oeil.secure.europarl.europa.eu/oeil/popups/ficheprocedure.do?reference=2021/0366(COD)&l=en> (accessed 11 March 2023)).

43 For the use of indicators in this Regulation, see *supra*, section 3.2.

44 Art. 1 of Directive 2014/95/EU of the European Parliament and of the Council of 22 October 2014 amending Directive 2013/34/EU as regards disclosure of non-financial and diversity information by certain large undertakings and groups (inserting Articles 19a and 29a in the text of Directive 2013/34/EU of the European Parliament and of the Council of 26 June 2013 on the annual financial statements, consolidated financial statements and related reports of certain types of undertakings, amending Directive 2006/43/EC of the European Parliament and of the Council and repealing Council Directives 78/660/EEC and 83/349/EEC).

in its internal management and, on the other hand, improve comparability within a sector or value chain. Therefore, a company should use general, sectoral and company-specific KPI. In addition, the Commission underlines the importance of using the same indicators over time. Finally, the Commission points to the importance of data collection and methodology of KPI, but it does not require disclosure on these issues[45]. These considerations show that indicators are seen as an important but not the only aspect of non-financial reporting, and that they should assure uniformity: uniformity in time, but also uniformity within the sector.

As the political focus shifted from general sustainability considerations to climate change, the European Commission published a supplement to the 2017 Guideline in 2019, dealing with reporting climate related information[46]. The 2019 supplement recommends a number of specific key performance indicators that companies should use "to support their climate-related disclosures"[47], with detailed descriptions on the calculation. For example, the supplement recommends four different indicators on Greenhouse Gas emissions, energy consumption and efficiency, exposure to physical risk resulting from climate change, products and services contributing to mitigation or adaptation of climate change, as well as green bond and green debt. Several of these indicators should show the proportion the company invests or is likely involved in climate change related policies. Its annex I provides further guidance with a big number of additional indicators for banks and insurance companies.

4.2 *The Push for Indicators in EU-Law Relating to Sustainable Finance*

As mentioned above (Section 2), the concept of ESG and the push for measurement in this area started in a discussion on sustainable finance. It is therefore not surprising that sustainable finance is the area in which the European Union has developed legal instruments dealing with or containing indicators most actively in recent years. In an effort to implement the UN Sustainable Development Goals as well as the Paris Climate Agreement, the European Commission has adopted an action plan on "Financing sustainable growth"

45 European Commission, 'Communication from the Commission. Guidelines on non-financial reporting (methodology for reporting non-financial information)' (2017/C 215/01), at point 4.5.

46 European Commission, 'Communication from the Commission. Guidelines on non-financial reporting: Supplement on reporting climate-related information' (2019/C 209/01).

47 European Commission, *supra* fn 46, at point 3.5.

in March 2018[48]. The implementation of this action plan gave rise to several instruments that deal with measuring corporate sustainability; the aim of the European instruments is to reorient investment decisions by promoting sustainable investment, to improve risk management and to increase transparency. Another aim of the regulation is to avoid so-called 'greenwashing', i.e. the sale of products/instruments as sustainable even if in fact they are not[49]. The following considerations will not deal with more detailed sector-specific regulations, but only refer to the general instruments.

In this field, the European Union has adopted legally binding instruments on three different issues relating to measurement: sustainability disclosures in the financial services sector, climate related and sustainability benchmarks, and a taxonomy for sustainable activities. The three issues show different ways to regulate measurement and indicators: the first one requires the use, or at least the consideration, of a number of indicators, the second one provides a regulation of performance measurement itself, by introducing a framework to ensure the accuracy of performance measurements, and the third one establishes tools to measure and assess sustainable activities and requires their use in certain contexts.

Adopted in November 2019, the Regulation (EU) 2019/2088 on sustainability-related disclosures in the financial services sector requires "financial market participants"[50] to inform on how they integrate sustainability risks in their investment decision-making process or advice (publicly, but also as a precontractual duty of information). The information requirements repeatedly refer to necessary information on the indicators used to measure the environmental or social impact. In addition, the Regulation provides for the creation of technical standards "on the content, methodologies and presentation of information" in respect of sustainability indicators (article 4(6) and (7)). Accordingly, the European Commission has adopted on 6 April 2022 a delegated regulation that specifies the information required in relation to indicators[51]. In its

48 European Commission, 'Financing sustainable growth' (COM(2018)97 final); on the context of the Action Plan, see, e.g., Markus Lange, 'Sustainable Finance: Nachhaltigkeit durch Regulierung' (2020) *Zeitschrift für Bank-und Kapitalmarktrecht* 216.

49 Rainer Baisch and Rolf H. Weber, 'Entwicklungen im Europäischen Finanzmarktrecht. «Sustainable Finance» and DLT Regulierung', in Astrid Epiney et al. (eds), *Schweizerisches Jahrbuch für Europarecht* (Schulthess 2022) 173, at 178.

50 As defined under article 2 (1) of the Regulation (EU) 2019/2088.

51 Commission delegated Regulation supplementing Regulation (EU) 2019/2088 of the European Parliament and of the Council with regard to regulatory technical standards specifying the details of the content and presentation of the information in relation to the principle of 'do no significant harm', specifying the content, methodologies and presentation of information in relation to sustainability indicators and adverse sustainability

annex I, it lists a number of adverse sustainability indicators relating to the "Statement on principal adverse impacts of investment decisions on sustainability factor" (Table 1), "Additional climate and other environment-related indicators" (Table 2) and "Additional indicators for social and employee, respect for human rights, anti-corruption and anti-bribery matters". The provisions of the delegated regulation require corporations to refer to these indicators on several occasions.

Regulation 2016/1101 on indices used as benchmarks in financial instruments and financial contracts or to measure the performance of investment funds[52] "introduces a common framework to ensure the accuracy and integrity of indices used as benchmarks in financial instruments and financial contracts, or to measure the performance of investment funds in the Union" (article 1). The Regulation does not establish benchmarks itself, but sets out a number of criteria that need to be applied when establishing a benchmark in order to ensure integrity and reliability of the benchmarks. These relate to governance and conflict of interest, oversight, control and accountability, methodology, source data/contributors (articles 4–16). More requirements exist for different types of benchmarks and for especially significant benchmarks

---

impacts, and the content and presentation of the information in relation to the promotion of environmental or social characteristics and sustainable investment objectives in pre-contractual documents, on websites and in periodic report.

52 Regulation (EU) 2016/1011 of the European Parliament and of the Council of 8 June 2016 on indices used as benchmarks in financial instruments and financial contracts or to measure the performance of investment funds and amending Directives 2008/48/EC and 2014/17/EU and Regulation (EU) No 596/2014, as amended by Regulation (EU) 2019/2089 of the European Parliament and of the Council of 27 November 2019 amending Regulation (EU) 2016/1011 as regards EU Climate Transition Benchmarks, EU Paris-aligned Benchmarks and sustainability-related disclosures for benchmarks; Regulation (EU) 2019/2175 of the European Parliament and of the Council of 18 December 2019 amending Regulation (EU) No 1093/2010 establishing a European Supervisory Authority (European Banking Authority), Regulation (EU) No 1094/2010 establishing a European Supervisory Authority (European Insurance and Occupational Pensions Authority), Regulation (EU) No 1095/2010 establishing a European Supervisory Authority (European Securities and Markets Authority), Regulation (EU) No 600/2014 on markets in financial instruments, Regulation (EU) 2016/1011 on indices used as benchmarks in financial instruments and financial contracts or to measure the performance of investment funds, and Regulation (EU) 2015/847 on information accompanying transfers of funds; Regulation (EU) 2021/168 of the European Parliament and of the Council of 10 February 2021 amending Regulation (EU) 2016/1011 as regards the exemption of certain third-country spot foreign exchange benchmarks and the designation of replacements for certain benchmarks in cessation, and amending Regulation (EU) No 648/2012.

(Title III). The Regulation then provides that a benchmark can in principle only be used if it is provided by a registered European Union or recognized third state administrator (Title IV) and establishes a framework for the registration and supervision of those (Title V). Finally, it provides the possibility for the European Commission to adopt delegated regulations. Thus, the regulation does not establish detailed measurement requirements, but it creates a framework that should ensure accuracy, transparency and accountability for the institutions that establish the measurement tools. The recent revision of the Regulation has added specific benchmarks relating to climate issues (such as the EU Climate Transition Benchmarks and EU Paris-aligned Benchmarks), and left it to delegated regulations to establish minimum standards.

The EU Taxonomy Regulation 2020/852[53] "establishes criteria" for assessing the environmental sustainability of an activity in order to "establish [...] the degree to which an investment is environmentally sustainable" (article 1(1)). In terms of measurement, the Regulation itself is a tool. It defines how to determine "the degree to which an investment is environmentally sustainable" (article 3) by identifying four criteria: substantial contribution to an environmental objective, absence of significant harm to an environmental objective, compliance with minimum safeguards and compliance with technical screening criteria. The technical screening criteria are the most detailed. The Commission Delegated Regulation 2021/2139[54] sets out a high number of criteria (indicators) for a wide range of activities. With almost 400 pages, it describes different economic activities as well as the way to assess their sustainability in an extremely detailed manner.

In its article 8, the Taxonomy Regulation also introduces an indicator that needs to be reported on in the context of Non-financial reporting (on which see above, Section 4.1). All undertakings subject to non-financial reporting

53 Regulation (EU) 2020/852 of the European Parliament and of the Council of 18 June 2020 on the establishment of a framework to facilitate sustainable investment, and amending Regulation (EU) 2019/2088.

54 Commission Delegated Regulation (EU) 2021/2139 of 4 June 2021 supplementing Regulation (EU) 2020/852 of the European Parliament and of the Council by establishing the technical screening criteria for determining the conditions under which an economic activity qualifies as contributing substantially to climate change mitigation or climate change adaptation and for determining whether that economic activity causes no significant harm to any of the other environmental objectives, as amended by Commission Delegated Regulation (EU) 2022/1214 of 9 March 2022 amending Delegated Regulation (EU) 2021/2139 as regards economic activities in certain energy sectors and Delegated Regulation (EU) 2021/2178 as regards specific public disclosures for those economic activities.

have to disclose if and to what extent their activities are associated with environmentally sustainable activities as defined under the Taxonomy Regulation. This is a clear requirement to measure. In addition, article 8(2) establishes key performance indicators[55]: non-financial undertakings have to disclose the proportion (of their turnover and capital and operating expenditure) that relates to environmentally sustainable activities (article 8 (2)). Also on these aspects, the Commission adopted a delegated act[56] that specifies the key performance indicators even more in detail in its annex I. These show how the taxonomy allows measuring: once an activity is qualified as environmentally sustainable, it is relatively easy to quantify its weight for a specific company in calculating the economic value that the company deploys or owns on the specific economic activity. In that context, the legal instruments speak about "taxonomy aligned activities".

While the Taxonomy Regulation deals only with environmental sustainability (and is therefore more limited in its approach than the other instruments discussed here), it provides an important example on how performance measurement is achieved in the area. In a first step, economic activities are identified as either environmentally sustainable or not. In a second step, the involvement with these activities can be quantified relatively easily. In that way, sustainability becomes measurable. It is clear, however, that the appropriateness of the measurement instruments depends entirely on the first step. It is behind the issue of whether and what activity is actually environmentally sustainable that the difficulties lie, as the size of the delegated acts relating to technical specifications proves.

4.3 *The Sustainability Reporting Directive*

The Sustainability Reporting Directive[57] that entered into force on 5 January 2023 and will be applied as of the financial year 2024 extends the reporting obligation to a wider range of large companies as well as to listed small and medium sized undertakings. The newly formulated article 19a requires in its paragraph 2 (h) that reporting includes "indicators relevant to the disclosures

55 According to the terminology in the delegated Regulation 2921/2178, preamble 1.

56 Commission delegated Regulation (EU) 2921/2178 of 6 July 2021 supplementing Regulation (EU) 2020/852 of the European Parliament and of the Council by specifying the content and presentation of information to be disclosed by undertakings subject to Articles 19a or 29a of Directive 2013/34/EU concerning environmentally sustainable economic activities, and specifying the methodology to comply with that disclosure obligation.

57 Directive (EU) 2022/2464 of the European Parliament and of the Council of 14 December 2022 amending Regulation (EU) No 537/2014, Directive 2004/109/EC, Directive 2006/43/EC and Directive 2013/34/EU, as regards corporate sustainability reporting.

referred to in points (a) to (g)". The same applies for consolidated reporting (article 29a). The Directive does not use the term key performance indicators, as it requires a more general use of indicators. It is only for the small and medium sized undertakings mentioned in article 19a paragraph 6 (i.e., undertakings that have limited reporting obligations) that the reporting can be limited to "key indicators" on the different points reported upon (article 19a paragraph 6 (e)).

With these changes in the reporting obligation, the Sustainability Reporting Directive extends and generalizes the requirement to use indicators in sustainability reporting. It does prepare the ground for an important additional step: it introduces the idea of Sustainability Reporting Standards, to be adopted by the European Commission. According to the Directive (article 29(b) paragraph 5), when adopting the standards, the Commission needs to take into account, amongst others, performance measurement tools developed in other contexts, such as indicators and methodologies set out in the legal framework relating to sustainable investment (point c and d)[58]. As discussed above (Section 4.2), the European law on sustainable finance has regulated the use of indicators to a very high degree.

A draft of the 'European Sustainability Reporting Standards' was published by EFRAG[59] in November 2022; EFRAG expects that the European Commission will adopt the delegated acts after a consultation process in June 2023[60]. The Draft European Sustainability Reporting Standards (ESRS) are a set of 12 different standards organized in two general parts and, taking up the terminology ESG referred to above, in 10 specific parts on Environment (E 1 to E5), Social (S1 to S4) and Governance (G1). The disclosure requirement it establishes covers reporting on four areas, one of them being "metrics and targets: how the undertaking measures its performance, including progress towards the targets it has set"[61]. Accordingly, every sector specific standard has one section on metrics and targets. This shows that measurement is an important part of

58 Regulation 2020/852 of the European Parliament and of the Council of 18 June 2020 on the establishment of a framework to facilitate sustainable investment, and amending Regulation (EU) 2019/2088; as well as its delegated act.

59 The EFRAG (originally the European Financial Reporting Advisory Group, but currently known only with the acronym) is a private association established with the encouragement of the European Commission; see <https://efrag.org/About/Facts> (accessed 11 March 2023).

60 See <https://efrag.org/lab6#subtitle4> (accessed 11 March 2023).

61 EFRAG, Draft ESRS 1, General Requirements, para 10, available at <https://www.efrag.org/lab6> (accessed 11 March 2023); the other areas are Governance, Strategy, and Impact, risk and opportunity management.

the standard. Interestingly, metrics (and therefore the indicators)[62] are generally geared to measure the "effectiveness of the delivery of the sustainability-oriented policies"[63]. This corresponds to the expectation set out in the UN Guiding Principles (on which see above, Section 2.1).

The importance of measurement varies, however, in each specific standard. The draft ESRS S 1 on the "Own work force", for example, has relatively detailed metric disclosure requirements on the employees, including the number of employees, breakdowns by gender, age and countries, the type of contracts, the coverage by collective bargaining agreements, benchmarks on wages, and many more. The draft ESRS S 3 on "Affected communities" is a lot less detailed on the indicators and measurement; it focuses mainly on possible targets and general principles (e.g., that targets be measurable) and only mentions a few examples such as the number of women community members to have been trained on how to become supplier to the undertaking, or the percentage of local employees. The draft ESRS S 2 on "Workers in the value chain" also contains relatively few requirements on what indicators to use and how to measure, as it only mentions a few examples (such as the living wages for supply chain workers and reduction in health and safety incidents).

The two draft general standards S 1 and S 2 are dealing with several general issues relating to measurement, e.g., when and how to use metrics in entity-specific disclosures[64], how to deal with uncertainty[65], and the external validity and labelling of the measurement results[66]. These considerations show the concern for the potential abuse or misuse of performance measurement in sustainability reporting.

To conclude, the new Sustainability Reporting Directive promotes the use of measurement and indicators even further. The strive for uniformity appears most clearly in the Sustainability Reporting Standards that the European Commission will adapt shortly. The draft refers to measurement mainly with a view to assessing the policies of undertakings. It also maps a range of indicators developed in other pieces of European Union legislation, mainly with regards to sustainable finance.

---

62 EFRAG, *supra* fn 61, para 21 (c): metrics refer to "qualitative and quantitative indicators".

63 EFRAG, *supra* fn 61, para 21.

64 EFRAG, *supra* fn 61, para 14 ff., addressing issues of validity, reliability and availability of context.

65 EFRAG, *supra* fn 61, para 91 ff.; EFRAG, Draft ESRS 2, General Disclosures, para 11, available at <https://www.efrag.org/lab6> (accessed 11 March 2023).

66 EFRAG, Draft ESRS 2, *supra* fn 65, para 71 ff.

4.4 *An Assessment: The Reference to Indicators in European Union Law*

European Union Law relating to sustainability has given rise to an impressive amount of regulation relating to measurement and indicators. While the first instrument merely required the use of key performance indicators in Non-Financial reporting, the legal instruments adopted in the last five years are focusing on different aspects relating to measurement. This development started in the area of sustainable finance and environmental reporting, where three different legal instruments regulate different aspects for measuring: the use of benchmarks, classification of activities in order to allow easier measurement and disclosure of environmental information, and finally, general standards for disclosure. The recently adopted general Sustainability Reporting Directive applies the logic of these instruments to sustainability reporting generally. It also introduces the 'European Sustainability Reporting Standards', that will regulate indicators and measurement to a great extent (though not exhaustively).

An important driver of the European Regulation is the willingness of the European Union to promote sustainability rather than imposing it. With the increasing public awareness of the issues, a high number of sustainability reporting initiatives has developed. Regulating how sustainability can be measured and reported is a way to translate the political willingness for action into regulatory measures without interfering with corporate activities themselves. In addition, this approach allowed the European regulator to build on previous (voluntary) initiatives. Regulating measurement is a way to promote trust in instruments that have the potential to be (mis)used for different purposes. The purpose of the standardization and regulation of different measurement instruments is to leave less room for marketing-oriented disclosures and greenwashing.

This shift from private (voluntary) measurement initiatives to public authoritative regulations of measurement will lead to a growing importance of the measurement related industry. When looking at the level of detail and complexity the current sustainability disclosure framework provides, compliance with it will require specialized knowledge. Sustainability reporting is becoming a sub-discipline of accounting, and, at the same time, a sector of economic activity. Sustainability reporting specialists will have their own interest. One challenge of this development is to avoid that the technicalities of the field, and the search for possibilities to measure, will hinder achieving the original objective – promoting sustainability. The validity of the indicators therefore needs to be continuously critically assessed.

Finally, European law also shows that measurement and indicators were – and still are – most prominently used in environmental reporting.

The methodologies and ways to measure are most developed and are relatively easy to be understood, though controversy might remain with regard to some aspects. One important reason lies in the scientific background of a lot of environmental information – emissions and pollution are easily measured. Social indicators are often less technical and developed. Measurement is often limited to a few instances and difficult to generalize. Most notably, there is no evidence that the classification and reflections developed on human rights indicators will be adapted to sustainability reporting on social issues. This might change when the focus will shift from the environment to the social world.

5 Final Remarks

The international and regional development shows an increasing use – and awareness of – measurement instruments in the area. While the UNGP promote the use of indicators on few instances only (with the main idea that measurement should allow corporations to track the effectiveness of their responses to their adverse impacts), the current framework at the European level requires the use of indicators and measurement generally, especially in the context of environmental sustainability.

Another common feature of the international and regional development is a unification movement or, in language of the market, a concentration towards a monopoly. While there was relatively little regulation on measurement and indicators in the field ten years ago, and on the international level a wide variety of initiatives co-existed, this variety is diminishing. On the international level, a unified standard is currently elaborated. On the European level, it was the regulator, i.e., the European Union, that started by regulating different aspects and tools of measurement and has now introduced a common reporting standard. The underlying idea is to facilitate reporting for corporations, to help investors compare the sustainability-related aspects of corporate activity, but also to increase trust. In other terms, while the initial phase saw in measurement as such a way to implement international sustainability requirements, the majority of stakeholders see the unification and/or regulation as necessary to increase trust and practicability.

The current regulations are of an increasing technical nature, and the regulator often delegates the task to specialists. This poses an issue when it comes to the legitimacy of the regulation and the oversight of the actual regulator. In addition, it is important to ensure the validity of the instruments – i.e. to guarantee that the measure or indicator actually refers to a relevant aspect relating to sustainability. The willingness to measure might also lead to neglect qualitative information. In other words, sustainability reporting needs to leave room – if not require – disclosure of non-measurable information. An example of ESG reports shows that some companies report qualitatively especially on social aspects. This might be due to the difficulty in finding appropriate indicators in this area[67]; at the same time, it allows for a bigger degree of discretion in the choice of information reported upon. The future will show whether and how the expected increase of regulation on measurement and social indicators (possibly along the lines of human rights indicators for States) will affect the practice of qualitative reporting.

---

67 The most frequently used indicator relating to human rights in the ESG reports of Volkswagen, UPM (a Finnish company with a prominent investment in Uruguay) and Glencore (a Swiss company in the commodities sector) is the number of human rights audits.

CHAPTER 15

The Role of International Organizations in the Production of Legal Metrics

Kevin E. Davis

1 Introduction

In September 2021, the World Bank announced that it was discontinuing production of the Doing Business report, a well-known compilation of worldwide data on business regulations and their enforcement[1]. The terse statement that announced the decision began with the sentence: "Trust in the research of the World Bank Group is vital"[2]. It went on to explain that the Doing Business report was being discontinued because the Bank's leaders had uncovered instances in which Doing Business data and the process that produced them could not be trusted. The statement explained that after irregularities in published data came to light, the Bank initiated a series of reviews, audits, and investigations which revealed that senior Bank staff had altered data in the report without following proper procedures in order to please powerful member countries that had financial dealings with the Bank. The investigation tarnished the reputation of the Bank and the individuals involved.

This remarkable series of events raises the question of whether the World Bank should ever have been trusted to produce the Doing Business report. It also raises the broader question of the extent to which any international organizations ought to be involved in the production of measures of the performance of legal institutions ('legal metrics'). As we shall see, a variety of actors produce these kinds of performance measures, including private and domestic actors. It is not immediately obvious whether it is necessary or appropriate for international organizations to add themselves to the list of producers of legal metrics. This question becomes urgent when we consider both the potential value of legal metrics and the power that their producers can wield.

1 World Bank, *World Bank Group to Discontinue Doing Business Report* (September 16, 2021), available at <https://www.worldbank.org/en/news/statement/2021/09/16/world-bank-group-to-discontinue-doing-business-report> (accessed 12 September 2022). I am grateful to the Filomen D'Agostino and Max E. Greenberg Research Fund for financial support.

2 Ibid.

 | DOI:10.1163/9789004680944_016

The first three sections of this chapter examine in turn how legal metrics are produced, the reasons why they might be valuable, and the power that producers of legal metrics wield. Section 4 considers whether it is efficient for international organizations to produce legal metrics. Section 5 discusses whether it is legitimate for them to play such a role. Section 6 briefly discusses the special challenges posed by metrics that qualify as 'indicators'. Section 7 suggests that the World Bank's experience producing the Doing Business report illustrates both the opportunities and risks associated with producing legal metrics. The final section concludes.

2 The Production of Legal Metrics

For the purposes of this chapter, we can define legal metrics broadly to include any data capable of being used to measure of the performance of legal norms or the organizations that administer them, or both. This includes both metrics that measure the characteristics of legal institutions themselves and those which purport to measure outcomes influenced by legal institutions. The data can reflect either the producer's own assessment of the relevant information or the beliefs of third parties.

An important sub-category of legal metrics are known as 'legal indicators'. Benedict Kingsbury, Sally Merry and I define an indicator as follows:

> An indicator is a named collection of rank-ordered data that purports to represent the past or projected performance of different units. The data are generated through a process that simplifies raw data about a complex social phenomenon. The data, in this simplified and processed form, are capable of being used to compare particular units of analysis (such as countries, institutions, or corporations), synchronically or over time, and to evaluate their performance by reference to one or more standards[3].

Legal indicators, naturally, are indicators that purport to represent the performance of components of a legal system. The difference between a legal indicator and any other legal metric lies in the fact that an indicator has been named to suggest that it represents a complex social phenomenon. Measures of the time and cost required to enforce contracts and incorporate a business are

3 Kevin E. Davis et al., 'Indicators as a Technology of Global Governance' (2012) 46 *Law & Society Review* 71.

metrics. The aggregation of those metrics into a single measure labelled "Ease of Doing Business" (as in the Doing Business report) is an indicator.

Production of legal metrics involves many discrete tasks, and those tasks can be distributed across multiple actors[4]. The production process begins with the conceptualization of the metric. This involves identifying what metric to produce and designing the remainder of the production process. The next steps are to collect and process the necessary data. Then comes promulgation, which involves naming and publishing the metric. Promulgation typically is followed by promotion, which involves a concerted effort to draw as much attention to the metric as possible, and may lead to criticism or contestation. Finally, the production cycle begins again with revision and updating of the metric.

Governments, quasi-governmental entities, universities, nonprofits, for-profits and international organizations are all involved in production of legal metrics, sometimes in combination with one another. Academics based in universities often are involved in conceptualization of metrics. Data collection often involves a variety of actors, including private market research firms, non-profits, governments and international organizations. Finally, all of these types of actors have been known to promulgate legal metrics. For example, until recently, Fundação Getulio Vargas, a private Brazilian educational institution, sponsored ICJBrasil, an indicator designed to measure public trust in the court system[5]. The Vietnam Chamber of Commerce and Industry together with the United States Agency for International Development produces the Vietnam Provincial Competitiveness Index, which covers both legal and non-legal aspects of the country's business environment[6]. The World Justice Project, a non-profit organization based in Washington, D.C., produces a large collection of data on respect for the rule of law in over 120 countries around the world, together with an aggregate Rule of Law Index[7]. Last but not least, in addition to the now-defunct Doing Business report – which it plans to replace – the

4 Kevin E. Davis, 'Legal Indicators: The Power of Quantitative Measures of Law' (2014) 10 *Annual Review of Law & Social Science* 37, 40–41.

5 Luciana Gross Cunha et al, *Relatório ICJBrasil: 1º semestre 2016* (FGV DIREITO SP 2016) 2, available at <https://bibliotecadigital.fgv.br/dspace/handle/10438/17204> (accessed 14 September 2022).

6 Edmund Malesky et al., *The Vietnam Provincial Competitiveness Index 2021: Measuring Economic Governance for Business Development* (2021), available at <https://pcivietnam.vn/en/publications/pci-full-report> (accessed 12 September 2022).

7 World Justice Project, *Rule of Law Index 2021* (2021), available at <https://worldjusticeproject.org/sites/default/files/documents/WJP-INDEX-21.pdf> (accessed 12 September 2022).

World Bank has produced several other legal metrics, including the Worldwide Governance Indicators[8].

3 Legal Metrics as Sources of Value

Legal metrics can be valuable in different ways to different constituencies[9]. The potential beneficiaries include not only the users of the metrics, that is to say, people who consciously refer to metrics and adjust their beliefs or actions accordingly, but also members of the society who are affected by those users' perceptions or actions.

A great deal of the value of legal metrics stems from their potential use in legal reform, that is to say, in altering legal systems with a view to improving their performance. There are two main ways in which decision-makers can consciously use legal metrics to reshape legal systems. First, metrics can be used in formal and informal incentive-based mechanisms that base officials' rewards or punishments on past performance. Second, metrics can be used to inform policymakers' decisions on whether to maintain or alter existing systems.

A range of actors might use legal metrics to effect legal reform. In democratic systems, voters can, in principle, both incentivize and prescribe public officials' behavior through their decisions at the ballot box. In hierarchical multilevel systems of government, officials at higher levels of government use information about the performance of lower-level governments in deciding how to exercise their powers of oversight. Government officials' peers might also rely on performance data in deciding whether to deliver praise or criticism. Self-motivated government officials will use the same data to determine whether and how to improve their own performance.

Legal metrics might be used for a range of purposes besides guiding legal reform. For instance, people trying to decide whether to move to or do business in a particular jurisdiction might use data about past performance of its legal system in order to predict future performance. It is generally reasonable

8 World Bank, *Worldwide Governance Indicators*, available at <https://info.worldbank.org/governance/wgi/> (accessed 12 September 2022); World Bank, *Business Enabling Environment* (*BEE*), available at <https://www.worldbank.org/en/programs/business-enabling-environment> (accessed 18 September 2022).

9 This section draws heavily on Kevin E. Davis, 'Data and Decentralization: Measuring the Performance of Legal Institutions in Multilevel Systems of Governance' (2018) 102 *Minnesota Law Review* 1619.

to assume that private parties benefit from use of metrics in these ways. If attracting investors, visitors or residents has broader social benefits, then this kind of private use of metrics will generate public as well as private benefits. In a similar vein, public actors might use legal metrics in the course of deciding how to deal with a given state. For example, donors who want to ensure that their donations are not misused might focus on metrics that measure the performance of anti-corruption laws. Alternatively, courts deciding whether to enforce a judgment from a foreign country might refer to metrics that purport to measure the integrity of the country's judiciary.

Different categories of potential users will tend to be interested in different types of performance measures. Members of the general public, such as voters and prospective residents, typically will have limited time or expertise to devote to analyzing governmental performance. Those users will tend to seek out indicators that report relatively large quantities of information in a highly simplified form. The Doing Business report's Ease of Doing Business Index was a good example of a highly simplified measure, as it purported to use a single number to capture the performance of all the portions of the legal system that bore on the ease of doing business in an entire country.

Several factors will determine the value of legal metrics. First, the value of a metric will generally depend on its validity and reliability. Validity concerns the extent to which a metric measures what it claims to measure; reliability is about whether it measures accurately. Validity is determined mainly by the label assigned to a metric. Reliability is determined by the quality of the data used to produce a metric and the care with which it is processed.

The value of a legal metric will also depend on how many units it covers. No matter how or by whom performance measures are used, there will be a premium on comparative data – data which permit a governmental unit to be analyzed in relation to either its own past performance or the performance of other units. By serving as a yardstick, comparative data can provide insight into the merits of outcomes that are difficult to evaluate in isolation. A New Yorker who has never been to Hong Kong might have no idea that it is possible for a subway system to be cleaner, safer, and more reliable than the New York subway system. Comparative data can also help to evaluate governments' actions. For instance, a comparison of policing tactics and crime rates, whether over time or across jurisdictions, can be used to figure out which tactics work better than others – as well as which governments have chosen those actions.

The availability of other metrics that measure the same phenomenon has ambiguous effects on the value of a legal metric. On the one hand, the alternative metrics may serve as substitutes for one another and thereby diminish the value of each one. On the other hand, the alternative metrics may serve as complements for one another, meaning that an increase in the availability of one increases the other's value(for instance, because they can be used to cross-check one another).

While it seems clear that legal metrics can influence legal reform and the allocation of resources, there is no guarantee those influences will be positive. Metrics that help to improve the law and allocate resources efficiently will have a positive impact. Metrics that prompt misguided reforms and misallocated resources can be enormously detrimental, to both the people who choose to rely on metrics and society as a whole.

Finally, assessment of the overall value of legal metrics requires taking into account their costs of production as well as their impact. The value of deploying the resources required to produce a particular metric in alternative uses may exceed the positive impact of the metric. In this case, it will not be efficient to produce the metric.

4 Legal Metrics as Sources of Power

Legal metrics used to reward and punish public officials, to direct investment, trade, and migration, or to guide legal reform, clearly influence the allocation of resources and regulate behavior. In other words, they qualify as modes of governance. This is why Benedict Kingsbury, Sally Merry and I refer to certain metrics used in the international context as "technologies of global governance"[10]. It is safe to generalize this statement and say that legal metrics typically qualify as "technologies of governance."

To the extent that legal metrics are technologies of governance it is appropriate to evaluate their production and use in terms of legitimacy, meaning, the extent to which they involve justifiable exercises of power. In assessing the implications of legal metrics for legitimacy, it is not sufficient to assess the legitimacy of decisions made by the users of legal metrics, i.e., the people who actually change laws or allocate resources. Sometimes users of legal metrics have little choice but to rely on producers' decisions, particularly when there are few alternative metrics. In those circumstances it seems reasonable to treat the producers of legal metrics as wielders of power and to ask whether they are acting legitimately.

Commentators have suggested several criteria for assessing legitimacy in global governance that can readily be applied to the production of legal

10 Davis et al., *supra* fn 3.

metrics[11]. One criterion is whether the relevant exercise of power produces, or at least aims to produce, beneficial consequences. Another consideration is whether the interests of all affected parties are given due regard. This criterion points to decision-making procedures that involve transparency, consultation, giving of reasons, and opportunities for recourse or review. Still another criterion is legality, that is to say, whether the exercise of power complies with applicable legal rules. The first of these criteria can be subsumed within the analysis of whether production of a metric is efficient. However, the criteria of due regard for affected parties and legality seem to require independent assessment.

With this evaluative template in hand, we can turn to the question of whether it is appropriate for international organizations to produce legal metrics.

5 The Efficiency of Production by International Organizations

For present purposes, we can define international organizations as mission-driven organizations that are ultimately governed by nation-states. These characteristics distinguish international organizations from other potential producers of legal metrics (such as national or sub-national governmental actors or private for-profit or nonprofit organizations) and have considerable bearing on how efficiently they are likely to produce legal metrics.

At the most general level, it seems fair to assume that an international organization will have an advantage in producing legal metrics to the extent that the production process overlaps with the organization's existing mission and draws upon its existing relationships with member states. Consider, for example, the International Monetary Fund (IMF), whose mission includes surveillance of the economic and financial policies of its member states. To fulfill this mandate, the IMF collects a broad range of data on member states' legal systems and maintains close relationships with key government ministries. As a result, the IMF should be able to collect the data required to produce legal metrics relating to fiscal and monetary policy at lower cost than virtually any other organization. The IMF's mission obviously also includes extensive processing and analysis of the data that it collects. The IMF should have an advantage in production of metrics based upon those analyses.

11 See generally, Eyal Benevenisti, *The Law of Global Governance* (Brill 2014); Richard Stewart, 'Remedying Disregard in Global Regulatory Governance: Accountability, Participation, and Responsiveness' (2014) 108 *American Journal of International Law* 211.

The idea that international organizations might capitalize on synergies between the production of legal metrics and their other activities carries over to the promulgation and promotion phases of metric production. Specifically, some international organizations' activities have left with them with extremely strong brands, meaning that their names are widely recognized and carry positive associations. Organizations with strong brands should have an advantage in promulgating and promoting legal metrics, or at least metrics that are sufficiently related to the activities linked to their brands.

The fact that international organizations are mission-driven organizations allows them to take a distinctive approach to the production of legal metrics from profit-driven organizations. To begin, profit-driven organizations will tend to ignore benefits from metric production that accrue to other actors, even if those benefits are very large. Production of legal metrics will often involve these sorts of 'externalities' because it is difficult for the producers to capture all of the benefits of production. This is in part because, like other information products, metrics can often be copied and redistributed without compensating the original producer (and without meaningful risk of liability). In addition, many of the benefits of producing legal metrics accrue to people who are not in a direct relationship with the producer or the user of the metric. For instance, metrics that are used for the purpose of guiding law reforms or deciding where to invest may benefit the entire population of a country, who may have no dealings with either the producer or user of the metric. A mission-driven organization will not necessarily ignore these sorts of externalities when making decisions about production and distribution of a legal metric. For instance, if the organization's mission calls for promoting economic development, then it is likely to produce suitable metrics even if it is unable to recoup the costs of production by charging the beneficiaries.

The fact that international organizations are mission-driven organizations does not necessarily mean that they will internalize all the relevant costs and benefits of producing legal metrics. First, an international organization dominated by a subset of its member states may neglect the interests of states outside the dominant coalition[12]. Second, the fact that these organizations are governed by member states creates a potentially inefficient bias in favor of the interests of states and the government officials who represent them. That statist bias might lead an organization to ignore the costs that production of a metric imposes on non-state actors. For instance, data collection can impose

---

12 Randall W. Stone, *Controlling Institutions: International Organizations and the Global Economy* (Cambridge University Press 2013).

costs on the people and organizations who provide the data; completing surveys and questionnaires can be time-consuming and respondents run the risk that their data will be used or transferred without their consent.

Mission-driven organizations governed by nation-states are prone to inefficiency in a broader sense. The vague nature of most international organizations' missions makes it difficult to develop incentive-based performance mechanisms and to hold their officials accountable for unsatisfactory performance. The problem is exacerbated by the fact that the states to which international organizations report are themselves mission-driven organizations whose officials are difficult to motivate. The states may also face collective action problems that impair their ability to collaborate on holding officials accountable. These factors combine to result in 'agency costs', a catchall phrase for the costs that arise when an agent's actions diverge the preferences of its principal[13].

In certain phases of metric production, an international organization may possess both advantages and disadvantages relative to other producers. For instance, in the conceptualization phase, the fact that an international organization has ties to multiple member states might give it an advantage over actors with ties to fewer countries in designing metrics that are internationally comparable. At the same time, producers with closer ties to specific locations may have an advantage in designing metrics that are suited to their local context.

Another reason why it is difficult to arrive at a comprehensive assessment of how efficiently international organizations will produce legal metrics is because many of their inherent advantages, such as their ability to exploit synergies with their existing operations and their brands, will tend to diminish the amount of competition they face. The presence of competing producers can serve to enhance the accountability of producers of legal metrics – it will be relatively easy to notice when an organization produces a metric that is clearly inferior to comparable metrics. Ironically, this implies that organizations with the greatest potential to produce legal metrics efficiently will tend to be the least accountable, which may compromise their actual efficiency.

13 Daniel L. Nielson and Michael J. Tierney, 'Delegation to International Organizations: Agency Theory and World Bank Environmental Reform' (2003) 57 *International Organization* 241.

6 The Legitimacy of Production by International Organizations

International organizations face many challenges in ensuring the legitimacy of their operations, and the production of legal metrics is no exception. In many cases the techniques for bolstering legitimacy that have been developed in other areas can be applied to the production of legal metrics.

Ensuring legitimacy in international organizations' production of legal metrics will be particularly important when they face little competition. For the reasons set out above, international organizations are likely to have a competitive advantage in producing metrics which are international in scope, rely on data uniquely accessible to states, concern topics closely related to the organization's mission, and whose use has the potential to generate diffuse benefits. In the absence of competition, organizations that produce these kinds of metrics will have considerable power to shape the decisions of users, thus raising the question of whether their power is being exercised legitimately.

A key threat to the legitimacy of metric production by international organizations is the risk that the production process will fail to afford due regard to the interests of all affected parties. As we have already seen, there are risks that the decision-making processes in international organizations will be captured by a subset of member states, or will have spillover effects on non-member states, or will unduly favor the interests of member states' governments over the broader public affected by their decisions. Thus, it is important to consider the extent to which these risks are mitigated by mechanisms for transparency, reason-giving, consultation, review, and recourse.

Some of the measures required to ensure due regard to affected person are relatively straightforward. In particular, transparency and reason-giving merely entail publishing the data and methods used to construct a metric. Most producers of legal metrics willingly publish this kind of information because it helps to convince potential users of the value of the metric.

By contrast, consultation about the production of legal metrics is relatively challenging as it may require reaching well beyond representatives of an international organization's member states. Sometimes those representatives can be tasked with organizing appropriate consultations within the states that they represent. As we have seen, however, on other occasions the representatives of member states cannot be trusted to represent the interests of all parties likely to be affected by the production of a particular metric. In these situations, the international organization itself will have to take charge of the consultation process. This can be an expensive proposition if the metric covers a large number of countries or affects a large proportion of the population, or both. Consultation of members of disempowered groups in a society without the cooperation of the local government is likely to be especially difficult.

Ensuring that metrics pay due regard to affected parties also requires establishing mechanisms for review and recourse. At a minimum, this means establishing a mechanism for challenging the accuracy of the data underlying a metric and the calculations involved in processing it. Designing this kind of review mechanism involves decisions such as who should be able to initiate a review, how many stages of review to provide, and how independent the reviewers at each stage ought to be from the producer. These decisions generally require tradeoffs between, on the one hand, enhanced accountability and, on the other hand, increased cost and delay.

Ideally, review mechanisms would extend beyond data collection and processing to include assessments of the overall impact of a metric. Periodic impact assessments should help to ensure that metrics live up to their initial expectations and may inform changes to production processes. These kinds of assessments not only ensure accountability to affected parties, they also enhance efficiency and 'output legitimacy'.

Another component of legitimacy is legality. Production of a legal metric might conceivably implicate legal norms designed to protect personal privacy, reputation, trade secrets or state secrets, as well as norms requiring good faith or due process when making decisions that affect other actors' interests. Respect for legality clearly implies that international organizations should ensure that production of legal metrics does not violate norms set out in their own constituting documents. It is less clear whether it is legitimate for an international organization to violate national or international laws that are not expressly incorporated into its constituting documents and from which it might have even negotiated immunity.

7 The Special Challenges of Legal Indicators

Two distinctive features of indicators, including legal indicators, give rise to risks that they will be produced inefficiently and illegitimately. First, the interest in viewing indicators is relatively high. Indicators promise quick insight into complex phenomena, an irresistible attraction for time-constrained users. Indicators also cater to human beings' innate interest in viewing rankings, even when they are not in a position to act on the results. In this sense, viewing indicators is akin to watching a sport. For-profit actors such as media organizations have incentives to publish rankings based on indicators and then monetize the attention they attract, typically by selling advertising or subscriptions.

This means that promulgators will find it relatively easy to attract attention to any indicators they produce. Whether or not they are motivated by financial returns, promulgators may benefit from the attention that indicators attract because the strength of their brand might be tied to widespread familiarity with their work.

A second distinctive feature of indicators is that their value is often low relative to what users expect based on the indicator's label. The potential for misunderstanding arises from both the extent to which indicators simplify complex phenomena and the fact that time-constrained and unsophisticated users often lack the ability to appreciate the consequences of those simplifications.

The combination of relatively high demand for indicators and relatively low value threatens both efficiency and legitimacy. Producers have incentives to produce indicators even when their social value is so low that production is inefficient. Worse still, producers have incentives to maintain interest in legal indicators by obfuscating their limitations. In other words, producers have incentives to compromise transparency in ways that tend to undermine the legitimacy of indicators.

There is no reason why the catalogue of risks generally associated with the production of indicators should not affect the production of legal indicators by international organizations. All of this implies that production of legal indicators – as opposed to other legal metrics – by international organizations warrants special scrutiny.

8 Application to the Doing Business Report

The production of the metrics contained in the now-defunct Doing Business report by the World Bank illustrates both the potential value and power of producing legal metrics and the associated risks. To be clear, the Doing Business report's metrics were not typical of legal metrics. In fact, they were arguably the most prominent legal metrics in the world. A study by Doshi, Kelly and Simmons found that from 2010 to 2017 the Doing Business report had a 65 per cent 'market share', measured in terms of media hits, among comparable global economic indicators[14]. The exceptional prominence of the Doing Business metrics makes them useful for illustrating the range of possible implications of producing legal metrics, but not the typical implications.

14 Rush Doshi, Judith G. Kelley, Beth A. Simmons, 'The Power of Ranking: The Ease of Doing Business Indicator and Global Regulatory Behavior' (2019) 73 *International Organization* 611.

One of the principal purposes of the Doing Business reports was to stimulate reform, and there is ample evidence that they achieved their goal. A review conducted by the World Bank's Independent Evaluation Group (IEG) just before the Doing Business report was discontinued concluded:

> Many governments establish explicit targets for progressing in their *DB* ranking, and many more incorporate reforms associated with improvements in *DB* scores into their development plans[15].

The IEG review went on to explain:

> In most cases, governments create or empower coordinating agencies explicitly focused on the *DB* reform agenda. Typically, such agencies use *DB* indicators to help elaborate an initial agenda, to set explicit targets, to spur coordination and consultation, and to monitor and then publicize progress[16].

Another earlier review noted that countries often adopted reforms in order to raise their scores, even when the reforms were contrary to the advice of World Bank experts[17].

The Doing Business report appears to have influenced reforms through several channels. According to the IEG review, "[c]hannels of influence range from direct influence on government leaders to indirect influence through donors, investors, civil society, and the press". It summarized this assessment graphically in the figure reproduced below (Figure 15.1)[18].

The IEG's figure suggests that in addition to driving legal reforms, the Doing Business report influenced the allocation of investment. This is in part because the metrics influenced investment by the World Bank itself. In a ten-year period from 2010 to 2020, the Doing Business report informed $15.5 billion of the World Bank's lending[19]. In addition, while there is little direct evidence that private investors used the Doing Business metrics in their decision-making,

---

15 World Bank Independent Evaluation Group (IEG), *The Development Effectiveness of the Use of Doing Business Indicators, Fiscal Years 2010–20* (World Bank 2022) 5.

16 IEG, *supra* fn 15, 17.

17 Laura Alfaro et al., *Doing Business: External Panel Review* (September 1, 2021), 9 <https://www.worldbank.org/en/news/statement/2021/09/20/report-on-external-panel-review-of-doing-business-methodology> (accessed 12 September 2022).

18 IEG, *supra* fn 15, 5–6.

19 IEG, *supra* fn 15, 31.

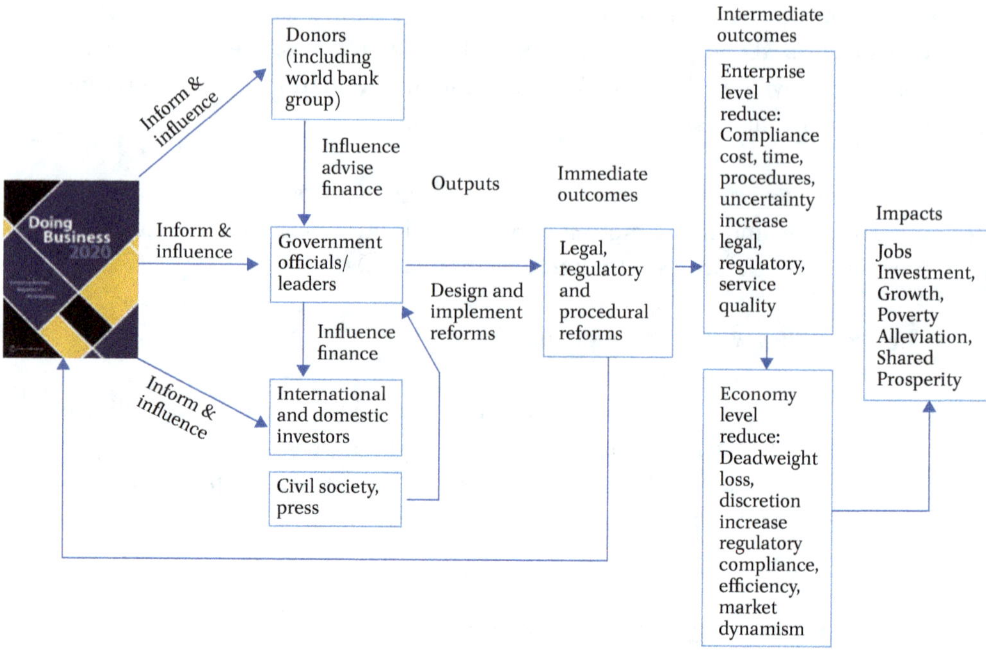

FIGURE 15.1 How *Doing Business* influences actions leading to development outcomes
SOURCE: WORLD BANK INDEPENDENT EVALUATION GROUP (IEG), *THE DEVELOPMENT EFFECTIVENESS OF THE USE OF DOING BUSINESS INDICATORS, FISCAL YEARS 2010–20* (WORLD BANK 2022) 6

there is indirect evidence. Doshi, Kelly and Simmons used a creative experimental framework to show that professional investors altered their perceptions of countries' suitability for investment based on the Doing Business metrics[20]. Just as importantly, there is abundant evidence that many government officials believed that the Doing Business metrics influenced foreign investors' decisions[21].

The power that the World Bank wielded by producing the Doing Business report was only underscored by the events that led to the project's demise. The investigations that preceded the discontinuation of the report revealed that one of the motivations for the data alterations was a desire to mollify Chinese government officials, who had repeatedly expressed concerns about their country's performance to the President of the World Bank and other senior

20 Doshi et al., *supra* fn 14.
21 IEG, *supra* fn 15, 22.

Bank officials[22]. The fact that a country as powerful as China cared enough about its scores on the Doing Business report to raise the matter personally with the President of the World Bank suggests that the report and the metrics it contained had material effects on the countries being measured.

The impact of the Doing Business report is consistent with the hypothesis that international organizations possess an advantage in the production of legal metrics that are closely related to their core operations. The World Bank is the world's largest development agency, known for sophisticated analysis of the economies of developing countries. When it launched the Doing Business report, the Bank did not have particular expertise in legal reform or in collecting the types of data that the report relies upon. However, it did have special expertise in analyzing the economies of developing countries. It also had strong relationships with the governments of many countries.

At the same time, it is difficult to say whether the World Bank's resources and expertise allowed it to produce metrics of higher value than the metrics that other organizations produced. It is even more difficult to say whether the Doing Business metrics are superior to metrics that other organizations would have been capable of producing if the World Bank had not occupied the field. At first glance, the Doing Business report's success in the 'marketplace' implies that it was a superior product. However, many users of metrics are either incapable of or uninterested in assessing their value as guides to legal reform. Accordingly, success in the market for metrics is not a guarantee of social value.

The World Bank's own assessments of the value of the Doing Business metrics as guides to legal reform have come to mixed conclusions. The IEG's 2022 report found that many of the metrics measured features of countries' legal systems associated with positive social outcomes[23]. At the same time, the IEG suggested that further research was needed on whether reforms that would lead to higher scores on some of the metrics were associated with unintended consequences. For example, improvements on the ease of getting credit indicator might result in exclusion of some borrowers[24]. The IEG went on to complain that the Doing Business reports contained many "weakly evidenced"

22 WilmerHale, *Investigation of Data Irregularities in Doing Business 2018 and Doing Business 2020: Investigation Findings and Report to the Board of Directors* (September 15, 2021), available at <https://www.worldbank.org/en/news/statement/2021/09/16/world-bank-group-to-discontinue-doing-business-report> (accessed 12 September 2022).

23 IEG, *supra* fn 15, 42–43.

24 Ibid., 43–44.

claims linking reforms measured by its indicators to outcomes such as job growth or economic growth[25].

The external review commissioned by the World Bank in 2021 was even more critical of the Doing Business metrics. The external panel considered many of the indicators to be of little value because they focused on de jure rules rather than the de facto experiences of businesses[26]. The panel also found that many of the metrics captured information that was not particularly relevant to the ultimate intended beneficiaries, namely, small and medium-sized firms in developing countries.

External reviewers have been particularly critical of the World Bank's efforts to synthesize its metrics into indicators, including the overall Ease of Doing Business Index[27]. The Bank's management argued that eliminating the indicators and the country rankings they made possible would reduce the Doing Business report's press coverage and influence. However, the external reviewers argued that given the arbitrary way in which they were constructed, the indicators were of dubious value. Moreover, the indicators were prone to misinterpretation. For example, the review panel noted:

> Notably, almost all Doing Business indicators have an exclusively domestic focus. Regulations affecting foreign direct investment are explicitly excluded. Nevertheless, media reports suggest that many audiences interpret Doing Business as a measure of a country's attractiveness to foreign investors[28].

Alongside concerns about the social value of the Doing Business metrics were concerns about their legitimacy. At first glance this might come as a surprise because the World Bank made considerable efforts to ensure that the process of producing the Doing Business report afforded governments of affected states adequate opportunities to participate and was transparent and subject to independent review. Governments were invited to participate in the data collection process by submitting data on legal reforms, and were notified via the Bank's Executive Directors of reforms that would be reflected in the data when the draft report and data were circulated within the Bank for review[29].

---

25 Ibid., 44–46.

26 Alfaro et al., *supra* fn 17, 23–28.

27 Alfaro et al., *supra* fn 17, 33–36.

28 Alfaro et al., *supra* fn 17, 10.

29 World Bank, *Review of Data Irregularities in Doing Business* (December 16, 2020), Annex 1: Doing Business Data Collection and Review Process, available at

Once the Report was published, the scores and underlying methodology (but not the underlying data) were all posted on the World Bank's website[30]. The website itself contained a notice inviting the general public to dispute the data and modifications to past years' data were acknowledged and posted on the website. On top of all that, there were periodic reviews of the Doing Business reports: by the IEG in 2008 and 2022 and by panels of independent experts in 2013 and 2021[31] (some of the transparency and participation mechanisms described above were adopted in response to these evaluations). Finally, in 2018 and 2021 the Bank undertook or requested five separate audits and investigations, three internal and two external, in response to allegations of data irregularities[32].

Notwithstanding these safeguards, significant concerns about legitimacy continued to surround the Doing Business report when the Bank made the decision to discontinue it. The main cause for concern was not the absence of participation by affected states but rather that certain states were influencing the production of the metrics in non-transparent ways that bypassed the Bank's elaborate formal processes. The investigations that followed the data alternation scandal identified three distinct channels of improper influence[33]. First, there were states that pressured Bank management to change scores after the period for making and reviewing such changes had passed[34]. Second, certain states entered into consulting arrangements with the team that produced the Doing Business metrics which might have effectively made the Bank's fees contingent on whether the states improved their rankings, thus incentivizing manipulation of the metrics[35]. Third, there were reports of states placing pressure on individuals who contributed data used to create the metrics[36].

<https://www.worldbank.org/en/news/statement/2021/09/16/world-bank-group-to-discontinue-doing-business-report> (accessed 12 September 2022).

30 The Doing Business website continues to be publicly available as an archive. See <https://archive.doingbusiness.org/en/doingbusiness> (accessed 12 September 2022).

31 The results of these reviews are summarized in IEG, *supra* fn 15, 7.

32 World Bank, *supra* fn 1.

33 Alfaro et al., *supra* fn 17, 72–74.

34 WilmerHale, *supra* fn 22. Although Wilmerhale found that changes were made to data for the *Doing Business 2018* report after the Bank-wide review, the investigators went out of their way to deny that there was an inappropriate conduct on behalf of Chinese or other government officials; Ibid, 2, n. 4.

35 WilmerHale, *supra* fn 22; Alfaro et al., *supra* fn 17, 74. Cf. IEG, *supra* fn 17 (finding that potential conflict of interest did not negatively influence client and stakeholder perceptions of the World Bank).

36 Alfaro et al., *supra* fn 17, 73–74.

Just a few months after discontinuing the Doing Business report, the World Bank announced that it would produce an alternative set of metrics to capture the business and investment climate in economies around the world[37]. Ensuring the value and legitimacy of the alternative metrics will entail the same challenges that arose in producing the Doing Business metrics.

9 Conclusion

Few if any legal metrics will ever be as influential as the Doing Business metrics. Still, the remarkable amount of attention the Doing Business metrics commanded, and the magnitude of their influence on lawmakers and investors, show that many people value legal metrics as guides to legal reform and allocation of resources. This, in turn, suggests that producers of legal metrics wield considerable amounts of power. International organizations are often well placed to produce metrics which realize that potential value by drawing upon synergies with their existing operations, and there are well-known methods of addressing the associated concerns about legitimacy. This suggests, all things considered, that international organizations should be encouraged to embrace opportunities to produce legal metrics. The balance of considerations is less clear, however, when it comes to production of legal indicators. There is a considerable risk that international organizations will be tempted to produce indicators that attract considerable attention but offer little value to society and become magnets for illegitimate influences. Thus, the saga of the Doing Business Report illustrates both the opportunities and perils that face international organizations that produce legal metrics, and especially metrics that qualify as indicators.

37 World Bank, *supra* fn 8.

CHAPTER 16

Quantification of Performance as a Regulatory Technique: A Comparative Appraisal

Mauro Bussani, Sabino Cassese and Marta Infantino

1 Introduction

The trend of measuring performances is global and pervasive. Although to different extents and in different ways, we all live in quantified societies, in which an ever-growing array of social activities in a range of fields – from education to health, from work to credit, from consumption to sustainability to justice – are in various ways assessed, controlled and governed according to quantitative techniques.

One of the simplest illustrations of the global pervasiveness of performance-based measurements, that we all experienced passively (and, as educators, actively), is the practice of grading students at schools. When students are large in number and diverse, grading offers a neutral and rapid tool for comparatively testing masses of disparate learners. It is no coincidence that, as early as the seventh century CE, the Chinese empire based the imperial examination system for the recruitment of state officials on comparative assessments of candidates' works[1]. In the West, it was only from the nineteenth century onwards, when access to education in Europe started to reach gradually beyond political and religious elites, that the need arose for tools that could objectively and rapidly manage the increasingly large and varied crowd of students: it was at this point that grading was adopted[2].

The example of student grades is telling for our purposes from many points of view. First, it shows that performance quantification can easily become

1 See, for all, Muzhou Li, Haifeng Liu, Wei-Chiao Huang, 'A Historical Investigation and Classification Analysis of Seven Controversies on the Reform and Abolition of the 1300-year Chinese Imperial Examination System' (2022) 114 *International Journal of Educational Research* 1–9, available at <https://doi.org/10.1016/j.ijer.2022.101976> (accessed 10 January 2023).

2 Marilyn Strathern, 'From Improvement to Enhancement. An Anthropological Comment on the Audit Culture' (1996/7) 19 *Cambridge Anthropology* 1–21, at 4–5; Neil Postman, *Technopoly. The Surrender of Culture to Technology* (Vintage Books 1993) 13, 139–140.

 | DOI:10.1163/9789004680944_017

normalized by those who are subject to and/or participate in it. Grading students is not the only possible approach to learning. Nevertheless, quantification of student performance has rapidly become the most common technique for managing education, and is rarely objected to[3]. Second, students' grading vividly illustrates how social quantification is a 'technology of distance': it is widely used in order to manage communities of strangers in which other techniques for guiding and controlling behavior (in particular those based on intimate knowledge and personal trust) are better replaced by objectified and standardized methods of social governance[4]. Third, it is clear from the example of grades that the choice in favor of quantification has broader consequences, many of which are unintended. We all know how grading changes the set of incentives for students, shifting the focus of learning from achieving knowledge to getting good grades[5]. Moreover, once grades exist, they often take on a life of their own, meaning that a large plethora of actors outside the education system rely on them as a proxy for personal merit. After all, it is much easier to examine past grades than to test people's actual abilities[6]. Fourth, the case of students' grading also demonstrates that performance measurement, despite being a common trait among contemporary societies, manifests itself in forms and with features that differ significantly from one place to another, being heavily dependent on the context in which quantification occurs. As will be well-known to anyone who has had the opportunity to be educated, or to teach, in more than one country, the style, the significance and the practices of grading vary greatly across borders[7].

---

3 "To say that [...] someone is a 7.2 on a sensitivity scale, or that this man's essay on the rise of capitalism is an A – and that man's is a C + – would have sounded like gibberish to Galileo or Shakespeare or Thomas Jefferson. If it makes sense to us, that is because our minds have been conditioned by the technology of numbers so that we see the world differently than they did": Postman, *supra* fn 2, 13.

4 This has been masterfully shown by the studies of Alain Desrosières, *La politique des grands nombres. Histoire de la raison statistique* (La Découverte 2000, 2nd edn; the first edition was also published in English as *The Politics of Large Numbers. A History of Statistical Reasoning* (translated by Camille Naish, Harvard University Press 1998)), and Theodore M. Porter, *Trust in Numbers: The Pursuit of Objectivity in Science and Public Life* (Princeton University Press 1995). See also, more recently, Nick Couldry and Ulises A. Mejias, *The Costs of Connection. How Data Is Colonizing Human Life and Appropriating It for Capitalism* (Stanford University Press 2019) 122–151; André Broome and Joel Quirk, 'Governing the world at a distance: the practice of global benchmarking' (2015) 41 *Review of International Studies* 819–841.

5 Among the many, see Thomas R. Guskey and Susan M. Brookhart, 'Introduction', in Thomas R. Guskey and Susan M. Brookhart (eds), *What We Know about Grading* (ASCD 2019) 1–12, at 3.

6 Ibid.

7 Cell Dilon, 'Grading Discrepancy in Global Education' (2018) 4 *PEOPLE: International Journal of Social Sciences* 1611–1624.

Yet, this book is not about students' grades. Chapters herein collected explore many forms of what we defined in the Introduction as 'legal metrics'[8]. As noted in the same Introduction[9], the performance-based measurements herein investigated sometimes have a clear legal focus, insofar as they assess the management of legal services or a person's compliance with legal norms. Suffice it to think of tools centering on the performances of public bodies, law schools, contractual parties in the platform economy, or on the overall quality of countries' legal infrastructure, or on the respect by corporations of 'environmental, social and governance' (ESG) criteria and 'corporate social responsibility' (CSR) standards[10]. Other times, however, the performance-based measurements scrutinized in the book involve sectors that at first glance are not legal: this is the case, for instance, of quantification initiatives in the broader area of education (beyond law schools) and of automated tracking of online users' behavior[11]. We were interested in these initiatives too, and included them in our notion of legal metrics. This is because, by channeling expectations and conducts in given directions, they may also effectively exert regulatory influence.

For the same reason, we included in our study performance-based measurements that are markedly different from one another in terms of source and form. This explains why some of the metrics here analyzed are officially established by national and/or international law[12], while others are developed and adopted by actors (international organizations, non-governmental organizations (NGOs), domestic agencies, corporations) with limited to no official rule-making power[13]. This also explains why the quantification initiatives covered

---

8 See Chapter 1, Section 2.

9 See Chapter 1, Section 2.

10 See Chapters 2 (Brazil), 3 (Mexico), 4 (India), 5 (Switzerland), 7 (Poland), 9 (China), 10 (Japan), 12 (UK), 14 (Europe/globe), 15 (globe).

11 See Chapters 6 (South Africa), 8 (Africa), 12 (Africa), 13 (Europe).

12 For instance, many measurements of judicial performances and of academic research are mandated by national laws: see Chapters in Part 1 of this book, and also below, in this Chapter, Section 2.1. As to international law, one of the most well-known examples is the obligation of states parties under article 31 of the United Nations Convention on the Rights of Persons with Disabilities (CRPD) "to collect appropriate information, including statistical and research data, to enable them to formulate and implement policies to give effect to the present Convention" (see <https://www.un.org/development/desa/disabilities/convention-on-the-rights-of-persons-with-disabilities/convention-on-the-rights-of-persons-with-disabilities-2.html> (accessed 10 January 2023)).

13 See for instance Chapters 6 (on initiatives undertaken by South African universities), 8, 12 and 13 (on algorithmic quantification by businesses), 14 (on the self-assessment by corporations of compliance with ESG/CSR standards), 15 (on the World Bank initiative for quantifying the openness to investment of countries' legal infrastructure).

by previous chapters come in many different shapes and shapes, ranging from more qualitative, analog and expert-driven tools to hyper-quantitative, automated and AI-powered assessments.

All the above makes it clear how contributors to this volume undertook the great effort of searching for quantitative measurements that, independently of their status and nature, perform regulatory functions, and to enter, with little guidance, into domains where few legal scholars dared venture before. Analyzing how performance-based measurements work as a regulatory technique, indeed, demands accepting that the law may be found in unusual places, and outside the umbrella of official institutions and sources. While many strands of scholarship – from informal international law to global administrative law, from transnational legal theory to legal pluralism[14] – are suggesting to move in this direction, how to examine areas that have been long neglected by legal scholars and left to the exclusive exploration by other social scientists remains a steep path. Engaging lawyers in thinking about metrics and its regulatory power is an original contribution of this volume to the debate on quantification of the social world – a debate that, as highlighted in the Introduction, has so far involved social scientists from a variety of disciplines, but very few legal scholars[15].

Another original contribution that this book brings to the broader debate on social quantification lies in its emphasis on difference: performance-based measurements and their impact are not inherently uniform across sectors and countries. Because of obvious constraints of time, space and competence of the people available, the book does not cover every possible field and legal system. As explained in the Introduction[16], we asked our contributors to focus on the use of metrics in one or more of following sectors: state-administered justice, education, policy-making, and market-related activity. As a result, and as usual in this kind of initiatives, the final picture we got is dependent on each author's take on the issue[17]. All these limitations notwithstanding, the picture confirms what we suspected when we launched this project: legal metric is on the rise everywhere, but its design and effects are uneven in different fields and places. While further research could achieve a more comprehensive

14 See Chapter 1, Section 2, fn 4.

15 See Chapter 1, Section 4.

16 See Chapter 1, Section 4.

17 For instance, contributors of this volume display varying degrees of enthusiasm and skepticism vis-à-vis legal metrics, which seem to be associated more with their own personal opinion than with objective features of what is studied. Cf. for instance the reading of algorithmic quantification in Africa in Chapters 8 and 12.

description of performance-based measurements and their regulatory potential, the chapters herein collected document the variety of forms and impacts that such measurements have and the need for adopting a comparative approach in exploring them.

In the following pages, we will build on the information and results collected in previous chapters, combining them with the available literature, in order to draw some general observations about comparative legal metrics. In particular, Section 2 will attempt to summarize the main features of performance-based measurements that have emerged from contributions to this book. On this basis, in Section 3 we will explain why legal metrics may qualify as a regulatory technique and how it can be framed and tamed. Section 4 will highlight the major conclusions and present possible directions for future research.

2 Comparative Findings

In spite of the limited substantive and geographical coverage of the essays herein collected, there are many general observations on performance-based measurements that can be drawn out of them.

In this section, we will complement the results contained in the previous chapters with illustrations and information available in the literature, in order to highlight where instances of legal metrics can be found (Section 2.1), what they focus on (Section 2.2), how, by whom and for whom they are made (Sections 2.3–2.4). The last two sub-sections will investigate the reasons for which legal metrics are adopted (Section 2.5) and what consequences they entail (Section 2.6).

2.1 *Where Legal Metrics Can Be Found*

We already noted that performance-based measurements producing legal effects are on the rise everywhere. What should be stressed is that 'everywhere' means any possible locus of law-making.

Many of the previous chapters explore instances of legal metrics adopted at the domestic level, either by state organs (through law or by ministries and agencies working in a regulatory capacity)[18] or by other actors, such as company-led social credit initiatives in China and quantitative-based assessments of

18 This is the case of national initiatives to assess the performance of courts (Chapters 1–5), of universities and academics (Chapter 7), and of administrative bodies or the state itself (Chapters 9–11).

admission policies by universities in South Africa[19]. Other authors highlight how legal metric is often requested and produced by international organizations, both regional (such as the Council of Europe, the European Union and the African Union)[20] and global (e.g., the World Bank)[21]. Still a few other contributors focus on performance measurements flourishing across, and independently from, national borders and international law regimes, in what may be called the transnational level of law-making[22]. This is notably the case for assessments of corporations' ESG/CSR obligations[23] and algorithmic-based measurements of the online behavior of market players (whether businesses or consumers)[24].

More data would be needed in order to understand whether there are patterns within the adoption of specific types of performance-based measures in given regions and spheres. What we can and should underline is that measurements existing in different places and on different levels rarely operate in isolation from one another. On the contrary, domestic, international and transnational initiatives constantly interact, compete and conflict with one another,

19 See respectively Chapters 9 (China) and 6 (South Africa).

20 See respectively Chapters 5 (Switzerland), 14 (Europe) and 8 (South Africa).

21 See Chapter 15.

22 On transnational law, from a variety of perspectives, cf. Peer Zumbansen, 'Transnational Law: Theories and Applications', in Peer Zumbansen (ed), *The Oxford Handbook of Transnational Law* (OUP 2021) 3–30; Mauro Bussani, 'Strangers in the Law: Lawyers' Law and the Other Legal Dimensions' (2019) 40 *Cardozo Law Review* 3125–3184, at 3146–3160; Larry Catá Backer, 'Next Generation Law: Data-Driven Governance and Accountability-Based Regulatory Systems in the West, and Social Credit Regimes in China' (2018) 28 *Southern California Interdisciplinary Law Journal* 123–172; Sabino Cassese, 'Beyond Legal Comparison', in Mauro Bussani and Lukas Heckendorn Urscheler (eds), *Comparisons in Legal Development. The Impact of Foreign and International Law on National Legal Systems* (Schultess 2016) 227–234; Lawrence M. Friedman, 'Erewhon. The Coming Global Legal Order', in Lawrence M. Friedman, Rogelio Pérez-Perdomo, Manuel A. Gómez (eds), *Law in Many Societies. A Reader* (Stanford University Press 2011) 308–316.

23 See Chapter 14. On this point, see also Larry Catá Backer and Matthew B. McQuilla, 'The algorithmic law of business and human rights: constructing private transnational law of ratings, social credit and accountability measures' (2022) 18 *International Journal of Law in Context* 1–19, available at <https://doi.org/10.1017/S1744552322000453> (accessed 10 January 2023); Tomáš Morochovič and Lucy Lu Reimers, 'Hidden in the Shades. Patterns of Entanglement within the Web of Corporate Social Responsibility Law', in Nico Krisch (ed), *Entangled Legalities Beyond the State* (CUP 2021) 318–350; Emily Webster and Laura Mai, 'Transnational environmental law in the Anthropocene' (2020) 11 *Transnational Legal Theory* 1–15; Graeme Auld and Lars H. Gulbrandsen, 'Private Regulation in Global Environmental Governance', in Robert Falkner (ed), *The Handbook of Global Climate and Environment Policy* (John Wiley & Sons 2013) 394–411.

24 Cf. Chapters 8 (South Africa), 12 (Africa), 14 (Europe).

and are also strengthened or influenced by one another. For instance, Sunder Raj and Basak explain how performance-based assessments of judicial performance have developed in parallel at the international and at the national level, sometimes in opposition and sometimes as complimentary to one another[25]. Jakubowski points out how the transnational quantification of scientific output by companies providing metrics on journal and researcher performances (such as Scopus, Web of Science and Google Scholar)[26] are increasingly relied on by domestic, state-led assessments of universities, thereby pushing national academics to adopt strategies that reinforce the significance of transnational, corporate measurements[27]. Davis talks about the World Bank (WB) Doing Business reports (DB), that, over their almost twenty years of existence, have gently induced governments around the world to adopt slightly under 4.000 national reforms of business law[28], and have inspired many other experiments with legal indicators, both by the WB itself[29] and by other actors (such

---

25 See Chapter 4 (India), Section 2.

26 See, respectively, <https://www.scopus.com/sources>, <https://clarivate.com/webofsciencegroup/solutions/web-of-science/> and <https://scholar.google.com/intl/it/scholar/metrics.html> (accessed 10 January 2023). On the overall effects of the metrics provided by these companies in the field of scientific research, see, among the many, Sarah Lamdan, *Data Cartels* (Cornell University Press 2023) 52–55, 63–66; Mario Biagioli and Alexandra Lippman (eds), *Gaming the Metrics. Misconduct and Manipulation in Academic Research* (MIT Press 2020); Imad A. Moosa, *Publish or Perish: Perceived Benefits versus Unintended Consequences* (EE 2018); Annie Vinokur, 'La normalisation de l'université', in Benoît Frydman and Arnaud Van Waeyenberge (eds), *Gouverner par les standards et les indicateurs. De Hume aux rankings* (Bruylant 2014) 235–261. Similar observations apply to the many private actors producing global rankings of academic institutions, such as THE, Quacquarelly Symonds and ARWU mentioned in Chapter 1, Section 3; on these rankings, see Barbara M. Kehm, 'Global University Rankings: Impact and Applications', in Biagioli and Lippman (eds), *supra* this fn, 93–100.

27 See Chapter 7 (Poland).

28 See Chapter 15, as well as World Bank, 'Doing Business 2020. Comparing-Business-Regulation-in-190-Economies' (2019) 25, available at <https://archive.doingbusiness.org/en/doingbusiness> (accessed 10 January 2023).

29 The DB reports inspired the creation of the 'Investing Across Borders' (IAB) index (published once in 2010 to measure countries' openness to foreign direct investments and then discontinued: see World Bank, 'Investing Across Borders 2010' (2010), at <https://openknowledge.worldbank.org/handle/10986/27883> (accessed 10 January 2023)), the 'Women, Business and the Law' (WBL) reports (established in 2010 with the aim of completing the DB with data and scores on women in the economy, and of overcoming the critique moved to the DB about its being gender-blind, and still ongoing: see the website <https://wbl.worldbank.org/en/wbl> (accessed 10 January 2023)), the 'Global Indicators of Regulatory Governance' (GIRG) (released once in 2016 to explore how governments interact with the public when shaping regulations that affect their business community, and then never published again: see the website <https://rulemaking.worldbank.org/en/about-us>

as the 'Fondation pour le droit continental', a French non-governmental organization, that attempted in the 2010s to build a concurrent initiative, the now extinct 'Index de la sécurité juridique')[30].

The case of the DB also shows well that tools for quantifying social phenomena are reactive to the environment in which they operate, and therefore often change through the repetition of their measurement cycles. For instance, the strong resistance voiced by France after early editions of the DB, which suggested that legal systems whose origins could be traced back to the British common law were more efficient than those whose origins lay in French law, prompted the WB to gloss over the significance of legal origins in later reports[31]. In 2009, harsh criticism by the International Trade Union Confederation and the International Labour Organization against the dimension 'Employing Workers' in the DB (which rewarded countries where firing workers was easier) obliged the WB to stop using it within the calculation for the final 'Ease of Doing Business' score[32]. Vociferous critiques from many quarters accusing the

---

(accessed 10 January 2023)), the 'Business Enabling Environment' (BEE) project (now under preparation, with the aim of taking up the legacy of the DB "to measure the business enabling environment in economies worldwide": see the website <https://www.worldbank.org/en/programs/business-enabling-environment/bee> (accessed 10 January 2023)).

30 The publication (for two editions only) of the 'Index de la sécurité juridique' was prompted by the shock provoked among French élites by the first editions of the DB reports, according to which French and French-inspired laws were inefficient. See Bruno Deffains and Michel Séjean (eds), *Index de la sécurité juridique. Rapport pour la Fondation pour le droit continental* (Dalloz 2018). For some critical remarks on this project, see Jonas Knetsch, 'Measuring Legal Certainty? Critical Feedback about the Development of an Index of Legal Certainty', in Mark Fenwick, Mathias M. Siems, Stefan Wrbka (eds), *The Shifting Meaning of Legal Certainty in Comparative and Transnational Law* (Bloomsbury 2017) 177–186. For further illustrations of counter-initiatives inspired by the DB, see Chapter 1, Section 4.2.

31 Marta Infantino, *Numera et impera. Gli indicatori giuridici globali e il diritto comparato* (Franco Angeli 2019) 147. Considering that the WB discountinued in 2021 the DB up after the discovery of some negotiations between the WB team and individual countries about their scores (see the website <https://www.worldbank.org/en/news/statement/2021/09/16/world-bank-group-to-discontinue-doing-business-report> (accessed 10 January 2023)), it is however fairly possible that the room for national influence of the DB reports was much larger than officially acknowledged.

32 On this story, cf. Henner Gött, 'The ILO's Model Under Pressure: The World Bank's Employing Workers Indicator', in Henner Gött (ed), *The Law of Interactions Between International Organizations. A Framework for Multi-Institutional Labour Governance* (Springer 2020) 67–95; Debbie Collier and Paul Benjamin, 'Measuring Labor Market Efficiency. Indicators that Fuel an Ideological War and Undermine Social Concern and Trust in the South African Regulatory Process', in Sally Engle Merry, Kevin Davis, Benedict Kingsbury (eds), *The Quiet Power of Indicators. Measuring Governance, Corruption, and*

DB of gender-blindness were the main reason underlying the establishment, in 2010, of a gender-based spin-off indicator called 'Women, Business and the Law' (WBL) reports[33]. Similarly, repeated complaints about the scant transparency of the measurement process, the fact that it was impossible to participate in it and the absence of any form of review, gradually led the WB to publish all supporting materials for the reports, to enable interested parties to submit relevant information, and to subject the reports to external audits[34].

These illustrations are just some examples, among the many possible ones, of what we stressed at the beginning of this section. Performance-based measurements exist at many different levels, which may be identified as the 'where' in which they operate, but they often also subsist in complex ecologies that cut across spheres of governance, constantly interacting with forces situated outside the boundaries of their own locus of activity. The case of the DB demonstrates that the feedback and reflexive cycles created by the repetition of measurements through time may extend well beyond the biunivocal relationship between the measurers and the measured, and may embrace any person who relies on the quantitative assessments of others' performances; as a result, external reactions to a measure end up pressuring the measure itself to change[35]. Through the linkages, interactions and feedback loops among all of the actors concerned – irrespective of where these actors are situated –, quantitative measurements of performance emerge, settle, adapt, sometimes change, and sometimes fall[36].

Rule of Law (CUP 2015) 284–316; Paul Benjamin, Haroon Bhorat, Halton Cheadle, 'The Cost of 'Doing Business' and Labour Regulation. The Case of South Africa', 149 *International Labour Review* 73–91 (2010).

33 On this indicator, see *supra* fn 29, as well as Catherine Powell, 'Gender Indicators as Global Governance: Not Your Father's World Bank', 17 *Georgetown Journal of Gender & Law* 777–807 (2016).

34 Infantino, *supra* fn 31, 243–244.

35 On this dynamics, cf. Zumbansen, *supra* fn 22, 15–22; Brian Z. Tamanaha, 'A Reconstruction of Transnational Legal Pluralism and Law's Foundations', in Nico Krisch (ed), *supra* fn 23, 449–477; Paul Shiff Berman, 'Understanding Global Legal Pluralism. From Local to Global, from Descriptive to Normative', in Paul Shiff Berman (ed), *The Oxford Handbook of Global Legal Pluralism* (OUP 2020) 1–35, at 2–12; Gregory T. Shaffer, 'Theorizing Transnational Legal Ordering' (2016) 12 *Annual Review of Law and Social Science* 231–253; Sabino Cassese, Elisa D'Alterio, Maurizia De Bellis, 'The Enforcement of Transnational Private Regulation: A Fictitious Oxymoron', in Fabrizio Cafaggi (ed), *Enforcement of Transnational Regulation: Ensuring Compliance in a Global World* (EE 2013) 331–371, at 347–355, 367–368.

36 See the authors quoted *supra*, fn 35.

2.2 *The Fields of Legal Metrics*

In light of the burgeoning production, at all levels, of performance-based measurements, the question naturally arises as to whether this tendency is evenly distributed among sectors.

As already noted, it is difficult to infer any generalizations from our limited data, especially considering that our results may be tainted by lawyers' preference to focus on metrics with a clear legal object, such as assessments of courts and evaluations of law schools. Moreover, any attempt at identifying certain fields as being more prone to quantification than others would have to be wary of the blurred lines and different understandings of the same domains across legal cultures. For instance, a correlation between the spread of quantification in some sectors and their public (or private) character would be largely meaningless. Areas that in some places are deemed to pertain to the core of the state's non-delegable duties may elsewhere be left in private hands, or in still other places may be managed in ways that defy classification according to the public/private dichotomy. Any attempt at generalization on the basis of the 'public versus private' distinction would fail on account of the different ways in which the divide is perceived and managed around the world[37].

With this caveat in mind, we may nevertheless note that performance-based measurements seem to flourish in some fields more than in others.

At the domestic level, several contributors, from countries as different as Brazil, China, India, Japan, Mexico, and Switzerland report on the development, in recent years, of some forms of performance-based measurement of justice[38]. One author, Jakubowski, explicitly focuses on the quantitative assessments for the quality of legal research (in Poland)[39], and refers to similar initiatives taking place elsewhere; there is indeed an ample literature

---

37 Aside from the fact that the public/private divide is difficult to reconcile with China's socialist market economy, one need only recall here that legal education and healthcare services are largely privatized in common law countries, while they are generally publicly funded and managed elsewhere. On the difficulties arising out from the application of the public/private divide across different cultures, see Couldry and Mejias, *supra* fn 4, 54–57; Xingzhong Yu, 'State Legalism and the Public/Private Divide in Chinese Legal Development' (2014) 15 *Theoretical Inquiries in Law* 27–52; Cassese, D'Alterio, De Bellis, *supra* fn 36, 342–347; Ignazio Castellucci, 'Rule of Law with Chinese Characteristics' (2007) 13 *Annual Survey of International & Comparative Law* 35–92, at 69–75; John Henry Merryman, 'The Public Law-Private Law Distinction in European and American Law' (1968) 17 *Journal of Public Law* 3–19.

38 See Chapters 2 (Brazil), 3 (Mexico), 4 (India), 5 (Switzerland), 9 (China) and 10 (Japan). Chapter 4 also contains references to many similar initiatives in other countries and at the international level.

39 See Chapter 7 (also mentioning similar experiences in other countries).

on the same trend affecting many other countries[40]. While few authors deal with performance-based measurements in the fields of education in general (beyond law schools and legal research)[41], academics know well the variety of tools quantifying and ranking the quality of universities, scientific journals and individual researchers[42]. Some of our contributors also mention instances of legal metrics being adopted to check how public law bodies and agencies perform their functions[43].

In the grey area between the domestic and the transnational domain, many authors note the increasing reliance by tech and digital companies on big data analytics and more or less sophisticated forms of algorithmic measurements of the online performance of businesses and people[44]. In the same dimension, Heckendorn explores the peculiarly soft forms of (self-)measurements of multinationals' compliance with ESG/CSR standards[45]. His observations about the specificities of quantitative assessments in the field resonate with the findings

40 See Rob van Gestel and Andreas Lienhard (eds), *Evaluating Academic Legal Research in Europe. The Advantage of Lagging Behind* (EE 2019).

41 See Chapters 6 (South Africa) and 9 (China).

42 See *supra* fns 26-27. The power of university rankings is confirmed by the recent scandal involving Columbia University. In the spring of 2022, a Columbia math professor, Michael Taddeus, denounced a pattern of inaccurate or misleading statements made by Columbia University to U.S. News and World Report for the production of the national universities ranking yearly produced by the latter (the complaint is available at <http://www.math.columbia.edu/~thaddeus/ranking/investigation.html> (accessed 10 January 2023)). Taddeus' complaint prompted U.S. News and World Report to downgrade Columbia from no. 2 to no. 18. See James Barron, 'Columbia Loses A-Plus Status in U.S. News Rankings' (14 September 2022) *New York Times*, available at <https://www.nytimes.com/2022/09/13/nyregion/columbia-loses-a-plus-status-in-us-news-rankings.html> (accessed 10 January 2023).

43 See Chapters 10 (on Japan) and 11 (on UK). Measuring public bodies' performances was indeed the main aim of the New Public Management movement discussed in Chapter 1, Section 4.1.

44 See Chapters 8 and 12 (on Africa), 9 (on China) and 13 (on Europe). A similar trend, often dubbed RegTech and SupTech, is noticeable among domestic and supranational regulatory and supervisory authorities, especially in the banking and finance sector, which increasingly tend to rely on performance-based technologies to monitor norm compliance: Laura Grassi and Davide Lanfranchi, 'RegTech in public and private sectors: the nexus between data, technology and regulation' (2022) 49 *Journal of Industrial and Business Economics* 441–479; John Ho Hee Jung, 'RegTech and SupTech: The Future of Compliance', in Jelena Madir (ed), *FinTech Law and Regulation* (EE 2021) 291–316; David Restrepo Amariles and Gregory Lewkowicz, 'Unpacking Smart Law: How Mathematics and Algorithms are Reshaping the Legal Code in the Financial Sector' (2020) 25 *Lex Electronica* 171–185.

45 See Chapter 14.

of those who have noted the multiplication of self-reporting, benchmarking and third-party certification initiatives to loosely monitor the activities of transnational corporations[46].

This takes us into a further area of diffusion of performance-based measurements that fluctuates between the transnational and the international sphere: that of quantification initiatives focusing on the performances of countries vis-à-vis a wide array of issues – from protection of human rights to the rule of law, from the fight against corruption and human trafficking to the creation of business-friendly legal environments. An example is the already mentioned WB's DB, with its annual measurement of investment climates around the world, but several others may be added. For instance, the 'Freedom in the World' index (by the New-York based NGO Freedom House) and the 'Global Rights' index (by the International Trade Union Confederation, an international federation of trade unions seated in Brussels) score countries for their respect of citizens' and workers' rights respectively[47]. The 'Rule of Law Index®' (published by the Washington-based NGO World Justice Project) evaluates how effectively states adhere to the rule of law[48]. The 'Corruption Perceptions Index' (by the Berlin-based NGO Transparency International) and the 'Trafficking in Persons' reports (by the United States Department of State) quantify the efforts of states in combating corruption and human trafficking[49]. As this minimal list makes clear, such a 'globalizing' kind of metrics is almost invariably produced by entities based either in Europe or (more frequently) in the US, claiming the authority to assess the compliance with allegedly universal standards by all the rest[50].

---

46 Tim Bartley, 'Power and the Practice of Transnational Private Regulation' (2021) 27 *New Political Economy* 188–202 (2021); Auld and Gulbrandsen, *supra* fn 23; Cassese, D'Alterio, De Bellis, *supra* fn 36, 337–339.

47 See the websites <https://freedomhouse.org/report/freedom-world> and <https://www.globalrightsindex.org/> (accessed 10 January 2023).

48 See the website <https://worldjusticeproject.org/rule-of-law-index/> (accessed 10 January 2023).

49 See the websites <https://www.transparency.org/en/cpi/> and <https://www.state.gov/trafficking-in-persons-report/> (accessed 10 January 2023).

50 Among the many who noted this, cp. Sarah Sunn Bush, 'The Politics of Rating Freedom: Ideological Affinity, Private Authority, and the Freedom in the World Ratings' (2017) 15 *Perspectives on Politics* 711–731, at 722–724; Jedidiah Kroncke, 'Law and Development as Anti-Comparative Law' (2012) 45 *Vanderbil Journal of Transnational Law* 477–555, at 479 and 538; Liam Clegg, 'Our Dream is a World Full of Poverty Indicators: The US, the World Bank, and the Power of Numbers' (2010) *New Political Economy* 473–492, at 474, 481; Strathern, *supra* note 2, 2.

Further research may highlight the proliferation of performance measurements in additional domains, and help understand why assessments of performances seem to be more frequent for some activities and not for others. What we can do is checking how the above-mentioned measures are made, and verifying whether and to what extent there are common patterns emerging within specific sectors.

2.3 *How Measurements Are Carried Out*

The performance-based measurements surveyed in this book come in a variety of shapes and sizes[51]: scores and scorecards, rankings, ratings, benchmarking, black/white-lists, big data analysis, hybrid quali-quantitative judgments, arrived at through analog or digital means (or both). We cannot enter into too much detail about the many forms that performance-based measurements can take; we will try to highlight some features that, amidst their great variety, these measures have in common.

Let us start from the issue of titles. Performance-based measurements often have bureaucratic names, but sometimes have nice titles or acronyms, which are supposed to make them travel smoothly in the world. The case just mentioned of the indexes named 'Freedom in the World' and 'Global Rights' are examples of this branding strategy at the global level[52]. FICO®, the formula that supports the vast majority of consumer credit assessments in the US, is the acronym of the corporation ('Fair, Isaac and Company') that devised it[53], while the system for consumers' social credit scores managed by the Chinese company Ant Financial (a member of the Alibaba group) is evocatively dubbed 'Sesame Credit' ('芝麻信用')[54]. Some Chinese cities have used catchy names

---

51 See above in this Chapter, Section 1.

52 On both these indicators, see above in this Chapter, Section 5.2.

53 See the website <www.fico.com> (accessed 10 January 2023); see also Janine S. Hiller and Lindsay Sain Jones, 'Who's Keeping Score?: Oversight of Changing Consumer Credit Infrastructure' (2022) 59 *American Business Law Journal* 61–121, at 71–77; Noah Vardi, *Creditworthiness and 'Responsible Credit'. A Comparative Study of EU and US Law* (Brill 2022) 89, 97.

54 See the website <https://www.zmxy.com.cn/#/home> (accessed 10 January 2023). There is a substantial literature on Chinese corporate social credit systems: cf. Abigail Devereaux and Linan Peng, 'Give us a little social credit: to design or to discover personal ratings in the era of Big Data' (2020) 16 *Journal of Institutional Economics* 1–19, at 5–6; Daithí Mac Síthigh and Mathias M. Siems, 'The Chinese Social Credit System: A Model for Other Countries' (2019) 82 *Modern Law Review* 1034–1071, at 1025–1053; Yongxi Chen and Anne S.Y. Cheung, 'The Transparent Self under Big Data Profiling: Privacy and Chinese Legislation on the Social Credit System' (2018) 12 *Journal of Comparative Law* 356–378, at 361–363.

for their municipal social credit systems, naming them after the cities' rivers, flowers and other meaningful local symbols, such as 'Qian River' ('钱江') score in Hangzhou, the 'Jasmine' ('茉莉') score in Fuzhou, the 'Litte Egret' ('白鹭') score in Xiamen and the 'Seashell' ('海贝分') score in Weihai[55].

Whether or not they have a nice title, all performance-based measurements are rooted in a methodology and a procedure, and several choices have to be made when determining them. These choices include decisions about what to count (and not to count), about the variables and dimensions that matter (and those that do not), and also about the proxies that capture information concerning these variables and dimensions (and those that do not). It is also necessary to decide on the weight assigned to each variable, dimension and proxy, the kind of data to be collected, the methods according to which non-quantitative data points should be obtained, rendered comparable with one another and transformed into numbers, and strategies for coping with noisy, missing or incomplete data. It is particularly important to establish what information (e.g., facts, opinions, perceptions) should be gathered and in what language, where the data should be taken from (e.g., through direct measurement, self-reporting, surveys, third parties' evaluations), how data are to be processed (e.g., by humans or by machine), and about who (or what) should bear concrete responsibility for the above steps[56].

As highlighted above, these elements are often revised over time, for every iteration of a measure provides an opportunity to learn from previous cycles[57]. Nevertheless, it must be underlined that all of the choices mentioned above are crucial, insofar as they all influence the type and quality of results that a measure can achieve[58]. Depending on their level of complexity, these steps

55 Marta Infantino and Weiwei Wang, 'Challenging Western Legal Orientalism. A Comparative Analysis of Chinese Municipal Social Credit Systems' (2021) 8 *European Journal of Comparative Law and Governance* 46–85, at 76.

56 For a tentative list of the technical steps that are required in order to design a system for measuring social performance, see David Restrepo Amariles and Julian McLachlan, 'Legal Indicators in Transnational Law Practice: A Methodological Assessment' (2018) 58 *Jurimetrics Journal* 163–209, at 183–190; David McGrogan, 'The Problem of Causality in International Human Rights Law' (2016) 65 *International & Comparative Law Quarterly* 615–644, at 631–633; Margaret L. Satterthwaite and Daniel Kacinski, 'Quantitative methods in advocacy-oriented human rights research', in Bård A. Andreassen, Hans-Otto Sano, Siobhán McInerney-Lankford (eds), *Research Methods in Human Rights* (EE 2017) 282–385, at 292–304. Needless to say, other layers of technical specialization have to be added when the quantification is partially automated, i.e., when it is largely embedded in algorithms: see, for all, Dan L. Burk, 'Algorithmic Legal Metrics' (2021) 96 *Notre Dame Law Review* 1147–1204.

57 See above in this Chapter, Section 5.1.

58 See the authors quoted *supra* fn 56.

may often demand an expenditure of time and money, the hiring and training of personnel with specific skills, and/or the establishment of dedicated offices[59]. The costs associated with setting up a quantification system explain why methodological choices are often dictated by practical constraints as much as (if not more than) they are determined by intentional design[60].

What emerges from the above list of issues is that many methodological options are available, and there is no perfect recipe for how to build a measure[61]. Every decision comes with its own pros and cons. For instance, reliance on human judgment ensures flexibility and context-sensitivity, but is also expensive, time-consuming, and exposed to errors and subjective bias – all the more so when the measure gathers sentiments about someone's performance. Suffice it to think of the naïveté (and blatant neglect of any basic comparative law teaching) transparently put forward by one of the major producers of sentiment indicators, the United Nations Economic Commission for Europe (UNECE): "[d]ata collection and reference periods may differ among countries. Different questions may be used and questions which are intended to measure the same phenomenon may be formulated in different ways. The perception of a phenomenon and questions related to this may also vary because of cultural and other differences and may influence the comparability across countries. [...] Such differences will, eventually, affect the comparability across countries. [...] However, it should also be noted that even if individual questions differ, if the sentiment indicator is composed from a set of many questions, these

59 See Chapter 1, Section 1.

60 It is often noted that measurements tend to count what can be easily counted, rather than counting what really matters. Among the many, see Sally Engle Merry, *The Seductions of Quantification. Measuring Human Rights, Gender Violence, and Sex Trafficking* (Chicago University Press 2016) 7; Kevin Davis, Benedict Kingsbury, Sally Engle Merry, 'Introduction. The Local-Global Life of Indicators: Law, Power, and Resistance', in Merry, Davis, Kingsbury (eds), *supra* fn 32, 1–24, at 13.

61 There is general agreement on this point. Cf. Sharmila Murthy, 'Translating Legal Norms into Quantitative Indicators: Lessons from the Global Water, Sanitation, and Hygiene Sector' (2018) 42 *William & Mary Environmental Law & Policy Review* 385–446, at 423–424; Satterthwaite & Kacinski, *supra* note 56, 290–292; Engle Merry, *supra* note 60, 7, 16–17; Davis, Kingsbury, Merry, *supra* note 60, 13; Broome & Quirk, *supra* note 5, 828; Tony Porter, 'Making serious measures: numerical indices, peer review, and transnational actor-networks' (2012) 15 *Journal of International Relations & Development* 532–557 (2012); Ralf Michaels, *Comparative Law by Numbers? Legal Origins Thesis, Doing Business Reports, and the Silence of Traditional Comparative Law*, 57 *American Journal of Comparative Law* 765–795, at 786–787 (2009).

differences may tend to cancel out so that the resulting indicator nevertheless may be used for international comparisons"[62].

To be sure, automated forms of measurements are cheaper, faster and more objective; yet the price to pay for these qualities is their enhanced rigidity and opacity, especially when the underlying algorithms are copyrighted (as is the case for both FICO® and Sesame Credit). Moreover, the possibility that the formula underlying the measure may be secret, coupled with the fact that automated metrics are often embedded in an interface that directly implements what the algorithm's suggestions and severely limits scope for double-checking and challenging its results[63].

We do not have enough data to suggest that certain methodological patterns are more common in some sectors than in others. What we may nevertheless note is that the performance-based measurements examined in this volume position themselves along a spectrum ranging from analog, expert-driven and more qualitative forms of assessments to algorithmic (or AI-driven), mechanical and more quantitative evaluation mechanisms. At one extreme, performance-based assessments of justice currently seem to dominated by quantitative-qualitative, analogic forms of evaluation[64] (although the introduction of robo-judges and digitalized justice may rapidly change this)[65]. At the other extreme, the digital domain is dramatically dominated by purely quantitative, machine-led measurements[66]. Measurements in other sectors lie somewhere in between these two poles, mixing qualitative, expert-driven judgments with automated, quantitative tools[67].

2.4 *Actors and Beneficiaries*

From what we saw, it is clear that performance-based measurements may be established by a plethora of actors for quantifying processes, activities and results attributable to an equally rich array of other actors. We saw examples of measurements set up by states, independent agencies, corporations, NGOs,

62 United Nations Economic Commission for Europe (UNECE), *Guidelines on producing leading, composite and sentiment indicators* (2019) 48, available at <https://unece.org/DAM/stats/publications/2019/ECECESSTAT20192.pdf> (accessed 10 January 2023).

63 This is particularly stressed by Chapter 13.

64 See Chapters 2 (Brazil), 3 (Mexico), 4 (India), 5 (Switzerland) and 9 (China).

65 Cf. Nyu Wang and Michael Yuan Tian, "Intelligent Justice': AI Implementations in China's Legal Systems', in Ariane Hanemaayer (ed), *Artificial Intelligence and Its Discontents. Critiques from the Social Sciences and Humanities* (Palgrave 2022) 197–222; Tania Sourdin, *Judges, Technology and Artificial Intelligence. The Artificial Judge* (EE 2021).

66 Cf. Chapters 8 and 12 (Africa), 9 (China), 10 (Japan) and 13 (Europe).

67 See Chapter 10 (Japan).

international organizations, and hybrids of all these types, focusing on the performances of individuals and entities, including universities, hospitals, companies, and states. Further, the analysis so far has shown that the dynamic initiated and supported by performance-based measurements often extends beyond the relationship between those who set up the measurement and the measured, involving wider networks of stakeholders. These stakeholders are sometimes interested in participating in the construction and the management of the measurement; at other times they may criticize and resist the quantification exercise; and still at other times they may embrace the initiative by imitating it or relying upon it for their own purposes. Be it as it may, the complexity of the network of actors surrounding performance-based measurements makes the answer to the question 'by whom and for whom are legal metrics made?' less obvious than it might appear to be at first sight.

Notwithstanding the limited data herein collected, we believe that the examples of performance-based measurements surveyed in previous chapters demonstrate that this question requires at least a bifurcated answer. When considered in the light of who measures, and for the benefit of whom, a neat (at least, in theory) distinction emerges between initiatives aiming to quantify one's own performance and initiatives quantifying the performance of others (although in practice the dividing line between the two types of metric is often unclear).

Many of our contributors presented scenarios in which someone – typically, a state, an agency or a company – measures its own performances or the performance of its own personnel. This is the case for measurements carried out by state authorities in the field of justice, legal research, education and public services, as well as for human rights self-assessments prepared by states and corporations[68]. Although these quantitative exercises may also send out a signal to interested stakeholders or to the general public, their primary aim seems to be self-improvement and self-regulation. In other words, the entity producing the measurement is the same as both the measured entity and the main beneficiary of the measurement. Consequently, initiatives of this kind raise few problems in terms of legitimacy, insofar as the power of self-measurement is included within the power of self-regulation.

The structure of the relationship between the actors affected by performance-based measurement becomes notably different in other cases.

68 Cf. Chapters 2 (Brazil), 3 (Mexico), 4 (India), 5 (Switzerland), 9 (China) and 10 (Japan) (on assessments of justice); Chapters 6 (South Africa), 7 (Poland) and 9 (China) (on assessments in the field of education); Chapters 11 (UK) and 14 (Europe/globe) (on human rights assessments).

Consider, for instance, universities, journals and researchers that are scored by specialized companies[69], of global indicators comparing the legal architecture of the world's countries[70], and the algorithmic profiling of businesses and individuals' online behavior[71]. Authors of these measurements notably differ from those who are subject to them: the rationale for quantification here is no longer self-improvement and self-regulation, but rather the improvement and regulation of others. Even more interestingly, in the vast majority of these scenarios, performance-based measurements are carried out by actors that have no connection with, and little to no authority over, the measured. In a limited number of instances, the measurement may still derive some legitimacy from the specific expertise of its author, or from its position vis-à-vis the measured (such as when the World Bank measures the business friendliness of the world countries or a food delivery platform measures the punctuality of its riders). However, in other cases (for instance the many NGO-led global indicators or the corporate tracking of online activities of net users), those who carry out the measurement have no expertise or status justifying their intervention. On the contrary, it is the very act of measuring that provides them with the experience and position to measure, thereby legitimizing ex post facto their power to quantitatively assess the performance of others[72]. It should be added that many of these measurements, especially those with a transnational or global scope, share the distinctive feature of being authored by actors based in the West (and, more often than not, in the US)[73]. These measurements may thus be useful for the measureds and for interested stakeholders. However, it is also certain that they help their authors to affirm and reinforce their own authority. We can go so far as to assert that those in power often measure as much as those who measure come to power.

69 See the cases mentioned *supra*, fns. 26 and 42.

70 See Chapter 15, as well as the illustrations provided above in this Chapter, Sections 5.1 and 5.2.

71 See Chapters 8 (South Africa), 12 (Africa) and 13 (Europe).

72 This paradoxical ex post facto legitimization has been noted by many. See Catá Backer and McQuilla, *supra* fn 23, 2; Broome and Quirk, *supra* fn 4, 823; Alexander Cooley, 'The emerging politics of international rankings and ratings. A framework for analysis', in Alexander Cooley and Jack Snyder (eds), *Ranking the World. Grading States as a Tool of Global Governance* (CUP 2015) 1–38, at 24; Espeland and Sauder, *supra* fn 42, 36. Well-known examples of this effect are the role and authority obtained in global governance by transnational NGOs measuring states' respective performances: for the examples of Freedom House and Transparency International, see *supra*, respectively fns 47 and 49.

73 See the authors quoted *supra* fn 50.

2.5 *Why Legal Metrics Are Adopted …*

The question about the actors and beneficiaries of legal metrics is of course associated with the question about why: what are the reasons underlying the establishment of performance-based measurements?

As we saw, if one leaves aside sector-specific rationales (such as better justice or more personalized services for online consumers), it seems at first glance that the most commonly recurring theme for measuring both one's own and others' performances is a somewhat underfined wish to promote (self-) improvement. The notion of improvement is of course a tricky one, insofar as it evokes the idea of progress and betterment, as if there were a universal consensus on the answer to questions about what improvement should be achieved, for whom, at what costs, and what for[74]. Yet, as vague as it may be, the ideology of improvement sustains the shared management-oriented belief that measuring processes and results unleashes efficiency gains, because, according to a frequently repeated catchphrase, 'what gets measured gets done'[75].

This belief in the improvement capacity of measures is rooted in well-known features of quantitative performance assessments. Metric is supposed to provide objective and impartial knowledge of social phenomena that can help carry out diagnostic analysis, highlight problems that needs to be fixed, identify patterns for corrective action and reward appropriate behavior. Furthermore, by repeatedly monitoring progress, by naming and shaming bad performers and by singling out good performers, metrics aim to foster change (either directly or through the pressure exerted by relevant stakeholders) in the behavior of the measured, stimulating competition among them, virtuously orienting their actions, and in any case making them accountable for how they perform[76].

Despites all these features, the capacity of performance-based measurements to stimulate improvement is much less straightforward than it might

74 There is not such a universal consensus. The notion of improvement carries the burden of ideology and history: see, for all, Paul Slack, *The Invention of Improvement: Information and Material Progress in Seventeenth-Century England* (OUP 2014) esp. 1–14.

75 'What gets measured gets done' is for instance the title of one of the sections of final reports by the United Nations on the MDGs: United Nations, 'The Millennium Development Goals Report 2015' (2015) 10, <https://www.un.org/millenniumgoals/2015_MDG_Report/pdf/MDG%202015%20rev%20(July%201).pdf> (accessed 10 January 2023).

76 Marta Infantino, 'Global Indicators', in Sabino Cassese (ed), *Research Handbook on Global Administrative Law* (EE 2016) 347–367, at 356; Kevin E. Davis, Benedict Kingsbury, Sally Engle Merry, 'Introduction: Global Governance by Indicators', in Kevin E. Davis, Angelina Fisher, Benedict Kingsbury, Sally Engle Merry (eds), *Governance by Indicators. Global Power through Quantification and Rankings* (OUP 2012) 3–28.

seem. At least three problematic aspects help to explain why this is the case – and why the myth of improvement through measurement is constantly retold in spite of the contradictory evidence supporting it.

A first problem arises with regard to the very definition of (good/bad performances and therefore) improvement. As noted a few lines above, the notion of improvement implies an ideal to be pursued. Especially in cases in which the measurers aim to nudge others into improvement (even though, as noted above[77], they often have little pre-existing expertise or authority in the field), that ideal may not be fully agreed upon or shared by all the actors involved. For instance, according to tech companies and data vendors, getting people to stay connected for longer and to spend more time engaging online, while data about their performances are constantly tracked, pursues the aim of providing them with better services and offers that are more 'personalized' (i.e., mass-customized on the basis of algorithmic correlations) in line with their needs. However, online tracking also furthers other goals – such as obtaining better knowledge from consumer data in order to exploit vulnerabilities, create unwanted needs, setting prices as high as consumers profiled are willing to pay, and also predict and manipulate desires and opinions –, not all of which could be defined as an improvement from the consumers' perspective[78]. In other cases, the ideal against which performance is measured may be tainted by bias or ideology. The DB again provides a good illustration of this point. The DB reports measured countries' performances in terms of the business friendliness of their legal architecture on the basis of a myriad of assumptions. Assumptions included the idea that the common law tradition is more conducive to economic growth than the civil law one, that all legal systems can be viewed as variations of either common law or civil law, that rules can be easily transplanted from one place to the other, that less regulation is always better, and that there is one 'right' answer to any business's legal problem, which invariably coincides with the common law solution[79]. These assumptions were

77 See above in this Chapter, Section 2.4.

78 The misalignment between online profiling and consumers' interest has been noted by many: cf. Christine Riefa, 'Protecting Vulnerable Consumers in the Digital Single Market' (2022) 33 *European Business Law Review* 607–634; Lauren E. Willis, 'Deception by Design' (2020) 34 *Harvard Journal of Law & Technology* 116–190; Burk, *supra* fn 56; Couldry and Mejias, *supra* fn 4, 83–112; Shoshana Zuboff, *The Age of Surveillance Capitalism* (Public Affairs 2019); Deborah Lupton, *The Quantified Self: A Sociology of Self-Tracking* (Polity 2016) 64–87.

79 See, among the many, André Broome, Alexandra Homolar, Matthias Kranke, 'Bad science: International organizations and the indirect power of global benchmarking' (2018) 24 *European Journal of International Relations* 514–539; Nuno Garoupa, Carlos Gómez Ligüerre, Lela Mélon, *Legal Origins and the Efficiency Dilemma* (Routledge 2016);

clearly in line with the WB's promotion of neo-liberal globalization; however, they were also all debatable, if not plainly wrong[80]. Unsurprisingly, many noted that countries' improved performances in the DB did not reflect improved performances in the real world – not even according to the limited meaning of 'improvement' embraced by the WB[81].

This leads us to a second, structural problem in using performance-based measurements as tools for improvement. No matter what notion of improvement is embraced, quantitative assessments invite those who are subject to them to focus their efforts on the metric being counted so as to produce better results. However, whatever is being counted always captures only a fraction (often, the most easily countable fraction) of what the measured is doing. As a result, what often happens is that the act of counting focuses the attention of the measured on a few variables, while interest is lost in any dimension that, although it may be crucial, is not being counted. By way of illustration, a measurement for legal research that only rewards English-language monographs and articles on indexed journals drives researchers to write in English and to submit papers to these journals, thereby underestimating the quantity and quality of research published in a different format or language[82]. The example also manifests how, in acting upon the world and changing the behavior of the measureds, the act of measurement easily generates self-fulfilling prophecies: the adhesion by (some of) the measured to the chosen variable confirms ex post, and reinforces, the formal validity of the variable, irrespective of its actual meaningfulness[83]. It is clear from this that measures often tell us little about, and lead to little change in, the dynamics underlying the process that is measured. Rather, what measures track (and stimulate) is improvement in *measured* performance. Performance-based measures monitor the measureds

---

Michaels, *supra* fn 61, 786–787; Bénédicte Fauvarque-Cosson and Anne-Julie Kerhuel, 'Is Law an Economic Contest? French Reactions to the Doing Business World Bank Reports and Economic Analysis of the Law' (2009) 57 *American Journal of Comparative Law* 811–829, at 814–815.

80 See the authors quoted *supra* fn 79, as well as those quoted *infra*, fn 81.

81 Cf. Gerard McCormack, 'Why 'Doing Business' with the World Bank May Be Bad for You' (2018) 19 *European Business Organization Law Review* 649–676; Amanda Perry-Kessaris, 'The re-co-construction of legitimacy of/through the Doing Business indicators' (2017) 13 *International Journal of Law in Context* 498–511; Benito Arruñada, 'How Doing Business Jeopardizes Institutional Reform' (2009) 10 *European Business Organization Law Review* 555–574; Benito Arruñada, 'Pitfalls to Avoid When Measuring the Institutional Environment: Is "Doing Business" Damaging Business?' (2007) 35 *Journal of Comparative Economics* 729–747.

82 Chapter 7 (Poland).

83 For all, see Espeland and Sauder, *supra* fn 42, 11–12.

with regard to chosen variables, rewarding good performers with higher results, but they are unable to appreciate whether these efforts came at a cost, whether unmeasured variables worsened, and whether the overall performance is (not only nominally better, but also) actually better – or even simply good[84].

A third additional reason why performance-based measurements may not improve performance (other than in relation to the measure itself) stems from the unintended effects of social quantification. As noted above, measurements tend to focus the attention of the measureds on what is counted, and to divert it from variables and aspects that are not counted. It is well-known that this mechanism generates, besides self-fulfilling prophecies, a number of side-effects. These are not limited to the rather rare cases in which the insistence on the measurement of certain variables exhausts the measured and triggers resistance, including, where this choice is available, disengagement from or active manipulation of the measure (a reaction often documented with self-tracking apps)[85]. There is a much more common unintended effect of performance-based measurements: measures stimulate the adoption by the measureds of gaming strategies and rank-seeking tactics – i.e., a behavior that formally conforms to the ideal embraced by the measure but that implies little or no change in practice[86]. After all, once a measure is in place, what the measured wants is better scores or, in other words, improvement certified by the measurement, as our initial illustration with students' grades reminds us[87]. Therefore, as every actual and former student knows, cheating is a viable option. Whenever one can obtain better scores through minimal or symbolic efforts, or through the manipulation of apparent data and numbers, gaming the measure may turn out to be the most efficient and cost-effective approach for dealing with it, as such a choice implies no change and no cost other than those required by the act of cheating itself. Needless to say, gaming strategies and rank-seeking tactics pollute measures, and increase the possibility that the 'improvement' captured by quantitative assessments will not be reflected by any improvement at all in the real world.

All the above takes us back to our initial question. Given that performance-based measures often fail to improve performance, why are they flourishing? In

84 See, for all, Espeland and Sauder, *supra* fn 42, 11–16.

85 Maiju Tanninen, 'Contested Technology: Social Scientific Perspectives of Behaviour-Based Insurance' (2020) *Big Data & Society* 1–14, at 8; Hugo Jeanningros and Liz McFall, 'The Value of Sharing: Branding and Behaviour in a Life and Health Insurance Company' (2020) *Big Data & Society* 1–15, at 9–11; Couldry and Mejias, *supra* fn 4, 193–194.

86 Espeland and Sauder, *supra* fn 42, 29–33.

87 See above in this Chapter, Section 1.

order to answer the question it would be necessary to reach beyond the mantra of measurements that result in efficiency gains, and looking for other rationales justifying the all-encompassing turn to social quantification. What we can do, on the basis of the information provided by the available literature and chapters herein collected, is point out to some of the most frequently occurring patterns for establishing measures of one's own or of others' performance.

Perhaps the clearest pattern of all is the following: measuring performance often allows someone to control what would otherwise be beyond anybody's control. To exemplify, in the West it is (in principle) not allowed to encroach upon judges' independence and researchers' scientific freedom, but it is permitted to measure their performance. Forcing states to adhere to standards that are only partially enshrined in international treaties (such as those on corruption, the rule of law, and openness to foreign investment) is not possible, yet the measurement of their performance against these standards is. Requiring multinational companies to abide by ESG/CSR obligations is impossible in the absence of any domestic or international obligation to do so, but involving them in (self-)measuring exercises is feasible and laudable. Manipulating people's desires is not commendable, while measuring online users' preferences and using this data to provide them with more 'personalized' services and offers is. From this point of view, measuring performance allows control (some would say: surveillance) to creep into areas in which regulation is either forbidden or unfeasible, while also reinforcing (or, as it often happens in cases involving the measurement of others' performances, actually creating) the authority of the measurer vis-à-vis the measured[88].

Beyond controlling what would otherwise be unchecked, many other rationales underly the spread of performance-based measurement. Especially when done in relation to one's own performance, measurement often offers a way of proving or advertising to the public one's more or less serious commitment to improvement[89]. Sometimes, especially when the performance of others

88 It is in this light that many commentators emphasize that measurements are a 'technology of governance': see, among the many, Judith G. Kelley and Beth A. Simmons (eds), *The Power of Global Performance Indicators* (CUP 2020); Nehal Bhuta, Debora V. Malito, Gaby Umbach, 'Introduction: Of Numbers and Narratives – Indicators in Global Governance and the Rise of a Reflexive Indicator Culture', in Debora V. Malito, Gaby Umbach, Nehal Bhuta (eds), *The Palgrave Handbook of Indicators in Global Governance* (Palgrave 2018) 1–29; Broome and Quirk, *supra* fn 4; Cooley, *supra* fn 72; Engle Merry, *supra* fn 60.

89 Suffice it to think of domestic measurements of justice and education: see Chapters 1–7 in Part 1. But this is also the case of self-assessments by corporations of their respect for ESG/CSR standards, which are often carried out in order to showcase companies' efforts and to capture the attention of ethically-minded consumers, while avoiding any real obligation: see Chapter 14 and Auld and Galbrensen, *supra* fn 23, 398.

is being measured, measurement is a commercial strategy that enables the measurer to exist or survive in a crowded and competitive marketplace[90]. On other occasions – no matter whose performances are measured –, some measures are created out of other pre-existing measures, as a way for the former to imitate or counter the latter[91]. And sometimes, quite simply, one measures because one can. The dataism affecting our contemporary societies actually invites the qualitative aspects of human experience to be converted into quantitative (and possibly computer-ready) information whenever possible[92].

2.6 ... *and What Effects They Produce*

We saw in the two previous sections that narratives of (self-)improvement and efficiency gains tell only part of the success story of performance-based measures. That story also includes other motives and rationales, many of which are not related (or are even inversely related) to modifying real-world performances. What we still have to see is what effects social measurements actually produce in practice. We will deal in this section with the most mundane consequences of performance-based measures, leaving to the next section an analysis of the broader impact of social quantification as a regulatory technique.

To our usual caveat about the limited and incomplete amount of information collected in this book, we should add here another caution. Tracing the effects of performance-based measurements is extremely hard, because in order to do so it would be necessary to demonstrate patterns of causality between the measure and some real-word change; however, these are often impossible to prove. There are several reasons for this[93]. Much of the effects of quantitative measures often remain invisible, involving imperceptible shifts in the identity and power of those who produce and use them, in the vocabulary

90 Cooley, *supra* fn 72, 21–22 ("An NGO or IO might also use rankings and ratings to 'flag-pant' or to brand themselves as the pivotal organizations advocating a particular cause or global concern. Generating a ranking, rating, or index about that issue can be an invaluable tool in staking the organization's claim to govern that issue and advance the solutions to the problems in question [22]. Branding is especially necessary in what is now a crowded market for advocacy organizations [...] [C]reating a unique index or ranking can establish the credibility of a particular NGO in an issue area and can be a critical vehicle for external fundraising").

91 For some illustrations about the spin-off projects and the alternative initiatives that the DB has generated, see above in this Chapter, Section 5.1, as well as Chapter 1, Section 4.2.

92 The meaning of dataism is not unequivocal, but is generally associated with the idea that data (is the only thing that) matters: Yuval Noah Harari, *Homo Deus. A Brief History of Tomorrow* (Penguin 2015) 428–462; Steve Lohr, *Data-ism: The Revolution Transforming Decising Making, Consumer Behavior, and Almost Everything Else* (HarperCollins 2015).

93 On these problems, see Infantino, *supra* note 76, 356–360.

of policy-making, as well as in the way in which problems are defined and responses are elicited. No matter how important these shifts are, their occurrence may be unconscious, unverbalized, undisclosed – and therefore very hard to document. The opposite may hold true as well: lip-service may be paid to measurements when justifying some change, even if these measurements played practically no role in that change. The adoption by the measureds of gaming strategies and rank-seeking tactics further complicates the picture, obliging to distinguish between *measured* change and *real-word* change. In addition, even when it is possible to detect some real-world modification, it is still difficult to unequivocally ascribe the observed modification to a measure, because change is always determined by a multiplicity of factors, of which performance-based measurements are but one. Last but not the least, investigating all of the above would require working with methodological tools that are beyond lawyers' (and surely our own) expertise.

Be it as it may, the previous chapters and the available literature provide us with some information about the real-world consequences of performance-based measurements. Let us try to summarize the results, starting from the effects of measurements on those who are subject to them and then looking at their effects on other actors.

As far as the measured are concerned, sometimes performance-based measurements clearly come with strings attached. Judges whose activity is not well evaluated may have their careers stall in Brazil, China, India, Mexico and Switzerland[94]. A law school whose members carry out (what the measure assesses as) outstanding research in Poland may secure special funding, and conversely faculties whose members do not perform well may be denied funding[95]. Chinese social credit initiatives reward good performers and deny or heighten the costs of access to services for bad performers[96].

---

94 See Chapters 2 (Brazil), 3 (Mexico), 4 (India), 5 (Switzerland) and 9 (China).

95 See Chapter 7 (Poland).

96 See Chapter 9 (China). Other examples include banks advising prospective or actual clients that their creditworthiness will be measured by FICO® or equivalent scores, or platforms, search engines and apps informing users through their terms and conditions about the collection, processing and uses of data relating to their behavior (subject to the special characteristic that, in such cases, users' acceptance of data collection is often the but-for condition, and in actual fact the consideration, for the service received). See, on all these points, Chapters 8 (South Africa) and 13 (Europe), as well as Couldry and Mejias, *supra* fn 4, 101–105; Catherine O'Neil, *Weapons of Math Destruction. How Big Data Increases Inequality and Threatens Democracy* (Crown 2016) 141–160; Frank Pasquale, *The Black Box Society. The Secret Algorithms That Control Money and Information* (Harvard University Press 2015) esp. 1–14.

Most often, however, measures do not trigger any official consequence: consider for instance the quantitative assessments of multinational companies' compliance with ESG/CSR standards, and the WB's measurement of states' performances in promoting foreign investments[97]. Nevertheless, the absence of foreseen consequences does not imply that such consequences do not exist. As highlighted in the Introduction[98] and repeatedly seen throughout this chapter[99], by combining apparently objective descriptions with evidence-based prescriptive suggestions, measures easily become performative, pressuring the measured, to the very least, to devise strategies to cope with them, ranging from compliance attempts to gaming techniques to resistance tactics[100]. Our contributors are divided as to their judgment on the overall ability of performance-based measurements to trigger beneficial effects for the measureds: some authors are more enthusiastic, while others are deeply critical[101]. The divide, however, seems to be associated more with the personal postures and beliefs of each author rather than with empirical evidence (that, as stated above, is often hard or impossible to get).

The impact of performance-based measurements on actors other than the measureds is quite a different issue. The uses (and effects) of quantitative measures by third parties may be intended or not: very often, those who measure their own performance conceive of the initiative as a purely internal procedure, while those who measure others' performances anticipate an interest in the measurement on the part of some stakeholders. This is particularly clear where quantitative assessments are only available upon subscription (as it is common in the field of academic rankings, ratings, and personal credit scoring), as well as in cases involving automated online profiling, since the transfer and re-use of data lie at the core of the digital economy. However, some

97 See Chapters 14 (Europe/globe) and 15 (globe).

98 Chapter 1, Section 1.

99 See above in this Chapter, Sections 2.1, 2.3–2.5.

100 The results of these strategies may sometimes be tragic. Juan Carlos Botero, Angela Maria Pinzon-Rondon, Christine S. Pratt, How, 'When and Why Do Governance, Justice and Rule of Law Indicators Fail Public Policy Decision Making in Practice?' (2016) 8 *Hague Journal on the Rule of Law* 51, 54–58, report how a quantitative incentive established in 2002 for policemen fighting against the Fuerzas Armadas Revolucionarias de Colombia (FARC) – and directly linking salary increases to the number of guerrilla fighters killed in action – resulted in the mass killings of innocent civilians whose corpses, dressed in FARC uniforms, were then claimed to be those of FARC combatants. The practice is known as the 'fake positive' scandal, for which Colombia was investigated before the International Criminal Court: see the website <icc-cpi.int/colombia> (accessed 10 January 2023).

101 Cf. for instance Chapters 3 (Mexico), 6 (South Africa), 10 (Japan) and 12 (Africa), with the findings in Chapters 2 (Brazil), 7 (Poland), 8 (Africa), 13 (Europe).

instances of measurements of others' performance explicitly forbid or caution against the re-use by third parties of the results obtained, as often occurs in relation to global measurements of states' performances[102]. Nonetheless, no matter what the position of the measurer is, uses by (and effects on) third parties of measures are frequent, and usually play a fundamental role in solidifying the success and the legitimacy of the measures themselves.

This is because, as simplified, decontextualized and easy-to-use information, measurements can travel long distances and end up in unforeseeable places. After they have been produced, quantitative assessments often take on a life of their own: they may be appropriated and used by anybody, for purposes that may be more or less distant from those that originally inspired their creation. Aside from the example of school grades[103], and surfing across the illustrations herein collected, we only need to consider how the numbers provided by corporate rankings of journals, articles and individual academics are relied upon by (researchers themselves, universities, publishers, and) domestic authorities in their own evaluations of the performance of higher education systems[104]. We already saw that the DB inspired several spin-off projects and even some concurrent initiatives[105]; what we should add now is that the scores produced each year by the DB were also used by WB offices for assessing countries' eligibility for loans, identifying areas for reform and verifying whether countries had implemented the conditions attached to loans[106]. Outside the examples made in this book, suffice it to think of how sovereign credit ratings are relied on by governments, central banks, investors, and voters on a daily basis to assess the trustworthiness of sovereign bond issuers and, more generally, the solidity of a given country's economy[107]. It is well-known, especially in common law countries, that a plethora of actors over and above banks (including employers, insurance companies, and landlords)

102 For some examples, see Infantino, *supra* fn 31, 215.

103 See above in this Chapter, Section 1.

104 See Chapter 7 (Poland).

105 See above in this Chapter, Section 2.1.

106 Tor Krever, 'Quantifying law. Legal indicator projects and the reproduction of neoliberal common sense' (2013) 34 *Third World Quarterly* 131–150, at 145. The scores of the WBL, one of the offshoots of the DB, are currently included in the formula used by the US development agency Millennium Challenge Corporation in order to distribute its funds: Powell, *supra* fn 33, 779.

107 Ahmed Naciri, *Sovereign Credit Rating: Questionable Methodologies* (Routledge 2017); Rawi Abdelal and Mark Blyth, 'Just who put you in charge? We did. CRAs and the politics of ratings', in Cooley and Snyder (eds), *supra* fn 72, 39–59; Mauro Bussani, 'Credit Rating Agencies' Accountability: Short Notes on a Global Issue' (2010) 10 *Global Jurist* 1–12.

resort to FICO® and similar credit scores for evaluating the overall creditworthiness of their prospective counterparties[108]. Similarly, where algorithms are used to measure online performances, it is equally well documented that these data are repeatedly re-sold, re-used and aggregated to help predict people's behavior (further heightening the risk of social conservativism, the perpetuation of historical and systemic bias, and social exclusion of the most vulnerable and disadvantaged)[109]. Sometimes uses of measurements by third parties may be counter-intuitive. One anecdote concerning an episode experienced directly by a Colombian colleague when she was conducting a field study for an NGO[110] is telling in this regard. While interviewing the NGO staff, she suddenly heard an employee of the NGO staff shout 'Hooray! We are a failed State!'. The employee was celebrating the fact that Colombia qualified (again) as a failed state according to the 'Fragile States Index' published by the American NGO Fund for Peace[111]. What was the reason for celebration? The bad result ensured that the Colombian NGO could continue to seek international funding.

It is clear that more research, possibly combining legal expertise with other methodological lenses, is needed to better trace the consequences of performance-based measurements, both for the measured and for other stakeholders. Our findings nevertheless enable us to highlight that measures often change the set of expectations and incentives for the actors concerned, producing effects that in many cases are comparable to, and even more effective than, those associated with regulation. The next section will investigate exactly how and to what extent performance-based measures relate to the law.

108 Burk, *supra* fn 56, 1163–1166; O'Neil, *supra* fn 96, 141–160; Pasquale, *supra* fn 96, 24–26; Citron and Pasquale, *supra* fn 109.

109 Among the many, see Burk, *supra* fn 56, 1163–1166, 1181–1186; Zuboff, *supra* fn 78; Safiya Umoja Noble, *Algorithms of Oppression. How Search Engines Reinforce Racism* (NYU Press 2018); Virginia Eubanks, *Automating Inequality. How High-Tech Tools Profile, Police and Punish the Poor* (St. Martin Press 2018); Solon Barocas and Andrew D. Selbst, 'Big Data's Disparate Impact' (2016) 104 *California Law Review* 671–732; O'Neil, *supra* fn 96; Danielle Keats Citron and Frank Pasquale, 'The Scored Society: Due Process for Automated Predictions' (2014) 89 *Washington Law Review* 1–33.

110 Lina Fernanda Buchely Ibarra, 'Indicators as a Form of Resistance' (2014) 25 *International Law Journal (Universidad Javeriana)* 225–265, at 226.

111 See the website <https://fragilestatesindex.org/> (accessed 10 January 2023).

3 Cross-Cutting Observations

It is apparent from the previous sections that social quantification in the form of performance-based measurement is widespread and operates as a technology of distance: it proliferates in communities of strangers, whenever the need arises for replacing other forms of social control with some neutral and rapid tool for managing and channeling social behavior[112]. We also saw that, once measures exist, they often trigger (intended and unintended) behavioral changes in the measureds and other relevant stakeholders, thus modifying the world in which they operate. Due to this tendency to become performative and to change (while also being changed by) the reality they apply to, social quantification studies have long noted that performance-based measures may easily turn into tools for governance and regulation, controlling and spreading standards for behavior in ways akin to (and often more effective than) what is traditionally conceived of as law[113].

In the pages that follow, Section 3.1 will survey the available literature, explaining in what sense legal metrics can be defined as a regulatory technique. Section 3.2 will examine and attempt to single out the characteristic features of performance-based measures as regulatory tools. By shedding light on the benefits and challenges that come with legal metrics, the analysis will prompt the question as to whether and how this regulatory power can be controlled. Section 3.3 will therefore investigate how and to what extent regulation through performance-based measurements currently is, and could in the future be, regulated.

3.1 *Legal Metrics as a Regulatory Technique*

It is well-known that people, including lawyers, use the words 'governance' and 'regulation' (not to speak about 'law') with quite different meanings. This is

---

112 See the authors quoted *supra* fn 4.

113 In addition to the authors quoted *supra* fn 88, see Pedro R. Borges Fortes, Pablo Marcello Baquero, David Restrepo Amariles, 'Artificial intelligence risks and algorithmic regulation' (2022) 13 *European Journal of Risk Regulation* 357–372; Lena Ulbricht and Karen Yeung, 'Algorithmic Regulation: A Maturing Concept for Investigating Regulation *of* and *through* Algorithms' (2022) 16 *Regulation & Governance* 3–22; Molly K. Land, 'The Problem of Platform Law: Pluralistic Legal Ordering on Social Media', in Berman (ed), *supra* fn 36, 975–994; Broome, Homolar, Kranke, *supra* fn 79; Mathias M. Siems and David Nelken, 'Global social indicators and the concept of legitimacy' (2017) 13 *International Journal of Law in Context* 436–449; Davis, Kingsbury, Merry, *supra* fn 76; Mireille Hildebrandt, *Smart Technologies and the End(s) of Law: Novel Entanglements of Law and Technology* (EE 2015) 11.

not the place to enter into the debate about the definition of these terms; for our limited purposes we embrace the authoritative suggestion that governance is "about providing, distributing, and regulating"[114], while regulation refers to a large array of elements, including politics, policies, (judicial, quasi-judicial, extra-judicial) nudges, institutions, compliance, and formal and informal controls[115]. What matters here is that performance-based measures have the ability to project their (often unarticulated) ideal views onto the measured as well as onto other stakeholders, and to stimulate from them reactions that reinforce the validity and cogency of these ideals. In this regard, insofar as they embody principles and values that are perceived of and enforced by the relevant community as binding, performance-based measures may well be said not only to be a governance technique, but also to have normative implications. To some extent, quantitative assessments may even be regarded as more powerful tools than regulation, insofar they simultaneously articulate a standard for behavior and apply it, rewarding compliance and sanctioning breaches[116].

This regulatory potential of legal metrics is indirectly confirmed by a circumstance that we repeatedly noted in the previous sections[117]: many of the performance-based measurements mentioned in the volume flourish in areas that are not disciplined by official law or in which the measurer has no official power or authority to intervene. These performance-based measurements seem therefore to work in the interstices of, and as a substitute for, traditional regulation in domains where the latter is absent or in which the measurer lacks regulatory power.

Most importantly, the conclusion that performance-based measurements may work as a regulatory technique resonates with the findings of the many social sciences studies on the implications of quantification[118], as well as of the few researches by legal scholars into measures in the social world[119]. For

114 John Braithwaite, Cary Coglianese, David Levi-Faur, 'Can regulation and governance make a difference?' (2007) 1 *Regulation & Governance* 1–7, at 3; see also David Levi-Faur, 'Regulation and Regulatory Governance', in David Levi-Faur (ed), *Handbook on the Politics of Regulation* (EE 2011) 3–21, at 3; Sabino Cassese, 'Administrative Law Without the State? The Challenge of Global Regulation' (2005) 37 *NYU Journal of International Law and Politics* 663–694.

115 See Richard H. Thaler and Cass R. Sunstein, *Nudge. Improving Decisions About Health, Wealth and Happiness* (1st edn 2008, Penguin 2021); Levi-Faur, *supra* note 114, 3 ff.

116 Davis, Kingsbury, Merry, *supra* fn 60, 18–19. This ability is particularly strengthened whenever the measurement is performed by an algorithm: see Burk, *supra* fn 56, as well as *infra*, fn 133.

117 See above in this Chapter, Sections 2.4, 2.5 and 3.

118 See the authors quoted *supra* fn 88.

119 See Chapter 1, Sections 4.2 and 4.3.

instance, the legal literature on indicators often notes that indicators "hold an intrinsic normative quality"[120], "function as implicit or even explicit standards"[121], operate as "regulatory devices"[122], are "comparable to law"[123] or even constitute "soft law"[124] themselves. The same kind of remarks are nowadays commonly made with regard to algorithmic and AI-driven quantification. The revolutionary intuition by Lawrence Lessig that code acts as law insofar as it provides a socio-technical infrastructure that determines what people can do and shapes their mutual expectations for interaction[125], is now routinely conveyed by the idea that code produces "algo norms"[126], "algorithmic law"[127] and "algorithmic regulation"[128]. We therefore stand on the shoulders of giants when we claim that performance-based measurements may qualify as "new forms of regulation [that] are fit subjects for legal research and teaching whether or not they are conceived of as 'law'"[129].

---

120 Debora V. Malito, Nehal Bhuta, Gaby Umbach, 'Conclusions: Knowing and Governing', in Malito, Umbach, Bhuta (eds), *supra* fn 88, 503–512, at 507.

121 Krever, *supra* fn 94, 132; along the same lines, see also Davis, Kingsbury, Merry, *supra* fn 76, 15; Davis, Kingsbury, Merry, *supra* fn 60, 18–19; Benoît Frydman, 'Prendre les standards et les indicateurs au sérieux', in Frydman and Van Waeyenberge (eds), *supra* fn 26, 5–68, at 21–25.

122 Sabino Cassese and Lorenzo Casini, 'The Regulation of Global Indicators', in Davis, Fisher, Kingsbury, Engle Merry (eds), *supra* fn 76, 465–474, at 466; see also Benoît Frydman and William Twining, 'Preface. A symposium on global law, legal pluralism and legal indicators' (2015) 57 *Journal of Legal Pluralism & Unofficial Law* 1–5, at 5.

123 Davis, Kingsbury, Merry, *supra* fn 60, 2; see also Judith G. Kelley and Beth A. Simmons, 'Politics by Number: Indicators as Social Pressure in International Relations' (2015) 59 *American Journal of Political Science* 55–70, at 59 (noting that indicators "have effects akin to regulation").

124 Murthy, *supra* fn 61, 390; see also Mauro Bussani, 'Deglobalizing Rule of Law and Democracy: Hunting Down Rhetoric Through Comparative Law' (2019) 67 *American Journal of Comparative Law* 701–744, esp. at 718–720; David Restrepo Amariles, 'Legal Indicators, Global Law and Legal Pluralism: An Introduction' (2015) 47 *Journal of Legal Pluralism and Unofficial Law* 9–21, at 17; Engle Merry, *supra* fn 60, 11.

125 Lawrence Lessig, *Code and Other Laws of Cyberspace, Version 2.0* (Basic Books 2006) esp. 77–84.

126 Håkan Hydén, 'AI, Norms, Big Data, and the Law' (2020) 7 *Asian Journal of Law and Society* 409–436.

127 Catá Backer and McQuilla, *supra* fn 23, 1; see also Hildebrandt, *supra* fn 113, 11–12.

128 Borges Fortes, Baquero, Restrepo Amariles, *supra* fn 113; Ulbricht and Yeung, *supra* fn 113; Karen Yeung and Martin Lodge (eds) *Algorithmic Regulation* (OUP 2019); Mireille Hildebrandt, 'Algorithmic Regulation and the Rule of Law' (2018) 276 *Philosophical Transactions of the Royal Society A: Mathematical, Physical and Engineering Sciences* 20170355; James Grimmelmann, 'Note, Regulation by Software' (2005) 114 *Yale Law Journal* 1719–1742.

129 Frydman and Twining, *supra* fn 122, 5.

3.2 *Ruling by Numbers: Features and Challenges*

As a regulatory technique, performance-based measures have some distinctive features, the strengths and weaknesses of which deserve to be highlighted.

Starting with the strengths, a first specificity of performance-based measures is related to the way in which the measurements act upon the world. As already recalled[130], performance-based measurements have the rare ability to embody a standard of behavior, to provide carrot-and-stick incentives to comply with that standard, and to verify the level of compliance, all at the same time (and all the more so where the measurement is automated).

A second strength of performance-based measures arises from the fact that they are usually conceived of as technical tools providing neutral, empirical and evidence-based knowledge about the social phenomena they apply to. The allegedly technical nature of quantification initiatives implies that the solutions they offer are often eagerly accepted by their addressees and relevant stakeholders as a reasonable basis for policy-making, decisions and actions.

Precisely because they are conceived of as technical exercises, a third strength of performance-based measures lies in their political agility (or invisibility, if you will). The establishment of a quantitative assessment does not typically require any political decision or diplomatic bargaining, and its management is not constrained by requirements of good regulatory governance such as transparency and participation, since "the traditional contentions inherent in the formation of policy choices and the legal structures that support them [are] transferred to the development of data, its analytics, and the algorithms that are meant to reflect judgment"[131]. Simply put, the alleged technicality of quantification helps to insulate it from political scrutiny and legal challenges[132]. Whenever quantification is automated, the significance of all these features – the combination of regulation-control-enforcement, the rapidity, technicality, invisibility and unchallengeability of the measuring process – increases exponentially[133].

As the three points of strength listed above suggest, performance-based measurements also have darker sides. Let us start by noting that, as is emphasized

130 See the authors quoted *supra* fn 116.

131 Catá Backer, *supra* fn 22, 166. Political invisibility may explain why, as already noted (see above in this Chapter, Sections 2.4, 2.5, 3 and 3.1), reliance on performance-based measurements is widespread in contexts that are not disciplined by official law.

132 On all these features, cf. Infantino, *supra* fn 76, 356; Davis, Kingsbury, Merry, *supra* fn 76.

133 Among others, see Burk, *supra* fn 56; Andrew D. Selbst and Solon Barocas, 'The Intuitive Appeal of Explainable Machines' (2018) 87 *Fordham Law Review* 1087–1139, at 1092–1096; Barocas and Selbst. *supra* fn 109, 671–731, at 677–694; Hildebrandt, *supra* fn 113, 11–12; Citron and Pasquale, *supra* fn 109, 5–6, 11–16; Grimmelmann, *supra* fn 127, 1729–1730.

by a plethora of researches on social quantification[134], measurements convey objective and empirical knowledge on what they measure only inasmuch as they are able to capture comprehensive information concerning the measured phenomena. More often than not, measures are not able to do so: as fast, top-down and routinized forms of control, performance-based measurements rely on standardized and simplified variables (e.g., the number of judgments rendered in a given time span, the impact factor of the journal in which a scientific article is published, web users' online browsing speeds) that require to erase context and complexity to be erased in order to obtain comparable results. Anything that does not fit in with the standardized categories is either forced into them or discarded. In this regard as well, the more quantitative and automated the assessment is, the more inflexible it tends to be, and the more information gets lost in the process.

What is lost in the process is notably a taste for quality: when measuring performance, it does not matter whether the outcome of a judicial opinion was fair, how good a scientific article is or the purpose of web browsing; at best, these aspects may be taken into account indirectly (for instance, by proxies adding to the picture whether the judgment was reversed, how many citations the article received, and which websites were visited). Measuring, in other words, shifts everybody's attention from the substance of what is done to the form of what can be counted as (having been correctly) done. An anecdotal illustration concerning the transformation of the regulation of university teaching in Italy in the last century shows very well what this shift means (and how it may also change the way in which official regulation is framed and expected to work). One hundred years ago, a 1923 statute regulating higher education in Italy mandated that "[u]niversity professors [...] should teach [...] as many hours a week as required by the nature and the size of the subject matter

---

134 In addition to the seminal works of Desrosières and Porter, cited *supra* fn 4, cf. Siddharth Peter de Souza, *Designing Indicators for a Plural Legal World* (CUP 2022) 27–50, 112–173; Malito, Bhuta, Umbach, *supra* fn 120, 503–512; Restrepo Amariles and McLachlan, *supra* fn 56; Broome, Homolar, Kranke, *supra* fn 79; Wendy Espeland, 'Narrating Numbers', in Richard Rottenburg, Sally Engle Merry, Sung-Joon Park, Johanna Mugler (eds), *The Making of Governmental Knowledge through Quantification* (CUP 2015) 56–75; Broome and Quirk, *supra* fn 4; Merry, *supra* fn 60, 27–43, 212–216; Jack Snyder and Alexander Cooley, 'Conclusion: Rating the ratings craze: From consumer choice to public policy outcomes', in Cooley and Snyder (eds), *supra* fn 72, 178–193; Morten Jerven, *Poor Numbers: How We Are Misled by African Development Statistics and What to Do About It* (Cornell University Press 2013); Davis, Kingsbury, Merry, *supra* fn 76; Krever, *supra* fn 94; Kerry Rittich, 'Governing by Measuring. The Millennium Development Goals in Global Governance', in Hélène Ruiz Fabri, Rüdiger Wolfrum, Jana Gogolin (eds), *Selected Proceedings of the European Society of International Law* (Hart 2010) 463–487; Espeland and Sauder, *supra* fn 42.

taught"[135]. After one century, the corresponding norm (enacted in 2010) provides that "[p]rofessor should teach no less than 350 hours per year"[136], further adding that "[t]he bylaws of each university determines how professors self-declare their own teaching activities and how the university checks professors' actual compliance with their teaching obligations"[137].

The above example also demonstrates how the shift from substance to form implies a heightened significance of evidence. Doing something bears little relevance for a measurement if there is no proof of what has been done. Usually, proof should be given using the standardized forms of evidence (e.g., self-reporting, third-party audits, log-ins, mechanical recordings) that are defined by the metrics themselves as the only relevant evidence. With respect to evidence too, whenever a measure incorporates some technological elements, the overall rigidity of the system increases. If performance has to be proved by filling out a form, which is then automatically checked by a machine, any failure to fill out the form or by the machine reading equates to a bad performance, no matter how good performance actually was. Additional side-effects of this emphasis on form and evidence are a rise in the costs of producing, checking and storing evidentiary requirements, and the ease with which the system can be gamed or manipulated by anyone who is sufficiently smart or well-resourced to do so.

We already noted that all of the methodological elements mentioned so far – the choice about which variables should be counted, and how, relying on which evidence, provided by whom, and so on and so forth – are important in determining the overall effects of measurements[138]. These choices are influenced by empirical and practical constraints as much as they are influenced by assumptions about what good/bad performance means, what factors are causally relevant in determining improvement, and what ideal world the measurement should strive to realize[139]. From this point of view, any performance-based measure embodies a specific stance vis-à-vis the measured phenomena that is determined by both the technical and political constraints that affect those who conceive of and manage the measures. The less transparent a measure is as regards its underlying choices, the more difficult it is to unpack and contest its results, all the more so where the measurement is expressed

135 Article 84 of the Italian royal decree of 30 September 1923, no. 2102 (Law on higher education).

136 Article 6(2), Law of 30 December 2010, no. 240, Law on the organization of universities.

137 Article 6(7), Law of 30 December 2010, no. 240, Law on the organization of universities.

138 See above in this Chapter, Section 2.4.

139 See above in this Chapter, Section 2.4.

in statistical language or performed automatically by algorithms and codes (whether copyrighted or not)[140].

The technicality characterizing analog and automated performance-based measurements has other consequences. As specialized and complex artifacts, measures typically require, and imply the formation of, a technocracy capable of conceiving them and a bureaucracy capable of managing them. Experts in social quantification are usually needed in order to conceive the quantitative assessment; after it has been established, measures have to be repeated, the methodology has to be fine-tuned, and the results have to be interpreted and packaged in a publishable format by dedicated personnel. Specialized personnel may also be required to manage the procedures for providing interested parties with rights of access, participation and review. However, the creation and involvement of a technocratic bureaucracy entail specific effects. On the one hand, the fact that many fundamental methodological choices are left in the hands of statisticians, programmers and data scientists not only depoliticizes decisions that may deserve to be politically negotiated, but also adds a further layer of opacity to the measuring process, because technical decisions often lay beyond the comprehension of laymen. On the other hand, the need for bureaucracy in order to manage metrics not only empowers invisible and politically unaccountable personnel, but also further entrenches a managerial mode of governance in which issues of substance and methodology are transformed into routinized controls to check that procedures and forms are respected. The side-effects produced by this managerial rule by experts may be limited when the empowerment of bureaucrats occurs within well-entrenched institutions whose conduct is constrained by clear administrative rules and practices. However, when bureaucratization occurs in the context of measures set up by other actors – such as international organizations, NGOs, and corporations – the power of technocracy may be constrained by nothing and may be accountable to none[141].

140 Among the many, see Burk, *supra* fn 56, 301–302; Catá Backer, *supra* fn 22, 166; Selbst and Barocas, *supra* fn 133, 1093–1094; Pasquale, *supra* fn 96, 8, 16; Grimmelmann, *supra* fn 133, 1736.

141 This point too has been noted by many: see, among others, de Souza, *supra* fn 134, 112–162; Catá Backer and McQuilla, *supra* fn 23, 16; Catá Backer, *supra* fn 22, 166–167; David McGrogan, 'Human Rights Indicators and the Sovereignty of Technique' (2016) 27 *European Journal of International Law* 385–408; Davis, Kingsbury, Merry, *supra* fn 60, 13–14; Merry, *supra* fn 60, 27–35; Snyder and Cooley, *supra* fn 134, 178; Davis, Kingsbury, Merry, *supra* fn 76, 19–21; Cassese and Casini, *supra* fn 122, 465–466; Restrepo Amariles, *supra* fn 124, 12–14; Jennifer Shkabatur, 'A Global Panopticon? The Changing Role of International Organizations in the Information Age' (2011) 33 *Michigan Journal of International Law* 159–214.

To sum up, performance quantification as a regulatory technique is based on a compliance-based analysis that conveys and enforces standards of behavior that are hardly visible, hardly negotiable, and hardly challengeable. It is reasonable to wonder whether there are ways to control what performance-based measurements do.

3.3 *Regulating Legal Metrics?*

When searching for legal rules applying to performance-based measures, it is necessary to make a distinction between legal metrics that are adopted by domestic actors, whether as state agencies, corporations or NGOs, and metrics adopted by actors that are not subject to domestic jurisdiction, such as international organizations and other hybrid subjects of international law.

Let us start from the latter case. In the current absence of any call for an international treaty on the field, and considering the general regulatory and jurisdictional immunity enjoyed by actors in the international arena, it seems that performance-based measures produced by international organizations and alike are bound by no rule other than self-made ones[142].

Quite different is the situation in the former case, since producers of domestic legal metrics are clearly subject to their own national laws. Although, to our knowledge, no legal system has adopted a set of rules specifically designed for performance-based metrics, a number of substantial and procedural obligations may arise from a variety of existing bodies of law, including constitutional and administrative law (whenever the measurer is a public authority), anti-discrimination provisions, privacy regulation and consumer protection laws. Moreover, many legal systems have enacted bans or imposed specific limitations on activities that are directly associated with performance-based measurements.

Bans are quite rare, but they do exist. A simple example comes from the rules that in many places, for historical or cultural reasons, forbid the collection of census data concerning, e.g., sex, religion and ethnicity[143]. Since the Chinese internet censorship has implemented the Great Firewall to block access from users in mainland China to a number of Western websites (such as, most notably, Alphabet's search engine and video repository, and Meta's social media

---

142 See especially Chapter 15.

143 Merry, *supra* fn 60, 14; Louis-Georges Tin, 'Qui a peur des statistiques ethniques', in Isabelle Bruno, Emmanuel Didier, Julien Prévieux (eds), *Stat-Activisme. Comment lutter avec des nombres* (La Découverte 2014) 155–166; William Seltzer and Margo Anderson, 'The Dark Side of Numbers. The Role of Population Data Systems in Human Rights Abuses' (2001) 68 *Social Research* 481–507, at 495.

and messaging application), many quantification activities routinely carried out by tech companies in the West are practically impeded – although similar activities are in practice performed by local actors[144]. With regard to AI-powered measurements, the proposal for a regulation of artificial intelligence currently under discussion in the European Union includes a few prohibitions; for instance, it prohibits the construction or use in the European market of AI systems "for the evaluation or classification of natural persons over a certain period of time based on their social behaviour or known or predicted personal or personality characteristics"[145] (provided that the social score leads to some unjustified discrimination), and "the use of 'real-time' biometric identification systems in publicly accessible spaces by law enforcement authorities or on their behalf for the purpose of law enforcement"[146].

More common is the adoption of selective limitations. Several countries have for instance adopted place rules aimed at limiting the conflict of interest and at fostering transparency in the credit rating industry[147]. In China, many cities that have implemented municipal social credit programs have also enacted regulations providing that the persons measured can check their own scores, report any information that they consider relevant for improving their social credit, and ask for the rectification of any error or mistake[148]. In the US, the Fair Credit Reporting Act requires any person or body that uses information collected by consumer reporting agencies for credit, insurance, or employment purposes, to notify the affected person when any adverse action is taken on the basis of those reports[149]. In the European Union, online platforms must now disclose to users, in an easily comprehensible manner, the parameters and criteria (including those related to the tracking and profiling of users' behavior) according to which the information contained in the platform is

144 For an updated list of the websites that cannot be accessed from mainland China, see <https://ltl-beijing.com/websites-banned-in-china/> (accessed 10 January 2023).

145 Article 5(1), lit (c), European Commission, Proposal for a Regulation of the European Parliament and of the Council laying down harmonised rules on artificial intelligence (Artificial Intelligence Act), July 2022 draft, at <https://artificialintelligenceact.eu/wp-content/uploads/2022/07/AIA-CZ-1st-Proposal-15-July.pdf> (accessed 10 January 2023).

146 Article 5(1), lit (d), European Commission, *supra* fn 145.

147 Cf. the Securities Exchange Act of 1934, Section 15E(d) (15 USCA. 7807) (as amended) in the US, the Regulation (EC) No 1060/2009 of the European Parliament and of the Council of 16 September 2009 on credit rating agencies (as amended) in the EU, and the Interim Measures for the Administration of the Credit Rating Industry adopted in 2019 in China. On the many limitations of these regulatory approaches, see Bussani, *supra* fn 107.

148 Infantino and Wang, *supra* fn 55, 80–85.

149 Fair Credit Reporting Act, 15 USC. §§ 1681–1681x.

prioritised and presented to them[150]. Still in the European Union, the above-mentioned proposal for a regulation of artificial intelligence imposes several obligations (concerning risk management, data governance, transparency, human oversight and accuracy)[151] on producers and users of (what the proposal defines as) high-risk AI systems. Many of these high-risk AI systems are classified as such exactly because they incorporate mechanisms for measuring performances. The list, for instance, includes: systems that could be used in work-related contractual relationships "for task allocation based on individual behavior or personal traits or characteristics and for monitoring and evaluating performance and behavior of persons in such relationships"[152], systems that could be "used by public authorities or on behalf of public authorities to evaluate the eligibility of natural persons for public assistance benefits and services"[153] or that could be used by anybody "to evaluate the creditworthiness of natural persons or establish their credit score"[154], and systems that could be "used by law enforcement authorities or on their behalf for making individual risk assessments of natural persons in order to assess the risk of a natural person for offending or reoffending"[155].

However, the potential of these rules in governing performance-based measurements adopted by domestic actors remains limited. Many of the above bans and obligations have a narrow scope and suffer of well-known shortcomings in their (public and private) enforcement even at the domestic level, i.e., in scenarios in which all the people involved belong to the same jurisdiction[156]. More importantly, the enforceability of domestic rules is seriously undermined

---

150 See Article 27 of the Regulation (EU) 2022/2065 of the European Parliament and of the Council of 19 October 2022 on a Single Market For Digital Services and amending Directive 2000/31/EC (Digital Services Act). According to its Article 93, the Regulation shall apply from February 17, 2024.

151 See articles 8–15, European Commission, *supra* fn 145.

152 Annex III, no. 4, lit (b), European Commission, *supra* fn 145.

153 Annex III, no. 5, lit (a), European Commission, *supra* fn 145.

154 Annex III, no. 5, lit (b), European Commission, *supra* fn 145.

155 Annex III, no. 6, lit (a), European Commission, *supra* fn 145.

156 Limited public and private enforcement is a well-known critique against rules on credit rating agencies, Chinese cities' regulations on social credit, and American rules on consumer credit reporting: Frank Partnoy, 'What's (Still) Wrong with Credit Ratings?' (2017) 92 *Washington Law Review* 1407–1472; Bussani, *supra* fn 107; Devereaux and Peng, *supra* fn 54, 4; Chen and Cheung, *supra* fn 54, 373; Alexandra P. Everhart Sickler, The (Un)Fair Credit Reporting Act (2016) 28 *Loyola Consumer Law Review* 238–296. Many have criticized the DSA and the current AIA proposal, in the EU, exactly on this very point: Catalina Goanta and Jerry Spanakis, 'Discussing The Legitimacy of Digital Market Surveillance' (2022) 2 *Stanford Computational Antitrust* 44–55; Martin Ebers, Veronica R.S. Hoch, Frank Rosenkranz, Hannah Ruschemeier, Björn Steinrötter, 'The European Commission's

whenever the problem arising out from the measure involves (parties belonging to) more than one jurisdiction. The applicability of national laws, indeed, depends on territorial sovereignty and therefore on the possibility of either enforcing them at home or of finding sufficiently strong reasons to have them applied elsewhere. In cases of performance-based measures made by domestic actors acting across national boundaries – think of quantitative assessments produced by transnational NGOs, credit ratings agencies, multinational corporations, tech companies[157] –, both these possibilities pose well-known, thorny legal issues of jurisdiction and conflict-of-laws that seriously undermine the prospect of relying on domestic rules to govern the transnational effects of measurements[158].

It may therefore seem that, besides the few cases in which legal metrics live enclosed in national boundaries, the chances of controlling through regulation performance-based measures made by international actors or with transnational effects are quite meagre. Before reaching such a conclusion, however, it is important to take into account the pioneering global administrative law (GAL) theory developed since the 2000s by scholars specifically interested in the governance of hybrid international and transnational actors[159].

According to this theory, global administrative bodies – a notion that includes formal and informal intergovernmental networks, national bodies operating within international regimes, hybrid and private bodies exercising transnational governance functions of public significance[160] – are increasingly complying, and should increasingly comply, with unwritten but

---

Proposal for an Artificial Intelligence Act – A Critical Assessment by Members of the Robotics and AI Law Society (RAILS)' (2021) 4 *J* 589–603, at 598–599.

157 See Chapters 8 (South Africa), 12 (Africa) and 13 (Europe).

158 This issue has been repeatedly underlined with regard to the enforcement of domestic regulations of online activities: Matthias C. Kettemann and Alexander Peukert, 'Conclusion: The Law of Global Digitality: Findings and Future Research', in Matthias C. Kettemann, Alexander Peukert, Indra Spiecker (eds), *The Law of Global Digitality* (Routledge 2022) 250–255, at 251–254; Luciano Floridi, 'The Fight for Digital Sovereignty: What It Is, and Why It Matters, Especially for the EU' (2020) 33 *Philosophy & Technology* 369–378; Marta Infantino and Weiwei Wang, 'Algorithmic Torts: A Prospective Comparative Overview' (2019) 28 *Transnational Law and Contemporary Problems* 309–362; Michael L. Rustad and Thomas H. Koenig, 'Harmonizing Cybertort Law for Europe and America' (2005) 5 *Journal of High Technology Law* 13–58.

159 Sabino Cassese, *An Advanced Introduction to Global Administrative Law* (EE 2021); Sabino Cassese, *A World Government?* (Global Law Press 2018); Cassese (ed), *supra* fn 76; Benedict Kingsbury, Nico Krisch, Richard B. Stewart, 'The Emergence of Global Administrative Law' (2005) 68 *Law and Contemporary Problems* 15–61.

160 Kingsbury, Krisch, Stewart, *supra* fn 156, 17.

well-recognized principles of global administrative law, such as access, transparency, reason-giving, participation, review and accountability. When looked through the GAL lenses, it is quite clear that the producers of many of the examples of legal metrics surveyed in this book may qualify as global administrative bodies, insofar as they are involved in a governance-by-knowledge activity and entrusted with a de facto regulatory power that is indifferent to national boundaries. Under this reading, producers of legal metrics are bound to comply with fundamental GAL standards: they should be transparent about their methodology, give reasons and provide effective review for their choices, allow participation in the measurement process, and accept accountability for the effects of their measurements[161]. Far from being a wishful thinking, this interpretation seems consonant with a few developments that can be detected in our field. We already mentioned that external criticism prompted the WB to implement through time several improvements in the DB's methodology and procedures, modifying the internal structure of the indicator in light of the critiques received, making available to the public the materials underlying the reports, allowing bottom-up participation, and voluntarily subjecting itself to external audits[162]. Similarly, under the (harder and softer) stimuli of a plethora of actors, big tech companies (in particular, Alphabet and Meta) have in recent years slowly but steadily increased the transparency of the algorithms underlying their recommenders' systems, increasingly allowed users to submit complaints and established clearer procedures for handling the disputes arising out from their services[163].

The GAL theory looks particularly promising, especially because of its aspiration to overcome traditional boundaries and to attach accountability to power, whatever its form. It may be objected that global administrative standards are per se not enforceable against global administrative bodies. However, as the illustrations made above show, spontaneous compliance with global administrative law principles is often spurred by expectations and demands by interested parties and by the public. To foster such demands and expectations, it is fundamental to enlarge awareness of the pervasiveness of social quantification, of its benefits and costs, and of its invisible regulatory power. We hope that, by shedding light on the number of performance-based measurements

161 Infantino, *supra* fn 76; Cassese and Casini, *supra* fn 122.

162 Infantino, *supra* fn 76, 363.

163 See Orit Fischman-Afori, 'Taking global administrative law one step ahead: Online giants and the digital democratic sphere' (2022) *International Journal of Constitutional Law*, avaiable at <https://doi.org/10.1093/icon/moac089> (accessed 10 January 2023).

with regulatory effects, this volume may contribute to foster awareness of social quantification and spur requests for its responsible use.

4 Conclusions

The above sections, as well as all the preceding chapters, show how ubiquitous quantification is. We live in societies where there is widespread collection of information, which is then used by different actors at various levels to make decisions that materially affect our everyday life. The shift towards quantification as a regulatory technique is undoubtedly here to stay.

What our research also showed is that there are different ways in which measures are made, used and consumed, and there are different ways in which measurement may be controlled. The burgeoning variety of performance-based assessments calls for more comparative researches on legal metrics. Quantification of performances does not produce the same effects always and everywhere. As the sections above show, similar measures affect the social world differently, including the daily management of the law, depending on who carries them out, how, for the benefits of whom and for what purposes. Measuring justice is different from assessing research quality; evaluating consumers' credit worthiness is one thing, profiling consumption preferences is another; none of these has much in common with measures of states' and companies' efforts to achieve sustainability. Yet, the variety we are referring to goes deeper than sectoral heterogeneity. Consider for instance the varied response to the DB reports. All the divisions of the WB readily embraced the DB, while many other international organizations attacked it; several countries took the DB seriously, adopting legal reforms to comply with its prescriptions; others attempted to game it or simply cheated; still others strenuously tried to resist it[164]. Other examples may readily follow. Measures of justice and research encroach upon judges' and researchers' independence to different extents in continental Europe, in Latin America, in common law jurisdictions and in East Asia[165]. The embracement of social credit in China has triggered fears of governmental surveillance in the West, where the same activities of gathering and relying on quantified performance data are often managed by corporate actors[166]. Many other illustrations may be added, but the point is that legal

164 See above, Section 2.1.

165 See Chapters 2–5 and 9–10 of this book.

166 Infantino and Wang, *supra* note 55, 51–53; Daithí Mac Síthigh and Mathias M. Siems, 'The Chinese Social Credit System: A Model for Other Countries?' (2019) 82 *Modern Law*

cultures, systems and orders internalize and react to the rise of performance-based quantification each in their own way. We need to understand more about which forms of quantitative measures are widespread, in which sectors and regions, made by whom and producing what regulatory effects. We also need to understand more about the existing and emerging legal rules that may apply to these measures, and the extent to which they affect the contents, style and impact of social quantification. The entire volume proves that this research is both urgent and topical.

We are aware that many of the arguments herein proposed may not be acceptable to all readers. We know, for instance, that many lawyers have understandings of legal sources that differ from the one adopted here, and may resist the idea of equating measurements to regulation (and even more so to law). However, no matter whether one (dis)agrees with the labels and qualifications that are used throughout the book, we hope we demonstrated that performance-based measurements are associated with great power. As the saying goes, with that power should therefore come great responsibility – or, to say it in lawyerish, more skeptical terms, with great power should at least come minimal accountability.

Review 1034–1071; Larry Catá Backer, 'Next Generation Law: Data-Driven Governance and Accountability-Based Regulatory Systems in the West, and Social Credit Regimes in China' (2018) 28 *Southern California Interdisciplinary Law Journal* 123–172.

Detailed Table of Contents

Index

www.ingramcontent.com/pod-product-compliance
Lightning Source LLC
LaVergne TN
LVHW010623300926
849162LV00001B/47